Africa
in World Politics

FOURTH
EDITION

Africa
in World Politics
Reforming Political Order

Edited by John W. Harbeson
and Donald Rothchild

Westview Press
A Member of the Perseus Books Group

Published by Westview Press,
A Member of the Perseus Books Group

Find us on the World Wide Web at www.westviewpress.com.

Designed by Trish Wilkinson
Set in 10.5 point Minion

Library of Congress Cataloging-in-Publication Data

Africa in world politics : reforming political order / edited by John W. Harbeson
and Donald Rothchild. — 4th ed.
p. cm.
Includes bibliographical references and index.
ISBN 978-0-8133-4364-8 (pbk. : alk. paper)
1. Africa—Politics and government—1960—Congresses. 2. World politics—
1989—Congresses. I. Harbeson, John W. (John Willis), 1938– II. Rothchild,
Donald S.
DT30.5.A3544 2009
960.3'3—dc22 2008003966

10 9 8 7 6 5 4 3 2 1

Contents

Tables and Figures

Tables

Figures

Africa

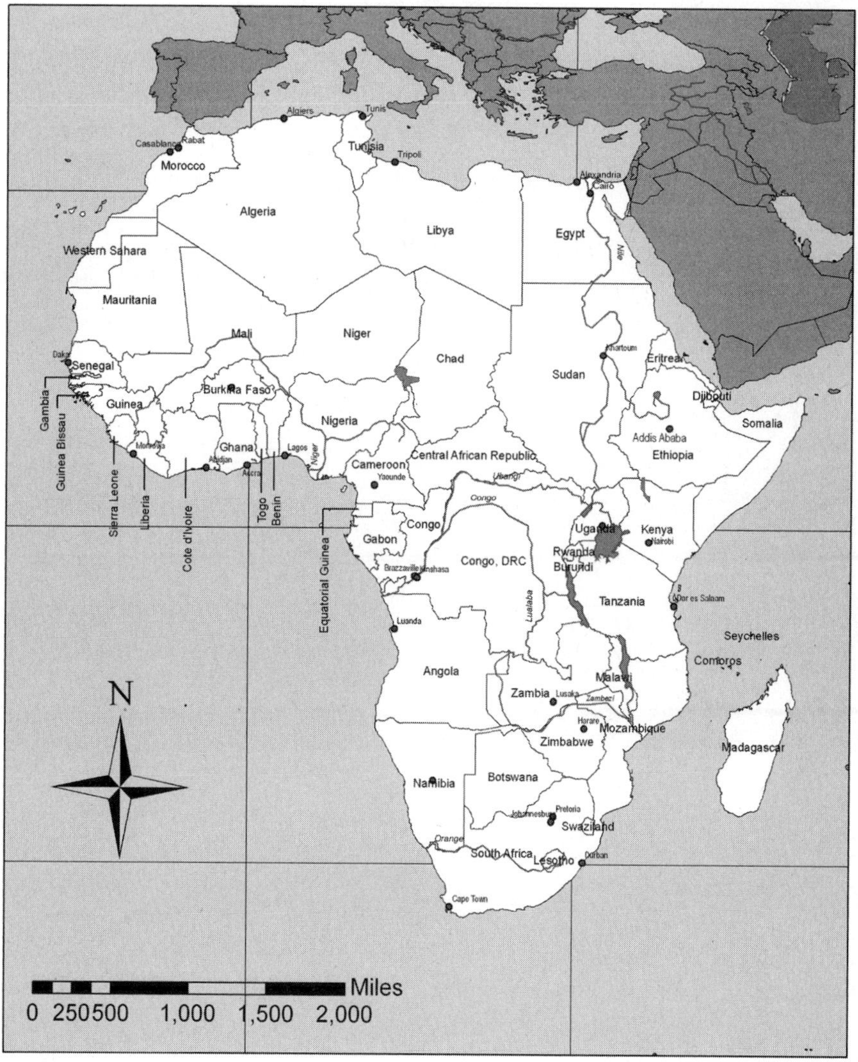
Algiers
Tunis
Casablanca
Rabat
Morocco
Tunisia
Tripoli
Alexandria
Cairo
Algeria
Libya
Egypt
Western Sahara
Nile
Mauritania
Mali
Niger
Dakar
Senegal
Chad
Khartoum
Eritrea
Sudan
Gambia
Burkina Faso
Guinea
Djibouti
Nigeria
Somalia
Guinea Bissau
Addis Ababa
Ethiopia
Monrovia
Ghana
Lagos
Niger
Abidjan
Accra
Cameroon
Yaounde
Central African Republic
Ubangi
Congo
Sierra Leone
Liberia
Cote d'Ivoire
Togo
Benin
Equatorial Guinea
Gabon
Congo
Uganda
Kenya
Nairobi
Rwanda
Burundi
Congo, DRC
Brazzaville
Kinshasa
Lualaba
Tanzania
Dar es Salaam
Luanda
Seychelles
Comoros
Angola
Malawi
N
Zambia
Lusaka
Zambezi
Harare
Mozambique
Zimbabwe
Madagascar
Namibia
Botswana
Johannesburg
Pretoria
Swaziland
Orange
South Africa
Lesotho
Durban
Cape Town
Miles
0 250500 1,000 1,500 2,000

Acronyms

ACP	African, Caribbean and Pacific States group
ADB	African Development Bank
ADFL	Alliances of Democratic Forces for the Liberation of the Congo
AEF	French Equatorial Africa
AFCOM	U.S. Africa Command
AfDB	African Development Bank
AGOA	African Growth and Opportunity Act (U.S.)
AIAI	Al-Itihaad al-Islaami
AIPPA	Access to Information and Protection of Privacy Act (Zimbabwe)
AMIS	Africa Union Mission
AMU	Arab Mahgreb Union
ANC	African National Congress (South Africa)
AOF	French West Africa
APF	Africa Union Peace Fund
APRM	African Peer Review Mechanism
AU	Africa Union
CDR	Coalition for the Defense of the Republic (Rwanda)
CEAO	West African Economic Community
CEEAC	Economic Union of the States of Central Africa
CfA	Commission for Africa (Blair Commission)
CFA	Communauté Financière Africaine
CFSP	Common Foreign and Security Policy (Europe)
CJTF-HOA	Combined Joint Task Force-Horn of Africa
COMESA	Common Market of East and Southern Africa

CPA	Comprehensive Peace Agreement
CSSDCA	Conference on Security, Stability, Development, and Cooperation in Africa
DANIDA	Danish International Development Authority
DATA	Debt, AIDS, Trade, Africa report
DFID	British Department of International Development
DRC	Democratic Republic of the Congo (Kinshasha)
EACU	East African Customs Union
EC	European Community
ECA	Economic Commission for Africa
ECOMOG	West African Military Observer Group
ECOWAS	Economic Commission of West African States
EPAs	Economic Partnership Agreements
EPLF	Eritrean People's Liberation Front
EPRDF	Ethiopian People's Revolutionary Democratic Front
ESCE	Economic Security and Cooperation in Europe
ESDI	Europe's Common Security and Defense Identity
EU	European Union
EUCOM	U.S. European Command
EUFOR	European Force
FDC	Forum for Democratic Change (Uganda)
FNLA	National Front for the Liberation of Angola
FOMWAN	Federation of Muslim Women's Associations of Nigeria
FRELIMO	Mozambique Liberation Front
FTAs	Free Trade Areas
G8	Group of eight leading industrial economies
GDA	Global Development Alliance
GFATM	Global Fund to fight AIDS, Tuberculosis, and Malaria
GLPF	Great Lakes Policy Forum
GPRA	Provisional Government of the Algerian Republic
GSPC	Salafist Group for Preaching and Combat
HIPC	Highly Indebted Poor Countries
IBRD	International Bank for Reconstruction and Development (World Bank)
ICG	International Crisis Group
IFIs	international financial institutions
IGAD	Intergovernmental Authority on Development (formerly IGADD)
IGADD	Intergovernmental Authority on Drought and Development (now IGAD)

IMF	International Monetary Fund
LIFG	Libyan Islamic Fighting Group
MDG	UN Millenium Development Goals
MDRI	Multilateral Debt Relief Initiative
MOSOP	Movement for the Survival of the Ogoni People
MSF	Medicin Sans Frontieres (Doctors Without Borders)
NANGO	National Association of Non-Governmental Organizations (Zimbabwe)
NANGOF	Namibia Non-Governmental Organisations Forum
NATO	North Atlantic Treaty Organization
NCP	National Congress Party (Sudan)
NEPAD	New Partnership for African Development
NIF	National Islamic Front (Sudan)
OAU	Organization of African Union (predecessor of AU)
ODA	Official Development Assistance
OECD	Organization for Economic Cooperation and Development
OIC	Organization of the Islamic Conference
ONLF	Ogaden National Liberation Front
OOTW	Operations Other Than War
OSCE	Organization for Security and Cooperation in Europe
PAGAD	People Against Gangsterism and Drugs (South Africa)
PEPFAR	Presidential Emergency Program for AIDS Relief
PMLA	Popular Movement for the Liberation of Angola
POSA	Public Order and Security Act (Zimbabwe)
PRSP	Poverty Reduction Strategy Paper
PSFU	Private Sector Foundation of Uganda
PSI	Policy Support Instrument
PTA	Preferential Trade Area
RBAs	Rights Based Approaches
RENAMO	Mozambique National Resistance Organization
RUF	Revolutionary United Front (Sierra Leone)
SACU	Southern African Customs Union
SADC	Southern African Development Council
SADR	Sahrawi Democratic Republic
SIDA	Swedish International Development Authority
SNA	Somali National Alliance
SPLM/A	Sudan People's Liberation Movement Army
SRSG	Special Representative of the Secretary General
SSA	Sub-Saharan Africa
SSLM	Southern Sudan Liberation Movement

TCSTI	Trans-Saharan Counter Terrorism Initiative
TFG	Transitional Federal Government (Somalia)
TRIPS	Trade Related Aspects of International Property Rights
UDEAC	Customs Union of the Central African States
UEAC	Economic Union of Central Africa
UEMOA	West African Monetary and Economic Union
UIC	Union of Islamic Courts (Somalia)
UNAIDS	Joint UN Program on HIV/AIDS
UNCTAD	UN Conference on Trade and Development
UNDP	United Nations Development Program
UNDRD	United Nations Declaration on the Right to Development
UNFPA	United Nations Population Fund
UNICEF	United Nations Children's Fund
UNITA	Union for the Total Independence of Angola
UNITAF	United Nations Task Force (Somalia)
UNODC	UN Office on Drugs and Crime
UNOSOM	United Nations Operations in Somalia
USAID	United States Agency for International Development
WHO	World Health Organization
WILDAF	Women in Law and Development in Africa
WTO	World Trade Organization

Preface

Donald Rothchild

We dedicate this fourth edition of *Africa in World Politics* to the memory of Donald Rothchild, who passed away on January 30, 2007. Conceiving and working together on the various editions of this book greatly deepened our professional collaboration and close friendship of more than forty years. He lived long enough for us to plan this edition together and to contribute his own chapter.

Donald Rothchild was one of the foremost scholars of African international relations. He was the author or editor of more than two dozen books and over seventy articles during a career spanning almost fifty years. He wrote perceptibly and with unfailingly exhaustive scholarship on a range of African international relationships, including conflict mediation, international political economy, U.S. foreign policy toward Africa, ethnic politics, international regimes, international security, and Africa's place in contemporary world politics. A scholar of great breadth, he also wrote insightfully in the area of comparative politics and produced important work on Ghana, civil society, Afro-Marxist regimes, state-society relations, and other topics.

Rothchild was much honored for his high quality and pathbreaking scholarship. A professor of political science at the University of California at Davis from 1965 until his death, he was awarded a University of California system Distinguished Professorship in 2003. He received fellowships and awards from the Ford Foundation, the Rockefeller Foundation, and the U.S. Institute of Peace. Rothchild's reputation for quality scholarship won him an international reputation. He taught for a time in four different African universities, in Ghana, Zambia, Uganda, and Kenya, and was twice elected to the presidency of an International Political Science Association research committee.

Donald Rothchild's stature as a scholar of international relations, with a particular emphasis on Africa, led him to be in great demand as a consultant. He served on numerous editorial boards, including the advisory board to Lynne Rienner Publishers and the *Western Political Quarterly*. But this was only the tip of the iceberg. He was constantly in demand for panels at African Studies Association conventions as well as meetings of the International Studies Association and the American Political Science Association, and he was instrumental in the formation of the African Politics Conference Group.

Rothchild was a Phi Beta Kappa graduate of Kenyon College and went on to receive his MA from the University of California–Berkeley and his PhD from Johns Hopkins University. Before coming to Davis, Professor Rothchild taught at Colby College. He met Edith, his wife of over fifty years, during his two years of military service. In addition to Edith, he is survived by two sons, Derek of Hermosa Beach, California, and Maynard of San Marino, California, and five grandchildren.

Don Rothchild was our wonderful colleague, collaborator, and great friend, as he was for legions of academics in political science and other fields and in many countries. He exemplified the academic community at its very best. With Don, scholarship and friendship were always seamlessly joined. He was unfailingly generous and unselfish in encouraging the academic pursuits of countless students, colleagues, and collaborators, who today support and build the study of international relations.

For all of us, he will remain a model and an inspiration.

John W. Harbeson
City University of New York

Part I

Introduction

1

Intimations of an African Renaissance

Recent Progress, Long-Term Challenges

JOHN W. HARBESON

Sub-Saharan Africa has shown clear signs that it may emerge from its long night of chronic marginalization in world politics at the beginning of its second half-century of independence. Indications of the beginnings of real domestic economic and political progress combined with new sub-Saharan African prominence on the world stage have cast in sharp relief both the potential benefits and the costs of the continent's possibly diminished marginalization and the profound long-term challenges to sustainable and significant progress that continue to confront it. This book examines the many dimensions and issues presented by these encouraging developments and the persistent omnipresent shadows cast over them. These shadows include the legacies rooted in the continent's colonial and postcolonial past and the ever-present hurdles to an enduring political and economic renaissance that remain.

Not for the first time have prospects for an African political and economic renaissance emerged only ultimately to be proven illusory wholly or in part. The mid-twentieth-century independence of nearly fifty African countries from colonial rule and exploitation itself created the expectation of a vastly expanded, culturally diversified global civilization accented by African commitment to nonalignment and self-reliance as between the Cold War alliances.

However, African nonalignment was qualified, at best, during the ongoing Cold War, and proclaimed self-reliance proved to be illusory, even as development progress bogged down and postindependence political institutions crumbled in a long season of coups and countercoups.

Multilateral commitment to economic growth with equity for poor majorities in African and other developing countries in the 1970s to overcome the failures of the first development decade foundered on the shoals of a U.S. economy weakened relative to others and a global economy disarrayed by diminished U.S. economic leadership, crises induced by the oil cartel, and failures of development policy design and implementation that led to unsustainable debt levels in developing countries. The subsequent strategy, led by the World Bank and the International Monetary Fund to attack the threatening debt crisis through comprehensive neoliberal reforms, by general agreement, produced, at best, mixed results for African countries by the close of the twentieth century. The broken implied promise of enlarged private investment streams, which were expected to accompany structural adjustment, served only to reinforce sub-Saharan Africa marginalization and vulnerability in an increasingly globalized post–Cold War economy.

The end of the Cold War marked the beginning of new, still uncertain, and only gradually emerging prospects for an African political and economic renaissance and for the continent's participation within the world community of nations from a more prominent and more secure position. Democracy's Third Wave (or "second" independence) has washed widely and deeply over African shores, leaving only a handful of stubbornly autocratic countries, reinforced by international commitment to support anticipated positive interconnections between economic and political liberalization. By the beginning of the twenty-first century, growing international commitment emerged for new efforts to greatly diminish the economic marginalization of many African and other developing nations. These initiatives included commitments to extensive debt forgiveness, broad-gauged assaults on poverty through the United Nations' Millennium Development Goals (MDG) project, and at least still flickering prospects for mutually beneficial trade liberalization from the Doha and direct European-African talks. By early 2008, multi-year growth rates for a number of African countries were the best in memory, although data indicated that African countries were behind schedule in meeting MDG goals set for 2015.

These encouraging manifestations of a significant African political and economic renaissance must be examined in the context of important emergent trends and developments (outlined below), whose long-term implications remained in the realm of speculation in early 2008.

STATE WEAKNESS, COLLAPSE, AND RECONSTRUCTION

First and foremost, by the mid-1990s, the campaign to shrink the role of African governments in directing and managing their economies in favor of much greater reliance upon market mechanisms gradually spawned awareness of the far deeper problem of fundamental state weakness. It became increasingly apparent that implementation of reduced *regime* direction of economies demanded measures to establish stronger, more resilient *states.* Irony and paradox accompanied this realization insofar as it had become conventional to treat regime and state as synonymous with one another.

Thus, one bitter legacy of the Cold War's end became the stark reality of collapsed and gravely weakened states wherein effective governance ceased, nearly vanished, or dissolved in civil war. Somalia remained stateless and in near anarchy almost two decades after the fall of dictator Siad Barre, although breakaway Somaliland made strides to restore stability in part of the country as it bid for recognized independence. The states of Liberia, Sierra Leone, and the Democratic Republic of the Congo (DRC) all but collapsed. Angola and Sudan remained mired in civil war, and Burundi and Rwanda exploded in genocidal ethnic civil war that engulfed eastern DRC as well. Côte d'Ivoire descended into de facto partition and near civil war following the death of its founding father, Félix Houphouët-Boigny, after his reign of more than thirty years. Iron-fisted and brutal resistance to multiparty democracy by the regime of Zimbabwe's aging founding ruler, Robert Mugabe, has left that country teetering on the brink of political and economic collapse. Eritrea became the first new state to emerge in postindependence Africa, but its long war to gain independence from Ethiopia shook the foundations of that ancient polity, which continued to struggle to define and establish a postimperial state. Many other African states experienced low-level domestic political violence, often ethnically inspired, and/or chronically weak capacity of ruling regimes to enforce their writs throughout still colonially defined borders.

Set against these manifestations of state weakness and collapse have been significant and heartening—if still problematic—examples of state renewal and successful transformation. South Africa and Namibia have become stable democratic states even as they labor to overcome the social and economic consequences of decades of apartheid oppression. Mozambique has made a stunning, if still incomplete, transition to democratic stateness and marked economic recovery from a colonial and postcolonial history of bitter and almost unending civil war. Angola, too, has begun to recover from the ravages of unrelieved postindependence civil war. With extensive international assistance, both Sierra Leone and Liberia have begun to rebuild democratic states from the ashes of prolonged civil war, while, at the beginning of 2008, de facto partitioned Côte d'Ivoire was in the early, promising stages of reconciliation leading to political reunification.

CORRUPTION AND THE QUEST FOR TRANSPARENCY

Directly related to these manifestations of state crisis and renewal have been persistent and endemic patterns of official corruption chronicled in global surveys by Transparency International and widely criticized in the literature on African politics and by the international financial institutions for its debilitating effects on both governance and economic reform. Its manifestations have included outright thefts of staggering proportions, shading into deeper patterns of neo-patrimonialism, sustained in part by deeply rooted societal clientelism. Diametrically at variance from politically neutral, rule-bound governmental administration, these departures from Weberian models of probity and neutrality have been deeply influenced by what Will Reno in his chapter terms the pervasive privatization of international relations associated with the spread of a global market economy.

The privatization of international relations appears to have potentially profound and long-term implications for sub-Saharan African nations, although the balance of its beneficial and malevolent effects has yet to be clearly established. On the one hand, there exists, in principle, the possibility that the privatization of international economic and political relations will result in at least somewhat greater diffusion of, and convergence on, standards of administrative behavior that characterize Western models, thereby strengthening both governance and economic management. On the other hand, there lies the possibility, contemplated by Reno in "The Privatization of Africa's International Relations," of increasing the marginalization of the state itself, and thereby its capacity to restrain as well as to exacerbate corruption, even to the point where the very Habermasian conception of the public sector dissolves in a vast global ocean of unaccountable privatized economic relations. Such a prospect was never envisioned by the international financial institution architects of structural adjustment, whose conception was of government assumed at least residually capable of regulating market relationships, albeit not directing or managing them. In this respect, state strength and regime governance, though analytically and importantly distinct, merge into one another.

DEMOCRATIZATION AND STATE STRENGTHENING

All but a handful of sub-Saharan African countries have democratized since 1990, at least to the extent of conducting competitive multiparty elections. As

I note in Chapter 5, sub-Saharan African countries as a group have made notable strides in the observance of civil and political liberties since 1990, and most have undertaken constitutional reform to some degree. One heartening manifestation of the new African constitutionalism has been the insistence by civil society in several countries that presidents honor, and desist from seeking to circumvent, two-term limitations on their tenure in office. Indeed, the number of African countries practicing democracy at or above global standards, as defined by several dimensions of democratization, has expanded from two prior to 1990—Mauritius and Botswana—to approximately one-third of all African countries, as measured by Freedom House, Polity IV, and the World Bank's *Governance Matters* surveys. The *Afrobarometer* surveys suggest a widespread, if variable, popular preference for democratic government over the obvious alternatives, although citizen satisfaction with the *efficacy* of new democratic institutions and practices has appeared to be qualified, at best, in these surveys.

However, the implications of democratization for the challenge of strengthening weak states in sub-Saharan Africa and elsewhere have become a subject of intense controversy that remains to be explored in the depth commensurate with its fundamental importance. Issues involving prevalent working definitions of both state and democracy have complicated the issue. On the one hand, there has been the relatively pessimistic anticipation that autocratic *anciens régimes* would survive electoral democracy and frustrate broadened democratization, that democracy would be hybridized with autocracy in forms termed electoral or competitive authoritarianism.[1] But that hypothesis has implicitly hinged on an empirical operationalization that reduces democracy to elections alone, to the virtual exclusion, *inter alia*, of civil society as one important manifestation of broader processes of democratization. Those broader processes of democratization have clearly differentiated the continent's group of, so far, leading democratizers from other countries on the continent. Aili Tripp's chapter in this volume, "In Pursuit of Authority: Civil Society and Rights-Based Discourses in Africa," details the broadening rights-based agendas of vibrant civil society in many African countries, belying the claims of civil society's critics. Those critics inaccurately presume that its defenders rely upon definitions of civil society that treat it as synonymous with what Western donors are charged to fund and support rather than grounding it in a broader understanding of civil society commensurate with realities on the ground in many countries.

On the other hand, Edward Mansfield and Jack Snyder have prominently asserted that democratization, implicitly defined to be synonymous with elections, has proven detrimental to the viability and stability of weak states.[2] Their contention that autocratic states must first take on *other* characteristics implicitly associated with democracy, such as the rule of law, acceptance of civil society, and transparent governance, has been criticized as unrealistic. But these criticisms have appeared to understate the possibility that democratic processes, broadly conceived to include these features, may be factors in the *creation* of state stability as well as democratization rather than simply *outcomes* of state stability. This may indeed be what has begun to occur in Africa's more successful democracies to date.

HIV/AIDS: DEVASTATION, RESILIENCE, AND COMMITMENT

HIV/AIDS, which burst on the world scene in the 1980s, has devastated sub-Saharan Africa more than any other world region. Beyond its catastrophic consequences in purely human terms lie unfolding, profound diminishment of the very human resources without which no political or economic renaissance would be possible. In Chapter 7, "The AIDS Crisis: International Relations and Governance in Africa," Alan Whiteside and Anokhi Parikh chronicle the incidence and consequences of this pandemic. The costs in lives lost, life expectancies foreshortened, and diminished human resources profoundly threaten the viability of African societies, economies, and polities in the long term, although it appears that they have been surprisingly resilient in the short term. Notwithstanding the significant current mobilization to address this crisis, the authors decry the absence, to date, of the requisite depth, scope, and uniformity of commitment, in Africa and worldwide, to arrest the spread of HIV/AIDS, treat the afflicted, and redouble the search for ultimate cures.

TOWARD STRENGTHENED AFRICAN INTERNATIONAL POLITICAL AND ECONOMIC ORGANIZATION: GROWING PAINS

A key factor in effecting reinforcing state strengthening and democratization in sub-Saharan Africa has been and continues to be the nature, quality, and extent of available external support. One important component of that external involvement is the support of African countries themselves. A singularly encouraging development of the new century has been the transformation of the Organization of African Unity (OAU) into the Africa Union (AU) and the formation by African leaders of a New Partnership for Africa's Development (NEPAD), one critically important dimension of which is the creation of the African Peer Review Mechanism (APRM). Together with older regional initiatives emanating from the Southern African Development Community (SADC) and the Economic Community of West African States (ECOWAS), these African organizations have represented a new and growing commitment by African states to assume collective responsibility for the stability and quality of governance by member states and for their shared relationship with the international community at large.

As described in Chapter 9, by William Zartman, these organizations reflect the ever-increasing breadth of African experience and capability in diplomatic negotiations, which began in earnest at independence itself in the mid-twentieth century with negotiations on constitutional and other terms for separation from the retiring colonial powers. Specifically, the APRM institutionalizes the commitment of participating states to conform to "agreed political, economic, and corporate governance values, codes and standards." Thus, the APRM serves to ground NEPAD's broader objectives, which are (1) to promote accelerated growth and sustainable development, (2) to eradicate widespread and severe poverty, and (3) to halt the marginalization of Africa in the globalization process.

These initiatives appear on their face to imply reinforcement of state strength and transparent governance in both the public and private sectors and thus would seem likely to diminish rather than deepen marginalization of the state in the face of greater privatization of international relations. But they are in their infancy, and what they will become in the future remains entirely to be seen. The AU has been severely challenged in seeking to address the crises of Darfur and Somalia, and its commitment of troops has proven manifestly insufficient for these purposes. As of early 2008, Sudan had taken advantage of the AU's weakness by relying upon it in such a way as to frustrate the larger UN peacemaking and humanitarian efforts to resolve the crisis. The AU's weakness in Somalia at the time of this writing has left Ethiopian troops exposed as the dominant force on the ground seeking to install a stable and viable government in that country for the first time in nearly two decades. More broadly, the substantially increased space for free political expression, which has been part and parcel of sub-Saharan African democratization, has both created opportunities for and served to mandate more purposeful ongoing negotiations within weak polities on acceptable terms for strengthened states.

NON-AFRICAN EXTERNAL ENGAGEMENT IN A TRANSFORMED GLOBAL ORDER: ASSISTANCE, NEGOTIATED REFORM, AND COMPETITIVE INTERVENTION

Prospects for a sustainable and enduring sub-Saharan African political and economic renaissance hinge critically upon the degree to which the continent diminishes its marginalization as it responds to a moment of markedly more widespread and intensified external engagement. This expanded external engagement has reflected a substantially transformed global order in the post–Cold War, post–September 11 era. In this new era, sub-Saharan Africa is confronted with a closely interconnected array of new potential pathways to enhanced development, but one that also entails corresponding risks of continued, even deepened, marginalization and economic malaise. A major contribution to this transformed global political and economic order has been the changing role and posture of the United States. The significance of its position as the sole superpower in military terms at the end of the Cold War has been eroded by the expanding multipolarity of the global economic order, the prominence of issues, particularly in Africa, for which conventional military power has proven to be inappropriate, and the alienation in a great many countries as a consequence of the increased propensity of the United States to act unilaterally on global problems that require multilateral engagement and cooperation.

Chapter 10, by the late Donald Rothchild, explains that U.S. initiatives to promote political stability, peace, democracy, and development in Africa have generally had a low profile, have relied upon soft power, and have often been effectively conducted through regional or global multilateral coalitions rather than unilaterally. He finds the explanations for this approach toward Africa in official perceptions that the credibility of the United States has not been at stake, that there has been limited public support for more energetic initiatives to effect political and economic outcomes in the continent, and that there was limited "usable power" for these objectives—points all dramatized by the failed humanitarian venture in Somalia in the early 1990s.

Over the past several years, however, a global order in the throes of profound political and economic transformation has been reshaping American posture toward sub-Saharan Africa. The events of September 11, 2001, and the growing presence of China have stimulated growing U.S. recognition that it does indeed have vital interests in the region and therefore a corresponding need for more direct, unilateral measures to project power and influence commensurate with them. Its initial efforts to do so have been complicated, and perhaps significantly compromised, by widespread dismay and opposition among many nations and peoples, including many in Africa, to what they view as a misguided, even counterproductive, venture in Iraq. Thus, there have been misgivings, as well as some acceptance, within Africa for the creation of a new U.S. African military command. Explained officially as a bringing together of military operations in Africa that were previously spread among three separate commands, and justified also as a means of supporting humanitarian and development assistance, there can be little doubt that a core objective is to undergird cooperation with African security forces to advance the U.S. global war on terror.

There is a risk, however, that the new U.S. Africa Command will conflict with or undermine ongoing nonmilitary U.S. assistance objectives in Africa. The danger is that African regimes will be encouraged to limit civil liberties by enacting legislation analogous to the U.S. Patriot Act as counter-terrorism measures just as those countries have begun to advance democratization through the expansion of civil and political liberties. Another risk is that groups opposed to regimes cooperating with AFRICOM will be labeled as terrorists and attacked militarily with AFRICOM support instead of encouraging these regimes to reconcile with opposition groups in the interests of strengthening weak states.

Chapter 11, by Princeton Lyman, addresses the challenge of achieving a proper balance—ideally complementarity—between needed enhancement of security programs and continued measures to encourage improved governance, relieve poverty, and extend democracy and human rights. "Any crackdown on terrorist activity," he observes, "has to be carried out with great sensitivity to the historic grievances of marginalized groups, the incipient struggle for human rights, and the relatively weak civilian oversight of the military and security institutions."

China's ascendancy as a major global economic power has dramatized the emergence of an increasingly multipolar global economic order, in which India, Brazil, and other economies have become significantly influential players. Chapter 13, by Denis Tull, highlights the challenges that China's rapidly expanding engagement with sub-Saharan Africa poses for the G8 countries as well as for the continent itself. As it has ever since African countries achieved independence, China has presented itself, in competition with India, as the champion of developing countries in their struggle to level the playing field with industrialized nations. In its current African démarche, however, China may have presented the continent with a Faustian bargain. Tull details the ways in which China has projected its own insistence on unfettered state sovereignty, thereby giving aid and comfort to African countries struggling with a range of Western political and economic conditionalities, including the reduction of poverty through the Millennium Development Goals. He warns that the result may be a reinforcement of elite interests against those of the poor. He also pinpoints the significant respects in which China is also an economic competitor and how it may be serving its own interests at the expense of those of African countries. In these ways, while appearing to be offering welcome benefits in the form of infrastructural development and aid with fewer strings attached, China may be replicating the same neocolonial practices against which it has purported to champion African resistance.

China's contrariness in its expanding engagement with Africa, from the standpoint of the Paris Club nations, clearly threatens to complicate significantly, the realization of their own profoundly evolving post–Cold War relationships with sub-Saharan Africa. The Paris Club approach to what had been endemic developmental malaise in sub-Saharan Africa has changed quite dramatically from initial single-minded insistence in the 1980s that African countries adhere to neoliberal structural adjustment medicine as a condition for economic assistance. They combined this "stick" with what turned out to be an unrealistic implied "carrot," a promise to African countries of expanded private investment as a reward for their adherence to these terms.

Chapter 3, by Thomas Callaghy, authoritatively traces the evolution of Paris Club approaches toward sub-Saharan Africa, from debt rescheduling to debt forgiveness, to a new commitment of aid for poverty alleviation. He attributes this transformation substantially to the emergence of nongovernmental organizations as players in international economic governance and to Africa's newly enhanced geostrategic importance since September 11, 2001. The new regime of debt forgiveness and the Millennium Development Goals, combined with continuing insistence on neoliberal political and economic reform, undoubtedly reflects a more nuanced sense by the industrialized nations of their own best interests. But it also reflects their deeply held convictions about what Africa requires in its own interests and that has come gradually to include the kinds of economic assistance African countries themselves have long demanded in resisting structural adjustment.

The key question, as Callaghy observes, is "whether Africa is ready to take full advantage of these new opportunities." He cautions against indulging in "analytic hurry"—seeing a desired trend as fact before the evidence shows that it is sustainable—particularly when donors perceive that trend to be vital to their interests. Prospects for realizing these strategically important outcomes depend critically upon more than the wisdom, determination and commitment of African countries to use these new resources wisely. Equally important will be the degree to which this increased aid for Africa will be administered and extended in line with best practices derived from more than half a century of often unhappy experience with aid packages. Will the aid promote sustainable, replicable development? Will it duly take into account the expressed interests and knowledge of the recipient peoples? Will it be free of inappropriate, unrealistic, debilitating, and unnecessary conditionalities?

Additionally, prospects for realizing the desired outcomes will also depend upon sustainable commitment by industrialized countries not only to increased aid but also to terms of trade that are more favorable to African economies. In this regard, Chapter 12, by Gilbert Khadiagala, sounds a note of warning and skepticism. The Cotonou Partnership Agreement of 2000 committed African states to economic partnership agreements (EPAs), which, in response to World Trade Organization pressure, signal the demise of nonreciprocal trade agreements calculated to give African countries favored access to European markets. But Khadiagala observes that European countries have used their continuing dominance in relationships with African countries to secure EPAs "while perennially reneging on G8 aid promises that ultimately seek to equip African countries to absorb and deal effectively with the EPAs."

THE STATE: COLONIAL LEGACIES, POSTCOLONIAL ACCOUNTABILITY, AND RECONSTRUCTION

At the end of the day, whether intimations of an early twenty-first-century African political and economic renaissance portend real and sustainable development hinges, to a very large extent, on what happens to the African state. In the last decade of the twentieth century and the first of the twenty-first century, its condition has been more at issue, and demands upon it for performance and accountability more extensive and complex, than at any time in the past. How African states, individually and collectively, respond to increasingly complex and energetic international engagement with the continent will critically influence to what extent and in what ways persistent marginalization of the continent will be significantly and sustainably diminished. To what extent will diminished marginalization in economic and political terms become commensurate with its growing global prominence in cultural and religious terms as examined in Ali Mazrui's chapter? At the same time, the measure of African states' performance will be their skill in utilizing, mediating, and adapting this increased and multifaceted international engagement in ways that reflect, enhance, and are accountable to the best interests of their citizens—not just ruling elites—as they understand those interests.

Chapter 2, by Crawford Young, documents the authoritarian practices of the African colonial state and their deep imprint and continuing influence on postindependence African states. At the moment of African independence, the insufficiency of coercive colonial-era rule for postindependence development was not adequately appreciated; the fragility of postindependence political institutions and their metastasis into patrimonial rule was neither foretold nor anticipated. But Young now anticipates that "perhaps nearly five decades after the great surge to independence in 1960, the colonial shadow will begin to fade," at just the moment when reformed states have become critical to the broadening and sustaining of tentative, preliminary signs of true improvement in the human condition in sub-Saharan Africa.

In Chapter 14, Francis Deng asserts that the cascading demands for domestic and external performance and accountability thrust upon the African state since the end of the Cold War amounted to "a formidable national identity crisis in which sovereignty is being contested by forces in internal confrontation and their external supporters." The fact that China is offering ways for African states to circumvent these demands clearly complicates the issue. Deng has long prescribed, as key to resolving this identity crisis, the concept of responsible sovereignty in the forms of domestic, regional, and international accountability by states for the security and welfare of their citizens. The chapters of this book underscore the importance and de facto reality of this fundamental amendment of Westphalian norms, for the extent to which the premise of noninterference by states in each other's affairs has been compromised by events, especially since the latter years of the twentieth century.

The question of how responsible sovereignty is to be established and realized in practice in the circumstances of sub-Saharan Africa is not susceptible to easy answers, nor is it readily apparent how the concept addresses what Deng considers to be the African state's identity crisis and the factors that have created it. It is a given that African states have become increasingly accountable to the international financial institutions and private investors for the quality of their economic management and, more generally, to the international community for adherence to international human rights and domestic democratic governance. But how are states to balance their accountability to their citizenries with their accountability to these powerful, if somewhat diffuse, regional and global actors?

At the core of the African state's identity crisis is a basic question: When all is said and done, whose state is it? Deng expresses an underlying paradox succinctly. He reminds us that "the irony, however, is that the principal modern agent of Africa's political and economic development and its interlocutor in the international arena is the state, itself a creature of foreign intervention." In what now has come to be termed sub-Saharan Africa's first independence, few, if any, of its peoples had any meaningful opportunities to deliberate on how, and in what ways, they wished to reconfigure their inherited colonial governance structures as independent states reflective of their values. Instead, their leaders negotiated the terms of independence with retiring colonial powers on their behalf, presumptively representing their interests as the voices of the nationalist movements.

The confluence of Deng's injunction that ruling *regimes* condition their legitimacy on accountability to their citizens for their security and welfare with the arrival of democracy's Third Wave in Africa has created a dual mandate. The mandate is that while African regimes must accept responsibility to the international community for commitments to democratization and human rights, they must also proactively enable their citizens to participate meaningfully in the reforming of the state to which those regimes must also be accountable at the moment of Africa's "second" independence, as the Third Wave in Africa has been described. African citizens have long deserved as direct and influential a voice as possible in reforming their *states*, an opportunity that was generally denied them half a century ago.

Thus, Deng's injunction implies a kind of "higher law," an obligation of regimes to citizens, which can best be made explicit and institutionalized domestically by treating states as differentiated from and superior to regimes. Implied is a conception of the state in which the Weberian properties of monopolies of coercion over compulsory, territorially defined communities acquire their requisite legitimation to the degree that they become tethered to overarching, agreed-upon terms for shared membership in a polity, established democratically on the basis of as much citizen participation as possible. Indeed, greater realization of this principle may distinguish the leading post–Cold War African democratizing states from others.

In this way, democratic participation in the reformation of the state, so conceived, becomes a key component of state strengthening and a potential bulwark against state descent into neo-patrimonialism, which was missing in Africa's first independence. It may indeed be a necessary foundation for sub-Saharan African states to meet the long-term challenges presented by escalating international engagement with the continent and an imperative for present intimations of an African economic and political renaissance to become durably sustainable.

NOTES

1. Andreas Schedler, ed., *Electoral Authoritarianism: The Dynamics of Unfree Competition* (Boulder: Lynne Rienner Publishers, 2006).

2. Edward D. Mansfield and Jack Snyder, *Electing to Fight: Why Emerging Democracies Go to War* (Cambridge: M.I.T. Press, 2005); Jack L. Snyder, *From Voting to Violence: Democratization and Nationalist Conflict* (New York: Norton, 2000).

Part II

Historical Parameters

2

The Heritage of Colonialism

CRAWFORD YOUNG

Africa, in the rhetorical metaphor of imperial jingoism, was a ripe melon awaiting carving in the late nineteenth century. Those who scrambled fastest won the largest slices and the right to consume at their leisure the sweet, succulent flesh. Stragglers snatched only small servings or tasteless portions; Italians, for example, found only deserts on their plate. In this mad moment of imperial atavism—in Schumpeterian terms, the objectless disposition to limitless frontier expansion—no one imagined that a system of states was being created. Colonial rule, assumed by its initiators to be perpetual, later proved to be a mere interlude in the broader sweep of African history; however, the steel grid of territorial partition that colonialism imposed appears permanent. Although the patterns of disorder and state collapse that emerged in the 1990s led some to call for a reconsideration of the existing territorial system, the stubborn resilience of the largely artificial boundaries bequeathed by the colonial partition remains astonishing.[1]

Colonial heritage is the necessary point of departure for analysis of African international relations. The state system—which is, transnational vectors notwithstanding, the fundamental structural basis of the international realm—inherits the colonial partition. A few African states have a meaningful precolonial identity (Morocco, Tunisia, Egypt, Ethiopia, Burundi, Rwanda, Madagascar, Swaziland, Lesotho, and Botswana), but most are products of the competitive subordination of Africa—mostly between 1875 and 1900—by seven European powers (Great Britain, France, Germany, Belgium, Portugal, Italy, and Spain).

AFRICAN COLONIAL HERITAGE COMPARED

The colonial system totally transformed the historical political geography of Africa in a few years' time, and the depth and intensity of alien penetration of subordinated societies continues to cast its shadow.[2] The comprehensive linkages with the metropolitan economies in many instances were difficult to disentangle. In the majority of cases in which decolonization was negotiated, the colonizer retained some capacity to shape the choice of postcolonial successors and often—especially in the French case—enjoyed extensive networks of access and influence long after independence was attained. The cultural and linguistic impact was pervasive, especially in sub-Saharan Africa, where the language of the colonizer continues to enjoy official status. Embedded in the institutions of the new states was the deep imprint of the mentalities and routines of their colonial predecessors. Overall, colonial legacy cast its shadow over the emergent African state system to a degree unique among the major world regions.

In Latin America, although colonial administrative subdivisions shaped the state system, Spain and Portugal swiftly ceased to be major regional players after Creole elites won independence in the nineteenth century. Great Britain and, later, the United States were the major external forces impinging upon the region. In Asia, the first target and long the crown jewel of the colonial enterprise, imperial conquest tended to follow the contours of an older state system; not all Asian states have a historical pedigree (the Philippines, Pakistan, Papua New Guinea), but a majority do. The circumstances surrounding Asian independence, the discontinuities imposed by the Japanese wartime occupation of Southeast Asia, and the larger scale of most Asian states and the greater autonomy of their economies all meant that the demise of the colonial order there was far more sharp and definitive than was the case in Africa.

Perhaps the closest parallel to Africa in terms of durable and troubled colonial impact on regional international relations is found in the Middle East. The partition of the Ottoman domains in the Levant between Great Britain and France and the imperial calculus employed in territorial definitions and structures of domination left in their wake a series of cancerous conflicts. The duplicity of incompatible wartime promises to Arabs and Zionists bore the seeds of inextricable conflict over whether the Palestine mandate awarded to Great Britain by the League of Nations would develop as a Jewish homeland or an Arab state; Great Britain invented Jordan as a territory for its wartime ally Prince Abdullah; Lebanese borders were drawn so as to maximize the zone of dominance for Maronite Christians; Sunni Arab nationalism in Syria was countered by heavy recruitment of minority Alawites for the colonial militia; and Kurdish state demands were denied so that oil-rich zones could be attached to the British-Iraqi mandate.[3] The unending turbulence in this region provides daily confirmation of the colonial roots of many intractable contemporary conflicts. But even here, colonial penetration of Middle Eastern Arab societies and economies was much less than was the case in Africa, and the erstwhile colonial connections weigh less heavily.

In the African instance, the shadow of the colonial past falls upon the contemporary state system in several critical features. The sheer number of sovereign units and the weakness and vulnerability of many due to their small scale are the most obvious. At the same time, the struggle for territorial independence always had an associated pan-African vision, which became a permanent vector in African international relations. The continuing importance of former economic and political colonial linkages, most of all for the twenty states formerly under French rule, significantly shapes regional politics—both as an active channel of influence and as a negative point of reference. Finally, and perhaps most important, the bureaucratic authoritarianism, which was the institutional essence of the colonial state, quickly resurfaced in the guise of single-party or military regimes, whose failure led to the widespread state crisis by the 1980s.[4] In this chapter, I will consider these components of the colonial heritage in turn.

FRAGMENTATION OF AFRICA

The African continent in 1993 (and its offshore islands) contained no fewer than fifty-three sovereign units (using U.N. membership as the criterion)—nearly one-third of the world total.[5] Although this large number has some advantages in guaranteeing a voice in international forums where the doctrine of sovereign equality assures equal voting rights for states large and small, this is little compensation for the disabilities of being tiny. Sheer economic weakness is one disadvantage. Most African states had a GNP less than the Harvard University endowment or the profits of a major multinational corporation. The limits of choice imposed by a narrow national market and circumscribed agricultural and mineral resource bases rendered most states highly vulnerable to the vagaries of commodity markets and the workings of the global economic system. Although some minuscule mercantile states elsewhere have achieved prosperity—Singapore is an obvious example—and tiny sovereignties perched on vast oil pools may accumulate enormous wealth—Kuwait, Bahrain, and Qatar are illustrations, now joined by Equatorial Guinea and São Tomé in Africa, of the microstates among Africa's fifty-three polities, only Mauritius, Equatorial Guinea, São Tomé and Príncipe, and to a lesser extent, Cape Verde, have prospered.

The full scope of the fragmentation of independent Africa was not apparent until the virtual eve of independence. Most of the vast sub-Saharan domains under French domination were joined in two large administrative federations: Afrique Occidentale Française (AOF) and Afrique Equatoriale Française (AEF). Political life, however, germinated first at the territorial level; the crucial 1956 *Loi-cadre* (framework law) located the vital institutions of African political autonomy at this echelon. Although some nationalist leaders dreamed of achieving independence within the broader unit, especially in the AOF, the wealthier territories (Ivory Coast, Gabon) were opposed to this. In the final compressed surge to independence, the interaction of divisions among nationalist leaders and movements, combined with French interests, resulted in twelve states of modest size rather than two large ones.[6] In the 1950s, Great Britain did promote federations of its colonial possessions as a formula for self-government in the West Indies, the United Arab Emirates, and Malaysia, as well as in east and central Africa, but with indifferent success. In east and central Africa, the fatal flaw was linking the project of broader political units to the entrenchment of special privilege for the European settler communities. Thus contaminated, the federation idea was bound to fail as a framework for independence, although the dream of an East African Federation was revived in the 1960s, and again at the turn of the century.[7] In instances in which large territories had been governed as single entities—Nigeria, Sudan, Congo-Kinshasa—independence as one polity was possible, although all three countries have, at times, been beset by separatist pressures.

Once sovereignty gave life to colonial territories as independent nations, the African state system has proven to be singularly refractory to broader movements of unification. The 1964 amalgamation of Tanganyika and Zanzibar to form Tanzania and the 1960 unification of British Somaliland and Italian-administered Somalia at the moment of independence remain the sole such cases. The Tanzania union with Zanzibar has been at times questioned, and in the wake of the collapse of a Somali state in 1991, Somaliland reemerged, although unrecognized by the international community, as a separate and functioning unit, in contrast to the prolonged anarchy in the rest of Somalia.

DREAM OF AFRICAN UNITY

The dream of a broader African unity persists, first nurtured by intellectuals of the diaspora and expressed through a series of pan-African conferences beginning in 1900, then embraced by the radical wing of African nationalism in the 1950s, above all, by Kwame Nkrumah of Ghana. The Organization of African

Unity (OAU) was created in 1963 to embody this dream, but even its charter demonstrated its contradictions. The OAU was structured as a cartel of states whose territorial integrity was a foundational principle. Rather than transcending the state system, the OAU consolidated it. Although the vocation of African unity was reaffirmed with the 2002 official launch of the African Union to replace an OAU deemed moribund, the ascendancy of states remains.

The urgency of regional and ultimately continental unification is nonetheless repeatedly endorsed in solemn documents. Innumerable regional integration schemes have been launched, of which the most important are the Union du Maghreb Arabe, the Economic Community of West African States, the Southern African Development Community, and the various customs and monetary unions of the francophonic West African states. But the goal of effective integration remains elusive; the impact of the colonial partition remains an enduring obstacle.

The colonial origins of most African states weighed heavily upon the consciousness of postindependence rulers. Initially, the fundamental illegitimacy of the boundaries was a central tenet of pan-African nationalism; the 1945 Manchester Pan-African Congress excoriated "the artificial divisions and territorial boundaries created by the Imperialist Powers." As late as 1958, the Accra All-African Peoples' Conference denounced "artificial frontiers drawn by the imperialist Powers to divide the peoples of Africa" and called for "the abolition or adjustment of such frontiers at an early date."[8] But once African normative doctrine was enunciated by the states rather than by nationalist movements, the tone changed, and the sanctity of colonial partition frontiers was asserted. The consensus of the first assembly of African independent states—also in Accra in 1958—was expressed by Nkrumah, the leading apostle of African unification: "Our conference came to the conclusion that in the interests of that Peace which is so essential, we should respect the independence, sovereignty and territorial integrity of one another."[9]

The OAU Charter made reference to territorial integrity no less than three times; at the Cairo OAU summit in 1964, the assembled heads of state made the commitment even more emphatic by a solemn pledge to actively uphold existing borders, a level of responsibility that goes significantly further than the mere passive recognition of the inviolability of frontiers.[10] Although a certain number of boundary disputes have arisen in independent Africa, the principle of the sanctity of colonial partition boundaries—the juridical concept of *uti possidetis*—remains a cornerstone of a solidifying African regional international law.[11] Most of the disputes have been resolved by negotiation, applying the colonial treaties as the point of juridical reference.[12] The enduring fear of the fragility of the African state system paradoxically endows the artificial, colonially imposed boundaries with astonishing durability. The one apparent exception—the independence of Eritrea from Ethiopia in 1993—can be said to prove the point. Eritrean nationalists grounded their claim to self-determination in the argument that Eritrea, as a former Italian colonial territory, should have had the opportunity for independence like all other former colonies, rather than being forcibly joined (in the Eritrean view) to Ethiopia by the international community. The same argument is advanced by the Western Saharan independence movement to contest Moroccan annexation justified by precolonial historic claims.

The colonial system profoundly reordered economic as well as political space. During their seventy-five years of uncurbed sovereignty, colonial powers viewed their African domains as veritable *chasses gardées* (private preserves). Metropolitan capital enjoyed privileged access; to varying degrees, other foreign investment was viewed with reserve or even hostility (especially by the Portuguese until the final colonial years). The security logic of the colonial state joined the metropolitan conviction that the occupant was entitled to exclusive economic benefits in return for the "sacrifice" of supplying governance services to foster trade and investment linkages, which tied African territories to metropolitan economies as subordinated appendages. Territorial infrastructures, particularly the communications systems, were shaped by the vision of imperial integration; road networks ran from the centers of production to the ports and colonial capitals. Although over time a shrinkage of the once-exclusive economic ties with the erstwhile colonizers has occurred, these bonds were so pervasive that they have been difficult to disentangle. It is no accident that regional economic integration schemes joining states once under different colonial jurisdictions have had only limited success; the most resilient mechanism of regional economic cooperation has been the Communauté Financière Africaine "CFA" franc zone, a product of the economic space defined by the former French empire in sub-Saharan Africa.

INFLUENCE OF FORMER COLONIZERS

The colonial occupation of Africa, which occurred relatively late in the global history of imperial expansion, was comparatively dense and thorough. The multiplex apparatus of domination, which was constructed to assure the "effective occupation" stipulated by the 1884–1885 Berlin Conference as a condition for the security of the proprietary title and to extract from the impoverished subjects the labor service and fiscal tribute to make alien hegemony self-financing, as metropolitan finance ministries required, was unlikely to dissolve instantly once the occupying country's flag was lowered on independence day. Over time, the many linkages—both manifest and submerged—binding the decolonized state to the former metropole have slowly eroded. They were a central dimension in the international relations of new states, especially in the early years of independence. Even five decades later, especially in the case of France, colonial connections still play a role.

Several factors influence the importance of ties with former colonizers. In those cases in which independence was won through armed liberation struggles rather than bargaining, the power transfer brought initial rupture (Algeria, Guinea-Bissau, Mozambique, Angola). In some other cases (Guinea, Congo-Kinshasa), the circumstances of independence brought immediate crisis and discontinuity in relationships; even though relations were ultimately restored, the degree of intimacy between the two countries could never be the same.[13] Generally, the smaller erstwhile colonial powers played a less visible role than did the two major imperial occupants, Great Britain and France.

Italy was largely eliminated by being on the losing side in World War II. Although it regained a ten-year trust territory mission in Somalia in 1950, Rome was never permitted to return to Libya and Eritrea and quickly ceased to be a factor in either territory. Spain was the last country to enter the colonial scramble, and it had only a superficial hold on its territories in northwest Africa (former Spanish Morocco, Ifni, Western Sahara, Equatorial Guinea). Its minor interests were swallowed up in postcolonial turmoil in its erstwhile domains (the Moroccan annexation of Western Sahara, the Macías Nguema capricious tyranny in Equatorial Guinea from its independence in 1968 until 1979). Emblematic of Spain's elimination from Africa was the affiliation of Equatorial Guinea with the French-tied CFA franc zone after Macías Nguema was overthrown in 1979.[14]

Belgium retained an important and uninterrupted role in its small former colonies of Rwanda and Burundi, but its economic interests in these states were not large. In Congo-Kinshasa, where the financial stake was considerable, relationships were punctuated with repeated crises.[15] The sudden and aborted power transfer left inextricably contentious disputes over the succession to the extensive colonial state holdings in a wide array of colonial corporations. These disputes were seemingly resolved several times, only to reemerge in new forms of contention.[16]

In the Portuguese case, an imperial mythology of the global Lusotropical multiracial community was a keystone of the corporatist authoritarianism of the Salazar-Caetano *Estado Novo*. However, the utter discrediting of this regime by its ruinous and unending colonial wars in Africa from 1961 to 1974 brought it repudiation.[17] More broadly, in the postcolonial era, a common element for the minor participants in the African partition was an abandonment of earlier notions that overseas proprietary domains validated national claims to standing and respect in the international arena.

Particularly intriguing has been the relative effacement over time of Great Britain on the African scene. Great Britain has long seen itself as a great power, although the resources to support such a claim silently ebbed away because of imperial overreach, according to one influential analysis.[18] In the 1950s, as the era of decolonization opened for Africa, conventional wisdom held that Great Britain was the most likely of the colonizers to maintain a permanent role in its vast colonial estates because of the flexible framework for evolution supplied by the British Commonwealth. This illusion proved to be based upon false inferences deduced from the older constellation of self-governing dominions, which had remained closely bound in imperial security relationships with London. Many thought the Commonwealth could preserve a British-ordered global ensemble beyond the formal grant of sovereignty in Asia and Africa. The illusion of permanence in which British imperialism so long basked dissipated slowly.[19] The doctrine enunciated at the 1926 Imperial Conference still dominated official thinking as the African hour of self-government approached. This document perceived the future as incorporating "autonomous communities within the British Empire, equal in status, in no way subordinate one to another in any aspect of their domestic or external affairs, though united by a common allegiance to the Crown and freely associated as members of the British Commonwealth of Nations."[20] As one of its commentators then wrote: "The British Empire is a strange complex. It is a heterogeneous collection of separate entities, and yet it is a political unit. It is wholly unprecedented; it has no written constitution; it is of quite recent growth; and its development has been amazingly rapid."[21] Membership is even open to countries never under British rule such as Mozambique, which joined in 1995.

These lyrical notions of a global commonwealth operating in a loose way as a political unit in world affairs so that Great Britain's claim to major power status might survive the decolonization of the empire eroded slowly. India's independence in 1947 was a crucial turning point; the true jewel in the imperial crown, its metamorphosis from the pivot of empire security to a self-assertive "neutralist" Asian power should have ended the illusion that an enlarged commonwealth could remain in any sense a "political unit." Yet when African members of the Commonwealth began joining with Ghanaian independence in 1957, some of the old mystique still persisted.

For most former British territories, joining the Commonwealth formed part of the *rite de passage* of independence; only Egypt and Sudan declined to enter its ranks.[22] Paradoxically, as Commonwealth membership became numerically dominated by Asian, African, and Caribbean states, it ceased to serve as a loose-knit, worldwide, British-inspired combine, and its meetings became occasions for heated attacks on British policy in Rhodesia and South Africa. Instead of the ingenious instrument for the subtle nurture of British global influence imagined by its designers, the Commonwealth thus seemed by the 1970s a funnel for unwelcome pressures upon British diplomacy. Even imperial nostalgia could not stave off recognition of these facts; waning British interest removed the Commonwealth's energizing center. In the words of one influential study, "The Commonwealth has survived only in [a] very attenuated form . . . [it is] still a useful argumentative forum for its governments, offering a place for small states to be heard, extending benefits (albeit on a modest scale) to its members, and providing opportunities for discussion of problems of common interest."[23] This adjustment in the British images of the Commonwealth goes hand in hand with the gradual reduction of London's self-perception—from global hegemon to middle-sized European power.

The diminishing mystique of the Commonwealth as the vessel for a global British role helps to explain the relative effacement of Great Britain on the African scene. In the first years of African independence, British disposition for intervention was still visible. In the army mutinies that swept Uganda, Kenya, and Tanganyika in 1964, British troops intervened to check the mutineers, at the request of the embattled regimes. In Nigeria, Great Britain initially had a defense agreement; however, this was annulled in 1962 due to Nigerian nationalist pressure. In a number of cases, national armies remained under British command for a few years after independence; in 1964, the British commander of the Nigerian army refused the solicitation of some Nigerian leaders to intervene after scandal-ridden national elections brought the country to the brink of disintegration. Security assistance and economic aid in modest quantities continue, and in a few cases—most notably Kenya—influence remains significant. But since 1970, the relatively subdued role of Britain, if set against the expectations of 1960, is what stands out. One striking recent exception was the energetic British military intervention under a UN cover in 1999–2000 in Sierra Leone, which put a final end to the macabre atrocities of the rebel Revolutionary United Front of Foday Sankoh.

THE FRENCH CONNECTION

The case of France, which has played a pervasive role in the seventeen sub-Saharan states formerly under its rule, is completely different from that of Great Britain. The political, cultural, economic, and military connection Paris has maintained with the erstwhile *bloc africain de l'empire* has been frequently tutelary, often intrusive, and sometimes overtly interventionist. The intimacy and durability of these linkages are as surprising as the eclipse of the United Kingdom. When African independence loomed on the horizon, France still suffered from its World War II humiliation and bitter internal divisions. The country was weakened by the chronic instability of the Fourth Republic, with one-third of its electorate aligned with the antiregime Stalinist French Communist party and its army locked in unending and unwinnable colonial wars—first in Indochina, then in Algeria. *France Against Itself* was the title of the most influential portrait of the epoch.[24] Few anticipated the recapture of its European status and sub-Saharan role as regional hegemon under the Fifth Republic.

In grasping the pervasive African role of the resurrected postcolonial France, one needs first to draw a sharp distinction between the Maghreb and sub-Saharan Africa, which is sometimes overlooked in the fascination with the French connection. In reality, French influence was shattered in what had been the most important parts of the former empire—North Africa and Indochina. In terms of the size of the economic stake, AOF (French West Africa federation) and especially AEF (French Equatorial Africa federation) were far behind the core regions of the imperial era. Psychologically, the heart of overseas France was Algeria, whose northern portions were considered to be full French departments. The savagery of the eight-year war for Algerian independence, especially the self-destructive fury of its final phases, compelled the exodus of most of the one million French settlers and the abandonment of much of their stranglehold on the Algerian economy.[25] The independent Algerian state pursued a consistently radical anti-imperial foreign policy until the 1990s, rendered financially possible by its relatively ample oil and natural gas revenues. Although Tunisia and Morocco were less assertive in international politics and leaned to Western positions in their nonalignment, neither accepted the degree of French tutelage that was common in sub-Saharan Africa.

Several factors explain the comprehensive nature of the French relationship with sub-Saharan states formerly under its domination.[26] The terminal colonial effort in this zone to construct an elusive "federalism" as permanent institutional bonding, although failing in its manifest goal of defining political status short of independence, had important consequences. The representation accorded emergent African leaders in the Fourth and (briefly) the Fifth Republics in French institutions, especially the Parliament, but also the cabinet of ministers, drew much of the sub-Saharan independence generation into the heart of French political processes. In the Algerian instance, Paris representation was dominated by settler interests and a small number of collaborating Algerians; Tunisia and Morocco, which had a different international legal status, were not given parliamentary seats.

Sub-Saharan Africans elected to French Parliament were far more representative of emergent political forces than the few Algerians who served in the

Paris Legislative Assembly. As early as the 1946 constitutional deliberations, Léopold Senghor of Senegal played an influential role. By the late Fourth Republic, African leaders held ministerial positions as well (for example, future presidents Félix Houphouët-Boigny of Ivory Coast, Modibo Keita of Mali). Until literally the eve of independence, the "federal" formula the Fifth Republic Constitution sought to institutionalize had the assent of most of the current francophone African political class, with the exception of the more radical intelligentsia—especially the students. The referendum approving the Fifth Republic Constitution in 1958, which proposed keeping the French-ruled sub-Saharan territories within a French sovereign framework, drew large, usually overwhelming majorities in all territories except Guinea, reflecting the strong wishes of the African leadership for its approval. Jarring as his words now sound, Houphouët-Boigny spoke for a political generation in his often-quoted 1956 statement: "To the mystique of independence we oppose the reality of fraternity." The degree of incorporation of the sub-Saharan African political elite into the French political world in the 1940s and 1950s has no parallel, and it left a lasting imprint on the texture of postcolonial relationships.[27] Successive French presidents from Charles de Gaulle to Jacques Chirac brought to office long-standing intimate ties with many sub-Saharan political leaders.

The original Fifth Republic concept of sub-Saharan territorial autonomy with an array of core sovereign functions (defense, money, and justice, for example) vested in the France-centered French community swiftly vanished.[28] In its place emerged an array of devices giving institutional expression to intimacy. Some form of defense accord was negotiated with fourteen sub-Saharan ex-colonies;[29] French troops were permanently garrisoned in Djibouti, the Central African Republic, Gabon, the Ivory Coast, and Senegal; and a reserve intervention force earmarked for swift African deployment was held in readiness in France. Except for Guinea, Mali, Mauritania, and Madagascar, all these ex-colonies remained within a French currency zone (and Guinea and Mali eventually sought reentry).

By the 1970s, Franco-African summit conferences became a regular and lavish part of the diplomatic landscape; often these attracted more heads of state than the OAU or AU summits. *Francophonie* as a cultural instrument finds expression in the French educational systems and linguistic policies; the nurture of the French language enjoys a priority in French diplomacy that is unique among former colonizers. In the Maghreb, *francophonie* competes with the active policies of affirmation of the Arab language and culture; in sub-Saharan Africa (excepting Madagascar and Mauritania), retention of French as the primary state vehicle has been internalized as a political value by most of the state class.[30] Even a populist socialist leader such as Alphonse Massemba-Débat of Congo-Brazzaville exclaimed in the late 1960s that the Congolese and the

French were "Siamese twins," separable only by surgery.[31] Senghor, who was the most intellectually brilliant member of the independence political generation, summed up the pervasive relationship as *francité* (Frenchness, Francehood).[32] His induction into the *Académie Française* was, in his own eyes, a crowning achievement in a splendid career. A neologism such as *francité* has plausible resonance in the Franco-African case, but its analogues would be preposterous in characterizing any other postcolonial ties.

A singular form of tutelary, or dependent, linkages results from this broad set of connections, not all of which are well captured in the visible aspect of politics or in the asymmetrical core-periphery economic flows to which "dependency theory" draws attention. The francophonic African community counts upon the senior French partner to defend its interests within the European Union and among the international financial institutions, both public and private. Priority access to French aid is assumed, including periodic budgetary bailouts for the more impoverished states.[33] French willingness to occasionally intervene militarily to protect clients is of crucial importance; between 1963 and 1983, Guy Martin tallies twenty instances of such intervention.[34] As then President Valéry Giscard d'Estaing stated, "We have intervened in Africa whenever an unacceptable situation had to be remedied."[35] Perhaps even more critical to the nurture of tutelary standing are French security services of a more clandestine nature. French intelligence services provide invaluable protection to rulers by their capacity to monitor and penetrate opposition groups and to foil potential conspiracies by providing early warning to incumbents. These security operations have always enjoyed high-level attention in Paris through such presidential advisers as the late éminence grise Jacques Foccart. François Mitterrand as president had entrusted these functions to his son, Jean-Christophe Mitterrand.

In the early years of the twenty-first century, there are signs that the silken threads binding francophonic Africa to France are fraying. France made no move to prevent the overthrow of Hissène Habré by armed insurgents enjoying Libyan support in Chad at the end of 1990, although French troops in Chad could easily have prevented the takeover. Nor did France lift a finger to avert the overthrow of Ivory Coast ruler Henri Bédié in December 1999 when he was forced out by a military coup. Supporting the CFA franc zone is more expensive and less profitable than it once was, and France engineered a large devaluation in 1994, in the face of heated opposition by a number of African clients. Pessimism has spread concerning Africa's infirm economic and political condition. Protection of friendly incumbents appears to have lost some of its attraction, as in early 1990, France softened its long-held view that single-party rule, with its corollary of life presidency, was the most "realistic" political formula for Africa. But the closely woven fabric of the French connection is too sturdy to quickly unravel, and France was more ambivalent toward democratization than the other former colonial powers.

STRUGGLE TO ELIMINATE COLONIAL INFLUENCE

The importance of the colonial past in shaping contemporary African international relations is thus beyond dispute. At the same time, the colonial system serves—paradoxically—as a negative point of reference for the African concert of nations. The legitimacy of the first generation of African regimes was rooted in the regimes' achievement—by conquest or negotiation—of independence. The two transcendent unifying principles of the pan-African movement from its inception have been opposition to both colonialism and racism, evils that were joined on the African continent. The independent states that assembled to create the OAU in 1963 were divided on many questions of ideology and interpretation of nonalignment; all could rally behind the combat to complete the liberation of Africa from colonial occupation and regimes of white racial domination. The elemental notion of African solidarity arose out of the shared experience of racial oppression, a point made explicit by W. E. B. Dubois many years ago.

> There is slowly arising not only a curiously strong brotherhood of Negro blood throughout the world, but the common cause of the darker races against the intolerable assumption and insults of Europeans has already found expression. Most of humanity are people of color. A belief in humanity means a belief in [people of color]. The future world will in all reasonable possibility be what colored men make of it.[36]

Nearly five decades later, Julius Nyerere translated these thoughts into African nationalist language: "Africans all over the continent, without a word being spoken, either from one individual to another, or from one African country to another, looked at the European, looked at one another, and knew that in relation to the European they were one."[37]

Indeed, at the moment of the OAU's creation, many of the most arduous independence struggles still lay ahead, such as those in the Portuguese territories, Zimbabwe, and Namibia, as well as the mortal combat with apartheid in South Africa. The OAU had a mediocre record in coping with conflicts within Africa (Somalia, Liberia, Eritrea, Western Sahara, the Nigerian civil war, the Congo rebellions, and Chad-Libya, for example). However, its anticolonial role has been important in providing a continental focus for African liberation diplomacy.

Within their own territorial domain, independent states faced a compulsion to demarcate themselves from their colonial past, to render visible the new status. The superficial symbolic accoutrements of independence—flags and postage stamps—might serve for a time. Africanization of the state apparatus might help as well, although over time, the perception could arise that the real benefits of this change accrued above all to state personnel.

The imperative of demarcation eventually spread to the economic realm. In the 1970s, a wave of seizures of foreign assets with potent colonial connotations swept through Africa: Idi Amin's "economic war" against the Asian community in 1972, Mobutu Sese Seko's "Zairianization" (Congolization) and "radicalization" campaigns of 1973 and 1974, Tanzania's socialization measures after the 1967 Arusha Declaration, the 1972 and 1976 Nigerian "indigenization decrees," the copper mine nationalizations in Zambia and Congo-Kinshasa, and parallel measures in many other countries. Measures of expropriation of foreign assets almost exclusively affected holdings associated with the colonial past. This partly reflected a distinction often made between postindependence investments, which involved contractual commitments (presumably) freely made by the African state, and those made under alien sovereignty, which lacked moral standing (and doubtless had been well amortized). More important, moves to indigenize the economy reflected pressures to move beyond purely political independence, which would be denatured if all the structures of economic subordination remained intact. By the 1980s, this surge of economic demarcation had run its course; the deepening economic crisis and heightened vulnerability to external pressures made such measures unfeasible. In addition, the measures were frequently discredited by the chaotic improvisation of their implementation and consequent dislocations (Congo-Kinshasa, Uganda) or by the perception that only narrow politico-mercantile classes had benefited (Nigeria).[38]

The compulsion for demarcation from the colonial past was driven by psychological as well as political and economic factors. Particularly in sub-Saharan Africa, the colonial era brought a broad-front assault upon African culture that was far more comprehensive than similar experiences in the Middle East and Asia. The "colonial situation," to borrow Georges Balandier's evocative concept,[39] was saturated with racism. African culture was, for the most part, regarded as having little value, and its religious aspect—outside the zones in which Islam was well implanted—was subject to uprooting through intensive Christian evangelical efforts, which were often state-supported. European languages supplanted indigenous ones for most state purposes; for the colonial subject, social mobility required mastering the idiom of the colonizer. In innumerable ways, colonial subjugation in Africa brought not only political oppression and economic exploitation but also profound psychological humiliation. In the nationalist response to colonialism, psychological themes are prevalent to a degree unique in Third World anti-imperialist thought. Frantz Fanon, the Martinique psychiatrist who supplied so powerful a voice to the Algerian revolution, was only the most eloquent such spokesman.[40] Such doctrines as *négritude* and "African personality" were central components in nationalist thought, asserting the authenticity and value of African culture. This dimension of African nationalism gave a special emotional edge to the postcolonial quest for demarcation, as well as to the fervor of African state reaction to racism and colonialism.

Colonial heritage as a negative point of reference also influenced the contours of Cold War intrusion into Africa. The United States and the Soviet Union both represented themselves as alternatives to exclusive reliance of African nations upon the erstwhile colonizers for succor and support, as has China more recently. Particularly in the early phases of independence, visible Soviet linkages served as a badge of demarcation. The extravagant fears of all colonizers—and of the West generally—regarding "Communist penetration" of Africa enhanced the value of Soviet relations, even if Soviet economic assistance was minimal. For those states that wanted (or felt compelled to undertake) a more comprehensive break with the Western colonial system, for a short period in the early 1960s and again in the 1970s, the Soviet bloc appeared to offer an alternative. The bargain proved to be rather fruitless, however, as the Soviet Union began to disengage from Africa in the early 1980s.[41]

AUTHORITARIAN LEGACY OF THE COLONIAL STATE

Finally, the defining attribute of the colonial state in Africa until its final years was the monopoly of central authority enjoyed by its almost entirely European top administration. The structures of a postindependence polity were grafted onto the robust trunk of colonial autocracy, which proved a much more enduring legacy than the hastily created and weakly rooted democratic institutions normally assembled at the final hour before independence. The command habits and authoritarian routines of the colonial state were in most countries soon reproduced in single-party or military-political monopolies.

In the final colonial years after World War II, the superstructure of imperial rule had become well professionalized, its European cadres trained in specialized institutes, and its African chiefly intermediaries now requiring literacy and competence as well as customary qualifications. The imperial administration enjoyed exceptional insulation from an emergent African civil society denied organizational scope till the eve of independence by repressive colonial legislation. The African colonial state was a pure model of bureaucratic authoritarianism.

Swelling postwar colonial revenues fueled by the global commodity boom, and for the first time significant metropolitan public investment, yielded rapid expansion of state services and social infrastructure in the final colonial decade. Though some authors, notably Jeffrey Herbst, argue that the colonial state was weak,[42] in my reading, in the form bequeathed to the African independence elite generation, the late colonial state was a robust and effective hegemonic apparatus habituated to a command relationship with its subject population. The African state weakness stressed in the introductory chapter is rather a product of political itineraries since 1960 than an immediate consequence of colonial legacy.[43]

Postcolonial rulers, inspired by a vision of high modernity to be swiftly realized, sought a rapid expansion in the mission and scope of the state.[44] African independence coincided with a moment of peak confidence in state-led development; the example of apparent centrally planned transformation of the Soviet Union and China stood as potent models. To release the developmental state from the constraints of democratic process, the fragile representative institutions belatedly created by the withdrawing colonizer for the transition to independence were set aside in favor of single parties or, when these lost public favor, military regimes restoring the colonial legacy of authoritarian rule.

However, effective centralization and monopolization of power and political space did not suffice to ensure the unhindered hegemony of the postcolonial state, which could never match the autonomy from society enjoyed by the imperial bureaucracy. The command state could not operate on the basis of impersonal authority and coercive force alone; indispensable were supplementary mechanisms translating state rule into personalized linkages with key intermediaries and their ramifying networks of clientele. By subtle metamorphosis the bureaucratic authoritarianism of the colonial state legacy became the patrimonial autocracy almost everywhere ascendent by the 1970s. As numerous works attest,[45] this pathway led to the economic and political bankruptcy afflicting most states by the calamitous 1980s, and the battered, delegitimated—and weak—state which faced the democracy moment of 1990, a tale beyond the scope of this chapter.

Thus, in various ways, the colonial heritage intrudes into postindependence African international relations. Perhaps nearly five decades after the great surge to independence in 1960, the colonial shadow will begin to fade. Important new trends that may tug colonial legacy further into the background will have a critical impact as the new century unfolds.[46] The end of the Cold War has already had a profound influence. The depth of the economic crisis and a widening consensus that regional integration that bridges the old colonial divisions is indispensable to overcoming them, which may lead to innovations in the state system that will begin to transcend the colonial partition. For the first forty-odd years of African independence, however, colonial heritage has powerfully shaped the African international system.

NOTES

1. Jeffrey Herbst, *States and Social Power in Africa: Comparative Lessons in Authority and Control* (Princeton: Princeton University Press, 1994).

2. For a more extended argument on the pathology of the African colonial state, see Crawford Young, *The African Colonial State in Comparative Perspective* (New Haven: Yale University Press, 1994).

3. In the extensive literature on these themes, I have found especially useful Charles Issawi, *An Economic History of the Middle East and North Africa* (New York: Columbia University Press, 1972); Peter Sluglett, *Britain in Iraq, 1914–1932* (London: Ithaca Press, 1976); William Roger Louis, *The British Empire in the Middle East, 1945–1951: Arab Nationalism, the United States, and Postwar Imperialism* (Oxford: Clarendon Press, 1984); George Antonius, *The Arab Awakening* (New York: Capricorn Books, 1965); and Mary C. Wilson, *King Abdulla, Britain and the Making of Jordan* (Cambridge: Cambridge University Press, 1987).

4. This argument is advanced in detail in Young, *The African Colonial State.*

5. This total does not include Western Sahara, which is recognized as a member state by the Organization of African Unity but not by the United Nations. Eritrea and South Africa were added in the 1990s.

6. The most careful political history of this process of fragmentation is Joseph-Roger de Benoist, *La Balkanisation de l'Afrique Occidentale Française* (Dakar: Nouvelles Editions Africaines, 1979). His study clearly demonstrates that the balkanization was less a product of Machiavellian French design than the outcome of a complicated interplay of African political competition and French improvised response. Resentment of the distant bureaucratic despotism of the AOF French administrative headquarters was common in the outlying territories. Those nationalist leaders who, at various times, fought to preserve the unit—Léopold Senghor, Sékou Touré, Modibo Keita—were constrained both by their own rivalries and by the absence of a strong popular attachment to the AOF as a geographical entity.

7. Among the works on this subject, see Arthur Hazlewood, ed., *African Integration and Disintegration* (London: Oxford University Press, 1967); Joseph S. Nye, *Pan-Africanism and East African Integration* (Cambridge: Cambridge University Press, 1965); Patrick Keatley, *The Politics of Partnership* (Harmondsworth: Penguin Books, 1964); Philip Mason, *Year of Decision: Rhodesia and Nyasaland in 1960* (London: Oxford University Press, 1960); and Donald S. Rothchild, *Toward Unity in Africa: A Study of Federalism in British Africa* (Washington, D.C.: Public Affairs, 1960).

8. Saadia Touval, *The Boundary Politics of Independent Africa* (Cambridge, Mass.: Harvard University Press, 1972), pp. 22–23, 56–57.

9. Ibid., p. 54.

10. Onyeonoro S. Kamanu, "Secession and the Right of Self-Determination: An O.A.U. Dilemma," *Journal of Modern African Studies* 12, no. 3 (1974), pp. 371–373.

11. *Uti possidetis* is derived from a Roman private law concept, which holds that pending litigation, the existing state of possession of immovable property is retained. Translated into international law, the phrase means that irrespective of the legitimacy of the original acquisition of territory, the existing disposition of the territory remains in effect until altered by a freely negotiated treaty. For a passionate attack on this doctrine by a Moroccan jurist, see Abdelhamid El Ouali, "L'uti possidetis ou le non-sens du principle de base de l'OUA pour le règlement des différends territoriaux," *Le mois en Afrique* 227–228 (December 1984–January 1985), pp. 3–19.

12. For major studies on African boundary issues, see, in addition to the previously cited Touval work, Ricardo René Larémont, *Borders, Nationalisms, and the African State* (Boulder: Lynne Rienner Publishers, 2005); Carl Gosta Widstrand, ed., *African Boundary Problems* (Uppsala: Scandinavian Institute of African Studies, 1969); A. I. Asiwaju, *Partitioned Africans: Ethnic Relations Across Africa's International Boundaries, 1884–1984* (London: C. Hurst, 1984); Ian Brownlie, *African Boundaries: A Legal and Diplomatic Encyclopedia* (Berkeley: University of California Press, 1979); and Markus Kornprobst, "Border Disputes in African Regional Sub-Systems," *Journal of Modern African Studies*, 40, no. 2 (2002), pp. 360–394.

13. For example, in the colonial Congo, the dominant financial combine was the Société Générale group. By the early twenty-first century, the Société Générale had completely redeployed its vast capital holdings out of Congo-Kinshasa.

14. On the limited nature of Spanish rule, see Ibrahim Sundiata, *Equatorial Guinea* (Boulder: Westview Press, 1989); and Tony Hodges, *Western Sahara: The Roots of a Desert War* (Westport, Conn.: Lawrence Hill, 1983).

15. For thorough detail, see Gauthier de Villers, "Belgique-Zaire: Le grand affrontement," *Cahiers du CEDAF* 1–2 (1990).

16. For detail on the *contentieux*, see Crawford Young and Thomas Turner, *The Rise and Decline of the Zairian State* (Madison: University of Wisconsin Press, 1985), pp. 276–325.

17. Patrick Chabal et al., *A History of Postcolonial Lusophone Africa* (Bloomington: Indiana University Press, 2002).

18. Paul Kennedy, *The Rise and Fall of the Great Powers: Economic Change and Military Conflict from 1500 to 2000* (New York: Vintage Books, 1987).

19. The phrase is drawn from the intriguing study by Francis G. Hutchins, *The Illusion of Permanence: British Imperialism in India* (Princeton: Princeton University Press, 1967).

20. Cited in Cecil J. B. Hurst et al., *Great Britain and the Dominions* (Chicago: University of Chicago Press, 1928), p. 9.

21. Ibid., p. 3.

22. South Africa, which had been a member since its accession to "dominion" status in 1910, quit in 1961 in the face of increasing attacks from the swelling ranks of African members but rejoined after the fall of the apartheid regime.

23. Dennis Austin, *The Commonwealth and Britain* (London: Routledge and Kegan Paul, 1988), pp. 62, 64.

24. Herbert Luthy, *France Against Itself* (New York: Meridian Books, 1959).

25. For a graphic account of the holocaust during the final year of the Algerian war, with a mutinous army and a murderous settler force—the Organization de l'Armée Secrète—see Paul Henissart, *Wolves in the City: The Death of French Algeria* (New York: Simon and Schuster, 1970).

26. Useful studies on this topic include Edward Corbett, *The French Presence in Black Africa* (Washington, D.C.: Black Orpheus Press, 1972); Guy Martin, "Bases of France's African Policy," *Journal of Modern African Studies* 23, no. 2 (1985), pp. 189–208; George Chaffard, *Les carnets secrets de la décolonisation* (Paris: Calmass-Levy, 1965); Pierre Pean, *Affaires africaines* (Paris: Fayard, 1983); and Charles-Robert Ageron, *Les chemins de la décolonisation de l'empire français, 1936–1956* (Paris: Editions du CNRS, 1986).

27. Victor T. Le Vine, *Politics in Francophone Africa* (Boulder: Lynne Rienner Publishers, 2004), pp. 61–102.

28. For a painstaking account by a highly informed French observer, see Joseph-Roger de Benoist, *Afrique Occidentale Française de 1944 à 1960* (Dakar: Nouvelles Editions Africaines, 1982).

29. Martin, "Bases of France's African Policy," p. 204.

30. One encounters some exceptions among the intelligentsia; one example was the late Cheikh Anta Diop of Senegal, a cultural nationalist of great influence who strongly urged promotion of the most widely spoken Senegalese language, Wolof. But overall, the commitment to French as the cultural medium is far more entrenched in the former French sub-Saharan territories than anywhere else in Africa.

31. Corbett, *The French Presence,* p. 66.

32. Léopold Sédar Senghor, *Ce que je crois: Négritude, francité et civilisation de l'universel* (Paris: B. Crasset, 1988).

33. In theory, financial injections to meet budgetary crises—most commonly, payments to civil servants—have long ceased; in practice, they continue to occur. For fascinating details on the process and its political importance, see Raymond Webb, "State Politics in the Central African Republic," Ph.D. diss., University of Wisconsin–Madison, 1990.

34. Martin, "Bases of France's African Policy," p. 194.

35. Ibid.

36. Quoted in Victor Bakpetu Thompson, *Africa and Unity: The Evolution of Pan-Africanism* (London: Longman, 1969), p. 36.

37. Lecture by Julius Nyerere at Wellesley College, Wellesley, Mass., April 1961; from my notes.

38. For details, see Crawford Young, *Ideology and Development in Africa* (New Haven: Yale University Press, 1982).

39. Georges Balandier, "The Colonial Situation," in Pierre van den Berghe, ed., *Africa: Social Problems of Change and Conflict* (San Francisco: Chandler Publishing, 1965), pp. 36–57.

40. See, for example, Frantz Fanon, *Black Skin, White Masks* (New York: Grove Press, 1967). On this theme, see also O. Mannoni, *Prospero and Caliban: The Psychology of Colonization* (London: Methuen, 1956), and A. Memmi, *Portrait du colonisé, précédé du portrait du colonisateur* (Paris: Buchet-Chastel, 1957).

41. Arnold Hughes, ed., *Marxism's Retreat from Africa* (London: Frank Cass, 1992).

42. Herbst, *States and Social Power.*

43. For a more extended argument, see Young, *The African Colonial State.*

44. James C. Scott, *Seeing Like a State: How Certain Schemes to Improve the Human Condition Have Failed* (New Haven: Yale University Press, 1998).

45. Among other sources, see Achille Mbembe, *On the Postcolony* (Berkeley: University of California Press, 2001); Mark R. Beissinger and Crawford Young, eds., *Beyond State Crisis? Postcolonial Africa and Post-Soviet Eurasia in Comparative Perspective* (Washington, D.C.: Woodrow Wilson Center Press, 2002); Patrick Chabal and Jean-Pascal Daloz, *Africa Works: Disorder as Political Instrument* (Oxford: James Currey, 1999); and Jean-François Bayart, *The State in Africa: The Politics of the Belly* (New York: Longman, 1993).

46. For analysis of some such trends, see Thomas Callaghy, Ronald Kassimir, and Robert Latham, eds., *Intervention and Transnationalism in Africa* (Cambridge: Cambridge University Press, 2001).

3

Africa and the World Political Economy

Still Caught Between a Rock and a Hard Place?

THOMAS M. CALLAGHY

MARGINALIZATION AND DEPENDENCE

Since the late nineteenth century, Africa's political economy has left it marginalized and highly dependent on outside actors and forces. There are, however, modest indications that this may be changing due to four major structural changes: (1) the basic health of the world economy in the mid- and late 2000s, especially high commodity prices, (2) the rise of China as a major economic and political power—possibly the single most important event of the past thirty years, (3) the rise of nongovernmental organizations (NGOs) as key players in international economic governance, which has led to major debt reduction and increased aid, and (4) the new post–September 11 international context, which has increased Africa's geostrategic importance. The question remains whether Africa is ready to take full productive advantage of these new opportunities.[1]

Increased Marginalization: "Post-neocolonialism"

From the mid-1980s to the late 1990s, the marginalization of most countries in sub-Saharan Africa actually increased. The decline was twofold—economic and politico-strategic—and both aspects were tightly linked. The first, primarily economic, aspect was that Africa was no longer very important to the major actors in the world economy (equity investors, multinational corporations, and international banks). The second aspect of Africa's marginalization was that with the end of the Cold War, African countries had less politico-strategic importance for the major world powers. Africa generated a declining share of world output, and the main commodities it produced were becoming less important or being more effectively produced by other developing countries. Trade was declining; few wanted to lend, especially in the private sector, and an even smaller number wanted to invest, except in narrowly defined mineral enclave sectors.

Africa's per capita income levels and growth rates declined after the first oil crisis in 1973, while its percentage of worldwide official development assistance rose from 17 percent in 1970 to about 38 percent in 1991. After 1970, nominal gross domestic product (GDP) for sub-Saharan African countries rose more slowly than that of other developing countries, while real GDP growth rates dropped dramatically.

Other developing countries performed better in spite of the poor world economic climate, especially in the 1980s. Cross-regional comparisons were quite revealing. For the period 1982–1992, average GDP growth for Africa was 2.0 percent; for South Asia, the most comparable region, it was 5.2 percent, while the East Asian rate was 8.0 percent. The rate for all developing countries was 2.7 percent. The GDP per capita rates were even more revealing: Africa, –1.1 percent; South Asia, 2.9 percent; and East Asia, 6.4 percent. At these rates of per capita GDP growth, it would be forty years before Africa got back to mid-1970s levels. The World Bank's baseline projections for Africa in the 1990s were more optimistic, but, as we shall see, its projections for the 1990s met with very mixed results.

In addition, African export levels stayed relatively flat or, actually declined after 1970, while those of other developing countries rose significantly. For example, the continent's share of developing country agricultural primary product and food exports declined from 17 percent to 8 percent between 1970 and 1990, while South and East Asian exports grew rapidly. If the 1970 share had been maintained, export earnings in the early 1990s would have been significantly higher. Average annual growth rates for all exports fared poorly.

Africa's marginalization became even more obvious when its performance was compared with that of other low-income countries. This was particularly true in regard to South Asia, with which Africa has the most in common. South Asia is composed of Bangladesh, Bhutan, Burma, India, Maldives, Nepal, Pakistan, and Sri Lanka. The difference in per capita GDP growth between the two regions was striking: Africa's declined dramatically, while that of South Asia rose slowly but steadily. Moreover, Africa's population growth rate continued to climb, while that of South Asia began to decline.

The most startling differences between the two regions related to the level and quality of investment. Africa's investment as a percentage of GDP declined in the 1980s, while that of South Asia continued to increase, despite the difficult economic conditions of the decade. South Asia followed better economic policies and, above all, provided a much more propitious socioeconomic and politico-administrative context for investment. This was most vividly manifested in the comparative rates of return on investment: Africa's fell from 30.7 percent in the 1960s to just 2.5 percent in the 1980s, while South Asia's increased slowly but steadily, if only marginally, from 21.3 percent to 22.4 percent in the same period.

Given this dismal economic performance, both substantively and comparatively, it was not surprising that world business leaders took an increasingly jaundiced view of Africa. As one business executive expressed it to me in 1990, "Who cares about Africa; it is not important to us; leave it to the IMF and the World Bank."[2] Some observers referred to this phenomenon as *post-neocolonialism*. For the most dynamic actors in a rapidly changing world economy, even a neocolonial Africa was not of much interest, especially after the amazing changes wrought in Asia and Eastern Europe in the late 1980s and early 1990s. According to this viewpoint, the African crisis really should be left to the international financial institutions as a salvage operation, and if that effort worked, fine; if not, so be it. The world economy would hardly notice.

Thus, Africa increasingly imposed enormous difficulties for potential international investors, including political arbitrariness, spreading civil war and other forms of strife, and administrative, infrastructural, and economic inefficiency. Foreign capital had considerable ability to select the type of state with which it cooperated, and therefore it was doubtful that Africa would play any significant role in the ongoing shifts in the patterns of production in the international division of labor, especially after the international economic crisis that began in Asia in 1997 and spread to Russia and parts of Latin America. For most external business people, Africa had become a voracious sinkhole that swallowed their money with little or no long-run return. Two arresting facts further underscored Africa's marginalization by the early 1990s: (1) the amount of external financing done in 1991 through bonds for East Asia was $2.4 billion, and for South Asia $1.9 billion, while it was zero for Africa; and (2) flight capital at the end of 1990 as a percentage of GDP was 14.9 percent for South Asia, 18.9 percent for East Asia, 27.8 percent for developing Europe and Central Asia, while it was 80.3 percent for Africa.

From this perspective, the laments of international organizations and development economists about the intractable underdevelopment of Africa were not a conspiratorial attempt to conceal the pillage of Africa, but rather a reflection of the fact (although they would not put it this way) that Africa, from the point of view of major private economic actors, was an underexploited continent with weak states and weak markets.

The second aspect of Africa's marginalization was politico-strategic and entailed negative economic consequences as well. Africa had become of much less interest to the major world powers after the end of the Cold War. As one senior African diplomat put it, "We are an old tattered lady. People are tired of Africa. So many countries, so many wars."[3] The rise of warlords in regional and civil wars similar to those in nineteenth-century Africa challenged the very notion of the nation-state borrowed at the time of independence in the 1960s.

At the same time, however, the dramatic changes of 1989, Africa's politico-strategic marginalization, and the search for a new foreign policy rationale by Western industrial democracies in the early 1990s meant that economic conditionality was joined by forms of political conditionality, under the assumption that economic and political liberalization must go hand in hand. Hence, along with economic marginalization, Africa was becoming more dependent on often quite intrusive external actors.

Increased Involvement: The New Neocolonialism

In the 1980s, Africa became more tightly linked to the world economy in two major ways: (1) an extreme dependence on external public actors, particularly the International Monetary Fund (IMF) and the World Bank, in the determination of African economic policy, and (2) the liberal or neoclassical thrust of this economic policy conditionality, which tried to push the continent toward more integration with the world economy. Both of these aspects were linked directly to Africa's debt crisis.

In 1974, total African debt was about \$14.8 billion; by 1992, \$150 billion, amounting to more than 100 percent of Africa's total GNP. South Asia's percentage debt was only 36.3 and East Asia's 27.9. Much of Africa's debt was owed to international financial institutions (IFIs), especially the IMF and the World Bank, and resulted largely from the borrowing associated with externally sponsored economic reform programs, usually referred to as structural adjustment. In 1980, IFI debt equaled 19 percent of the total; by 1992, it accounted for 28 percent, and by 1998, it reached 32 percent. Until 1996, this debt could not be formally rescheduled or diminished, and significant arrears accumulated, with the result that some countries were cut off from IMF and

World Bank assistance. Much of the rest of Africa's debt was bilateral or government-guaranteed private medium- and long-term debt, and thus was rescheduled by Western governments through the Paris Club, not by private banks, as was the case in Latin America and Asia. A key norm of the debt regime was that countries could not obtain Paris Club rescheduling relief without being in the good graces of the IMF and the World Bank.

This difficult external debt burden and the resulting desperate need for foreign exchange made African countries very dependent on a variety of external actors, all of whom used their leverage to "encourage" economic liberalization. This process, which some have referred to as the new neocolonialism, meant intense dependence on the IMF, the World Bank, and major Western countries for the design of economic reform packages and the resources needed to implement them. This leverage was converted into economic policy conditionality—specific economic policy changes in return for borrowed resources. The primary thrust of these economic reform efforts was to try to integrate African economies more fully into the world economy by resurrecting the primary-product export economies that existed at the time of independence and making them work properly this time by creating a more "liberal" political economy.

One good indicator of this increased international involvement was the number of African countries with ongoing relationships with the IMF and the World Bank. Between 1970 and 1978, African countries accounted for 3 percent of total assistance from IMF-approved economic reform programs. Their share of the total number of IMF programs for this period was 17 percent; by the end of 1979, it rose to 55 percent. In 1978, only two African countries had agreements with the IMF; in March 1990, twenty-eight African countries had agreements with the IMF (constituting 60 percent of all agreements). Despite the large number of new members from Eastern Europe and the former Soviet Union, African countries still accounted for 38 percent of the agreements in September 1993. By February 1999, 41 percent of the agreements were with African countries, despite an increased number of programs due to the Asia crisis. Most of these countries also had agreements with the World Bank. Lastly, African countries had the highest number of repeat programs of any region of the world.

In sum, Africa's dismal situation was not caused predominantly by its relationship with the world economy or with dominant countries or actors in the international state system. Clearly, however, what happened to Africa was the *combined* result of the effects of world market forces, the international state system and its international financial institutions, African socioeconomic structures, and the nature and performance of African state structures. Africa had always been relatively marginal in the world economy. In many respects,

Africa was lost between state and market. It wandered between an ineffective, sometimes collapsing state and weak markets, both domestic and international, and the latter were increasingly indifferent.

THE POLITICAL ECONOMY OF ATTEMPTED ECONOMIC REFORM IN THE 1980s AND 1990s

By the early 1980s, the key question was not whether Africa had a serious economic crisis, but what to do about it. Avoiding the problem and policy drift were common reactions despite external warnings and pressure. Much of the African response was to rail against the prescriptions of external actors. For those governments that did decide—out of conviction or a desperate need for foreign exchange and debt rescheduling—to attack the problem, the dilemmas were enormous, the risks great, and the uncertainties pervasive. Throughout the 1980s and early 1990s, economic reform did take place in Africa in large and small ways. Many countries went through the motions or at least appeared to do so, resulting in a series of small reforms. Few cases of large reform—that is, multisector and sustained over time—appeared, however.

Ghana and Uganda were the only clear-cut examples, and they illustrated the enormous difficulties. Dr. Kwesi Botchwey, Ghana's longtime finance minister, portrayed them vividly:

> We were faced with two options, which we debated very fiercely before we finally chose this path. I know because I participated very actively in these debates. Two choices: We had to maneuver our way around the naiveties of leftism, which has a sort of disdain for any talk of financial discipline, which seek refuge in some vague concept of structuralism in which everything doable is possible . . . . Moreover, [we had to find a way between] this naiveté and the crudities and rigidities and dogma of monetarism, which behaves as if once you set the monetary incentives everybody will do the right thing and the market will be perfect.[4]

As the Rawlings regime in Ghana and the Museveni regime in Uganda discovered, neither position is fully correct: Everything is not possible, and policy incentives do not ensure that markets will work well. In addition, a revenue imperative exists no matter what path is chosen. Resources have to come from somewhere. A quite rare conjuncture of factors allowed the economic reform in Ghana and Uganda to be sustained, and their success at large reform—which is still fragile—was rare on the continent.

Economic Reform and the Implicit Bargain

Africans had long maintained that substantial resource flows and debt relief were required for sustained reform. One of the lessons of Ghana and Uganda was that they were certainly necessary but not sufficient conditions for resurrecting Africa's economy. By the early 1990s, external actors began to realize that increased resource flows and debt relief were going to be required for Africa. This realization began to sink in as the enormous obstacles to reform and the possibility of widespread failure became increasingly apparent.

A larger problem existed, however, that was directly linked to Africa's increasing marginalization from the world economy. An implicit bargain was struck between the IFIs and the major Western countries, on the one hand, and African countries, on the other. The provisions of the bargain were that if African countries successfully reformed their economies in a neo-orthodox direction with the help and direction of the IMF and the World Bank, new international private bank and bond lending and equity and direct foreign investment would be available to underpin and sustain the reform efforts.

By the early 1990s, this implicit bargain was very far from being upheld. It was not really the fault of the IMF and the World Bank, both of which worked to increase voluntary lending and direct foreign investment, or of reforming African governments. It was a legacy of Africa's thirty-year history of dismal economic performance, a track record that banks and investors did not forget easily. More importantly, structural shifts in the world economy and state system made other areas of the world more attractive to investors. Even if the African end of the bargain were fulfilled, and it rarely was, the bargain would hold only if other areas of the world did not provide better opportunities. The "flight to safety" that followed the onset of the Asia crisis in 1997 demonstrated that, under conditions of uncertainty and shattered expectations, capital would return to the heartland of the world economy and not go to marginalized areas such as Africa except for oil and some minerals.

Structural adjustment was an enormously difficult and politically sensitive task in Africa, especially as the benefits were often uncertain and came quite far down the road. Reform was often complicated by other factors, such as drought, famine, civil and regional wars, political destabilization, weakening states, and AIDS.

A link clearly existed between debt and structural adjustment in Africa, but it was not predominantly a causal one. The need for structural adjustment long predated the debt crisis despite the views of many Africans. The debt crisis merely brought the structural adjustment crisis to a head. Even if the debt crisis had miraculously been solved, the structural adjustment crisis would have remained. The case of Nigeria showed that massive amounts of new resources could intensify rather than ameliorate economic decline.

For Africa, the task of confronting this decline was enormous, much more so than for any other region of the world with the possible exception of Central Asia. External actors learned that Africa was a special case; it had not responded as neoclassical theory predicted it should. The World Bank observed that:

> The supply response to adjustment lending in low-income countries, especially in SSA [sub-Saharan Africa], has been slow because of the legacy of deep-seated structural problems. Inadequate infrastructure, poorly developed markets, rudimentary industrial sectors, and severe institutional and managerial weaknesses in the public and the private sectors have proved unexpectedly serious as constraints to better performance—especially in the poorer countries of SSA. Greater recognition thus needs to be given to the time and attention needed for structural changes, especially institutional reforms and their effects.[5]

Note the revealing use of *unexpectedly*: It indicates a changed perception—that Africa was a particularly difficult case. It was not just a case of reordering policies, but rather one of constructing a whole new context—what the World Bank called an "enabling environment."

In a sense, both the structuralist and neoliberal sides were correct: As the structuralists maintained, there were enormous economic and social structure obstacles to development in Africa; and as the adherents of neoliberalism maintained, the state was also an impediment. Both sets of obstacles inhibit both import substitution industrialization and export-oriented economic activity, public and private. The structuralists were correct that socioeconomic obstacles prevented neoclassical monoeconomics—the presumption that economic processes work the same everywhere—from being fully operative in Africa, as the World Bank had "unexpectedly" discovered; and the neoliberals were correct that the nature of the state in Africa made import substitution industrialization ineffective and wasteful, as many African structuralists still had not admitted.

Structuralists did have a theory of reform; it was just a weak one, however, because its primary instrument of reform—the state—was itself terribly ineffective in Africa. Yet in the course of attempted reform, the external proponents of neoclassical change confronted an orthodox paradox—in order to implement such reform, they, too, had to use what they perceived to be the major obstacle to reform—the African state—as the primary instrument of reform. Many people knew what kind of state was needed, but nobody knew how to obtain it. Other than getting the state out of the economy, the neoclassical strategists did not have a theory of state reform, and they found that getting the state out of the economy was much more difficult than expected—politically, administratively, and technically. In addition, the adherents of neo-orthodoxy learned that their own proclaimed instrument of reform, the market, was also terribly weak in Africa. Over time, it became clear that nobody understood the functioning of African economies; even the basic data set for the formal economy was extremely limited and unreliable, and systematic data on the informal economy was nearly nonexistent. After forty years of independence, most of Africa was neither effectively socialist nor capitalist; it was not even competently statist. Africa was caught between a rock and a hard place.

Doubts and Debates

Despite the learning that occurred by the end of the 1980s—with obstacles to reform apparent on all sides—the key question remained: What should Africa do to cope with its devastating economic crisis? The answer of the external actors, led by the IMF and the World Bank, was to persevere with the neoliberal thrust of reforms, with modifications to make them work more effectively. Many Africans remained unconvinced. This fundamental disagreement simmered quietly throughout the 1990s, while the IFIs claimed there was an increasing consensus around a modified neo-orthodox position. What was taken as consensus by powerful external actors was, in fact, a quiet waiting game generated by the desperate need of African countries for external resources and the hope of a major bailout through substantial debt relief, higher export prices, greatly increased bilateral and multilateral aid, commercial bank lending, or direct foreign investment. Amazingly, by 2007 much of this had taken place.

In the meantime, the debate had flared up again in 1993. This time, the IMF and the World Bank had to defend themselves on a wider variety of fronts, most urgently at the annual Fund-Bank meetings. Africa was a major topic of discussion because, compared to other regions, economic reform was not doing well. The IMF and the World Bank now conceded that reform had been modest and that it was taking longer than they had expected. They admitted that in the decade between 1980 and 1990, half of the IMF programs in Africa had broken down, as had two-thirds of the World Bank structural adjustment loans. By their own reckoning, only one of twenty-six countries in Africa with reform efforts in 1990–1991 did well, while the results in fourteen other countries were only fair. In eleven countries, results were poor to very poor.

One of the major structural changes in the international system was the emergence of development NGOs, as a policy force to be reckoned with. Oxfam issued a stinging attack on structural adjustment entitled *Africa Make or Break: Action for Recovery*,[6] supported by additional critiques from the Environmental Defense Fund, Development Gap, Christian Aid, and others. Oxfam declared bluntly that IMF reform in Africa had failed and that if the Fund did not undergo major reform, it should withdraw from Africa. Legislators in some Western countries also complained about the marginal reform results in Africa, funded by the taxes of their citizens. At the same time, academics and Asian governments insisted that there were statist lessons to be learned from the East Asian experience. Japan held a major conference on Africa in Tokyo in October 1993 in which it pushed these views, while making no new pledges of assistance. At the same time, it was also clear that African views about structural adjustment had not changed much either. It was still largely seen as an externally imposed evil, and many Africans believed that the world should accept an African alternative *and* pay for it.

But what was this African alternative? Had it evolved and become more coherent, more viable? The answer was no. A viable African alternative to IMF and World Bank reform did not exist, especially given the weak state capabilities. An East Asian statist option was also clearly not possible. Desires for transformation do not an alternative make. The Fund/Bank strategy was a second-best one, but a modified version of it was probably the most viable option. As Ghana's Kwesi Botchwey was fond of saying, "Structural adjustment is very painful, but structural maladjustment is much worse."[7] This became very clear with the rising number of flailing and failing states.

The Rise of Political Conditionality: Governance and Democracy

Part of the modified version of structural adjustment, based on the poor track record of the 1980s, was the new notion of good governance. The World Bank's emphasis on governance emerged from its learning about the primary importance of creating a more facilitative sociopolitical context for economic reform in Africa. Due to the dramatic political changes in the world in 1989–1990 and the search for a new foreign policy thrust to replace containment (what the Clinton administration called "enlargement" of the world's free community of market democracies), governance was quickly transformed by the major Western industrial democracies into political conditionality focusing on the promotion of democracy and civil society. The convergence of these two policy thrusts—one largely technocratic from the World Bank, the other distinctly political from the major powers—posed a real dilemma for African leaders.

But was political conditionality a good idea, especially regarding the prospects for major economic change? The presumption of the mutually reinforcing character of political and economic reform in Africa relied on an extension of neoclassical economic logic: economic liberalization creates sustained growth; growth produces winners as well as losers; winners would organize to defend their newfound welfare and would create sociopolitical coalitions to support continued economic reform. This logic, however, did not seem to hold for much of Africa. Successful economic reform in Africa was rare and required a special conjuncture of factors. The progress of democratization in Africa was also very uneven, especially in its relationship to economic reform, which proved to be far weaker than the advocates of double reform asserted. Was this version of the "thesis of the perverse effect"[8]—that political liberalization might not have a positive impact on the chances for sustained economic reform—likely to hold across the board for Africa? Not necessarily, but it was important to assess particular cases carefully. A probabilistic rather than a deterministic perverse effect was more likely to operate. If not handled properly, political conditionality linked to democratization might impede rather than facilitate the productive relinking of Africa to the world economy. The widespread emergence of what Richard Sklar called "developmental democracies" was not likely in Africa anytime soon.[9]

Undue Expectations Yet Again: Africa's "Renaissance" in the Mid-1990s

Nonetheless by early 1998 a new African renaissance was being widely proclaimed by the IFIs, one based, however, on relatively narrow data. Key external actors rushed to proclaim that Africa had turned the corner after only three years of improved growth, and they projected that it would continue. Undue bursts of cheerleading that quickly become hollow do not do anybody any good; this is a lesson that appears very hard for powerful external actors to learn. Given Africa's marginalization, it was relatively insulated from the devastating blows of the Asia crisis, with the exception of South Africa. As one IMF analyst put it, "Given the rudimentary state of financial markets in most sub-Saharan African countries and the rather limited amounts of private capital flowing into them, the financial contagion from the Asia crisis was effectively limited to South Africa."[10] Many Africans, however, bitterly resented the enormous Western rescue packages for Asia and the preemptory one for Brazil from the IFIs, given that these countries had been saying they did not have more resources for Africa. Despite the comparatively modest relative impact of the Asia crisis on Africa, there was an even more sobering lesson learned from the crisis—the imperative to have solid and internationally capable banking sectors. Even if large private resource flows were to come to Africa, structural impediments such as extremely weak banking sectors would inhibit the effective use of them.

DEBT AND NEW GLOBAL ECONOMIC GOVERNANCE: THE HIPC INITIATIVE

The Asia crisis was seen by many analysts, including mainstream economists, as a major challenge to the legitimacy of the IMF and the World Bank. also evidenced by quite vigorous public differences between the two. Like the onset of the Latin American debt crisis in 1982, the Asia crisis set off a major and quite varied flurry of proposals for a "new international financial architecture." Precisely because of its marginality, however, Africa had in fact been quietly leading the way in the 1990s toward new financial architecture and broader forms of global economic governance.[11]

One of the primary results of structural adjustment in Africa was a rising level of external debt. In 1998, Africa's long-term debt was $176 billion. Unlike most other regions of the world, this debt was mostly "official" debt owed to major Western countries, the International Monetary Fund, and the World Bank. Africa owed an incredible 76 percent of its debt to bilateral and multilateral creditors (44 percent and 32 percent respectively)—itself a major indicator of marginalization. Since the late 1950s, bilateral debt has been rescheduled by creditor countries, organized into a mechanism that came to be known as the Paris Club, while multilateral debt could not be rescheduled. The Paris Club became the core of the international debt regime for official debt.

Debt rescheduling was one of the easiest and quickest ways to provide badly needed foreign exchange to countries in economic, social, and political trouble, but Paris Club relief was at the center of a complicated set of nested games. Rescheduling was possible only if the debtor country had an economic reform program in good standing with the IMF. In addition, London Club private bank rescheduling was supposed to come only after Paris Club rescheduling, and Consultative Group aid coordination was also linked to prior Paris Club rescheduling.

While Paris Club debt relief was contingent on maintaining an economic reform program with the IMF, and usually also with the World Bank as well, the debt owed to these "multilateral" institutions was not reschedulable. This norm was meant to protect the "preferred creditor" status of these institutions. In short, the international debt regime did not cover multilateral debt. Given the high dependence of African countries on loans from the IMF and the World Bank, multilateral debt became an increasingly severe problem over the 1980s, and a seriously threatening one in the 1990s.

The practices of the debt regime evolved in important ways beginning in the late 1980s. By the early 1990s, it had become increasingly clear that many of the poorest states that came before the international regime for official debt relief had an insolvency rather than a liquidity problem. This was a realization too long in coming, because the debt did not pose a major short-run threat to the stability of the world economy. The debt crisis emerged first in Africa, signaled by Zaire's first rescheduling in 1976, but it went largely unnoticed until the mid-1980s. By 1996, the IMF and the World Bank had designated forty-one of their members as "heavily indebted poor countries" (HIPCs) whose debt was not likely ever to be repaid. The debt of these countries, mostly public or official rather than private, rose from $55 billion in 1980 to $183 billion only a decade later and to $215 billion by 1995—more than twice their export earnings. Of these forty-one countries, thirty-three were sub-Saharan African countries. Most of the HIPCs had high levels of poverty and limited domestic resources, and, in effect, came close to constituting an international underclass of states on the margins of the globalizing world economy. All but six fell into the United Nations Development Program's lowest human development category. According to development NGOs, these countries have been locked in a vicious circle of economic and social decline.

Although important, the Group of Eight (G8) governments, including the United States, were *not* the main driving force of change in the debt regime. It was necessary to look elsewhere to explain the nature and process of this evolution, especially to advocacy and development NGOs. At the core of the evolution of the debt regime was the broadening of the processes of international economic governance, especially the role of new actors and ideas and the institutional contexts that supported them. The emergence of the Heavily Indebted Poor Country Debt Initiative (HIPC) in 1996 brought striking and important, but ultimately limited, change to the debt regime for a specifically designated group of countries that for the first time had more uniform rules developed for them. The striking innovations included the partial treatment of multilateral debt, developing the notion of debt sustainability, focusing debt relief on poverty reduction after the revision of the program in 1999 under NGO pressure, and, in the process, quietly shifting the center of gravity of the debt regime from the Paris Club of bilateral creditors to the IMF and the World Bank, institutions that were now more open and accountable than in the past. As we shall see, the later emergence of the Multilateral Debt Relief Initiative (MDRI) in 2005 became another major step in this attempt to make debt relief more effective, under the widely held view that more debt relief was a good idea.

These changes in the debt regime were brought about by a confluence of factors: (1) slow and uneven learning by bilateral and multilateral creditors about the existence of a group of countries that were not benefiting much from structural adjustment, while greatly increasing their debt loads; (2) the growing pressure, influence, and effectiveness of a new set of actors in international economic governance—networks of NGOs (including Jubilee 2000, Jubilee USA, Eurodad, and Oxfam) that believed the existing situation was unjust and untenable and had new ideas and proposals of their own, plus a social movement to back them up; (3) the influence of a group of economists, both inside and outside creditor institutions, who provided knowledge, advice, and technical understanding about this issue; (4) the leadership of a group of small creditor states and eventually several members of the G8, especially Britain; (5) leadership at the World Bank that was more open to new ideas; and (6) eventually tough negotiations among all major creditor countries, the IMF, the World Bank, and to a lesser extent, some of the major NGOs. This outcome was not inevitable, however; a change in one or two of these factors, such as different G8 governments, leadership at the Bank, or the absence of NGO pressure might have led to a quite different outcome.

The major path of the evolution of the treatment of sovereign debt was from debt collection, to debt rescheduling, to aid and structural adjustment, to debt "sustainability," to small-scale forgiveness and poverty reduction, and finally, to major debt cancellation for a set of poor countries—what one official called the slippery slope of debt relief. The original aim of the HIPC initiative was to provide debt sustainability that would help to remove a major constraint on investment and growth and be a spur to further adjustment, in part by galvanizing increased private external investment. It was not at all clear that this happened. By the time the "enhanced" HIPC initiative emerged in 1999, the focus had shifted quite exclusively to poverty reduction. By 2005, the emphasis had shifted to nearly complete cancellation of debt owed to the IMF, the World Bank, and the African Development Bank (AfDB). On the donor side, the hope was that this expanding debt relief process would strengthen the legitimacy and "ownership" of structural adjustment programs without cutting the heart out of them. It soon became clear that this would be difficult to accomplish. The complex Poverty Reduction Strategy Paper (PRSP) process that emerged out of the enhanced HIPC initiative required each debtor country to put together a plan based on consultation with domestic civil society, business, and the legislature for fighting poverty using funds derived from debt relief and other sources.

HIPC was not a magic bullet; it was important for a number of countries but very far from turning Africa and other poor countries around, far from making a major dent in Africa's structural dilemma. In this context, it was not clear that an exclusive focus on poverty is the correct approach. By enhanced HIPC in 1999, there was a clear sense that the process had acquired multiple objectives but still had only one instrument. The objectives included debt sustainability, regularization of relations with creditors, poverty reduction, and growth. There was also an increasing perception that debt relief was but one part in a much larger picture, one that needed to be dealt with for real debt sustainability to be achieved. But an even larger question remained: Was it possible, as the new Bush administration came to power in 2001, especially after the tragedy of September 11, to go beyond enhanced HIPC?

FROM HIPC TO MDRI: THE GEOPOLITICS OF DEBT RELIEF

The Bush administration came to power with a policy of "drop the debt and stop the debt" (i.e., write off the debt and substitute grants for loans. It was not enthralled by HIPC, for both ideological and practical reasons, including moral hazard, and spent much of its first three years pursuing two policy tracks simultaneously: (1) containing the cost of HIPC as well as any new incremental policy innovation—its feeble version of "drop the debt," and (2) pushing a proposal to significantly increase the ratio of grants to loans—the "stop the debt" part. The first track eventually encountered serious geostrategic issues and intense G8 politics over a concept that the Bush administration had openly scorned—"odious debt."

NGO coalitions were working toward much more dramatic change in the strategic relationship between Africa and powerful external actors. With great consistency, they maintained their demand for full debt cancellation *and* an end to structural adjustment, while arguing for substantial increases in aid, especially grants, to meet the Millennium Development Goals. They linked these issues to AIDS, the larger African health crisis, increased war and violent conflict, declining state services and infrastructure, and unfair trade practices by the industrial democracies. Oxfam even charged that the G8 was content to have debt remain the focus of debate in order to keep systematic attention away from major trade reform. September 11 and its aftermath stalled efforts for greater debt relief, but by early 2004, major pressure for additional debt relief had been recreated as HIPC was scheduled to expire at the end of the year. This pressure came from NGOs and African governments, as well as a number of smaller European governments, but also from some parts of the World Bank and a couple of major states. Gordon Brown, then British Chancellor of the Exchequer, announced in April 2004, "There is now a window of opportunity to make progress on this issue, and I'm hopeful that when we meet at the annual meetings we'll have made the most of this opportunity."[12] Brown believed this opportunity existed because the Bush administration, in its efforts to get major debt relief for Iraq, appeared to be softening its position on HIPC reform and debt relief in general. Others were less optimistic, but then geopolitics kicked in.

Not long after the U.S. invasion of Iraq, the Bush administration realized that despite having the world's second largest oil reserves, Iraq needed major relief on its roughly $120 billion external debt. The administration argued that Iraq deserved a 90–95 percent reduction of its $40 billion Paris Club debt, relief for which it was not qualified under existing Paris Club rules, despite earlier rule-breaking deals for Poland, Egypt, and Russia. Former Secretary of Treasury and Secretary of State James A. Baker became a special envoy whose task was to travel the world to persuade countries to at least join a *financial* "coalition of the willing." Holding a relatively small proportion of Iraq's debt, all of a sudden the United States did not hesitate to characterize Saddam Hussein's borrowings as "odious debt."

Canada supported the American demand for 90–95 percent debt relief, as did Britain, but major G8 opposition emerged from France, Germany, Japan, and Russia. President Chirac of France asserted that Iraq should not get a better deal than the world's heavily indebted poor countries, making it clear that little progress would be made on Iraq until more was done for these countries. He insisted that Iraq should get no more than a 50 percent reduction, a position supported by much of the rest of the G8. At the Sea Island, Georgia, G8 meeting in June 2004, President Bush presented a stunning proposal to cancel *all* the multilateral debt that HIPC countries owed to the IMF, World Bank, and AfDB. The tacit quid pro quo would be support by the other creditors for the American position on the Iraqi debt. The proposal was presented as an example of "compassionate conservatism" in the larger context of the Millennium Development Goals. Under Secretary of the Treasury for International Affairs, John Taylor said, "We need to *complete* the 'drop and stop the debt' vision put forth by President Bush at the start of his administration" by focusing more on debt reduction.[13]

The British had a similar proposal, which Gordon Brown had formulated prior to the 2004 G8 meeting. They took the additionality (debt relief should not come out of existing aid resources) issue very seriously by offering to cover 10 percent ($180 million) of the tab to the World Bank and the AfDB, while insisting that the IMF portion be financed using its gold reserves. The United States rejected these positions and remained silent about how to finance its own debt relief proposal. Any decision was put off until the annual IMF/World Bank meetings in Washington in early October 2004.

At the annual meetings, HIPC was extended for the third time, to the end of 2006, to allow eleven more African HIPC countries, all with serious conflict and/or arrears problems, to enter the process. The Bush administration was desperate to get a deal on the Iraqi debt, but it wanted a deal on the cheap, while swallowing its often-voiced concerns about moral hazard—the worry that debt relief would only encourage more borrowing because of the debtor's assumption that more debt relief would be forthcoming. Facing an enormous budget deficit and a huge, growing cost of the Iraq war, the United States, unlike the British, wanted the World Bank and the IMF to finance this major new debt relief out of their own resources.

Many observers saw the U.S. proposal for what it was—a geopolitical ploy. As one European diplomat put it, "When the United States asked us for so much debt relief for Iraq, we said the answer was to also relieve the debt of the poorest nations. Now the Americans are trying to come along with debt relief for the poor but we are afraid they will dry up the money . . . that these poor countries deserve."[14] Intense discussions at the Fund-Bank meetings failed to reach an agreement, bogging down in quarrels about how to finance any new multilateral debt relief. It was only agreed that the G8 would report on its discussions by the end of the year.

The British were scheduled to take over the presidency of the G8 in 2005, and Gordon Brown was committed to having Britain lead the G8 into major new debt relief by the next summit in Scotland, although the details of his plan were not yet public. Most observers viewed the British proposal as more responsible and remained critical of the American position. Many of these NGOs supported major debt relief for Iraq because of the obvious "odious debt" precedent that it would set, at least in their eyes, and one pushed by the world's major power out of geopolitical desperation. The United Nations joined the chorus, with various agencies calling for full multilateral debt relief for poor countries—including the Secretary General, UNCTAD, and UNAIDS, among others.

After President Bush was reelected in November 2004, the United States redoubled its efforts to get major debt relief for Iraq while remaining silent on its surprising and unexpected June Sea Island debt cancellation proposal. A compromise Paris Club deal was reached on November 21 that would cancel 80 percent of Iraq's debt in three stages over four years *if* it lived up to the standard economic conditions, primarily reestablishing macroeconomic stability. A number of NGOs noted the rapid movement on debt relief for Iraq and the slow movement toward more debt reduction for African and other poor countries. Germany and France wanted some reconciliation with the reelected Bush administration that would appear positive and not be military in nature. Russia, however, remained the last hold out, and it took all-night negotiations to reach a Paris Club deal for Iraq. The Russians subsequently made it clear that its support was linked to a "mutual understanding" about the handling of Russia's own debt to the Paris Club and better treatment for its companies in Iraq. The NGOs, which had previously met with Paris Club officials to argue for an immediate moratorium on Iraqi debt service, did not believe the Paris Club agreement went far enough, with some calling it scandalous. In an early December report, Oxfam warned that the "war on terrorism" threatened to bring back an era when assistance was determined by "security considerations rather than developmental need." Max Lawson, its chief policy advisor, noted that "debt relief for Iraq shows that rich countries can find the resources for foreign aid if they need to."[15] As we will see with Nigeria, geopolitical factors were indeed back.

The Iraq Paris Club deal left the U.S. position on debt relief for Africa up in the air. The Bush administration remained silent on the issue as it approached the end of its G8 presidency, leaving the issue to the British instead. Britain was very anxious for major movement on poor country, especially African, debt, and development assistance more generally while it led the G8 in 2005. In a speech to the Council on Foreign Relations in New York, Brown finally made the details of his proposal public. He identified the countries that would be eligible—the fifteen HIPC countries that had completed the full HIPC process, twelve of them African, and six other low-income countries—Albania, Armenia, Mongolia, Nepal, Sri Lanka, and Vietnam. As usual, however, the devil really was in the details, especially those concerning financing. The British proposal was billed as a core part of a new Marshall Plan meant to support the Millennium Development Goals.

Most of the major NGOs supported the British plan, albeit with some modification, and spent considerable energy campaigning for it in the lead-up to the G8 summit in Gleneagles, Scotland, in early July 2005. Major pressure was aimed at the Bush administration to honor its 2004 Sea Island G8 proposal now that it had achieved its desperately sought-after Paris Club deal for Iraq. This was made all the harder by its stubborn unilateralism in foreign affairs. In the end, the United States agreed to the creation of the Multilateral Debt Relief Initiative (MDRI), but only after getting most of its way about financing it, which meant that the Bush administration had to put up very little money.

MDRI is separate from HIPC but linked to it operationally. Under MDRI, the World Bank's International Development Association, the IMF, and the AfDB's African Development Fund would provide upfront, irrevocable 100 percent debt relief on eligible debts to countries having reached the HIPC completion point. Although MDRI is an initiative common to the three international financial institutions, the decision to grant debt relief was ultimately the separate responsibility of each institution, and the approach of each to coverage and implementation varied somewhat.

NGOs criticized MDRI for applying only to HIPC countries, plus a few non-HIPCs, rather than to all poor countries; for covering debt only up to the end of 2004 for the Fund and to the end of 2003 for the Bank; and in addition to HIPC conditionality, for requiring a "once off" assessment of economic performance after having reached the HIPC completion point. In the initial assessments, Mauritania did not make the list but was added after making required policy changes. In early September 2006, for example, Malawi reached its HIPC completion point, receiving \$1.1 billion in debt relief from its Paris Club creditors, the Fund, and the Bank, and an additional \$1.4 billion in MDRI debt relief from the Fund, the Bank, and the AfDB. Assuming no additional debt accumulation, Malawi now had a much more sustainable debt service burden of about \$5 million a year between 2006 and 2025.

After all this effort, how much debt relief has the HIPC/MDRI process actually provided for African countries? Figure 3.1 shows the before and after impact on debt as a percentage of GDP for fourteen of the now eighteen African countries that had completed the combined HIPC/MDRI process as of April 2007; the other four are Cameroon, Malawi, São Tomé, and Sierra Leone. The amount of debt reduction has clearly been substantial. The debt stock of the thirty countries (twenty-six African) that had either entered or completed the combined HIPC/MDRI process had been reduced by 85 percent by mid-2007, with more relief to come. The debt stock of these countries

FIGURE 3.1 Debt burdens before and after HIPC and MDRI debt relief

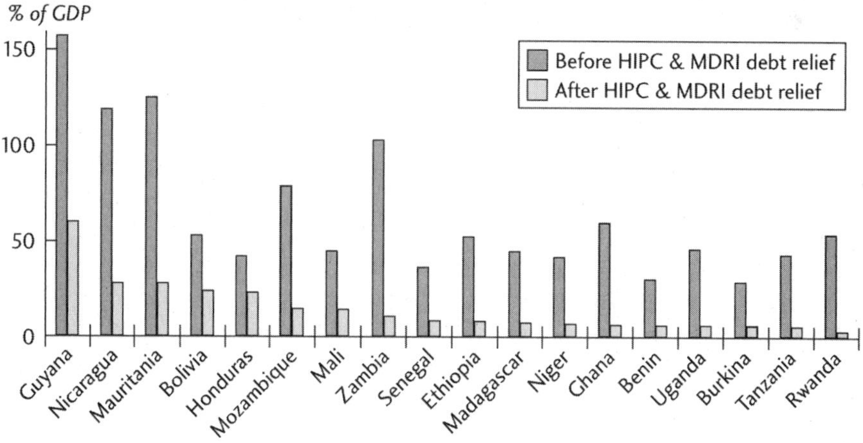

Source: International Bank for Reconstruction and Development/World Bank, *Global Development Finance 2006: The Development Potential of Surging Capital Flows* (Washington, D.C.: World Bank, June 2006), p. 94.

before HIPC in 1996 was $75 billion; after initial HIPC relief, it dropped to $38 billion, while HIPC-related Paris Club debt reduction provided another $3 billion. MDRI debt reduction dropped the total to $11 billion. In other words, by mid-2007, HIPC had provided $37 billion in relief, and MDRI another $24 billion, for a total of $61 billion. Adding in the $3 billion HIPC-related Paris Club relief, the total debt reduction came to $64 billion. MDRI also brought the AfDB into the multilateral debt reduction process. The institutional breakdown of MDRI relief for the twenty-two countries (eighteen African) that had completed the HIPC process and been approved for MDRI relief by mid-2007 was 75.2 percent from the World Bank, 8.3 percent from the IMF, and 16.5 percent for the AfDB. By 2006, the debt service-to-exports ratio for these countries had dropped to 6 percent, close to the average of 5 percent for all of the world's low-income countries. More HIPC/MDRI debt relief is likely, however; by mid-2007, eight countries had not yet completed the HIPC process but would receive MDRI multilateral debt reduction when they do; seven of them are African—Burundi, Chad, both Congos, Gambia, Guinea, and Guinea-Bissau. In addition, eight African HIPC countries that had not yet entered the process—Central African Republic, Comoros, Côte d'Ivoire, Eritrea, Liberia, Somalia, Sudan, and Togo—would also eventually get substantial debt reduction. There is some evidence that HIPC countries that have entered or completed the process increased their poverty reduction spending on average from 6 percent in 1999, when HIPC was enhanced, to 9.8 percent by 2006. Both the IMF and the World Bank have processes for monitoring poverty-related spending after debt relief is granted, although most institutions and NGOs working on debt agree that these efforts still have a long way to go.

NEW OPPORTUNITIES AND A WINDOW OF OPPORTUNITY

Where then does Africa stand nearly a half century after independence, with its high levels of marginalization and dependence and weak record of economic reform? Are its marginalization and dependence beginning to diminish in the opening decade of the twenty-first century?

Africa's Place in the World Economy

The World Bank described 2005, declared by the British as head of the G8 to be the "Year of Africa," as part of a move toward a "Decade of Africa," a switch "from promises to results."[16] Compared to the 1980s, growth rate of 1.8 percent, with a per capita growth of –1.1 percent, the 1990s brought 2.4 percent and 0.2 percent respectively. By contrast, 2000–2004 brought growth rates of 4.0 percent and 1.6 percent. Exports grew at 0.0 percent, 5.0 percent, and 3.7 percent for the three periods respectively. The growth rate for 2005 was 5.3 percent, marking "a sharp departure" from the weak and volatile growth of the 1980s and 1990s: "2005 was the fifth year in a row that regional growth was at least 3.5 percent, and ended the first 5-year period since the 1960s that per capita growth remained positive in every year."[17] Growth rates for 2004, 2005, and 2006 were 5.3 percent, 5.8 percent, and 5.6 percent—three years of over 5 percent, based on impressive world economic growth (especially high commodity prices), better African macroeconomic balance, strong aid flows, increased capital flows, and improved political stability. Yet these rates should be compared with South Asia rates of 8.0 percent, 8.7 percent, and 8.6 percent, respectively. Variation in growth rates among African countries, however, is as important as the regional averages. As Table 3.1 shows, the World Bank designates categories of little growth, slow growth, sustained growth, and oil-exporting countries.

While this improvement is notable, despite doubts about its sustainability, one should keep longer-run comparative performance levels in mind. As Figure 3.3 shows, Africa in 2004 was still 40.4 percent below other low-income countries in per capita GDP. The key difference is lower productivity growth, as investment in Africa still yields less that half the return in other developing regions. Comparative rates of growth in output per worker are also revealing. For 1990–2003, the rate for Africa was –0.09 percent, 3.10 percent for South Asia, 3.12 percent for East Asia without China, and 8.51 percent for China. A similar story holds for growth in total-factor productivity in these years: Africa, 0.44 percent; South Asia, 1.38 percent; East Asia without China, 0.58 percent; and China, 4.72 percent. The other major factor is the rate of investment. Africa's level remains only half the share of GDP of other developing countries, with African economies obtaining growth only one-third to one-half that of other regions from this investment. Capital inflows did increase from $28.9 billion in 2005 to $39.8 billion in 2006, a surge that may well continue, given the renewed role of geostrategic factors and the stunningly increased presence of China in Africa. At the same time, Africa's share of net developing country capital flows remained steady at a low 6.7 percent, which, however, exceeded bilateral aid grants for the first time since 1999, while net official lending declined by $1 billion. On the other hand, net equity flows rose from $7 billion to $31 billion, and net private lending doubled to $10.6 billion. Two-thirds of the net 2006 increase of $2 billion in foreign direct investment was concentrated in only five countries—Nigeria, Sudan, Angola, Equatorial Guinea, and South Africa—in short, invested in oil and the subcontinent's only industrial economy.

TABLE 3.1 Divergent African growth paths

Average annual GDP growth 1996–2005 (%)

Little or no growth countries Average: 1.3 percent 20 percent of African population		Slow growth countries Average: 3.4 percent 16 percent of population		Sustained growth countries Average: 5.5 percent 25 percent of population		Oil-exporting countries Average: 7.4 percent 29 percent of population	
Swaziland	2.8	Namibia	4.0	Mozambique	8.4	Equitorial Guinea	20.9
Kenya	2.8	Zambia	3.6	Rwanda	7.5	Angola	7.9
Lesotho	2.7	Guinea	3.6	Cape Verde	6.5	Chad	7.8
Eritrea	2.2	Niger	3.5	Uganda	6.1	Sudan	6.4
Comoros	2.0	Togo	3.3	Mali	5.7	Nigeria	4.0
Seychelles	2.0	Madagascar	3.3	Botswana	5.7	Congo, Rep.	3.5
Côte d'Ivoire	1.5	Malawi	3.2	Ethiopia	5.5	Gabon	1.7
Burundi	1.2	South Africa	3.1	Tanzania	5.4		
Sierra Leona	1.1	São Tomé Principe	3.1	Mauritius	4.9		
Central African Republic	0.9			Mauritania	4.9		
Guinea-Bissau	0.6			Benin	4.8		
Congo, Dem. Rep.	0.0			Ghana	4.7		
Zimbabwe	−2.4			Senegal	4.6		
				Burkina Faso	4.6		
				Gambia, The	4.5		
				Cameroon	4.5		

Note: Data on growth rates are not presented for Liberia and Somalia, but they are included in the denominator in the calculation of population shares.

Source: International Bank for Reconstruction and Development and World Bank, *African Development Indicators 2006* (Washington, D.C.: World Bank, 2006), p. 3.

FIGURE 3.2 Comparative income levels: Africa risks falling behind

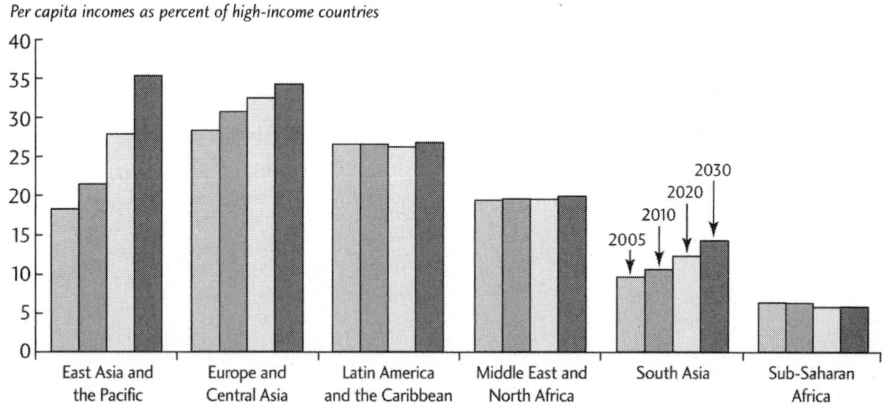

Source: World Bank, *Global Economic Prospect 2007: Managing the Next Wave of Globalization* (Washington, D.C.: World Bank, December 2006), p. xvii.

FIGURE 3.3 GDP per capita: Sub-Saharan Africa and other regions, 1960–2004

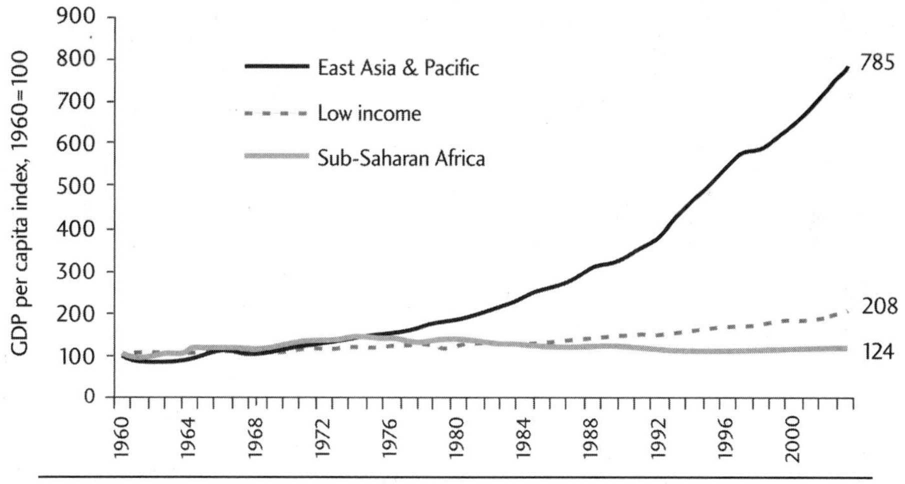

Source: Benno Ndulu, *Challenges of African Growth: Opportunities, Constraints, and Strategic Direction* (Washington, D.C.: World Bank, 2007), p. 5.

Yet bonds remain a key indicator of Africa's continued marginalization from the global economy: Gross bond flows to Africa in 2005 were estimated at $2.3 billion, *all* of it to South Africa, compared to $5.3 billion for South Asia, $20.3 billion for East Asia, and $43.0 billion for Latin America. A comparable trend holds for private bank lending: Africa, $11.9 billion; South Asia,

$12.2 billion; East Asia, $34.5; and Latin America, $46.3 billion. In 2006, the Seychelles became the second African country to issue international bonds (South Africa was first), although Ghana, Kenya, Nigeria, and Zambia, and possibly even Côte d'Ivoire were expected to do so in 2007. Foreign aid, not counting debt relief, rose from $7.7 billion in 2002 to $13.2 billion in 2005, but then fell in 2006, despite the 2005 promise by the G8 in Gleneagles that they would double their aid to $50 billion by 2010. (As I discuss below, this pledge was not fulfilled.) They also pledged to provide significant debt relief, which was achieved, and to open their markets to African products, which has not occurred, with the Doha trade round essentially dead. A key underlying factor is the delayed demographic transition in Africa, despite increased deaths from war and disease. Some studies claim this delayed transition accounts for two-thirds of the difference between Africa and other regions. Poverty levels remain very high, with one-third of the world's poor living in Africa, while life expectancy has declined from 49 to 47 years since 1990. As Figure 3.3 shows, the projected long-term effect of this is stunning.

Nonetheless, by the late 2000s, African countries had more resources at their disposal. They had a huge portion, more than $60 billion, of their bilateral and multilateral debt simply written off by the Paris Club, HIPC, and MDRI, while non-HIPC African countries also received significant debt reduction from the Paris Club, including a unique deal giving Nigeria alone $18 billion (and an overall reduction of debt stock of $30 billion), signaling the return of geostrategic economic logic to Africa. The NGOs continue to campaign for a total debt write-off, which may not be a good thing. When used properly and in feasible limits, debt can be a major tool of development, and African states need to learn to manage their debt loads and use these resources productively.

One of the most useful things to come out of the debates about debt has been the Debt Sustainability Framework developed by the World Bank and the IMF, which provides a mechanism for managing the risks associated with additional borrowing. Many fear that African countries will merely start running up their debt loads again with the expectation that the debt will get written off again—a classic example of moral hazard at work. There are indications that African states are looking for, and finding, places to borrow from that do not have the conditionality that comes with official creditor and IFI borrowing.

As part of a large worldwide trend among developing countries, including some African countries, is the buildup of foreign reserves as a hedge against external shocks *and* as a way to avoid having to go to the IMF or the World Bank. This applies to African oil producers in particular, but not exclusively.

In 2007, for example, Angola refused to borrow from the IMF because of the conditionality involved and borrowed instead from China. In 2004–2006, 20 percent of global South-South private lending went to African countries, three-quarters of which was from Chinese banks and with no conditionality. Only 6 percent of Africa's borrowing consisted of North-South private lending, which is not formally conditioned, though it is carefully assessed for risk. For African and other countries that want a seal of approval from the IMF without borrowing from it, the Fund created the Policy Support Instrument (PSI). The first one was for Nigeria as part of its stunning 2005 Paris Club deal. Uganda, Cape Verde, Tanzania, and Mozambique have signed up for PSIs, while Angola refused one. In part, the PSI was designed to facilitate the turn or return of low-income countries to global private markets for loans, bonds, equity capital, and foreign direct investment.

As financial globalization accelerates and becomes more complex, however, with private resources and instruments proliferating at a rapid rate, Africa will begin to feel more of its effects, both positive and negative. One of the recent negative ones is that some low-income countries have become targets of "vulture funds," which buy up distressed sovereign debt sold by creditor states at a deep discount in secondary markets. Vulture funds then sue the debtor. Virgin Islands–based Donegal International, for example, partly owned by an American firm, bought debt that Zambia owed to Romania with a face value of $42 million for a mere $3.2 million and then sued Zambia in a London court for $55 million in full payment plus interest and legal fees, wiping out part of the debt relief Zambia received from the Paris Club, HIPC, and MDRI. Donegal sued precisely because it knew Zambia was now in a better position to pay a court judgment or negotiate a settlement. The London court ruled that Zambia must pay $15.5 million, about a third of its debt relief for 2007. The case remains in litigation, and several donor countries are paying Zambia's legal fees. A number of other African countries, including Uganda, which has had to pay out $30 million to six vulture funds, are waging similar battles. Altogether, a third of HIPC counties have been sued by more than thirty-eight vulture funds, and some have settled. Britain's Gordon Brown called vulture funds "scandalous" and promised to take action. Major debt relief NGOs, including Oxfam, Jubilee UK, and TransAfrica Forum, have also taken up the cause, while the U.S. Congress has held hearings, and the Paris Club pledged to help. The World Bank extended its Debt Reduction Facility, which has helped poor countries deal with commercial debt problems. One of its vice presidents called vulture funds "a threat to debt relief efforts," admonishing that "their increasing litigation against countries receiving debt relief will penalize some of the world's poorest countries."[18]

The Role of the G8 and New Forms of Global Governance

At the British "Year of Africa" G8 meeting in Scotland in 2005, seven of the eight countries pledged to double aid to Africa by 2010 and to provide major new debt relief. The latter pledge was kept; the former was not. The difference this time was that a rare timetable was established, and a panel was appointed to report on progress. The African Progress Panel—chaired by former UN Secretary General Kofi Annan, made up of prominent private citizens, and paid for by the Gates Foundation—reported just prior to the 2007 G8 meeting in Germany that the target would not be met by the deadline unless significant additional efforts were taken. Reports were also issued by Oxfam, OECD, the World Bank, and Bono's NGO, Debt AIDS Trade Africa (DATA). Oxfam claimed that at current trends, the G8 would miss the pledge by $30 billion. The United States, Britain, and Japan were close to doing their part, while Canada was actually ahead, but Germany, France, and Italy were seriously behind. Russia did not join in the 2005 pledge. A high-level World Bank official said, "The record so far indicates that apart from debt reduction, African countries haven't realized the benefits promised at the G8 meeting two years ago, during the Year of Africa."[19] The DATA report claimed that less than half the amount needed to make good on the promise had been contributed.

All of these groups and some smaller creditor countries pressed Germany to make good at the 2007 meeting, but all that was achieved was a recommitment to the original promise without any specifics this time. Many NGOs pushed for additional debt relief, which was not forthcoming; in fact, some G8 members contended that debt relief should count as fulfilling their 2005 promise, a claim not generally accepted. The differences from the past are the public deadline, the assessment reports, and the political and social movements behind them. As Bono put it, "I want to grow the social movement. It's no coincidence that in the countries where churches and students are out on the streets—that's where the numbers are getting better."[20] Billionaire philanthropists are also becoming a major source of additional resources for Africa, with the efforts of people such as Bill and Melinda Gates and Warren Buffet, who also have ties to Bono's One Campaign, the Clinton Foundation, older mainstream foundations, and activist NGOs. Africa is likely to benefit from these changes in global governance processes.

China's Resurgence in Africa: A Window of Opportunity for Africa

The year 2006 was China's "Year of Africa." In November it held a major summit with African leaders in Beijing, organized by the Forum on China-Africa

Cooperation, which pledged major new financial and economic support. The summit was attended by forty-eight African countries, including thirty-five heads of state. The Chinese promised $36 billion in concessional loans for 2007–2009, plus $2 billion in concessional buyer's credits. China announced the establishment of a China-Africa Development Fund, which would provide $5 billion in capital for Chinese companies operating in Africa; it went into effect in June 2007 with $1 billion from the Chinese Development Bank. In reality, the summit was an elaborate public validation of a process that had begun in the early 1990s, as China reemerged as a major player in Africa, driven largely, but not exclusively, by its need for resources and markets to fuel its amazing transformation into an economic superpower in less than thirty years. China was poised to overtake Germany and become the world's third-largest economy, accomplishing one of the most important changes in the international political economy since the end of World War II. China's key motto had become "business is business, politics is politics," and the two should not have to meet. Oil, of course, is at the center of these efforts.[21]

China's new role as a source of trade, capital, and investment is largely welcomed by African governments because of the absence of IMF-like conditionality attached to it, as well as the speed and flexibility of the Chinese. This is in stark contrast to the operation of the IFIs and the "donors." As Aboulaye Diop, Senegal's finance minister, put it at the 2007 annual meeting of the African Development Bank, quite unusually held in Shanghai, "The Chinese treat us like adults." In the same vein, a leading Angolan economist said of the IFIs and the donors, "For them we should have ears, but not a mouth."[22] China may well quickly become a bigger lender to Africa than the World Bank.

China's trade with Africa, consisting primarily of oil and metals, amounted to about $12 million a year in the late 1980s, $3 billion in 1995, $10 billion in 2000, $40 billion in 2005, and $55.5 billion by 2006, up 40 percent in a single year. China is now Africa's second-largest trading partner, after the United States ($91 billion) and ahead of France ($47 billion); Africa may well become China's largest trading partner within five years. This has the potential to reverse the long-term decline of Africa's share of world trade, with some estimates predicting that China-Africa trade will rise to $100 billion by 2010. Eighty-five percent of Africa's exports to China consist of oil, metals, and agricultural raw materials, which are sourced primarily from five countries: Angola, Sudan, Nigeria, Congo-Brazzaville, and Equatorial Guinea. Thirty percent of China's oil now comes from Africa, and this figure will rise quickly. Angola overtook Saudi Arabia as the largest supplier of oil to China, and Sudan is now the second-largest African supplier, with 65 percent of its oil going to China. In addition, China is now exploring in more than seven other African countries. From 2000 to 2004, China was responsible for 40 percent of the world's increased demand for oil. The Chinese also import copper from Zambia, copper and cobalt from Congo-Kinshasa, uranium from Namibia, manganese from Ghana, bauxite from Liberia, iron ore from South Africa, and timber from Liberia, Cameroon, and Congo-Brazzaville. More than 440 African goods can now enter China duty free.

The summit's Beijing Action Plan was to double African assistance by 2009, including $36 billion in concessional, nonconditional loans. The core institution of this effort is China's new Export-Import Bank, already the largest such institution in the world, but all of its help is "tied" assistance, something Western countries have haltingly moved away from. The Export-Import Bank lent $7 billion between 2004 and 2006 and plans to lend $20 billion more in 2007–2010. Chinese foreign direct investment in Africa was less than $5 million in 1995, rose to $1.2 billion by 2000, approached $12 billion in 2007, and took place in forty-nine African countries, which were also home to close to 800 aid projects. Most of this investment and assistance was focused on infrastructure projects, something the IFIs and donors had long ago moved away from, and was financed by concessional loans to Chinese companies or African governments. High-level visits by numerous Chinese officials have become commonplace. President Hu Jintao made an eight-country trip to Africa in February 2007, his third in recent years. China also canceled some African debt, $80 million for Sudan alone in February 2007, and total cancellation may eventually approach $26 billion.

China's "business is business" approach produced charges of supporting genocidal regimes like Sudan, especially in regard to Darfur, where China has only been partially and intermittently helpful, and dictatorships presiding over failing states like Zimbabwe, and of general disregard for good governance in general. Many Western firms have complained about nimble and subsidized competition from Chinese companies. Dumping charges have come from a number of African states, especially regarding textiles shipped to South Africa, Ghana, and Zambia. In a tactical response, China moved to limit some textile exports to parts of Africa. The Chinese have also been accused of exploiting workers in Zambia, Cameroon, and other places. Thabo Mbeki warned about falling into a "colonial relationship" with China, similar to that between Africa and Europe, while he bargained aggressively with China on numerous economic fronts, and South African firms did a booming business in China. At the same time, African civil society groups complained about diminished pressure for good governance, fearing that China's ongoing surge would facilitate a reconsolidation of older African political patterns, despite some democratic and governance gains.

A major concern of the IFIs and the Western donors has been the effect on African debt sustainability, given the deep and costly debt reduction many

African countries have received. A related fear has been that new Fund-Bank lending or Official Development Assistance (ODA) might be used to repay Chinese loans, with the World Bank going so far as to charge China with free riding. The World Bank tried to negotiate these issues with the Chinese, with little effect except for a World Bank–China cooperation agreement that may be just a tactical deflecting move by the Chinese. These issues were also raised in U.S.-China discussions, again to little effect. G8 finance ministers warned China in May 2007 about undermining debt sustainability efforts in Africa, specifically mentioning large concessional nonconditional loans to Angola and Sudan. A senior U.S. Treasury official asserted that "it is crucial that both borrowers and creditors agree on an approach to debt sustainability that prevents the reemergence of debt distress."[23] In particular, there was substantial criticism of a huge Chinese loan to Angola, which, along with its huge oil revenues, made it possible for Angola to keep the IMF at bay by refusing even a PSI agreement; yet there was no criticism of a $200 million loan to Angola by Standard Charter, Barclays, and the Royal Bank of Scotland or lending to Angola by Germany, Brazil, Russia, Portugal, and Israel. Angola was also servicing its Paris Club debt, including clearing $2.3 billion in principal and interest arrears in early 2007, in order to avoid Paris Club insistence on an IMF agreement. Angola may well end up negotiating a prepayment of all of its remaining Paris Club debt, as Russia and Macedonia have done. The Chinese have certainly broken, or at least loosened, the hold of the IFI/donor cartel in Africa, bringing market competition to foreign aid, lending, trade, and investment. In the long run, this may not be a bad thing for all parties concerned.

The influence of a loose Chinese development model may also be an important consequence of China's new role in Africa. It is characterized by flexibility, experimentation, pragmatism, selective learning and borrowing based on local conditions, an export orientation and willingness to engage in globalization, openness to outside investment, considerable room for markets and entrepreneurship, working through existing imperfect institutions while reforming them, political and macroeconomic stability with a key productive role for the state, and above all, safeguarding policy space so that a country can make its own decisions about when and how to do things, including when to borrow ideas and money from others. It also includes proper sequencing of policies—easy reforms before hard ones, rural reforms before urban ones, and economic ones before political ones. African universities are beginning to open up Chinese study programs that will allow a closer examination of this Chinese "model." As Ellen Johnson-Sirleaf, a former World Bank official who is the newly elected president of Liberia, noted, "I expect all of Africa will look at China's great transformation, and we'll see the cooperation that is now going on and identify new means by which we can support each other."[24] Learning on all sides may well be possible; the IFIs and donors may reassess their procedures and conditionality practices, China may learn that some conditionality is necessary for stable long-term economic relations with Africa, and African countries may learn to bargain effectively with both sides while defending their own policy space. However, one should not expect that all of these potentialities will become full-fledged realities. The *Financial Times* may have put it best: "The less China behaves like the west of old and the more Africa behaves like the China of today, the more likely this relationship is to benefit both sides."[25]

A Positive Legacy of Thirty Years of Structural Adjustment

While the track record of structural adjustment in Africa has been meager and rocky, especially in regard to more difficult structural reforms, significant, if uneven, learning has taken place regarding the importance of macroeconomic balance. A key indicator is the level of international reserves. As Figure 3.4 shows, African reserves have grown 500 percent over the past ten years, from $21 billion in 1996 to an estimated $131 billion in 2007. Africa's performance has outdone the recent developing world average, but as Figure 3.5 indicates, the trend began in the mid-1980s and accelerated in the mid-1990s. Much of the money that would have been wasted in the past is now being saved; it seems to be a new habit bred by long years of structural adjustment and the example of other, mostly Asian, countries following the Asia crisis of 1997. In addition, it holds for oil-importing countries as well as oil-exporting ones. Uganda, for example, had reserves equivalent to the value of six months of exports in 2007.

This policy trend helps to hedge against risk and external vulnerabilities but also provides some policy space that decreases dependence on the IFIs and donor countries. Africa's reserves are growing faster than foreign trade and have been facilitated by substantial debt reduction, discussed above, as well as by higher commodity prices and the presence of major new actors like China, India, South Korea, and Malaysia. In 1998, Zambia's reserves amounted to less than 1 percent of its foreign debt, but by 2007, they were the equivalent of 28 percent, a good omen for debt sustainability. With the exception of stunning disasters like Zimbabwe, whose economy has nearly halved since 1999, as nearly a quarter of its people have fled to neighboring countries and inflation has soared to 4,500 percent, African countries have been pursuing better policy and management of public finances.

CONCLUSION

Given the factors discussed in this chapter, it is clear that Africa really has the possibility of a second chance, a perhaps short window of opportunity to step

FIGURE 3.4 Sub-Saharan African international reserves, 1996–2007

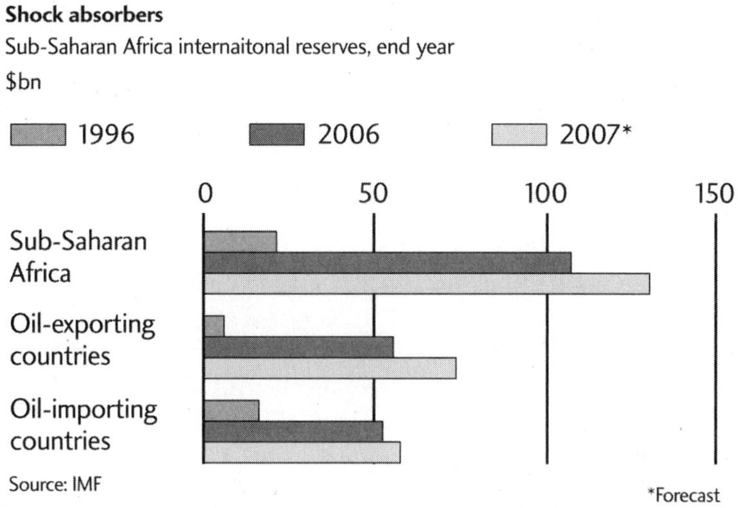

Source: "Africa Buys Itself a Bit of Insurance," *The Economist*, June 30, 2007, p. 84.

FIGURE 3.5 Sub-Saharan African international reserves, 1985–2006

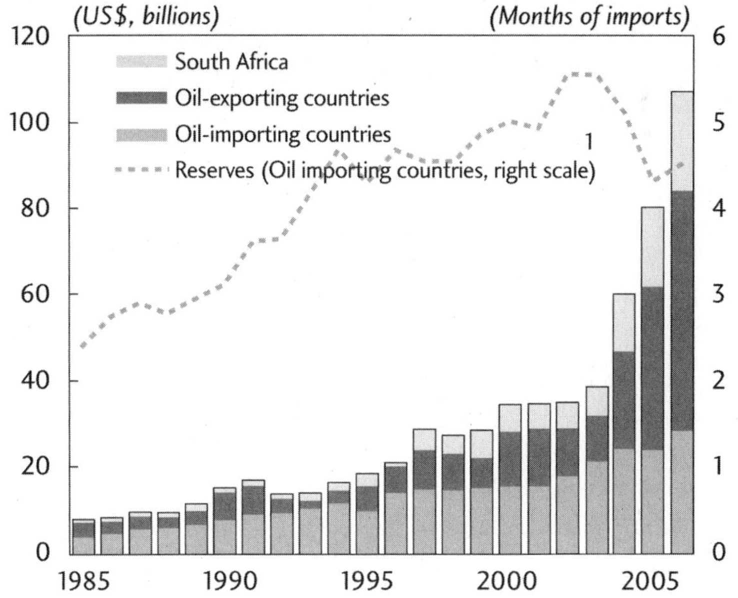

Source: International Monetary Fund, *Regional Economic Outlook: Sub-Saharan Africa* (Washington, D.C.: IMF, April 2007), p. 7

up and do what needs to be done for its own development. After more than thirty years of structural adjustment, African leaders, governments, and civil societies must stand up and prove they can do what is required. They have a chance to take the responsibility they have so long claimed they want. Not all of them will or will be able to do so; this is after all not just economics, but rather political economy, and serious political obstacles remain. Thus, we should not fall victim to the fault of analytic hurry—seeing a trend we really want to take place as real before there is hard evidence that it is actually sustainable. But it is a window of opportunity that has not existed for a long time. The leaders and governments who do stand up deserve all the help the international community can provide them. So, is Africa still caught between a rock and a hard place? Given the current conjuncture of forces laid out here, a possible answer is "not as much as we thought." Africa's marginalization and dependence could at least begin to diminish, but much of it depends on how Africans respond to their new opportunities. It is not clear whether this latest bout of optimism may be dashed as quickly as past ones.

NOTES

1. Note that the term Africa is used in this chapter to mean sub-Saharan Africa.

The economic and financial data in this chapter come from the following World Bank publications: the 1989–1998 editions of *World Development Report*; the 1991–1999, 2006–2007 editions of *Global Economic Prospects*; the 1999, 2006–2007 editions of *Global Development Finance*; *World Development Indicators* (1999); *Africa Development Indicators* (2006); *Sub-Saharan Africa: From Crisis to Sustainable Growth* (1989); *Africa's Adjustment and Growth in the 1980s* (1989); Benno J. Ndulu, *Challenges of African* Growth (2007); Harry Broadman, *Africa's Silk Road: China and India's New Economic Frontier* (2006). Other sources include publications by the IMF, including *World Economic Outlook* (1999) and *Regional Economic Outlook: Sub-Saharan Africa* (2007), and various issues of *IMF Survey*. Additional sources include online data from the Web sites of the IMF and the World Bank, and various issues of the *Financial Times*, 1993–2007.

2. Confidential interview, New York, April 26, 1990.

3. B. A. Kiplagat, quoted in "Africa Fears Its Needs Will Become Secondary," *New York Times*, December 26, 1989.

4. Quoted in "Ghana: High Stakes Gamble," *Africa News* 31/2 (January 23, 1989), p. 10.

5. World Bank, *Adjustment Lending* (Washington, D.C., World Bank, 1988), p. 3.

6. Oxfam, *Africa Make or Break: Action for Recovery* (London: Oxfam, 1993).

7. Quoted in Edward Balls, "Structural Maladjustment and the CFA Franc," *Financial Times*, November 15, 1993.

8. On the "thesis of the perverse effect," see Albert O. Hirschman, "Reactionary Rhetoric," *Atlantic Monthly* 263, 5 (May 1989), pp. 63–70.

9. See Richard L. Sklar, "Democracy in Africa," in Patrick Chabal, ed., *Political Domination in Africa* (Cambridge: Cambridge University Press, 1986), pp. 17–29.

10. Elliot Harris, "Impact of the Asia Crisis on Sub-Saharan Africa," *Finance and Development* 36, no. 1 (March 1999), p. 15.

11. In addition to the sources in Note 1, this section is based on confidential interviews with current and former officials of the IMF, the World Bank, and the U.S. and British governments and representatives of NGOs conducted in Washington, New York, London, and Brussels in 1997–2007.

12. Quoted in Christopher Swann and Ed Crooks, "World Bank: Low Levels of Aid for Poor 'Unacceptable,'" *Financial Times,* April 26, 2004.

13. Speech at the Senate "Poverty and Debt Relief Photo Exhibit," October 14, 2005; italics added.

14. Quoted in Elizabeth Becker, "Guess Who's Invited to Dinner," *New York Times,* September 23, 2004.

15. Quoted in Andrew Balls, "Foreign Aid Threatened by Anti-terrorism, Says Oxfam," *Financial Times,* December 6, 2004.

16. World Bank, *Africa Development Indicators 2006,* p. 1.

17. World Bank, *Global Development Finance 2006,* p. 22.

18. Quoted in "World Bank to Increase Support to Curb Vulture Fund Actions," World Bank Press Release No. 2007/415/PREM, May 31, 2007.

19. Quoted in "G8 Breaking the Aid Contract," *PRS Watch,* June 6, 2007, p. 1.

20. Quoted in Celia W. Dugger, "Rock Star Still Hasn't Found the African Aid He's Looking For," *New York Times,* May 15, 2007, p. A6.

21. It is important to note that other Asian countries are also involved, especially India, South Korea, and Malaysia; see Broadman, *Africa's Silk Road.*

22. Quoted in Steve Daly, "G8: Who's Pulling Africa's Purse Strings?" *Spiked,* June 7, 2007, www.spiked-online.com; quoted in "China in Africa: Never Too Late to Scramble," *Economist,* October 28, 2006, p. 54.

23. Quoted in "G8 Ministers Put Africa in Focus," BBC News, May 20, 2007, http://news.bbc.co.uk.

24. Quoted in Richard McGregor, "African Leaders' Summit Promises to Be Triumph of Diplomacy for Beijing," *Financial Times,* November 3, 2006.

25. Editorial, "No Panacea for Africa: China's Influence Is Not an Alternative to Neo-liberalism," *Financial Times,* February 6, 2007.

4

Africa and Other Civilizations

Conquest and Counter-Conquest

Ali A. Mazrui

INTRODUCTION: CULTURAL RECEPTIVITY

One of the most intriguing aspects of the historical sociology of Africa since the early twentieth century has been its remarkable cultural receptivity. For example, Christianity has spread faster in a single century in Africa than it did in several centuries in Asia.[1] European languages have acquired political legitimacy in Africa more completely than they have ever done in formerly colonized Asian countries like India, Indonesia, and Vietnam. Indeed, while nobody talks about "English-speaking Asian countries" or "Francophone Asia," African countries are routinely categorized in terms of which particular European language they have adopted as their official medium (Lusophone, English-speaking, and Francophone African states).

If we examine the preceding millennium, North Africa and much of the Nile Valley were not only converted to the Muslim religion; millions of the inhabitants were linguistically transformed into Arabs. Elsewhere in Africa, the Muslim faith has continued to make new converts in spite of the competitive impact of Euro-Christian colonial rule following the Berlin conference of 1884–1885.[2]

Linguistic nationalism in favor of indigenous languages in postcolonial Africa has been relatively weak. Only a handful of African countries allocate much money toward developing African languages for modern needs. On the other hand, most African governments south of the Sahara give high priority to the teaching of European languages in African schools.[3]

No African country has officially allocated a national holiday in honor of the gods of indigenous religions. All African countries, on the other hand, have a national holiday either in favor of Christian festivals (especially Christmas) or Muslim festivals (for example, Idd el-Fitr) or *both* categories of imported festivals. The Semitic religions (Christianity and Islam) are nationally honored in much of Africa; the indigenous religions are at best ethnic occasions rather than national ones.

TOWARD CONQUERING THE CONQUERORS

Africa's readiness to welcome new cultures is both its strength and its weakness. There is an African preparedness to learn from others; but there is also the looming danger of Africa's dependency and intellectual imitation.

What has so often been overlooked is the third dimension of this equation. Africa's cultural receptivity can over time make others dependent on Africa. There is a cyclic dynamic at play. Those who have culturally conquered Africa have, over time, become culturally dependent upon Africa. The biter has sometimes been bitten; the conqueror has sometimes been counter-conquered. This chapter is about this boomerang effect in acculturation and assimilation. Africa has sometimes counterpenetrated the citadels of its own conquerors.

This process of Africa's counterpenetration has sometimes been facilitated by Africa's political fragmentation in the egalitarian age. The majority of the members of the nonaligned movement are from Africa. The largest single group of members of the Organization of the Islamic Conference are African and also members of the African Union. Much of the agenda of the Commonwealth of Nations since the 1960s has been set by its African members—as they have used the "Britannic" fraternity to help liberate Southern Africa, dismantle apartheid, and address the challenges of globalization such as the debt crisis. Although African countries comprise about a third of the Commonwealth members, they have been by far the most influential regional group in shaping its agenda and its decisions. In the 1990s, African influence was for a while enhanced by the election of the first African Secretary-General of the Commonwealth, Chief Eleazar Emeka Anyaoku of Nigeria. South Africa's readmission under majority rule brought the whole story full circle. And when Mozambique was admitted in 1995, the Commonwealth ceased to be an exclusively anglophone club.

In the United Nations, countries from Africa were also almost a third of the total global membership until the Soviet Union and Yugoslavia collapsed, and Czechoslovakia split into separate UN members. Africa's fragmentation in an egalitarian age had for a while helped Africa's voting power in the General Assembly. Africa's percentage of the total membership has declined in the 1990s—closer to a quarter of the membership.[4]

On the other hand, Africa has had two successive Secretaries-General of the United Nations—Boutros Boutros-Ghali and Kofi Annan—partly as a result of the wider rivalries of world politics. On the negative side, the United States and Great Britain also succeeded in hounding out of power the first African Director-General of UNESCO, Amadou-Mahtar M'Bow of Senegal.[5] Even in this relatively egalitarian age in human history, real power continues to be decisive—when there is enough at stake to invoke it. In the first half of this twenty-first century will Africa provide another Director-General of UNESCO?

Even Africa's weakness has—on other occasions—been a source of power. As we indicated, Africa's territorial fragmentation has translated into voting influence even in UNESCO, in spite of what happened to Dr. M'Bow. And the General Assembly of the United Nations continues to take into account the liberation and egalitarian concerns of the African group.

Similarly Africa's cultural receptivity—though often excessive and a cause of Africa's intellectual dependency—has sometimes become the basis of Africa's counterinfluence on those who have conquered her. This chapter on Africa's counterpenetration is illustrative rather than exhaustive. I examine Africa's relationship with two interrelated civilizations—Arab and Islamic. I then examine the French connection as an illustration of Africa's potential in counter-influencing the Western world. I then examine Africa's interaction with India—with special reference to the legacies of Mahatma Gandhi and Jawaharlal Nehru. I conclude with Africa's conquest of Africa—the full circle of autocolonization.

The Arab factor in Africa's experience is illustrative of the politics of *identity.* The Islamic factor is illustrative of the politics of *religion.* With the French connection we enter the politics of *language.* The Afro-Indian interaction is examined through the politics of *liberation.* Finally, I examine the future politics of *self-conquest.* Let us now turn to the four case studies (Afro-Arab, Afro-Islamic, Afro-French, Afro-Indian and Afro-African) in greater detail.

AFRICA CONQUERS THE ARABS

In the seventh century CE, parts of Africa were captured by the Arabs in the name of Islam. Three factors speeded up the Arabization of North Africa and the Lower Nile Valley. One factor was indeed Africa's cultural receptivity—a remarkable degree of assimilability. The second factor that facilitated Arabization was the Arab lineage system, and how it defined the offspring of mixed marriages. The third factor behind Arabization was the spread of the Arabic language and its role in defining what constitutes an Arab.

At first glance the story is a clear case of how the Arabs took over large chunks of Africa. But on closer scrutiny the Afro-Arab saga is a story of both conquest and counterconquest. It is comparable to the role of the British in colonizing North America. Much later, imperial Britain was being protected and led by her former colonies, the United States of America.

But there is one important difference in the case of reciprocal conquest between the Arabs and the Africans. The actual creation of *new Arabs* is still continuing. Let us examine this remarkable process of "Arab-formation" in Africa across the centuries more closely.

The Arab conquest of North Africa in the seventh and eighth centuries initiated two processes—Arabization (through language) and Islamization (through religion). The spread of Arabic as a native language created new Semites (the Arabs of North Africa). The diffusion of Islam created new monotheists, but not necessarily new Semites. The Copts of Egypt are linguistically Arabized, but they are not, of course, Muslims. On the other hand, the Wolof and Hausa are preponderantly Islamized—but they are not Arabs.

The process by which the majority of North Africans became Arabized was partly biological and partly cultural. The biological process involved intermarriage and was considerably facilitated by the upward lineage system of the Arabs. Basically, if the father of a child is an Arab, the child is an Arab, regardless of the ethnic or racial origins of the mother. This lineage system could be described as *ascending miscegenation*, since the offspring ascends to the status of the more privileged parent.

This is in sharp contrast to the lineage system of, say, the United States where the child of a white father and a black mother *descends* to status of the less privileged race of that society. Indeed, in a system of descending miscegenation like that of the United States, it does not matter whether it is the father or the mother who is black. An offspring of such racial mixture descends to black underprivilege. The American system does not therefore co-opt "impurities" upward across the racial barrier to high status. It pushes "impurities" downward into the pool of disadvantage.

It is precisely because the Arabs have the opposite lineage system (*ascending* miscegenation) that North Africa was so rapidly transformed into part of the Arab world (and not merely Muslim world). The Arab lineage system permitted considerable racial cooptation. "Impurities" were admitted to higher echelons as new full members—provided the father was an Arab. And so the range of colors in the Arab world extends from the whites of Syria and Iraq to the browns of Yemen, from blond-haired Lebanese to the black Arabs of Sudan.

Within Africa the valley of the White Nile is a particularly fascinating story of evolving Arabization. The Egyptians were, of course, not Arabs when the Muslim conquest occurred in the seventh century CE. The process of Islamization in the sense of actual change of religion took place fairly rapidly after the Arab conquerors had consolidated their hold on the country.

On the other hand, the Arabization of Egypt turned out to be significantly slower than its Islamization. The Egyptians changed their religious garment from Christianity to Islam more quickly than they changed their linguistic garment from ancient Egyptian and ancient Greek to Arabic. And even when Arabic became the mother tongue of the majority of Egyptians, it took centuries before Egyptians began to call themselves Arabs.

But this is all relative. When one considers the pace of Arabization in the first millennium of Islam, it was still significantly faster than average in the history of human acculturation. The number of people in the Middle East who called themselves "Arabs" expanded dramatically in a relatively short period. This was partly because of the exuberance of the new religion, partly because of the rising prestige of the Arabic language, and partly due to the rewards of belonging to a conquering civilization. Religious, political, and psychological factors transformed Arabism into an expansionist culture that absorbed the conquered into the body politic of the conquerors. In the beginning there was an "island" or a peninsula called "Arabia." But in time there were far more Arabs outside Arabia than within. At the end of it all there was an "Arab world."

Along the valley of the White Nile, Northern Sudan was also gradually Islamized—and more recently has been increasingly Arabized. But as the crisis of Darfur has illustrated, many Northern Sudanese may learn the Arabic language as a second language—and fall short of seeing themselves as Arabs.[6] But other Sudanese people who were not originally Arabs have come to see themselves more and more as Arabs.

The question that arises is whether there is a manifest destiny of the White Nile—pushing it toward further Arabization. It began with the Egyptians and their gradual acquisition of an Arab identity. The Northern Sudanese have been in the process of similar Arabization. Are the Southern Sudanese the next target of the conquering wave of Arabization within the next hundred to two hundred years? Will the twin forces of *biological mixture* (intermarriage between Northerners and Southerners) and *cultural assimilation* transform the Dinkas and Nuers of today into the black Arabs of tomorrow?

It is not inconceivable, provided the country as a whole holds together. As racial intermarriage increases, Northern Sudanese will become more black in color. As acculturation increases in the South, Southerners may become more Arab. Biological Africanization of the North and cultural Arabization of the South will reinforce each other and help to forge a more integrated Sudan, provided peace is restored to the country. Without peace the country will break up sooner or later.

Southern Sudanese are the only sub-Saharan Africans who are being Arabized faster than they are being Islamized. They are acquiring the Arabic language faster than they are acquiring Islam. This is in sharp contrast to the experience of such sub-Saharan peoples as the Wolof, the Yoruba, the Hausa or even the Somali—among all of whom the religion of Islam has been more triumphant than the language of the Arabs. This rapid Arabization of the Southern Sudanese linguistically has two possible outcomes in the future. The Southern Sudanese could became Sudan's equivalent of the Copts of Egypt—a Christian minority whose mother tongue would then be Arabic. Or, the Arabization of the Southern Sudanese could be followed by their religious Islamization—in time making Southern and Northern Sudanese truly intermingled and eventually indistinguishable.

Meanwhile, the Swahili language has been creeping northward toward Juba from East Africa as surely as Arabic has been creeping southward from the Mediterranean. The Swahilization of Tanzania, Kenya, Uganda, and eastern Zaire has been gathering momentum.[7] With Arabic coming up the Nile toward Juba and Kiswahili down the same valley, Southern Sudanese will find themselves caught between the forces of Arabization and the forces of Swahilization. Historically, these two cultures (Arab and Swahili) can so easily reinforce each other. It is because of this pattern of trends that the manifest destiny of the Valley of the White Nile appears to be a slow but definite assimilation into the Arab fold over the next century or two. Ironically, the Arabization of Southern Sudan may continue even if the South breaks away and forms a separate country.

Nevertheless, racial ambivalence will maintain a linkage with Africanity. Indeed, the Southern Sudanese are bound to be the most negritudist of all Sudanese—even if they do become Arabized and do not secede. There is a precedent of black nationalism even among Northern Sudanese. It is not often realized how much "negritude" sentiment there is among important sectors of Northern Sudanese opinion. Muhammad al-Mahdi al-Majdhub has been described as "probably the first Sudanese poet to tap the possibility of writing poetry in the Arabic language with a consciousness of a profound belonging to a 'Negro' tradition."[8]

The poet al-Mahdi has indeed affirmed:

> *In the Negroes I am firmly rooted though the Arabs*
> *may boastfully claim my origin . . . My tradition is:*
> *beads, feathers, and a palm-tree which I embrace,*
> *and the forest is singing around us.*[9]

Muhammad Miftah al-Fayturi is another Arab negritudist. Information about his ancestry is somewhat contradictory. His father was probably Libyan and his mother Egyptian but of Southern Sudanese ancestry. In his words:

> *Do not be a coward*
> *Do not be a coward*
> *say it in the face*
> *of the human race:*
> *My father is of a Negro father,*
> *My mother is a Negro woman,*
> *and I am black.*[10]

In some notes about al-Fayturi's early poetic experiences, there is the anguished cry: "I have unriddled the mystery, the mystery of my tragedy: I am short, black and ugly."

Then there are the Arab negritudists who sometimes revel in the fact that they are racially mixed. They can also be defiant and angrily defensive about their mixture. Salah A. Ibrahim, in his piece on "The Anger of the Al-Hababy Sandstorm," declared:

> *Liar is he who proclaims:*
> *'I am the unmixed'. . . Yes, a liar!*[11]

In the Sudan of the future there may be even less room for such "lies" than there is at present. After all, Arabization is, almost by definition, a process of creating mixture—and its relentless force along the White Nile is heading southward toward Juba and beyond.

How has the boomerang effect worked in relation to the Arabization of Africa? In what sense has there been an Africanization of the Arab world? In what way has the whole process been cyclic?

It is worth reminding ourselves that the majority of the Arab people are in Africa. Over 60 percent of the population of the Arab world is now west of the Red Sea on African soil. The largest Arab country in population is Egypt, which in 1989 and 1993 became the presiding country in the Organization of African Unity, while its president was at the same time seeking a resolution of the Palestinian-Israeli impasse during both years.

The headquarters of the Arab League is in Africa. From 1979 to 1989 it was located in Tunis, having previously been in Cairo. In 1990 it was decided to return the Arab League to Cairo. If the headquarters of the Arab League symbolizes the capital of the entire Arab world, then the capital of the Arabs in the second half of the twentieth century was located on the African continent.

When the Palestine Liberation Organization and its warriors were expelled from Lebanon by the Israeli military invasion of 1982, the headquarters of the Palestinian movement also moved to Africa. Major decisions about the Palestinians, including the declaration of the Palestinian state in exile, were now made on African soil—from Tunis. Partly because of this evolving Afro-Palestinian solidarity, Yassir Arafat was in Lusaka in 1990 to embrace Nelson Mandela when the latter made his first trip outside South Africa in thirty years.

The largest city in the Arab world is located on its African side. The population of Cairo is more than the native population of Saudi Arabia as a whole.

Cairo also has become the cultural capital of the Arab world. The greatest singers and musicians of the Arab world—including the incredible Umm Khulthum, affectionately known as "the Star of the East"—used to mesmerize the Middle East from the studios of the Voice of the Arabs Broadcasting System in Cairo. Israelis even invented one more anti-Arab joke—"O yes, the Arabs have at last found unity—every Thursday night when they all tune in to listen to the voice of Umm Khulthum." Her funeral in 1975 was second only to President Nasser's burial in 1970 in terms of the size of the crowds and the passions and public grief displayed.[12]

The most famous Arab musical composer of the twentieth century has also come from the African side of the Arab world. Al-Ustadh Muhammad Abdul Wahab was in his younger days primarily a singer and instrumentalist. His musical compositions were initially modest, though they suited his vocal power. After deeper study of Western classical music—with special reference to Beethoven—Muhammad Abdul Wahab took Egyptian music into new levels of cross-cultural complexity. He developed new styles of Arab orchestral and even symphonic music. He was doing all this innovative work from the African side of the Arab world.

Culture has its technological and professional infrastructure. Egypt is by far the most important film-making country in both Africa and the Arab world. Egyptian shows feature prominently on cinema screens and television programs on both sides of the Red Sea.

There are other skills of the Arab people that also disproportionately emanate from the African side. Dr. Boutros Boutros-Ghali, when he was Egypt's Minister of State for Foreign Affairs, estimated that Egypt's technical assistance to other Arab countries was sometimes as high as two million Egyptians scattered in the region.[13] Boutros-Ghali later became Secretary-General of the United Nations, as stated earlier.

All this is quite apart from the importance of Egypt in the Arab military equation in at least four of the Arab-Israeli wars. Until the 1973 war, the Arab armies were no match for the Israelis. And even in 1973, Arab triumphs were mainly at the beginning of the conflict. What is clear is that the nearest thing to an Arab military credibility against Israel came from the African side of the Arab region. This is why the United States invested so heavily in the Camp David Accords and the neutralization of Egypt as a "confrontation state" against Israel. In exchange for American largess, Egypt is no longer prepared to defend either Palestinians or Lebanese militarily.

In 639 CE, the Arabs had crossed into Africa and conquered Egypt. By the second half of the twentieth century Egypt had become the most important pillar of the military defense of the Arab world. History has once again played its cyclic boomerang game in the interaction between Africa and her conquerors. The ancestral home of the Arabs in Asia is now heavily dependent culturally and militarily on the African side of the Arab nation. However, there are more petrodollars to the east of the Red Sea than to the west.

In His infinite wisdom, Allah has so far permitted the ancestral home of Islam—Saudi Arabia—to retain a preponderance of oil reserves and petropower. Perhaps only the petro-factor has prevented the African side of the Arab nation from attaining complete preponderance. Arabized Africa now leads the way demographically, culturally, technologically, militarily, and artistically. Allah has permitted the birthplace of the Prophet Muhammad to lead the way in petro-power for the time being.

AFRICA: THE FIRST ISLAMIC CONTINENT?

Why are Islam and Christianity continuing to spread so fast in sub-Saharan Africa? Why has *religious* receptivity in Africa been so remarkable?

The spread of Christianity during Africa's colonial period was particularly spectacular. The Christian gospel spread faster in a single century in Africa than it did in several centuries in places like India and China. Indeed, Christianity in southern India is virtually two thousand years old—going back to the days of the disciples of Jesus. Yet to the present day the Christian population in the whole of India is little more than 20 million in a country that has a total population of more than one billion.[14]

When we turn to Islam, there is just the chance that Africa will become to Islam what Europe has been to Christianity—the first continent to have a preponderance of believers. Europe was the first continent to have a majority of Christians. Is Africa becoming the first continent to have a majority of Muslims?

Since independence two issues have been central to religious speculation in Africa—Islamic expansion and Islamic revivalism. Expansion is about the spread of religion and its scale of new conversions. Revivalism is about the rebirth of faith among those who are already converted. Expansion is a matter of geography and populations—in search of new worlds to conquer. Revivalism is a matter of history and nostalgia—in search of ancient worlds to reenact. The spread of Islam in postcolonial Africa is basically a peaceful process of persuasion and consent. The revival of Islam is sometimes an angry process of rediscovered "fundamentalism."

In Arab Africa there is little Islamic expansion taking place—although some Egyptian Muslim militants regard the Coptic Church as a historical anachronism that ought to end.[15] For North Africa as a whole, Islamic revivalism is the main issue. It probably cost President Anwar Sadat his life in 1981 and has sometimes threatened the ruling regimes of Tunisia, Algeria, and Morocco. Indeed, Algeria was plunged into an ugly civil war when the military aborted an election that the Islamists were set to win in 1992.[16] Outside Arab Africa the central issue concerning Islam is not merely its revival but also the speed of its expansion. We are back to the issue of receptivity. It is not often realized that there are more Muslims in Nigeria than in any Arab country, including Egypt.[17] Muslims in Ethiopia are not a small minority either; they are probably half the population.[18] Islam elsewhere in Africa has spread—however unevenly—all the way down to the Cape of Good Hope. Islam in South Africa is three hundred years old, having first arrived not directly from Arabia but from Southeast Asia with "Malay" immigrants.[19]

The largest countries in Africa in terms of population are Nigeria, Egypt, Ethiopia, and the Democratic Republic of the Congo (DRC). Between them, these four countries account for nearly 200 million Muslims. (The Islamic part of the Congo is mainly in the east.) Virtually half the population of the continent is now Muslim.[20]

But religion in Africa does not of course exist in isolation. The world of religious experience in Africa is rich in diversity. It is even affected by the rivalry between the written word and the oral tradition. The written word and literacy are often regarded as allies of modernization. But the written word can also be an adversary to modernization. This is particularly so in situations where a holy book or sacred text commands so much loyalty that it hinders the process of secularization. The primordial power of the Qur'an on Muslim believers has tended to make "modernization" in the Muslim world more difficult—for better or for worse.

Religions of the oral tradition, on the other hand, tend to be more receptive to new religious influences. African traditional religions especially are particularly ecumenical. The same African individual may combine either Islam with his or her ethnic religion or Christianity with that indigenous religion. This is what so-called syncretism is all about. However, while an African may be both a Muslim and a follower of a traditional creed, an African is unlikely to be both a Muslim and a Christian. One religion of sacred text (for example, Islam) can be combined with a religion of oral message (for example, Yoruba religion). But it is rare that two religions of sacred text (Sunni Islam and Roman Catholicism) can be adhered to by the same individual. Religions of sacred text tend to be mutually exclusive. Shiite Muslims are unlikely to be simultaneously Methodists or Greek Orthodox.

Of the three principal religious legacies of Africa (indigenous, Islamic, and Christian), the most tolerant on record must be counted to be the indigenous tradition. It is even arguable that Africa did not have religious wars before Christianity and Islam arrived. Indigenous religions were neither *universalist* (seeking to convert the whole of the human race) nor *competitive* (in bitter rivalry against other creeds). Christianity and Islam, on the other hand, were both universalist and competitive—perhaps especially in Black Africa. In that arena south of the Sahara, Christianity and Islam have often been in competition for the soul of the continent. Rivalry has sometimes resulted in conflict.[21]

Indigenous African religions, on the other hand, are basically communal rather than universalist. Like Hinduism and modern Judaism—and unlike Christianity and Islam—indigenous African traditions have not sought to convert the whole of humankind. The Yoruba do not seek to convert the Ibo to Yoruba religion—or vice versa. Nor do either the Yoruba or the Ibo compete with each other for the souls of a third group, such as the Hausa. By not being proselytizing religions, indigenous African creeds have not fought with each other. Over the centuries, Africans have waged many kinds of wars with each other—but hardly ever religious ones before the universalist creeds arrived.

But what has this to do with cultural receptivity in contemporary Africa? The indigenous toleration today has often mitigated the competitiveness of the imported Semitic religions (Christianity and Islam). Let me illustrate with Senegal, which is over 90 percent Muslim.[22] The founder president of this predominantly Islamic society was Léopold Sédar Senghor. This Roman Catholic presided over the fortunes of postcolonial Senegal for two decades (1960–1980) in basic political partnership with the Muslim leaders of the country, the Marabouts.[23]

Contrast this phenomenon with the history of the United States as a predominantly Protestant society. In spite of a constitution that ostensibly separated church from state from the eighteenth century, it was not until 1960 that the American electorate was ready to elect a Roman Catholic as president. When will the United States elect a Jew to that highest office? Although U.S. Jews have occupied some of the highest offices of the land (and have been represented on the Supreme Court), it seems unlikely that there will be a Jewish president of the United States for at least another decade.

Muslims in the United States may now equal the Jews in numbers (although not in influence and power).[24] Although the Constitution still insists on separating church from state, for the time being, the prospect of a Muslim president of the United States of America remains mind-boggling.

And yet, newly independent Senegal could in 1960 calmly accept a Roman Catholic to preside over the fortunes of a basically Muslim country. Senghor belonged to an entirely different faith from most Senegalese, unlike Kennedy, who was a fellow Christian to most Americans but from a different sect. And yet he was president of a stable Muslim country for some twenty years.

His successor as president (partly sponsored by him) was Abdou Diouf—a Muslim ruler of a Muslim society, at last. But the tradition of ecumenical tolerance continued in Senegal. The first lady of the country—Madame Elizabeth Diouf—was Roman Catholic. And several of the ministers serving under the new president were, from time to time, Christian.

Senegalese religious tolerance has continued in other spheres. What might be regarded as provocative in other Islamic countries has been tolerated in Senegal. There have been occasions when a Christian festival like the First Communion—with a lot of feasting, merrymaking, and singing—has been publicly held in Dakar right in the middle of the Islamic fast of Ramadan. The feast has coexisted with the fast. And the Christian merrymakers have been left undisturbed.[25]

To summarize the argument so far, predominantly Muslim countries south of the Sahara have sometimes been above average in religious toleration. The capacity to accommodate other faiths may to some extent be part of the historical Islamic tradition in multireligious empires. But far more religiously tolerant than either Islam or Christianity have been indigenous African traditions—especially since these do not aspire to universalism and are not inherently competitive. In Black Africa this indigenous tolerance has, as I indicated, often moderated the competitive propensities of Christianity and Islam.

As President of Uganda in his first administration, Milton Obote (a Protestant) used to boast that his extended family in Lango consisted of Muslims, Catholics, and Protestants "at peace with each other." Obote's successor—Idi

Amin Dada (a Muslim)—also had a similarly multireligious extended family and even once declared that he planned to have at least one of his sons trained for the Christian priesthood. Amin may have reconsidered the matter when—upon losing office—he found political refuge in Saudi Arabia as a guest of the custodians of the Islamic holy cities of Mecca and Medina. And as indicated above, the first Muslim president of Senegal, Abdou Diouf, had a Roman Catholic first lady. Religious ecumenicalism and cultural receptivity continue to moderate the sensibilities of contemporary Africa.

When we place Islam in the context of the African continent as a whole, the cultural cyclic boomerang effect is once again discernible. The most influential Islamic university in the world—Al-Azhar University—is on the African continent. Al-Azhar in Cairo is credited with some of the most important *fatwas* under the Sharia (legal opinions under Islamic law) in the past six hundred years.

Al-Azhar was founded by the Fatimids more than a thousand years ago in 970 CE. This makes it one of the oldest and most durable universities in the world. The basic program of studies through the ages has been Islamic law, theology, and the Arabic language. Other subjects have more recently been added, especially since the nineteenth century. Women have been admitted since 1962. The university has continued to attract Muslim students from as far afield as China and Indonesia. It is widely regarded as *the* chief center of Islamic learning in the world.[26]

Islamic modernism has also been led from the African side of the Muslim world. The Egyptian thinker Muhammad Abduh (1849–1905) is still widely acclaimed as the chief architect of the modernization and reform of Islam. Born in the Nile Delta, he was later influenced by the great Pan-Islamic revolutionary Jamal al Din al-Afghani, who had settled in Cairo before being expelled for political activity in 1879. Abduh himself also suffered exile more than once. He lived to become the leading jurist of the Arab world, a professor at Al-Azhar University, and eventually *Mufti* of Egypt (chief Islamic chancellor). His doctrinal reforms included freedom of will in Islam, the harmony of reason with revelation, the primacy of ethics over ritual and dogma in religion, and the legitimacy of interest on loans under Islamic law.[27]

A much more recent disciple of Abduh and al-Afghani was the Sudanese scholar Mahmoud Muhammad Taha. Taha's own version of Islamic modernism in Sudan earned him a punishment more severe than what Abduh and al-Afghani suffered in nineteenth century Egypt. Under the presidency of Jaafar el-Nimeiry in Sudan, Mahmoud Muhammad Taha was executed in his old age in January 1985 on charges of apostasy and heresy.[28]

While this history of Islamic modernism includes personal tragedy as well as intellectual originality, there is no doubt about Africa's role in the reformation of Islam. Africa has often been the very vanguard of Islamic innovation and doctrinal review.

Africa's remarkable presence in the global Islamic equation includes the scale of Africa's membership in the Organization of the Islamic Conference (OIC). Until the collapse of the Soviet Union, almost half of the members of this global Islamic organization were also members of the Organization of African Unity. Africa has produced some of the leaders of the OIC. The late Ahmed Sékou Touré of Guinea (Conakry) was Chairman of the OIC when he attempted to mediate between Iraq and Iran in the earlier phases of their own Gulf war.

In distribution, Islam is indeed an Afro-Asian religion. Almost all Muslim countries are either in Africa or in Asia. In this new millennium, the Muslim population of the world has been estimated at 1.2 billion people. Before the middle of this new century, the Muslim population of the globe may reach a quarter of the human race. In a television address to the American people in August 1998, President Bill Clinton estimated that Muslims were already a quarter of the world's population, but that was probably premature.

The fastest rate of increase of the Muslim population of the world is currently in Africa. This is partly because Africa is undergoing the fastest rate of Islamic conversion of any major region on earth. It is also because natural fertility rates in Africa are higher than anywhere else. Moreover, Muslims in Africa are reproducing at a faster rate than most other Africans, as in many other regions.[29] This trend was confirmed in an earlier study:

> The single most remarkable demographic aspect of Islamic societies is the nearly universal high level of fertility—the average of childbearing in Islamic nations is 6 children per woman. . . . Fertility rates are highest for those Islamic nations in sub-Saharan Africa—an average of 6.6 births per woman. Furthermore, African Islamic nations south of the Sahara have higher fertility on average than do other developing nations in that region.[30]

There is evidence not only that Muslim women are married significantly earlier than other women in developing countries,[31] but also that Muslim women aspire to have more children. Kenya now has slowed its population growth, but until the concluding decades of the twentieth century, Muslim women aspired to an average family size of 8.4 children: "This was the highest of any religious grouping, with Catholic women preferring 7.1 children and Protestant women an average of 7.0 children."[32]

Although Asia still has many more millions of Muslims than Africa, the demographic indicators show that the African continent is narrowing the gap dramatically. In the twenty-first century, Africa may already have become the only continent of the world with an absolute Muslim majority.[33] This second-largest continent, in terms of area, may have become the first in Muslim preponderance. A part of Asia once conquered Africa in the name of Islam. Africa is now repaying the debt by overshadowing Asia in the fortunes of Islam. The cultural boomerang effect has once again been at work.[34] Once again we have a full circle.

History is in the process of playing out a remarkable prophetic destiny. The first great muezzin of Islam was a black man—the great Bilal, son of Rabah of Ethiopian extraction. Today we might compare his great voice with that of Paul Robeson. Bilal called Muslim believers to prayer in seventh-century Arabia.[35]

Symbolically, Bilal's Islamic call to prayer has echoed down the centuries. In this twenty-first century, has Bilal been heard particularly clearly in his ancestral continent of Africa? Perhaps the cultural boomerang effect has now taken the form of echoes of an African muezzin reverberating back across the centuries. What of the echoes from that other great civilization in Africa's destiny—the Western heritage? Our case study here concerns the French version of the idea of "Eurafrica." Let us explore this area.

EURAFRICA: THE FRENCH CONNECTION

France invented the concept of "Eurafrica"—asserting an organic relationship between Europe and Africa, deep enough to transform the two continents into a single integrated international subsystem. How does this concept relate to the French language?

The majority of French-speaking people in the world are in the Western world—mainly in France itself. However, the majority of French-speaking *states* are in Africa. Over twenty members of the African Union are French-speaking in the sense of having adopted French as an official language. These are Algeria, Benin, Burundi, Chad, Cameroon, Central African Republic, Comoros, Congo, Côte d'Ivoire, Djibouti, Burkina Faso, Gabon, Guinea, Madagascar, Mali, Mauritania, Mauritius, Morocco, Niger, Rwanda, Senegal, Réunion, Togo, Tunisia, and Congo (Kinshasa).[36]

Without Africa, the French language would be almost a provincial language. The Democratic Republic of Congo (formerly Zaire) is the largest French-speaking country after France in terms of population—and it is destined to be *the* largest absolutely by about the middle of the twenty-first century.[37] If the Congo (DRC) succeeds in stabilizing itself, and in assuming effective control over its resources, it may one day become France's rival in influence and power in French-speaking Africa as a whole.[38]

When we look at the global scene, the French language is shrinking in usage in the Northern Hemisphere. On the other hand, French is still spreading and gaining in influence in the Southern Hemisphere, especially in Africa. Let us take each of these propositions in turn. Why is French declining in Europe and the North as a whole?

The most important challenge to the French language in the Northern Hemisphere has been caused by the vast expansion of American influence in the twentieth century. The language has of course been English. While the spread of the English language in Africa has been mainly due to the impact of imperial Britain, the spread of the English language in Europe, and its expanding role in international affairs, has been largely due to the new American hegemony in the Northern Hemisphere. The triumph of the English language globally has ranged from increasing usage in diplomacy to its preeminent role as the supreme language of aviation and air-control.[39]

A related reason for the shrinkage of French in the Northern Hemisphere concerns the computer revolution and the Internet. The amount of information circulating in English is so much greater than what is transmitted in French that English is gaining the ascendancy even further. The old adage that "nothing succeeds like success" has now been computerized. The global influence of American computer firms initiated this Anglo-computer revolution.

At the other end of social concerns is the decline of the cultural influence of the upper classes in Europe. Royal houses in continental Europe as a whole had once preferred to use the French language extensively. In the aftermath of the Russian Revolution in 1917 and the subsequent development of social egalitarianism in Europe, linguistic snobbery declined, and linguistic pragmatism became the norm. Aristocratic linguistic snobbery had once favored French; egalitarian linguistic pragmatism in continental Europe was later to favor the English language.[40]

The fourth factor behind the decline of French in the Northern Hemisphere was Britain's entry into the European Economic Community (later, European Union). This made English more decisively one of the official languages of the community. English became increasingly influential in the affairs of the European Union, both written and oral. Smaller members of the EU have more frequently turned to English rather than French in the post-Gaullist era of European affairs.[41]

The fifth factor behind the decline of French in the Northern Hemisphere is linked to the decline of the power of the French-speaking Walloons in Belgium. The days of French preeminence in Belgium were coming to an end in the 1980s, although francophone Brussels still remained the capital of the country. Belgium moved toward a neofederal structure, rooted in the principle of linguistic parity between French and Flemish.[42]

It is arguable that in North America the French language has made some gains as a result of greater recognition of bilingualism in the whole federation of Canada. On the other hand, there has been a decline of linguistic nationalism in Quebec since the old militancy of the 1960s.[43]

The decline of the role of German in Europe has also tended to favor English rather than French. When the Scandinavian countries regarded German as virtually their first foreign language, there was a tendency to invest in the French language as well for a sense of balance. But when Scandinavians turned more decisively to the English language as their first foreign tongue, it was not just German that suffered; it was also French. Since English was in any case of wider international utility than German, its adoption by Scandinavians as the premier foreign language reduced the need to "balance" it with French.

Of course, Scandinavians are greater linguists than average. Their schools are still sensitized to the importance of French and German as well as English. But linguistic priorities have indeed changed in the Nordic syllabi and curricula—and in class enrollments. The English language has definitely been the main beneficiary of the decline of German, and the French language has also sustained a decline in educational emphasis.

Japan is also part of the Northern Hemisphere. It too has experienced shifts in emphasis that have demoted German and French—and raised the role of English in educational and linguistic priorities. Between the Meiji Restoration in 1868 and Japan's defeat in World War II in 1945, Japan's main Western role models were indeed Germany and France. This Franco-German orientation not only affected Japan's curricula and syllabi but also profoundly influenced its legal system and civil code.

It was the American occupation of Japan (1945–1952) that decisively shifted Japan from a Franco-German role model to the Anglo-Saxon alternative. The United States' continuing special relationship with Japan after the postwar occupation consolidated Japan's cultural reorientation. Although the Americans under Douglas MacArthur imposed upon Japan in 1947 a national constitution basically drawn from continental European experience, much of the rest of the Westernization of Japan has been a case of cultural Americanization—from Japanese introduction to baseball to Japanese enthusiasm for American pop stars. The very economy of Japan has interlocked itself with the American economy. The confirmation of the English language as Japan's first Western language in the postwar era has been part of this American phase of Japan's transformation. The decline of French and German languages in Japanese priorities was an inevitable consequence of the Americanization of Japan.[44]

If these have been the main factors that have resulted in the decline of the French language in the Northern Hemisphere, which factors have contributed to its expansion in the South?

What must be emphasized in the first instance is that the Southern expansion is mainly in Africa. On the whole, the distribution of the French language is *bicontinental*—a large number of French-speaking *individuals* in Europe, and a large number of French-speaking *states* in Africa. Europe and Africa are by far the primary constituencies of the French language.

Of course, there are smaller francophone constituencies in Quebec, Lebanon, Syria, Indochina, and elsewhere. But these are peripheries of the francophone world. The main theater of action is in Europe and Africa.

Factors that have favored expansion in Africa have included the type of states that French and Belgian imperialism created during the colonial period. These were often multi-ethnic countries that needed a lingua franca. Colonial policy chose the French language as the lingua franca—and the entire educational system and domestic political process consolidated that linguistic choice.[45]

A related factor was the assimilationist policy of France as an imperial power. This created an elite mesmerized by French culture and civilization. A surprising number still retained dual citizenship with France even after independence. If President Bokassa was anything to go by, some African heads of state may secretly still be citizens of France. Annual holidays in France continue to be part of the elite culture of francophone West and North Africa.

With some subsidies and technical assistance, the French language is also featuring more and more in classrooms in anglophone Africa. Before independence, British educational policymakers were more committed to the promotion of indigenous African languages than to the promotion of the rival French legacy in British colonies. Nor were French offers of language teachers for schools in British colonies welcome.

The global French fraternity of Francophonie now has a secretariat in Paris, which was for a while headed by Boutros Boutros-Ghali. The Francophonie club now enlists not only countries that have adopted French as a national language but also those that have been persuaded to teach more French in their schools.

The difference that Africa's independence has made partly consists in greater readiness on the part of anglophone governments to accept France's offers of teachers of the French language. Many an African university in the Commonwealth of Nations has been the beneficiary of technical assistance and cultural subsidies from the local French embassy or directly from France.

France's policy in Africa is consolidated partly through an aggressive cultural diplomacy. Considerable amounts of money are spent on French-style syllabi and curricula in African schools, and on the provision of French teachers, advisors, and reading materials. A residual French economic and administrative presence in most former French colonies has deepened Africa's orientation toward Paris.

In addition, every French president since Charles de Gaulle has attempted to cultivate special personal relations with at least some of the African leaders.

There is little doubt that French-speaking African presidents have had greater and more personalized access to the French president than their anglophone counterparts have had to either the British prime minister or the British head of state, the Queen of England, in spite of Commonwealth conferences.

Here again is a case of reciprocal conquest. There is little doubt that the French language and culture have conquered large parts of Africa. Many decisions about the future of Africa are being made by people deeply imbued with French values and perspectives.

Moreover, French is expanding its constituency in Africa, in spite of reverse trends in Algeria. It is true that the postcolonial policy of re-Arabization in Algeria is designed to increase the role of Arabic in schools and public affairs at the expense of the preeminent colonial role of the French language. The rise of Islamic militancy in Algeria may pose new problems to aspects of French culture. It is also true the late Mobutu Sese Seko's policy of promoting regional languages in the former Zaire (Lingala, Kikongo, Tshiluba, and Kiswahili) was partly at the expense of French in Zairean (now Congolese) curricula. Since 1994, French has also suffered a setback in Rwanda, led by anglophone Tutsi originally educated in Uganda. But such setbacks for French in Africa are the exception rather than the rule. On the whole, French is still on the ascendancy in Africa, though the speed of expansion has drastically declined.

However, when all is said and done, France's aspiration to remain a global power requires a cultural constituency as well as an economic one. It seems likely that the 2000s will continue to signify a change in France's economic priorities in favor of the new pan-European opportunities of an enlarged European Union and against the older investments in Africa. But it seems equally certain that a more open Europe after the end of the Cold War is favoring the English language at the expense of the French language even within France itself. As custodian of the fortunes of French civilization, France could not afford to abandon the cultural constituency of Africa entirely in favor of the more open Eastern Europe. The collapse of the Soviet empire has been a further gain for the English language. France may need Africa more *culturally*, but less *economically*.

As France's cultural constituency in Europe has been declining, its cultural constituency in Africa has become more valuable than ever. A remarkable interdependence has emerged—still imperfect and uneven, but real enough to make Africa indispensable for the recognition of France as a truly global power, and the acceptance of the French language as a credible *world* language. *Eurafrica* as a concept gets its maximum meaningfulness in the destiny of the French language. But is there also a concept of *Afrindia* worth exploring? And how does this relate to the legacies of Gandhi and Nehru?

AFRINDIA: BETWEEN GANDHI AND NEHRU

Quite early in his life Mahatma Mohandas Gandhi saw nonviolent resistance as a method that would be well suited for the African as well as the Indian. In 1924 Gandhi said that if the black people "caught the spirit of the Indian movement their progress must be rapid."[46]

In 1936 Gandhi went even further: "It may be through the Negroes that the unadulterated message of nonviolence will be delivered to the world."[47] And to understand his claim one should perhaps link it up with something that was later said by his disciple Jawaharlal Nehru, who said, "Reading through history I think the agony of the African continent . . . has not been equaled anywhere."[48]

To the extent then that the black man had more to be angry about than other men, he would need greater self-discipline than others to be "passive" in his resistance. But by the same token, to the extent that the black man in the past three centuries had suffered more than any other, passive but purposeful self-sacrifice for the cause should come easier to him. And to the extent that the black man had more to forgive the rest of the world for, that forgiveness, when it came, should be all the more weighty. Perhaps it was in response to these considerations that Gandhi came to the conclusion by 1936 that it was "maybe through the Negroes that the unadulterated message of non-violence will be delivered to the world."[49]

And so it was that in America the torch came to be passed to Martin Luther King Jr. In South Africa, where Gandhi first experimented with his methods, it was passed to Albert Luthuli and later Desmond Tutu. In Northern Rhodesia (Zambia after independence) Kenneth Kaunda became a vigorous Gandhian—"I reject absolutely violence in any of its forms as a solution to our problems."[50]

In the Gold Coast (Ghana before independence) Kwame Nkrumah translated *Satyagraha* (soul force) into a program of "Positive Action," which he defined as "non-cooperation based on the principle of absolute non-violence, as used by Gandhi in India."[51] In 1949 the *Morning Telegraph* of Accra went as far as to call Nkrumah the "Gandhi of Ghana."[52]

African conceptions of dignity now seemed very different from what was implied by that old ceremonial affirmation of young Kikuyu initiates that Kenyatta once told us about—the glorification of the spear as "the symbol of our courageous and fighting spirit." But these new conceptions of dignity could now also be differentiated from the submissive virtues of early missionary teachings.

Yet one question remained to be answered: Could passive resistance survive the attainment of independence? Would Gandhism retain political relevance once its immediate objective of liberation from colonialism was achieved?

It is perhaps not entirely accidental that the two most important Indian contributions to African political thought were the doctrines of nonviolence and nonalignment. In a sense they were almost twin doctrines. Gandhi contributed passive resistance to one school of African thought; Nehru contributed nonalignment to almost all African countries. We should note how Uganda's President Milton Obote put it in his tribute to Nehru on his death in 1964. Obote said: "Nehru will be remembered as a founder of nonalignment. . . . The new nations of the world owe him a debt of gratitude in this respect."[53] However, Gandhi and Nehru both taught Africa and learned from it.

But how related are the two doctrines in their assumptions? For India, Gandhi's *nonviolence* was a method of seeking freedom, while Nehru's *nonalignment* came to be a method of seeking peace. And yet nonalignment was, in some ways, a translation into foreign policy of some of the moral assumptions that underlay passive resistance in the domestic struggle for India's independence.

As independent India's first prime minister, Nehru's *armed* ejection of Portuguese colonialism from Goa in 1961 had a different impact on Africa. India's Foreign Minister Krishna Menon, speaking at the UN, described colonialism as "permanent aggression."[54] Particularly "permanent" was the colonialism of those who regarded their colonies as part of the metropole—as Portugal had pretended to do. In such a situation where colonialism threatened to be "permanent," the military solution was a necessary option.

Nehru's use of armed force against the Portuguese in Goa set a grand precedent for an Africa still shackled by Portuguese imperialism in Angola, Mozambique, and Guinea-Bissau. Had Gandhi's *Satyagraha* been replaced in 1961 by Nehru's *Satya-Goa?* Was there a Hegelian negation of the negation? Was Nehru's negation of nonviolence a legitimation of the violence of liberation?[55]

If Gandhi had taught Africa civil disobedience, had Nehru now taught Africa armed liberation? Had the armed ejection of Portugal from the Indian subcontinent strengthened Africa's resolve to eject Portugal from Angola, Mozambique, and Guinea-Bissau?

The impact of India upon twentieth-century Africa goes beyond even such towering figures as Mahatma Gandhi and Jawaharlal Nehru. But there is no doubt about the special significance for Africa of Gandhi's strategies of civil disobedience and Nehru's principles of both nonalignment and armed liberation. Gandhi's *Satyagraha* inspired African political figures as diverse as Nobel laureate Albert Luthuli of South Africa and Ivorian president Houphouët-Boigny. Nehru's ideas about what used to be called "positive neutralism" helped to shape African approaches to foreign policy in the early decades of the postcolonial era.

AFRICA'S REVERSE IMPACT ON GANDHI AND NEHRU

What has seldom been adequately examined is the reverse flow of influence from Africa into both Gandhi's vision of *Satyagraha* and Nehru's concept of nonalignment. Experience in the southern part of Africa must be counted as part of the genesis of Gandhi's political philosophy. And the 1956 Suez War in the northern part of Africa was probably a major influence on Nehru's vision of nonalignment.

South Africa was the cradle—and threatened to be the grave—of passive resistance as a strategy for Africa's liberation. Gandhi first confronted the problem of politicized evil in the context of racism in South Africa, where he lived for more than twenty years—from 1893 to 1914. Racial humiliation in that part of the continent helped to radicalize him and therefore prepared him for his more decisive historical role in British India from 1919 onward.[56]

Gandhi's political philosophy developed from both the world of ideas and the world of experience. Moreover, in the realm of ideas, he relied heavily on both Western liberalism and Indian thought, but what helped to radicalize Gandhi's own interpretation of those ideas was the power of experience. And within that crucible of experience we have to include Gandhi's exposure to sustained segregation in South Africa—a deeper form of racism than even the racist horrors of British India at that time.[57]

Under the stimulus of activated evil and the need to combat it, Gandhi reinterpreted in radical ways important concepts in Indian thought. For example, he reinterpreted *Ahimsa*—transforming it from nonresistance to passive resistance. This provoked the criticism of such Western students of Indian philosophy as Albert Schweitzer, who was also deeply fascinated by Africa. Schweitzer objected to Gandhi's reformulation of *Ahimsa* on the following grounds:

> Gandhi places Ahimsa at the services of world-affirmation and life-affirmation, directly to activity within the world, and in this way it ceases to be what in essence it is. Passive resistance is a non-violent use of force. The idea is that, by circumstances brought about without violence, pressure is brought to bear on the opponent and he is forced to yield. Being an attack that is more difficult to parry than an active attack, passive resistance may be the more successful method. But there is also a danger that this concealed application of force may cause more bitterness than an open use of violence. In any case the difference between passive and active resistance is only quite relative.[58]

Schweitzer and Gandhi were both profound humanitarians—and both retained a fascination with Africa. But while Schweitzer sought to serve humanity ultimately by curing the physical body of disease, Gandhi sought to serve humanity by curing the social condition of injustice. Schweitzer approached his physiological mission through medical work in Gabon. Gandhi approached his sociological mission through passive resistance, first in South Africa—and later, of course, in British India.

If Gandhi's *Satyagraha* was a response to the moral confrontation between good and evil, Nehru's nonalignment was a response to the militarized confrontation between capitalism and socialism. If Gandhi's political philosophy was originally a response to racial intolerance, Nehru's nonalignment was originally a response to ideological intolerance. The regime in South Africa became the symbol of racial bigotry for Gandhi. The Cold War between East and West became the essence of ideological bigotry for Nehru.

That South Africa was an inspiration for Gandhi is well documented. North Africa as an inspiration for Nehru's nonalignment has been less explored.

Two wars in North Africa in the 1950s were particularly important in Afro-Asian interaction. The Algerian War from 1954 to 1962 took African resistance beyond the passive level into the militarized active domain.[59] African Gandhism was in crisis. Had *Satyagraha* been rejected as no longer relevant for the struggle against colonialism?

The second great war in North Africa in the 1950s was the Suez conflict of 1956.[60] If the Algerian War marked a possible end to *Satyagraha* as a strategy for African liberation movements, the Suez War marked a possible birth of nonalignment as a policy of the postcolonial era. Gamal Abdel Nasser was economically punished by the United States, Britain, and the World Bank for purchasing arms from the Communist bloc. Washington, London and the Bank reneged on their commitment to help Egypt build the Aswan High Dam. Nasser's nationalization of the Suez Canal was an assertion of self-reliance, directing its revenue toward the construction of the "Great Dam." Egypt's sovereign right to purchase arms from either East or West was not for sale. In retrospect, Nasser's nationalization of the Suez Canal was a kind of unilateral declaration of nonalignment. This was before the nonaligned movement itself was formally constituted.[61]

Before the actual outbreak of the Suez hostilities, the diplomatic division at the level of the Big Powers was indeed East/West. Socialist governments were also neatly in support of Nasser, while the capitalist world was alarmed by his nationalization of the canal. However, when Britain, France, and Israel actually invaded Egypt, the Western world was divided. The United States was strongly opposed to the military action taken by its own closest allies.[62]

However, the Soviet Union went further than merely condemning the aggression by Britain, France, and Israel against Egypt. When the Western powers withdrew their canal pilots in an attempt to sabotage Egypt's efforts to operate the canal after nationalization, the Soviet Union lent Egypt its own pilots until Nasser could train his own. And in the wake of the West's reneging on the commitment to build the Aswan High Dam, the Soviet Union stepped into the breach—and became the builder of the dam.[63] What emerged from the entire experience was the value of trying to balance traditional Egyptian dependence on the West with readiness to find areas of cooperation with the East. The central principle of nonalignment was in the process of conception at Suez.

Jawaharlal Nehru helped to mobilize Third World opinion on the side of Gamal Abdel Nasser during the whole crisis. Although there was not as yet a nonalignment movement in world politics, the Suez conflict was part of the labor pains of its birth—and Jawaharlal Nehru was the leading midwife in attendance.

These factors made the Suez crisis part of the genesis of Pandit Nehru's diplomatic thought and vision—just as racism in South Africa was part of the genesis of Mahatma Gandhi's principle of *Satyagraha* (soul force). Suez was, at that time, the most dramatic test of a Third World country, being invaded by two members of NATO (France and Britain). Never before Suez had a Third World country been the subject of aggression by *two* members of NATO—and yet with the leader of NATO, the U.S.A., protesting against its allies. Nehru was both a teacher in and a learner from this crisis.

What all this meant eventually was that while Mahatma Gandhi had, in the first half of the twentieth century, inspired many Africans to pursue the path of passive resistance, Nehru's liberation of Goa in 1961–1962 converted still more Africans south of the Sahara to the possibilities of military action. Gandhi was the prophet of nonviolence; Nehru became the symbol of armed struggle. Were the two Indians contradicting each other in the corridors of history? Or were passive resistance and armed struggle two sides of the same coin of liberation?

The answer probably lay in the final struggle in the Republic of South Africa in the concluding years of the twentieth century. Both armed struggle and nonviolence played a part in South Africa—and the two forms of struggle appeared to be at once complementary and contradictory. As noted above, in a sense, South Africa was the cradle of Gandhi's *Satyagraha*. Was it about to become the graveyard of passive resistance, as racial violence loomed larger? Or would *Satyagraha* receive a new moral validation in the process of dismantling apartheid? Both liberation theology and armed struggle operated in South Africa. Political apartheid has now been abandoned, but economic apartheid is alive and well. Can soul-force end economic apartheid?

The answer lies in the womb of history. Two things about South Africa were predictable. When the fires of struggle were put out, a new black-led republic would join the community of nations. This has now happened. Almost equally predictable was the foreign policy that the new Republic of South Africa would adopt; it was going to be nonalignment. When the Republic of South Africa joined the nonaligned movement, the heritage of Gandhi and the legacy of Nehru were at last fused on the very continent on which they were once separately born. Morally, Afrindia was about to be vindicated.

South Africa would be indeed the last testing ground of nonalignment. From that perspective, if India was the brightest jewel of the British crown, Africa is now the richest source of all jewels.

And six Africans or men of African descent—all of whom were influenced by Gandhi—have won the Nobel Prize for Peace:

Ralph Bunche (1950)
Albert Luthuli (1960)
Martin Luther King Jr. (1964)
Anwar Sadat (1978)
Desmond Tutu (1984)
Kofi Annan (2001)

Two were black Americans, two black South Africans, one Egyptian, and one Ghanaian. By a strange twist of fate, Mahatma Gandhi himself never won the Nobel Prize. His black disciples did.

Africa's capacity to turn weakness into a form of influence has found a new arena of fulfillment. Fragmentation and excessive cultural receptivity are weaknesses. And weakness is not an adequate currency in the marketplace of power. But quite often the power of the weak is, in human terms, less dangerous than the weakness of the powerful—their arrogance and all.

And yet, when all is said and done, the ultimate conquest is Africa's conquest of itself. The ultimate colonization is *self-colonization* under the banner of *Pax Africana*. It is to this subject that we now turn.

TOWARD AN AFRICAN CONQUEST OF ITSELF

Is the process of Africa's decolonization reversible? As the postapartheid era has begun to emerge, the question has seriously arisen as to whether Africa is creating conditions that will sooner or later result in some kind of *recolonization*. And who will be the new colonizer?

In the 1990s, a thousand people a day were dying in the ongoing Angolan civil war. Somalia is torn between chaos and clanocracy (rule on the basis of clans). Burundi has a long history of brutal ethnocracy (rule by a particular ethnic group). Rwanda collapsed into genocide and civil war in 1994. Liberia and Sierra Leone had a tumultuous decade in the 1990s. The Congo and Darfur are in intensive care.

In the nineteenth century, imperialism justified itself by claiming to end tribal wars, hence *Pax Britannica.* In some parts of Africa the real tribal wars have come *after* colonial rule rather than before. *Pax Britannica* created future conflicts rather than ending old tribal feuds. And yet the specter of recolonization remains.

The issue has arisen as to whether colonization and decolonization are unilinear. We had previously assumed a neat sequence. There was a precolonial period covering millennia of African history. Then there was about a century of European colonial history, of immense economic, political, and cultural consequences. And then there would be the postcolonial period, ostensibly extending into infinity.

International intervention in African conflicts since the 1990s has raised the question of whether our complacency about neat periodization is indeed justified. Is there really a neat unilinear sequence of precolonial, colonial, and postcolonial periods?

Is *recolonization* feasible?[64] Indeed, could colonization itself be part of yet another cycle rather than unilinear experience? Could colonialism have different incarnations—a kind of transmigration of the imperial soul?

The imperial soul had previously resided in separate European powers—Britain, France, Portugal, and Belgium, among others. Has the imperial soul transmigrated to the United States? Or is the soul trying to decide whether to settle in the bosom of the United States or become part of the United Nations? Is this a period of cosmic imperial indecision between the United States and the United Nations as voices of "the world community"?

The next phase of colonialism could be *collective* rather than through individual powers. It may indeed be the transmigration of the soul of the United Nations Trusteeship Council to some new UN decision-making machinery. Will Africa play a role both as guardian and as ward?

A new form of UN trusteeship started in 1960 when things fell apart in the former Belgian Congo as the imperial power withdrew; on that occasion, the UN intervened to oppose Katanga's secession from the Congo. Officially, the United Nations ceased to be a trusteeship power in Africa as recently as 1990 when Namibia became independent. In Somalia, since the 1990s, the UN has so far ignored the self-proclaimed separatist Republic of Somaliland, which has declared its independence from the rest of Somalia. But if the problem of stability and anarchy in Somalia turns out to be insurmountable, the sanctity of Somalia's borders may one day be reexamined. Separatist Somaliland may yet survive to enjoy a legitimate UN seat—if not this time around, then after the next collapse of the Somali political patchwork. External recolonization under the banner of humanitarianism is entirely conceivable. Countries like Congo (Kinshasa), Somalia, and Sierra Leone, where central control has collapsed, have invited inevitable intervention. But by whom in the future?

Although colonialism may be resurfacing, it is likely to look rather different this time around. A future trusteeship system will be more genuinely international and less Western than it was under the old guise. Administering powers for the trusteeship territories could come from Africa and Asia, as well as from the rest of the membership of the UN. For example, might Uganda be officially invited by the UN to administer a fragile Rwanda? Might Nigeria be officially invited to administer Sierra Leone for a while on behalf of the United Nations or on behalf of a reconstituted Organization of African Unity?

Ethiopia was once a black imperial power, annexing neighboring communities. The future may hold a more benign imperial role for it, though this may take a century to evolve. The recolonization of the future will not be based on "the white man's burden" or the "lion of Judah." It may instead be based on a shared human burden: Ethiopia as an administering power on behalf of the UN or the African Union to help nurture the sovereignties of its smaller neighbors. But can Ethiopia be trusted to be altruistic when it intervenes in Somalia?[65]

However, regional hegemonic power can lose influence as well as gain it. Just as there is *subcolonization* of one African country by another, there can be sub-*de*colonization as the weaker country reasserts itself.

This is part of what happened between Egypt and Sudan in the 1990s. Sudan, under the Bashir Islamic regime, started asserting greater independence from Egypt—more than at any time since the Mahdiyya movement under Seyyid Muhammad el Mahdi in the nineteenth century.

Relations between Somalia and Egypt in the era after Siad Barre may also be a case of sub-decolonization—the reassertion of the weaker country (Somalia) against the influence of its more powerful brother (Egypt). When he was UN Secretary-General, Boutros-Ghali's problems with Mohamed Farah Aidid were perhaps part of the same story of sub-decolonization. Boutros-Ghali was seen more as an Egyptian than as the chief executive of the world body.

If subcolonization of one African country by another is possible, and sub-decolonization has also been demonstrated, what about sub-*re*colonization? Will Egypt reestablish its Big Brother relationship with Sudan and Somalia? Will there be another full circle? As the Arabs would affirm, *Allahu Aalam* (Only God knows).

In West Africa the situation is especially complex. Nigeria is a giant of over 135 million people. Its real rival in the region was never Ghana under Kwame Nkrumah, or Libya under Muammar Qaddafi or distant South Africa. The real rival to postcolonial Nigeria has all along been France. By all measurements of size, resources, and population in West Africa, Nigeria should rapidly have become what India is in South Asia or South Africa has been in southern Africa—a hegemonic power. Nigeria was marginalized not only by civil war in 1967–1970 but also by its own chronic incompetence and by the massive French presence in West Africa, mainly in its own former colonies but also in Nigeria itself.

In this twenty-first century, France will be withdrawing from West Africa as she gets increasingly involved in the affairs of Eastern, Central, and Western Europe. France's West African sphere of influence will be filled by Nigeria—a more natural hegemonic power in West Africa. It will be under those circumstances that eventually Nigeria's own boundaries are likely to begin threatening the Republic of Niger (the Hausa link), the Republic of Benin (the Yoruba link), and conceivably, Cameroon (part of which in any case nearly became Nigerian in a referendum in 1959).

The case of postapartheid South Africa also raises questions about a regional hegemonic power. On the positive and optimistic side, this will make it possible to achieve regional integration in Southern Africa. Regional unification is easier where one country is more equal than others—and can thus provide the leadership.

On the negative side, postapartheid South Africa could be a kind of subimperial power—and questions of subcolonization, sub-decolonization, and sub-recolonization may become part of the future historical fate of the smaller countries of Southern Africa. Another full circle.

Another African giant is the Democratic Republic of Congo. It is already the largest French-speaking country in the world after France; in the course of the twenty-first century, it will become, as indicated above, absolutely the largest French-speaking country in the world. In mineral resources it is already the richest French-speaking country. If Congo attains stability, it may become the magnet for the whole of French-speaking Africa. Will its boundaries remain the same? Congo (Brazzaville) may work out a federal relationship with Congo (Kinshasa) in the course of the twenty-first century. It would help the transition now that Zaire has reverted to its own older name of Congo (Kinshasa). A confederal relationship among the former Zaire, Burundi, and Rwanda is also conceivable later in the twenty-first century. All three were once ruled by Belgium. However, a more stable federation may be one among Burundi, Rwanda, and Tanzania, rather than Congo.

If I have presented some frightening possibilities, it is because some African countries may need to be temporarily controlled by others. The umbrella of *Pax Africana* is needed—an African peace enforced by Africans themselves. Africa may have to conquer itself.

A thousand lives a day were being indeed lost in the civil war in Angola at one time. If South Africa had already been black-ruled, it could have intervened—benevolent subcolonization could have been attempted for the greater good. It would have been comparable to India's intervention in East Pakistan in 1971, when the Pakistani army was on the rampage against its own Bengali citizens. India intervened and created Bangladesh. But India had a vested interest in dividing Pakistan, whereas a postapartheid South Africa might have intervened in a civil war in Angola for humanitarian and Pan-African reasons, and still preserved the territorial integrity of its smaller neighbors. South Africa's intervention in Lesotho in 1998 was bungled and inept, but the basic principle of *Pax Africana* behind it was sound!

New possibilities are on the horizon. We may yet learn to distinguish between benevolent intervention and malignant invasion in the years ahead. Africa could conquer itself without colonizing itself.

CONCLUSION

I have sought to demonstrate in this chapter the paradox of counterpenetration and the cyclic boomerang effect in Africa's interaction with other civilizations. Africa's cultural receptivity to its Arab conquerors has now tilted the demographic balance and changed the Arab cultural equation. The majority of the Arabs are now in Africa—and the African side of the Arab world has become the most innovative in art and science.

Africa's receptivity to Islam may make Africa the first truly Islamic continent. What Europe was to Christianity may turn out to be what Africa becomes to Islam—the first continent to have a preponderance of believers. African Islam since the nineteenth century has also been the vanguard of the Islamic reformation and modernism—especially since the Egyptian thinker, Muhammad Abduh. The fatal martyrdom of Mahmoud Muhammad Taha in Nimeiry's Sudan in 1985 is part of the story of daring innovation within the African constituency of the Islamic *ummah*. (The *ummah* is the worldwide Muslim community, basically followers of Sunni or Shi'a denominations, who account for more than 90 percent of the world's Muslim population.)

Africa's cultural receptivity to the French language and culture has already made Africa the second most important home of French civilization after France itself. The majority of French-speaking countries are already in Africa.

And Congo (Kinshasa) stands a chance of one day becoming a rival to France in leading the French-speaking part of the world. Congo (Kinshasa) is in the process of closing the population gap and the resource gap with France.

Africa's response to Gandhian ideas, reinforced by Christian pacifism, has already given Africa more Nobel Prizes for peace than India. Gandhi himself had once predicted that the torch of *Satyagraha* would one day be borne by the black world. Black winners of the Nobel Prize for Peace in the second half of the twentieth century have included two South Africans (Albert Luthuli and Desmond Tutu) and two African Americans (Ralph Bunche and Martin Luther King), but Mahatma Gandhi himself was never awarded the Nobel Prize.

Africa's response to Nehru's ideas of nonalignment have now resulted in a plurality of the nonaligned countries being from Africa. Africa was in fact the first continent to become almost completely nonaligned. If nonalignment once penetrated Africa, Africa has now truly penetrated the nonaligned movement.

But in the future, Africa's *cultural receptivity* has to be more systematically moderated by *cultural selectivity.* Counterpenetrating one's conquerors may be one worthy trend. But at least as important for Africa is a reduced danger of being excessively penetrated by others.

Perhaps one day the sequence of cultural penetration will be reversed. Instead of Africans being Arabized so completely that the majority of the Arabs are in Africa, the Arabian Peninsula may become increasingly Africanized. Instead of the Democratic Republic of the Congo being the largest French-speaking nation after France, Brazil will be counted the second-largest "African country" after Nigeria.

Meanwhile, Africa has to conquer itself, if it is to avoid further colonization by others. Africa needs to establish a *Pax Africana*—an African peace promoted and maintained by Africans themselves. One day each African person will look in the mirror—and recognize the human species as a whole. Amen.

NOTES

1. For an overview of Christianity in Africa, see Bengt Sundkler and Christopher Steed, *A History of the Church in Africa* (Cambridge and New York: Cambridge University Press, 2000).

2. On this conference, consult H. L. Wesseling, translated by Arnold J. Pomerans, *Divide and Rule : The Partition of Africa, 1880–1914* (Westport, Conn.: Praeger, 1996), pp. 113–119.

3. On the resistance to African languages by the elite and their attraction to foreign languages, see M. Ekkehard Wolff, "Language and Society," in Bernd Heine and

Derek Nurse, eds., *African Languages : An Introduction* (Cambridge and New York: Cambridge University Press, 2000), p. 342.

4. Montenegro becoming the 192nd member of the United Nations in July 2006 seemed to cap the explosion of UN membership among the former states of the Soviet Union and Yugoslavia. There are 53 member states of the Africa Union.

5. The United States was of course the real power in this conflict; a discussion of U.S. interaction with UNESCO may be found in W. Preston Jr., E. S. Herman, and H. I. Schiller, *The United States and UNESCO, 1945–1985* (Minneapolis: University of Minnesota Press, 1989).

6. The confusion over the identity politics of Darfur is exacerbated by several examples of intermarriage between those considered "Arab" and those considered "African," as illustrated in a story by Emily Wax, "A Family Torn by Sudan's Strife," *Washington Post,* September 29, 2004.

7. Relatedly, consult Alamin M. Mazrui, *Swahili Beyond the Boundaries: Literature, Language, and Identity* (Columbus: Ohio University Press, 2007).

8. See Muhammad Abdul-Hai, *Conflict and Identity: The Cultural Poetics of Contemporary Sudanese Poetry,* African Seminar Series No. 26 (Khartoum: Institute of African and Asian Studies, University of Khartoum, 1976), pp. 26–27.

9. *Nar al Majadhib* (Khartoum: Dar al-Jil and Shariakat al-Muktabah al-Ahliyah, 1969) pp. 195, 287; see also p. 24.

10. Cited by Abdul-Hai, *Conflict and Identity,* pp. 40–41.

11. *Ghadhbat al Hababy* (Beirut: Dar al Thaqafah, 1968); and Abdul-Hai, *Conflict and Identity,* p. 52.

12. For a discussion of this singer, see Virginia Danielson, *The Voice of Egypt: Umm Kulthûm, Arabic Song, and Egyptian Society in the Twentieth Century* (Chicago: University of Chicago Press, 1997).

13. Dr. Boutros Boutros-Ghali, interviewed by the author in Cairo, 1985.

14. V. A. Panadiker and P. K. Umashaker, "Politics of Population Control in a Diverse, Federal Democratic Polity: The Case of India," conference paper presented at the international symposium on "The Politics of Induced Fertility Change," sponsored by the University of Michigan, Villa Serbelloni, Rockefeller Foundation Conference Center, Bellagio, Italy, February 19–23, 1990.

15. Relatedly, see Daniel Williams, "Attacks on Copts Expose Egypt's Secular Paradox," *Washington Post,* February 23, 2006.

16. An overview of this conflict may be found in Robert A. Mortimer, "Islamists, Soldiers, and Democrats: The Second Algerian War," *Middle East Journal 50* (Winter 1996), pp. 18–39. By mid-2007, Algeria appeared to be limping back to some kind of normalcy, if not democracy; see the report by Craig Whitlock, "Algeria's Voters Uninspired as Limited Democracy Slowly Evolves," *Washington Post,* May 16, 2007.

17. Because of religious and political issues over the implications of population numbers, the estimation of the numbers of Muslims in Nigeria is quite contentious. Moreover, population estimates are quite unreliable. However, based on the U.S. State

Department's *2006 Report on International Religious Freedom,* the Muslim population of Nigeria may be between 70 and 75 million, while that of Egypt may be estimated to be about 67 million.

18. In Ethiopia today, Muslims may constitute a plurality (45–50 percent) while Ethiopian Orthodox Christians may constitute 35–40 percent; see the CIA World Factbook, at https://www.cia.gov/cia/publications/factbook/geos/et.html, accessed February 8, 2007.

19. Historically, three waves of Muslims are recorded as coming to South Africa; exiles from Southeast Asia, slaves from other areas of Africa, and indentured laborers from the Indian subcontinent. See Charlotte A. Quinn and Frederick Quinn, *Pride, Faith, and Fear: Islam in Sub-Saharan Africa* (New York: Oxford University Press, 2003), pp. 127–135; and Mervyn Hiskett, *The Course of Islam in Africa* (Edinburgh: Edinburgh University Press, 1994), p. 174. Shamil Jeppie has questioned the ascribing of "Malay" identity to the first wave of exiles; see Jeppie, "Commemorations and Identities: The 1994 Tercentenary of Islam in South Africa," in Tamara Sonn, ed., *Islam and the Question of Minorities* (Atlanta: Scholars Press, 1996), pp. 78–79.

20. There are more than 350 million Muslims in Africa, according to "Number of Followers of Major World Religions," *Current Events* 105, no. 21 (March 10, 2006), p. 4.

21. For an earlier elaboration of this thesis, see Ali A. Mazrui, "African Islam and Competitive Religion: Between Revivalism and Expansion," *Third World Quarterly* 10, no. 2 (April 1988), pp. 499–518.

22. One estimate of the percentage of Muslims in OIC countries puts the Senegalese figure at 97 percent; see Saad S. Khan, *Reasserting International Islam : A Focus on the Organization of the Islamic Conference and Other Islamic Institutions* (Karachi, Pakistan: Oxford University Press, 2001), p. 325.

23. On Senghor and Senegalese accommodation with Islam, consult Janet G. Vaillant, *Black, French and African: A Life of Léopold Sédar Senghor* (Cambridge: Harvard University Press, 1990); and Robert Fatton, *The Making of a Liberal Democracy: Senegal's Passive Revolution, 1975–1985* (Boulder: Lynne Rienner Publishers, 1987).

24. According to one study conducted by Professor Ihsan Bagby of Shaw University in Raleigh, North Carolina (as part of a larger study of American congregations called "Faith Communities Today"), and coordinated by Hartford Seminary's Hartford Institute for Religious Research, there are approximately 6 million Muslims in the U.S. with over 2 million of these being regularly participating adult attenders at the more than 1,209 mosques/masjids in the United States. The full report is available at http://www.cair-net.org/mosquereport/, accessed April 19, 2004. One estimate puts the number of Jews in the U.S. population at 6.06 million, amounting to about 2.2 percent of the U.S. population, according to a table in *The Statistical Abstract of the United States* (Washington, D.C.: Bureau of the Census, January 2002), p. 56.

25. Consult Susan MacDonald, "Senegal: Islam on the March," *West Africa* (London), no. 3494, August 6, 1984, p. 1570.

26. On this venerable university, consult Bayard Dodge, *Al-Azhar: A Millennium of Muslim Learning* (Washington, D.C.: Middle East Institute, 1974).

27. For a discussion of this important figure in modern Islamic intellectual history, consult Mahmudul Haq, *Muhammad Abduh: A Study of a Modern Thinker of Egypt* (Aligarh, India: Institute of Islamic Studies, Aligarh Muslim University, 1970).

28. See Mahmud Muhammad Taha's book, *The Second Message of Islam* (Evanston, Ill.: Northwestern University Press, 1987).

29. At a Pew Forum on Religion and Public Life on "The Coming Religious Wars? Demographics and Conflict in Islam and Christianity," May 18, 2005, Brian Nichiporuk pointed out, "Muslim regions tend to have significantly higher fertility rates than many other parts of the world." But he also pointed to the complex and diverse nature of these fertility rates. The event transcript is available at http://pewforum.org/events/print.php?EventID=82.

30. John R. Weeks, "The Demography of Islamic Nations," *Population Bulletin* (publication of the Population Reference Bureau, Inc.) 43, no. 4 (December 1988), p. 15.

31. More than a quarter (28.75 percent) of women in African Muslim countries between the ages of 15 and 19 are married, according to statistics from the United Nations, "Statistics and Indicators on Women and Men," at http://unstats.un.org/unsd/demographic/products/indwm/ww2005/tab2a.htm, accessed February 2, 2007.

32. Weeks, "The Demography of Islamic Nations," p. 20.

33. According to an estimate of the UAE Ministry of Islamic Affairs and Awaqf, 59 percent of Africa's population (in 1996) was Muslim; see http://www.fedfin.gov.ae/moia/english/e_growingreligion.htm, accessed May 28, 2004.

34. It is widely believed in African Muslim circles that Islam is already the majority religion on the African continent. This claim was often repeated at an international conference on Islam in Africa held in Abuja, Nigeria, in November 1989. See "Islam in Africa," *Africa Events* (London) 6, no. 2 (February 1990), pp. 23–37.

35. A biography of this towering figure in Islam may be found in H. A. L. Craig, *Bilal* (London and New York: Quartet Books, 1977).

36. This list is drawn from Arthur Banks, Thomas Muller, William Overstreet, eds., *Political Handbook of the World* (Binghamton, N.Y.: CSA, 2003); and David Crystal, ed., *The Cambridge Encyclopedia of Language* (Cambridge: Cambridge University Press, 1997).

37. See the map in Dennis Ager, *Identity, Insecurity, and Image: France and Language* (London: Multilingual Matters, 1997), p. 157.

38. Notably, even French public policy accepts that the demographic future of the French language rests in Africa; see Ager, *Identity, Insecurity, and Image*, p. 175.

39. A report in the *Economist* (December 20, 1986) titled "The New English Empire," pp. 127–131, describes this new dominance of the English language. For a fascinating history of the world's languages, see Nicholas Ostler, *Empires of the Word: A Language History of the World* (New York: HarperCollins, 2005); and for a comparative study of English and French, see Ronald Wardhaugh, *Languages in Competition:*

Dominance, Diversity, and Decline (Oxford; New York; and London: B. Blackwell and A. Deutsch, 1987).

40. For the Russian example, see the discussion in J. N. Westwood, *Endurance and Endeavor: Russian History, 1812–1992* (Oxford: Oxford University Press, 1993), p. 12.

41. See the column by Charlemagne, "Linguistic Follies," *Economist* (July 19, 2007) on the dominance and rise of English even in the affairs of the European Union.

42. Belgium's path toward relative amity between the regions is detailed in Lisbeth Hooghe, "Belgium: Hollowing the Center," in Ugo M. Amoretti and Nancy Bermeo, eds., *Federalism and Territorial Cleavages* (Baltimore: Johns Hopkins University Press, 2004), pp. 55–92; and Rolf Falter, "Belgium's Peculiar Way to Federalism," in Kas Deprez and Louis Vos, eds., *Nationalism in Belgium: Shifting Identities, 1780–1995* (Houndmills, Basingstoke, Hampshire, UK; and New York: Macmillan Press & St. Martin's Press, 1998), pp. 177–197. For an overview of Belgian regional cleavages, see John Fitzmaurice, *The Politics of Belgium: Crisis and Compromise in a Plural Society* (New York: St. Martin's Press, 1983); and also consult Alexander B. Murphy, *Regional Dynamics and Cultural Differentiation in Belgium: A Study in Cultural Political Geography* (Chicago: University of Chicago, Committee on Geographical Studies, 1988).

43. The tensions between Quebec and Canada are detailed in Kenneth McRoberts, *Misconceiving Canada: The Struggle for National Unity* (Oxford: Oxford University Press, 1997).

44. The two periods of Japanese transformation are detailed in Anne Waswo, *Modern Japanese Society, 1848–1994* (Oxford: Oxford University Press, 1996).

45. For a portrait of French colonialism in Africa in the early part of the twentieth century, see Jean Suret-Canale, *French Colonialism in Tropical Africa, 1900–1945* (London: C. Hurst, 1971).

46. *Young Indian,* August 21, 1924 (Madras: S. Ganesan, 1927), pp. 839–840. Consult also Pyarelal, "Gandhi and the African Question," *Africa Quarterly* 2, no. 2 (July–September 1962). See as well the selection from Gandhi titled "Mahatma Gandhi on Freedom in Africa," *African Quarterly* 2, no. 2 (July–September 1962). For a more extensive discussion by Gandhi on nonviolence, consult Gandhi, *Non-Violence in Peace and War*, 2nd ed. (Ahmedabad: Navajivan Publishing House, 1944).

47. This statement was reported in the *Harijan* (March 14, 1936); see Sudarshan Kapur, *Raising Up a Prophet: The African-American Encounter with Gandhi* (Boston: Beacon Press, 1992), pp. 89–90.

48. Jawaharlal Nehru, "Portuguese Colonialism: An Anachronism," *Africa Quarterly* 1, no. 3 (October–December, 1961), p. 9. See also Nehru, "Emergent Africa," *Africa Quarterly* 1, no. 1 (April–June 1961), pp. 7–9.

49. *Harijan* (March 14, 1936); this essay is also indebted to Mazrui, *The Africans: A Triple Heritage* (New York: Little Brown; and London: BBC Publications, 1986.)

50. See Colin M. Morris and Kenneth D. Kaunda, *Black Government? A Discussion between Colin Morris and Kenneth Kaunda* (Lusaka: United Society for Christian Literature, 1960).

51. Kwame Nkrumah, *Ghana: The Autobiography of Kwame Nkrumah* (New York: International Publishers, 1957), p. 112.

52. *Morning Telegraph,* June 27, 1949.

53. See *Uganda Argus,* May 29, 1964; and Ali A. Mazrui, *Africa's International Relations: The Diplomacy of Dependency and Change* (London: Heinemann Educational Books; and Boulder: Westview Press, 1977), pp. 117–121.

54. Menon's view of the Goa affair and Western criticism of Indian action is described in Michael Brecher, *India and World Politics: Krishna Menon's View of the World* (New York: Praeger, 1968), pp. 121–136.

55. For two views on the Goa affair, see P. D. Gaitonde, *The Liberation of Goa: A Participant's View of History* (London and New York: C. Hurst and St. Martin's Press, 1987); and P. N. Khera, *Operation Vijay: The Liberation of Goa and Other Portuguese Colonies of India* (New Delhi: Ministry of Defence, 1974).

56. Some of the early incidents of Gandhi's encounters with racist South Africans are described in J. N. Uppal, *Gandhi: Ordained in South Africa* (New Delhi: Ministry of Information and Broadcasting, 1995), pp. 23–30.

57. In addition to Uppal, *Gandhi: Ordained in South Africa,* also see Shanti Sadiq Ali, *Gandhi and South Africa* (New Delhi: Hind Pocket Books, 1994); and Maureen Swan, *Gandhi: The South African Experience* (Johannesburg: Ravan Press, 1985).

58. Albert Schweitzer, *Indian Thought and Its Development,* trans. by Mrs. C. E. B. Russell (New York: H. Holt, 1936), pp. 231–232. Consult also George Seaver, *Albert Schweitzer: The Man and His Mind* (London: Adam and Charles Black, 1951), p. 275.

59. The bloody war between France and Algeria is described in John E. Talbott, *The War Without a Name: France in Algeria, 1954–1962* (New York: Random House, 1980).

60. A full treatment of the Suez crisis can be found in a collection of essays edited by William Roger Louis and Roger Owen, *Suez 1956: The Crisis and Its Consequences* (Oxford: Clarendon, 1989).

61. The first conference of the group of countries that would later become the non-aligned movement was held in Bandung, Indonesia, in April 1955.

62. A portrait of the principal U.S. actors in the Suez crisis and their roles may be found in Robert R. Bowie, "Eisenhower, Dulles, and the Suez Crisis," in Louis and Owen, *Suez 1956,* pp. 189–214.

63. See Peter Woodward, *Nasser* (New York: Longman, 1992), pp. 59 and 87.

64. For an earlier, ominous article on recolonization, see Paul Johnson, "Colonialism's Back—Not a Moment Too Soon," *New York Times Magazine,* April 18, 1993, pp. 22–23 and 43–44.

65. Relatedly, see Stephanie McCrummen, "Ethiopia Finds Itself Ensnared in Somalia," *Washington Post,* April 27, 2007.

Part III

African States and the State System

Reinvention and Reconstruction

5

Promising Democratization Trajectories in Africa's Weak States

JOHN W. HARBESON

One of the least explored dimensions of twenty-first-century sub-Saharan African politics has been the evidence of significant differences in the progress of African countries toward achievement of stable, sustainable democratic stateness. Since democracy's Third Wave reached African shores with the end of the Cold War, evidence has begun to emerge that a number of sub-Saharan African countries have made notable, across-the-board progress toward sustainable and comprehensive democracy. Their progress, however, remains incomplete, fragile, and by no means irreversible. In this progress, however, they have begun to join long well-established democracies Botswana and Mauritius.

More generally, this same evidence has indicated that even countries that started from entrenched autocratic regimes or emerged from civil war in this period have demonstrated recognizable democratic progress, although they still fall short of significant overall democratic achievement. Moreover, nearly one-third of sub-Saharan African countries have made noteworthy progress across several, albeit not all, dimensions of democratic stateness. Just as important, the evidence also reveals that very few countries have become *less* democratic over the same period. Overall, however, a majority of sub-Saharan African countries remain in an intermediate position, demonstrating neither significantly improved overall levels of democratization nor substantial democratic retreats.

This chapter first reviews and probes the evidence that since the end of the Cold War, sub-Saharan African countries have indeed begun to evolve significantly divergent democratization trajectories characterized by significant advance, retreat, or continued mixed performance as democratic states. It then explores some implications of these findings, one of the most important of which is the bearing that nascent democratization may have on the strength and viability of chronically weak sub-Saharan African states. Specifically, contrary to literature contending that democratization tends to undermine weak states, this evidence suggests that democratization in sub-Saharan Africa has been at least compatible with, and may even have been important in, strengthening state viability and stability.[1]

Further comparative research, beyond the scope of this chapter, on the "whys" and "hows" of more and less successful democratization in sub-Saharan Africa may offer evidence potentially leading to the amendment of what have been prevalent empirical theories of democratization and its relationship to state strength. Though tacitly and commonly presumed to be universally applicable, these theories have generally continued to remain disproportionately shaped by the experience of only one or two world regions, including sub-Saharan Africa only rarely at most. Specifically, the empirical evidence may test reigning, still rarely examined, assumptions embedded in these theories concerning the relationship between democratization and state strengthening.

Although much of the evidence suggesting diverging democratization trajectories in sub-Saharan Africa is quantitative, it is also much more extensive and detailed than the overall Freedom House rankings, which have been nearly the sole quantitative points of reference in scholarly assessments of democratization in the region to date.[2] The evidence now available probes many of the specific *component* elements of democratization undergirding the overall Freedom House estimates of political and civil liberties. Similarly, component elements of the overall Polity IV scores have not been widely analyzed.[3] In addition, the World Bank *Governance Matters* surveys on six dimensions of democratization and governmental performance and the increasingly comprehensive Afrobarometer surveys of African public opinion on democratic performance have yet to be fully considered in relationship to Freedom House and Polity IV data.[4] The availability of this wider array of data relating to the issue of democracy and governmental behavior establishes at least the potential for a greater degree of reliability and validity for these quantitative estimates. The large number and wide range of collective perceptions aggregated in several, sometimes overlapping, surveys to arrive at these statistics do seem to support the hypothesis that markedly different, if still tentative, trajectories of democratic progress and regression have indeed emerged in sub-Saharan Africa.

The overall Freedom House scores themselves reveal modest but nonetheless significant improvement by sub-Saharan African countries as a group in their observance of political and civil liberties since the onset of democracy's Third Wave in the early 1990s. Moreover, as Table 5.1 makes clear, sub-Saharan African countries have improved in their observance of political and civil liberties more rapidly than have all countries worldwide over the same time period, moving from about 45 percent of the Freedom House worldwide average score in 1990 to nearly 77 percent of that average in 2005. This figure is counterbalanced only in part by the statistical anomaly that many countries outside Africa had less distance to travel to reach the top possible scores than almost all of those of sub-Saharan Africa. In addition, there has been a noteworthy increase in the number of countries that have scored above the worldwide average over the same period, a pattern of improvement that has largely counterbalanced declines of corresponding magnitude over the preceding fifteen year period.

Fifteen sub-Saharan African countries have set the pace with combined political and civil liberties scores above the average for all countries. These countries include not only Botswana and Mauritius, which have remained democratic since independence, but also Benin, Cape Verde, Ghana, Kenya, Lesotho, Madagascar, Mali, Namibia, Niger, São Tomé, Senegal, Seychelles, and South Africa.

TABLE 5.1 Trends in sub-Saharan African political and civil liberties, 1975–2005

	2005	2000	1990	1975
All countries	7. 56	7.39	7.75	7.02
Sub-Saharan Africa	5.79	5.20	3.50	3.79
Africa as % of all countries	77	70	45	54
African countries above all-country average	15	12	4	3
African countries below all-country average	33	36	44	45

Source: Compiled from data available at Freedom House, at http://www.freedomhouse.org.

Note: Freedom House ranks countries from 1 (high) to 7 on both political and civil liberties, the top combined score being 2, the lowest 14. A country with a rating of 1 or 2 on a political or civil liberties is considered free, 3–5 partially free, 6–7 unfree. Countries with combined scores of 2 to 5 are considered free, 6 to10 partially free, 11 to14 unfree. This table inverts numbers so that 12 (14 minus 2) is high. Hence, scores of 9 to 12 = free, 4 to 8 partially free, 0 to 3 unfree.

Only quite recently has Freedom House elected to release the data for the *components* of its political and civil liberties scores. The components of its political liberties scores include (1) the freeness and fairness of the election processes; (2) the extent of permitted political pluralism; and (3) the degree to which government functions accountably, free of corruption, and on the basis of policies chosen by elected officials. Civil liberties scores are based on (1) the degree to which freedom of expression and belief is respected; (2) the extent to which associations and organizations are free to organize, advocate, and engage in public discussions; (3) the extent to which the rule of law is upheld in civil and criminal proceedings, is applied by an independent judiciary, honors equality before the law, and is uncompromised by terror or insurgency; and (4) personal autonomy in the forms of political space for citizens to travel, own property, conduct business relations, marry and raise children as they please, and to be free of gender discrimination. Freedom House evaluates countries on each of these sub components, although it does not publish the sub component scores.

An examination of the scores for the components of the overall Freedom House political and civil liberties ratings (available on the Freedom House Web site) indicates that its overall assessments are reliable as a shorthand for estimating a country's democratic status. However, the component scores also facilitate more nuanced assessments of democratic progress by making it possible to analyze the *interrelationships* among the several components of democratic advancement. Table 5.2 lists the Freedom House component scores for 2006.

Several significant hypotheses about trajectories of democratization in the region are suggested by the data in Table 5.2. First, the 2006 component scores show clearly that although the region has advanced significantly in democratization by global standards since 1990 (as shown in Table 5.1), sub-Saharan Africa continues to be below average based on scores for all seven components probed by Freedom House assessments.

Second, the data suggest that *some* sub-Saharan African countries have a record of achievement that places them significantly *above* global averages on several dimensions of democratization. Bold-faced scores in Table 5.2 indicate scores that are one-half of a standard deviation or more above or below the global average. Although thirty-four sub-Saharan African countries scored below or significantly below the global overall average, fourteen scored *above* the global overall average. Eight of these exceeded the global average by one-half of a standard deviation or more, up from two—Mauritius and Botswana—prior to 1990. Joining those two countries are Cape Verde, South Africa, Ghana, Benin, São Tomé, and Namibia. The other six countries that scored above the global overall average, though by less than one-half of a standard deviation, are Senegal, Mali, Lesotho, Seychelles, Niger, and Kenya.[5]

TABLE 5.2 Freedom House component scores for sub-Saharan Africa, 2006

Country	PL	CL	Status	A	B	C	D	E	F	G	H
Cape Verde	1	1	F	**12**	**15**	**10**	**15**	**11**	**14**	**13**	**90**
Mauritius	1	2	F	**11**	**15**	**11**	**15**	**12**	**13**	**12**	**89**
South Africa	2	2	F	**12**	**14**	**9**	**15**	**12**	**12**	**12**	**86**
Ghana	1	2	F	**12**	**15**	**10**	**14**	**11**	**12**	10	**84**
Benin	2	2	F	**10**	**15**	8	**15**	**12**	**12**	10	**82**
São Tomé	2	2	F	**11**	**14**	8	**15**	**10**	**12**	10	**80**
Botswana	2	2	F	**11**	11	**9**	**14**	**10**	**13**	10	**78**
Namibia	2	2	F	**10**	12	**9**	**15**	**12**	10	9	**77**
Senegal	2	3	F	**11**	**13**	**9**	**15**	**10**	9	9	76
Mali	2	2	F	9	12	**9**	**16**	9	10	9	74
Lesotho	2	3	F	9	12	**9**	**15**	8	**11**	9	73
Seychelles	3	3	PF	8	10	7	10	9	**11**	11	66
Kenya	3	3	PF	9	11	5	**14**	9	8	8	64
Niger	3	3	PF	**11**	10	8	11	9	9	6	64
Sierra Leone	4	3	PF	9	10	**4**	12	8	8	9	60
Zambia	4	4	PF	8	11	6	11	8	8	**7**	59
Madagascar	3	3	PF	7	9	7	10	8	9	9	59
Malawi	4	3	PF	7	10	6	11	8	9	**7**	58
Tanzania	4	3	PF	6	10	6	11	7	10	8	58
Mozambique	3	4	PF	7	11	7	11	7	7	8	58

TABLE 5.2 *(continued)*

Country	PL	CL	Status	A	B	C	D	E	F	G	H
Liberia	3	4	PF	9	10	5	11	7	7	8	57
Guinea-Bissau	4	4	PF	9	9	**4**	11	8	8	**6**	55
Comoros	3	4	PF	9	11	**4**	10	**6**	8	**6**	54
Burkina Faso	5	3	PF	**5**	8	**4**	14	9	**6**	**7**	53
Nigeria	4	4	PF	6	9	6	11	7	**5**	**7**	51
Gambia	4	4	PF	6	**7**	**4**	10	**6**	**7**	8	**48**
Uganda	5	4	PF	**4**	**7**	**4**	11	**6**	**7**	**7**	**46**
Mauritania	5	4	PF	6	**7**	**4**	10	8	**6**	**5**	**46**
Burundi	3	5	PF	9	**9**	**4**	**8**	**5**	**4**	**6**	**45**
C.A.R.	5	4	PF	7	**7**	**3**	10	9	**3**	**4**	**43**
Gabon	6	4	PF	**2**	**5**	**3**	10	**6**	**6**	**5**	**37**
Djibouti	5	5	PF	**4**	**5**	**3**	**7**	**5**	**5**	**6**	**35**
Congo-B	6	5	NF	**3**	**5**	**3**	**9**	7	**2**	**6**	**35**
Ethiopia	5	5	PF	**5**	**5**	**4**	**7**	**3**	**4**	**6**	**34**
Rwanda	6	5	NF	**3**	**3**	**4**	**7**	**3**	**6**	**7**	**33**
Guinea	6	5	NF	**2**	**5**	**2**	**8**	**5**	**4**	**6**	**32**
Togo	6	5	NF	**2**	**4**	**2**	**7**	**5**	**3**	**6**	**29**
Angola	6	5	NF	**2**	**5**	**1**	**8**	**6**	**4**	**3**	**29**
Cameroon	6	6	NF	**3**	**5**	**3**	**7**	**3**	**2**	**4**	**27**
Congo-K	5	6	NF	6	**6**	**2**	**6**	**5**	**0**	**1**	**26**

TABLE 5.2 *(continued)*

Country	PL	CL	Status	A	B	C	D	E	F	G	H
Chad	6	5	NF	**3**	**1**	**2**	**7**	**5**	**1**	**3**	**22**
Swaziland	7	5	NF	**0**	**1**	**1**	**8**	**3**	**4**	**5**	**22**
Côte d'Ivoire	6	6	NF	**1**	**2**	**2**	**5**	**4**	**3**	**4**	**21**
Sudan	7	6	NF	**0**	**4**	**3**	**4**	**3**	**0**	**0**	**14**
Eritrea	7	6	NF	**0**	**1**	**2**	**2**	**0**	**2**	**6**	**13**
Zimbabwe	7	6	NF	**1**	**3**	**0**	**5**	**2**	**1**	**1**	**13**
Equatorial Guinea	7	6	NF	**0**	**1**	**0**	**5**	**0**	**1**	**3**	**10**
Somalia	7	7	NF	**0**	**0**	**1**	**3**	**0**	**0**	**0**	**4**
Africa averages	4.2	4.0		6.2	8.0	4.9	10.1	6.8	6.6	6.7	49
Standard deviation	1.8	1.4		3.8	4.2	2.9	3.6	3.2	3.9	3.0	23
World averages	3.3	3.1		7.7	10.1	6.6	11.4	7.9	8.6	9.7	62
Standard deviation	2.1	1.8		4.3	5.2	3.7	4.4	3.8	4.8	4.1	29

Source: Compiled from data available at Freedom House, at http://www.freedomhouse.org.

Note:

A = free elections
B = political pluralism
C = government accountability
D = free expression
E = associational rights
F = rule of law
G = personal autonomy
H = total
Boldface = 1/2 standard deviation above or below world mean
PL = political liberties
CL = civil liberties

Third, comparing the component scores for all sub-Saharan African countries as a group with those for all countries worldwide, it appears that sub-Saharan African countries most closely approximated global averages in the areas of freedom of expression and freedom of association, two areas in which they averaged 88 percent and 86 percent of global averages on these components, respectively. By contrast, they lagged global scores most in the area of personal autonomy, with sub-Saharan Africa's average coming in at only 69 percent of the global average for this component. This evidence suggests that although the conduct of free and fair elections has received by far the greatest attention in the academic and policy arenas—and sub-Saharan Africa has indeed made notable progress in this area—it is in the broader area of political liberalization—that is, successful assertion of the right to speak and to advance civil society—that progress has been at least as significant. The relatively weak performance in the area of personal autonomy suggests the importance of greater attention to the "output" side, as distinct from the "input" side of democratic stateness.

Correspondingly, a striking characteristic of some contemporary literature on less-developed countries has been a tendency implicitly to reduce democratization to electoral performance, on the basis of which to anticipate unfavorable, yet partially contradictory, outcomes from the interaction of fledgling democratic initiatives and weak states. On the one hand, it has been anticipated that authoritarian rulers are likely to be able to stall, subvert, or survive competitive multiparty elections. On the other hand, it has also been hypothesized that electoral democracy will undermine not only authoritarian regimes but the states over which they preside, to the degree that they may already be weak.[6]

However, the more detailed Freedom House data make clear that those sub-Saharan African countries that have begun to distinguish themselves from others on the continent as newly democratizing countries have done so by demonstrating capability not only to conduct reasonably free and fair multiparty elections but also to broaden political space beyond electoral competition to include more effective individual political expression, exercise of associational rights, and substantially increased political pluralism. Moreover, these data suggest that this much broader scope for democratic political action has included some strengthening and reform of the state through more accountable democratic governance and more reliable observance of the rule of law, even if much yet remains to be accomplished in these areas. In short, for the leading sub-Saharan African democratizers, competitive, relatively free, and fair elections have taken place *in conjunction with* other important dimensions of democratization, and as a consequence, democratization has also appeared to result in at least some improved democratic *governance*. Thus, democratization may need not necessarily await prior state strengthening but may itself be a *means* to state strengthening, as well as state reform.

Fourth, as encouraging as has been the marked increase in the number of sub-Saharan African countries that have achieved democratization records above average by global standards, equally important and revealing is the scope and pace of democratic improvement. From 1990 to 2005, a total of eighteen sub-Saharan African countries improved their overall performance by a combined total of four or more points on the Freedom House scale of political and civil liberties, all but two (Burundi and Guinea-Bissau, one each in civil liberties) by significant degrees in both categories. As Table 5.3 indicates, ten of these are among the fourteen leading democratizers. The others, except for Ethiopia, have emerged from the ranks of those deemed unfree countries by Freedom House measures to join the category of partially free countries: Liberia, Burundi, Malawi, Mozambique, Tanzania, Sierra Leone, and Guinea-Bissau.

The countries that have made the greatest strides in emerging from authoritarian rule are a diverse group, rarely considered together in other ways, but they appear to share a record of democratization with relative alacrity. A striking characteristic of this group is that its members have overcome very different sets of problems in coming rapidly and increasingly to share common democratic political attributes. What processes and circumstances might these countries have shared that has enabled them to democratize, even as they were rebuilding their states? What has distinguished them from other countries still relatively mired in political disarray and/or nondemocratic rule? This is one of the more important and yet least researched questions concerning African democratization to date.

One possible factor in this achievement may be that some of the continent's smallest countries are included: Seychelles, Guinea-Bissau, Cape Verde, São Tomé, and Benin. Might this suggest that venerable figures in the history of political philosophy, notably Rousseau, were accurate in believing that the likelihood of democracy varies inversely with size of country in terms of both population and territory?

A second pattern in this group is that several of these countries have become more democratic as they have simultaneously struggled to recover from civil war, although the course of their civil wars and the mode of their resolution have differed markedly. These include South Africa, Liberia, Burundi, Mozambique, Sierra Leone, and Ethiopia.[7] A third possibly significant factor may be that all the countries in this subgroup have benefited from external involvement in their recovery, in various forms and to varying degrees, although many countries not on this list have also been recipients of international intervention.

TABLE 5.3 Most improved performance in political and civil liberties, sub-Saharan Africa, 1990–2005 (minimum of four points higher in 2005)

Country	Political Liberties	Civil Liberties	Total
Ghana	5	3	8
Cape Verde	4	4	8
Mali	4	3	7
Lesotho	4	2	6
South Africa	4	2	6
Seychelles	3	3	6
São Tomé	3	3	6
Liberia	3	3	6
Kenya	3	3	6
Benin	4	2	6
Burundi	4	1	5
Malawi	3	2	5
Niger	3	2	5
Mozambique	3	2	5
Tanzania	2	2	5
Sierra Leone	2	2	5
Guinea	3	1	4
Ethiopia	2	2	4

Source: Compiled from data available at Freedom House, at http://www.freedomhouse.org.
Note: Freedom House ranks countries from 1 (high) to 7 in both categories.

A fourth possibly significant factor is that in many of these eighteen countries intense internal deliberations took place among governing elites and societal groups on revised terms for continued or resumed shared membership in the states bequeathed to them by departing colonial powers a generation earlier. With the benefit of significant international assistance in many cases, they have conducted these deliberations *prior* to their first multiparty elections. This group includes countries that experienced national conventions (Benin and Mali) and one that benefited from an all-party, United Nations–sponsored conference to design a transition from authoritarian to democratic rule (Malawi). International intervention also figured prominently in the cases of Kenya and Lesotho—the former from the Paris Club of donor governments, the latter from South Africa.

While still well below average in democratic accomplishment in comparison to the others, both Burundi and Ethiopia have nonetheless been judged to have made significant strides, even considering the postelection violence and governmental overreaction in Ethiopia during 2005.[8]

Fifth, by norming the scores for each democratization component as presented in Table 5.2, it becomes possible to delineate more clearly leading and lagging democratization sub-sectors vis-à-vis global averages, although this does not demonstrate specifically how these components have interfaced. Although many more African countries have continued to perform below global averages than performed above them, the fourteen leading democratizers as a group performed above global norms on each of the seven dimensions except for personal autonomy, where they matched the global average. Similarly, for all sub-Saharan African countries as a group, Table 5.2 establishes that they fell below global averages least in the areas of the exercise of free political expression (0.88 of the global average), realization of associational rights (0.86), notwithstanding persistent problems with free media, and in the conduct of free and fair electoral processes (0.80). Notwithstanding endemic problems of corruption, their record in accountable democratic governance was, rather surprisingly, close behind (0.79).

One of the most illuminating findings of the expanded Freedom House data is that the leading democratizers, as well as all sub-Saharan African countries as a group, lagged global averages most in the area of acceptance of important dimensions of personal autonomy (0.69), a category that includes freedom to travel, to own property and establish businesses, to realize gender equality and other social freedoms, and to experience equality of economic opportunity. Although establishment of the rule of law clearly continues to be an area where much remains to be done, these data suggest that a more serious problem with governmental performance lies, fundamentally, in persuading governments to allow citizens, within the law, to live their lives as they choose. The problem is broader and deeper than enabling citizens to engage freely in economic competition in line with principles of liberal political economy. Rather, it extends to realizing economic *opportunity*, securing property ownership, eradicating invidious social discrimination, and allowing freedom of movement.

In general, these data suggest that African democratization has advanced most broadly in the area of opportunities for political participation, notably in the representation of women in legislatures. Rwanda leads the world in percentage of women in parliament (49 percent), while Burundi, South

Africa, Mozambique, Uganda, and Tanzania are all in the top twenty worldwide. By contrast, sub-Saharan African democratization has advanced least in the areas of enabling citizens to conduct their political and socioeconomic lives free of governmental interference. In this, African countries collectively appear to have lagged most in an area of democratic achievement that is stronger, relative to other components, among all countries worldwide. Overall, weaker democratic governmental performance counterbalanced stronger performance on other dimensions of political expression, while performance in upholding the rule of law and associational freedom counterbalanced, to a lesser degree, greater weakness in recognizing claims to personal autonomy.

Although the Polity IV data have been widely cited, relatively little attention has focused on the individual components that are used to assess democratic performance.[9] The Polity IV data estimate the viability of rules and regulations governing democratic processes, whereas the Freedom House estimates gauge the extent of political and civil freedoms. The major components of the Polity IV include restraints on executive power, regulations securing open and competitive elections for heads of government, and the orderliness of processes for free expression. Table 5.4 presents Polity IV estimates for overall performance in sub-Saharan African countries and for the component elements in 1990 and 2004. Estimates are normed against the performance of all nations.

Notwithstanding evidence of backsliding in some areas, the Polity IV data provide further evidence that several African countries have reached levels of democratic performance well above global averages. Many African countries have registered striking levels of improvement, whereas only Zimbabwe, Togo, Uganda, and the Gambia have notably regressed over the period from 1990 to 2005. While only Mauritius scored a standard deviation or more above global averages overall in both years, seventeen other sub-Saharan African countries registered above average overall scores in 2004, in comparison to only three in 1990, again in addition to Mauritius and Botswana. Ten others moved from significantly below global standards in 1990 to levels approaching global averages in 2004, led by Tanzania and Djibouti, both of whom scored above average on orderly regulation competition of executive office.

A striking finding of the Polity IV estimates for democratic performance in sub-Saharan Africa has been that one-third of all countries recorded near global average or above global average performance on all three components, whereas in 1990 only five countries did so (Mauritius, Botswana, Namibia, Comoros, and the Gambia). Thus, almost all of the countries in this group reached near average or above average performance overall and on all three components in 2004, after having been significantly below average overall and on each of these components in 1990.

TABLE 5.4 State reform in sub-Saharan Africa, 1990 and 2004

	2004				1990			
	Polity	Const	ExReg	PolCom	Polity	Const	ExReg	PolCom
Mauritius	**0.83**	**0.84**	**0.78**	**0.85**	**0.89**	**0.89**	**0.84**	**0.90**
South Africa	**0.79**	**0.84**	**0.78**	**0.76**	0.23	**0.89**	**0.84**	0.28
Botswana	**0.79**	**0.84**	**0.78**	**0.76**	**0.83**	**0.79**	**0.84**	**0.84**
Lesotho	**0.75**	**0.84**	**0.78**	0.53	0.16	0.10	0.25	0.13
Ghana	**0.75**	**0.70**	**0.78**	**0.76**	0.16	0.10	0.25	0.13
Kenya	**0.75**	**0.70**	**0.78**	**0.76**	0.16	0.32	0.14	0.13
Senegal	**0.75**	**0.70**	**0.78**	**0.76**	0.41	0.32	0.14	**0.84**
Madagascar	**0.70**	0.52	**0.78**	**0.76**	0.19	0.32	0.14	0.20
Mozambique	**0.65**	0.33	**0.78**	**0.76**	0.16	0.32	0.14	0.13
Benin	**0.65**	0.52	0.62	**0.76**				
Mali	**0.65**	0.52	**0.78**	0.53	0.16	0.10	0.40	0.13
Malawi	**0.65**	0.70	0.62	0.65	0.10	0.10	0.14	0.13
Comoros	**0.65**	**0.84**	0.28	**0.76**	**0.67**	0.65	**0.72**	0.58
Namibia	**0.65**	0.52	0.62	**0.76**	**0.75**	0.65	**0.72**	**0.84**
Sierra Leone	0.59	0.52	0.62	0.53	0.16	0.32	0.14	0.13
Zambia	0.59	0.52	0.62	0.53	0.10	0.10	0.14	0.13
Nigeria	0.53	0.52	0.62	0.28	0.23	0.10	0.25	0.28
Niger	0.53	0.52	0.62	0.28	0.16	0.32	0.14	0.13
Tanzania	0.41	0.18	0.62	0.53	0.16	0.32	0.14	0.13
Djibouti	0.41	0.18	0.62	0.53	0.13	0.19	0.14	0.20
Ethiopia	0.35	0.18	0.62	0.40	0.13	0.19	0.14	0.13
Burkina Faso	0.30	0.18	0.28	0.65	0.16	0.10	0.25	0.13
Guinea	0.25	0.18	0.28	0.40	0.16	0.10	0.25	0.13

TABLE 5.4 *(continued)*

	2004				1990			
	Polity	Const	ExReg	PolCom	Polity	Const	ExReg	PolCom
Guinea-Bissau	0.25	0.08	0.15	0.53	0.13	0.19	0.14	0.13
Central African Rep.	0.25	0.08	0.15	0.53	0.16	0.10	0.25	0.13
Angola	0.21	0.18	0.07	0.65	0.16	0.32	0.14	0.13
Chad	0.21	0.08	0.28	0.40	0.16	0.10	0.25	0.13
Togo	0.21	0.08	0.28	0.40	0.47	0.10	0.40	0.13
Rwanda	0.17	0.18	0.28	0.11	0.16	0.10	0.40	0.13
Uganda	0.13	0.18	0.28	0.06	0.47	0.10	0.25	0.13
Gabon	0.13	0.08	0.28	0.11				
Cameroon	0.13	0.08	0.07	0.40	0.13	0.19	0.14	0.13
Equatorial Guinea	0.10	0.08	0.28	0.06	0.16	0.10	0.25	0.13
Gambia	0.10	0.08	0.28	0.06	**0.3**	0.65	**0.84**	**0.90**
Mauritania	0.08	0.18	0.07	0.06	0.16	0.32	0.14	0.13
Sudan	0.08	0.03	0.15	0.06	0.16	0.10	0.25	0.13
Zimbabwe	0.06	0.08	0.07	0.06	0.19	0.32	0.14	0.20
Eritrea	0.06	0.08	0.07	0.06				
Swaziland	0.03	0.08	0.03	0.03	0.08	0.10	0.07	0.13

Source: Compiled from data available at Polity IV, at http://cidcm.umd.edu/polity/data.

Note:
Polity = democratic characteristics minus autocratic ones.
Const = institutionalized powers and restraints on executive power
ExReg = openness and competitiveness of executive recruitment
PolCom = structures, openness, competiveness, orderliness of political expression
Boldface = 1/2 standard deviation or more above averages for all countries

Scores are normed against those for all countries:
Polity 2004 average = .49, std. 33; 1990 average .51, std. 32;
Const 2004 average = .49, std. 32; 1990 average .50, std. 32;
ExReg 2004 average = .50, std. 32; 1990 average .48, std. 34;
PolCom 2004 average = .50, std. 32; 1990 average .47, std. 34.

Beyond these quite remarkable levels of improvement themselves is what these data suggest about the relationships between democratization and state strengthening. Considered together, the Freedom House and Polity IV data suggest that democratization processes have at a minimum moved *in tandem* with those of state strengthening, where the latter is evidenced by viable rules regulating democratic political processes. Implicit in this observation is an important hypothesis: At least in the context of democratization in what have been chronically weak states in sub-Saharan Africa, in time it may turn out to be the case that the institution of working fundamental rules of the game that gain general public adherence may prove to be at least as important to public order as the Weberian requirement of a legitimate monopoly of the means of coercion. Perhaps it is gaining general public adherence, if not active *consent,* to working fundamental rules of the game that is the key to *legitimizing* that monopoly of the means of coercion rather than de facto possession of such a monopoly per se.

The tentativeness of these quantitatively estimated indications of progress in both democratization and strengthened stateness is apparent when the Freedom House and Polity IV data are considered together. Whereas the Polity IV data indicate marked progress in rule-based governance, the Freedom House estimates indicate areas of improvement in their implementation, which may be critical tipping points determining whether these improvements become sustainable and durable over time. The Freedom House data record weaknesses in the areas of accountable democratic governmental performance, in applying the rule of law, and in honoring and upholding the ability of individuals and organizations in civil society to operate within the law free of governmental interference inconsistent with basic human rights. Moreover, these same data suggest that increased spaces for political expression, political pluralism, and free and fair democratic elections have yet to be fully translated into areas of governmental performance needed for these improvements to be sustainable and to reduce risks that the public may experience in exercising these rights.

The World Bank's *Governance Matters* surveys paint a distinctively more mixed picture of sub-Saharan African democratization, stateness, and governmental performance since 1990.[10] They make clear the tentativeness, fragility, and potential reversibility of the apparent gains suggested by the Polity IV and Freedom House surveys. Yet they, too, indicate that some of the same sub-Saharan African countries have begun to rise above others in the region in achieving democracy, more effective governance, and greater state stability. Gleaned from a wide range of surveys in more than two hundred countries worldwide, the World Bank data focus more on governmental performance and state stability, whereas the Polity IV data probe the status of rules governing political expression and competition for executive leadership, and the Freedom

House surveys concentrate on the status of civil and political liberties. The components of the *Governance Matters* surveys include the status of opportunities for political expression and participation, state stability, governmental effectiveness, quality of governmental regulatory activity, rule of law, and corruption control. The *Governance Matters* surveys, initially conducted biennially (now annually), gauge changing patterns of democratic governance since 1996, that is, from the early stages (though not the very beginning) of post–Cold War democratization in sub-Saharan Africa.

The *Governance Matters* data indicate both important overall advancement and retreats in sub-Saharan African democratic governance between 1996 and 2006. Thirty-one sub-Saharan African countries advanced significantly by global standards in at least one important dimension of democratic governance (ten or more percentage points), while all but three (Liberia, Cameroon, and Rwanda) retreated in at least one key area during this ten-year period. The data indicate very little overall change in the level of democratic governance during this decade, with about half the countries registering net overall advances (25) and the other half registering net overall declines (23). However, significantly improved performances in strengthening stability and, interestingly, in governmental effectiveness overshadowed backsliders in these areas to produce noteworthy overall regional improvement in both areas.

Table 5.5 summarizes some of the key World Bank *Governance Matters* findings. It pairs overall democratic governance courses for sub-Saharan African countries in 1996 and 2006 together with tallies of changing performance on each indicator, each normed against the behavior of all countries over the same period.

Measures of significant net improvement and decline were numerous among sub-Saharan Africa states but were distributed widely throughout the list, with improvements by no means limited to the overall best performers identified in the Freedom House and Polity IV surveys. Nor were significant declines concentrated solely among the worst performers. Notwithstanding weakened performance by São Tomé and Benin, the countries previously identified as best performers were generally among the leaders in the *Governance Matters* surveys as well. Improvements by Rwanda, Tanzania, Mozambique, Cape Verde, and Liberia were counterbalanced by eleven countries that showed sharp overall declines in levels of democratic stateness. One of the countries showing the most pronounced decline in democratic stateness, Benin, registered significant retreats in every area except corruption control. While slipping, consequently, from a ranking of above average to that of near average in the *Governance Matters* estimates, Benin nevertheless remained among the above average performers on the Polity IV and Freedom House

TABLE 5.5 Changing patterns of democratic government in sub-Saharan Africa, 1996 and 2006

	2006	Tot	V/A	Sta	Gov	Reg	Rule	Corr	1996
Botswana	74.1	2.6	-6.4	22.6	6.6	-13.6	-2.9	9.3	71.5
Mauritius	72.6	2.1	0.8	8.1	-1.9	8.3	2.4	-5.3	70.5
Cape Verde	66.5	5.5	0.8	-3.4	5.6	18.1	0.0	26.2	61.0
South Africa	64.7	7.4	-4.0	30.7	7.1	19.0	-3.3	-5.3	57.3
Namibia	61.7	-2.6	-4.5	15.4	-13.8	10.3	-6.2	-17.0	64.4
Seychelles	55.5	11.2	1.7	1.5	22.8	14.1	-13.3	-6.3	44.3
Ghana	54.9	14.0	19.9	16.3	16.5	-2.5	12.9	20.8	40.9
Madagascar	48.1	10.5	-10.3	2.4	35.5	18.5	30.4	-13.5	37.6
Lesotho	47.9	0.7	10.8	-10.1	-17.5	5.8	4.8	3.9	47.2
Senegal	44.0	4.4	6.0	2.4	-6.2	11.7	7.1	5.3	39.7
Mali	43.6	-3.1	-10.2	-19.2	16.1	-15.6	46.2	-40.8	46.7
Mozambique	42.7	10.9	-4.1	45.2	-2.8	14.6	14.8	-2.5	31.8
Benin	41.7	-19.3	-10.3	-42.1	-26.0	7.0	-7.1	-6.4	61.0
Tanzania	41.4	12.7	12.2	6.7	23.2	-4.9	5.3	33.5	28.8
São Tomé	40.6	-10.3	-11.2	-18.3	-5.2	-6.4	-2.8	0.9	50.9
Burkina	37.1	-1.3	1.6	22.9	0.4	-3.4	-2.3	0.5	38.4
Gambia	36.8	-2.1	12.1	7.2	-14.2	32.7	-15.7	-34.4	38.9
Mauratania	35.0	-3.2	1.1	-26.4	-34.2	21.5	24.3	-18.5	38.2
Zambia	34.0	1.9	6.4	27.9	-3.8	-30.7	0.0	10.7	32.1
Malawi	33.8	-2.0	-9.4	9.6	-2.4	-10.7	9.0	-8.3	35.8
Rwanda	32.9	26.2	2.4	22.6	33.2	20.0	29.5	35.9	6.7
Gabon	31.7	7.8	-12.8	15.9	17.5	-6.8	16.2	17.0	23.9
Uganda	31.7	-0.4	0.2	1.5	3.8	-12.7	10.0	-5.4	32.2
Swaziland	30.7	-16.4	-1.8	-1.0	-17.5	-23.5	-47.6	-18.4	47.1
Niger	28.2	4.3	23.6	-7.7	15.6	16.1	2.4	-24.3	23.9
Kenya	27.3	2.2	20.4	-8.6	-19.9	12.7	1.4	7.3	25.1
Djibouti	24.8	-11.0	-4.6	-11.6	1.4	-22.5	-21.5	4.3	35.7

TABLE 5.5 *(continued)*

Comoros	23.7	-19.1	-6.0	-40.4	-21.8	-14.1	10.0	26.2	42.8
Ethiopia	23.6	10.5	-6.2	-8.6	20.4	15.1	12.9	29.6	13.0
Cameroon	22.3	11.8	7.8	27.0	10.9	4.9	9.5	10.7	10.5
Guinea-Bissau	18.6	-8.1	-6.0	0.4	-16.1	-36.1	7.6	1.9	26.7
Sierra Leone	18.1	3.6	8.3	28.4	-16.6	-4.8	1.0	5.3	14.5
Eritrea	17.5	-21.1	-14.3	-32.7	-28.9	-35.2	-32.0	-22.3	38.5
Liberia	14.1	12.0	19.3	12.0	6.1	4.4	11.0	18.9	2.2
Togo	13.8	-12.2	-8.1	-6.2	-21.8	-44.4	6.6	1.0	25.9
Nigeria	13.3	6.4	22.7	-3.9	11.4	5.8	1.0	1.4	6.9
Angola	12.9	6.4	3.4	25.4	6.6	1.4	3.3	-1.5	6.4
Burundi	12.8	1.3	10.1	5.3	-6.7	2.9	-3.3	4.9	11.5
Congo-B	12.2	-4.7	-15.3	-2.4	1.0	-4.4	2.4	-9.3	16.9
Eq.Guinea	11.9	-0.2	-3.8	9.2	3.8	-0.2	-1.5	-9.2	12.0
Guinea	10.5	-15.5	-2.8	-2.9	-5.7	-33.2	-0.5	9.9	26.0
C.A.R.	9.2	-24.8	-18.1	-34.2	-12.3	-22.9	-42.8	3.9	34.0
Chad	8.2	-10.6	-14.8	-16.3	-19.4	-7.3	-13.8	-7.7	18.8
Sudan	7.8	4.6	2.8	1.0	9.0	8.3	4.3	2.4	3.1
Côte d'Ivoire	7.1	-37.7	-18.1	-36.5	-57.4	-29.3	-23.8	-61.1	44.8
Zimbabwe	5.1	-27.0	-23.0	-11.6	-33.7	-19.5	-26.2	-48.0	32.1
Congo-K	3.3	0.5	-0.9	-4.8	0.5	4.3	0.9	2.9	2.8
Somalia	0.3	-1.0	-0.4	-1.9	-0.5	-1.0	-0.5	-1.5	1.2
South Africa	30.3	-0.8	-0.6	5.3	13.6	-2.6	1.1	-0.4	31.1

Source: Compiled from data available at World Bank Institute, 2007, at http://info.worldbank.org/governance/wgi2007/mc_countries.asp.

Note:

V/A = voice and accountability
Sta = political stability
Gov = governmental effectiveness
Reg = regulatory quality
Rule = rule of law
Corr = corruption control

measures. At the same time, Liberia, Gabon, Rwanda, and Ethiopia, among the weakest overall democratizers, registered strong gains on four of the six *Governance Matters* survey indicators, as did Tanzania among the middle-range performers on the other surveys. Ethiopia's gains were in the areas of governmental performance rather than state stability, and voice and accountability declined as a result of the violence in the aftermath of the 2005 elections. Rwanda's scores were weakest in the area of voice and accountability because of restrictions on opposition politics.

These patterns of mixed performance are perhaps to be expected, given the magnitude of the challenges facing any country in transition from long-entrenched autocratic rule. They serve to leaven unrealistic expectations concerning prospects for rapid, comprehensive, and sustainable democratic stateness, even as the Manichean tug-of-war between democratic advance and retreat they portray suggests the importance of maintaining or increasing external support for democratic stateness. Overall, however, there is little in this data to suggest that democratic initiatives have undermined political stability or the quality of governance, contrary to the thesis posited by Edward Mansfield and Jack Snyder, who insist that the state must acquire certain elements of democracy, such as the rule of law, prior to holding competitive elections.[11]

The key to this outcome, as the Freedom House and Polity IV data suggest, appears to be that intense electoral competition has been part and parcel of a broader arena of democratic expansion, including more acceptance of political pluralism, increased assertion of association rights, and broadened acceptance of free political expression. Indeed the *Governance Matters* data suggest that improvements in political stability and governmental effectiveness may have outpaced all these dimensions of democratization in at least some countries. An important, frontier research question, well beyond the scope of this chapter, underlies these findings. That issue is to what extent civil society pressure successfully exerted on many African presidents not to seek third terms may be an indicator that strengthening of these broader dimensions of democratization has been a factor in these manifestations of strengthened political stability as well as improved democratic governance.

The important exceptions to this assessment appear to be Rwanda and, especially, Kenya, which at this writing is experiencing violence in response to credible evidence of vote rigging in the 2007 elections. Kenya, however, bears closer examination. The Kenya case does suggest the importance of democratic sequencing, the underlying claim of the Mansfield-Snyder thesis, but not in the way they suggest.[12] Mansfield and Snyder insist in effect that the state acquire certain elements of democracy, such as the rule of law, prior to competitive elections, but they don't explain *how* that is supposed to happen.

The Kenya case suggests not that state reform must precede democratization but, rather, that democratic processes directed toward building consensus on constitutional reform should precede multiparty electoral competition to replace the authoritarian *ancien régime*. This is what happened in many of the countries that have emerged as the leading sub-Saharan African democratizers. Implied in this contention is a definition of democratic processes that includes negotiations among representatives of contesting groups concerning such fundamental rules of the game as those governing competitive electoral process. Kenya's embarking on competitive multiparty elections before building consensus democratically on a revised constitution has been at the root of its flawed democratic performance. The country was propelled into multiparty elections in 1992 at the insistence of donors. Lengthy, tortuous negotiations on constitutional reform took place only after these elections. That sequencing explains much of the turmoil that has afflicted Kenya politics in the multiparty era. It helps to explain the fact that not only the autocratic *ancien régime* of Daniel arap Moi but the opposition party regime elected in 2002 found themselves targets rather than products of democratic constitutional reform. It is also key to understanding (a) the violence preceding the 1997 elections, (b) the rejection of a democratically formulated constitutional reform by even an opposition coalition elected to replace the autocratic Moi regime in 2002 (and the voters' subsequent rejection of this regime's alternative draft), and (c) the new regime's desperate attempt to retain power by vote-rigging in 2007.

Overall, close to one-third of all sub-Saharan African countries made above average progress toward democratic stateness, on the basis of the surveys discussed above that assess somewhat different but overlapping and complementary perspectives on the subject. Table 5.6 summarizes these findings. Included are the eighteen countries that have registered above average performance and/or rates of improvement on at least two of the most recent surveys. As might be expected, this group includes the well-established democratic states of Botswana and Mauritius. Four of the continent's smallest countries are on the list: Benin, São Tomé and Principe, and Seychelles, as well as Mauritius, again bringing to mind the noteworthy strain in the literature of liberal political philosophy extolling the importance of small size to the well-being of democracy.

At least three factors appear to have interacted with each other in complex and yet to be fully understood ways to enable these countries to emerge as distinct leaders in achieving democratic stateness. First, in different forms and circumstances, Benin, Namibia, South Africa, Mali, Ghana, Malawi, and Mozambique all undertook significant constitutional deliberations and achieved critical degrees of political consensus on the fundamental rules of the game prior to launching initial multiparty national elections.

TABLE 5.6 Leading sub-Saharan African democratizers

	FH	FH up	Polity	WBI	WBI up	No.
Ghana	84	8	75	54.9	14	5
Cape Verde	90	8	79	66.5		4
Mauritius	89		83	72.6		4
South Africa	86	6		64.7		3
Benin	82	6	65			3
Botswana	78		79	74.1		3
Namibia	77		65	61.7		3
Mali	74	7	64			3
Lesotho	73	6	75			3
Seychelles		6		55.5	11.2	3
Mozambique	5	65		10.9	3	
Tanzania		5			12.7	2
Ethiopia		4			10.5	2
Madagascar		70		10.5	2	
São Tomé	80	6				2
Senegal	76		75			2
Liberia		6			12	2
Malawi		5	65			2

Source: Tables 5.2–5.5 infra.
Criteria for inclusion: Above-average performance in two categories.
Note:
FH = Freedom House 1990–2005
Polity = Polity IV
WBI = World Bank Institute Governance Matters 1996–2005
FH up = Point increase, 1990–2005
WBI up = Point increase, 1996–2006
No. = number of WBI categories in which a country scored above average and/or improved significantly from 1996 to 2006

Second, active pressure from domestic civil society was also an important factor in each of these cases. Benin and Mali conducted far-reaching national conferences in the wake of widespread and overt opposition to the *anciens régimes* in both countries. South Africa and Namibia benefited from sustained international opposition to apartheid in both countries and the good offices of the external actors in arriving at working consensus on constitutional arrangements for a transition to democratic governance. At the same time, however, that support did not diminish the importance of fierce, active insurgent opposition by community-based organizations in the townships, along with sustained involvement by urban middle-class nongovernmental organizations that were factors of at least equal importance in the South African victory over apartheid.

Third, extensive external engagement (including the Economic Community of West African States, the Africa Union, and leaders of individual African countries as well as representatives of industrialized countries) was an essential ingredient together with intensive negotiations on rules of the game prior to the holding of initial competitive multi-party elections, and active civil society pressure to set these countries apart. The Community of Sant'Egidio in Italy hosted intensive and ultimately successful negotiations between Renamo and the ruling Frelimo on terms by which to end their civil war in Mozambique, participate in national elections, and continue their competition on a civilian and democratic basis. Active external assistance in these negotiations and financial assistance to Renamo to enable it to compete on more equal terms with Frelimo proved to be indispensable factors that permitted Mozambique to become democratic and free from civil war for almost the first time in its history from colonial times onward. In Ghana, Jerry Rawlings was persuaded by strong international pressure to allow the formation of a generally representative Consultative Assembly, which was then able to hammer out a constitution for a future democratic government.

As a counterpoint to the foregoing factors that appear to have been building democratic stateness, it is at least arguable that *lack* of sustained international engagement was a factor in Ethiopia's failed transition to competitive multiparty democracy and (as explained above) to Kenya's ongoing difficult struggle to reform an independence-era constitution barnacled by authoritarian amendments during the Moi era. In Ethiopia, a nearly all-party conference on a post-authoritarian transition foundered because it was conducted in haste, the Ethiopian People's Revolutionary Democratic Front's innovative confederal constitutional dispensation was a *premise* of the conference more than a consensus outcome emerging from it, and arrangements for demobilizing collaborating militias and building an inclusive security force were not made. In the case of Kenya, several years of deliberations on a revamped post-Moi authoritarian-era constitution have foundered due to a failure to agree on whether and how to limit the power of the president. But unlike elsewhere in the continent, donors contented themselves with insisting on competitive multiparty elections, while relaxing pressure on further dimensions of democratization.

One key outstanding question has been how democratization processes in weak states have fared in the minds of the citizens who have experienced and helped to activate these processes. The Afrobarometer surveys have probed citizens' perceptions of democracy, stateness, the condition of the economy, and quality of life in society generally. Most of the eighteen countries in which the third-round Afrobarometer surveys were conducted in 2005 are among the eighteen countries singled out by the Freedom House, Polity IV, and *Governance Matters* surveys as above average performers in the quest for stable democratic stateness.[13]

Self-evidently, it is difficult to gauge what these levels of citizen approbation, or lack of it, may mean absent close comparisons with responses from citizens to comparable questions in mature democratic states with strong economies. That said, support for democracy, endorsement of state legitimacy, approval of still nascent democracy, and satisfaction with the level of quality of life in society generally in these eighteen sub-Saharan African countries seem to be modest, with a significant nonaffirming minority on several key questions. From this perspective, the Afrobarometer surveys point to the tentativeness, fragility, and potential reversibility of democratic progress achieved by the leading democratizers.

The Afrobarometer surveys have seemed to yield only modest approving majorities by citizens for democracy, juxtaposed to non-affirming minorities of significant size on many key questions, bearing in mind that democratic stateness has progressed further in these states than others in the estimates of the other surveys.

Only about 50 percent of those surveyed in the fifteen countries included in the second-round Afrobarometer surveys were prepared to forswear all other alternatives to democracy, led by the citizens of Cape Verde and Ghana at 69 and 67 percent, respectively. Lesotho brought up the rear at a mere 30 percent, although that figure represented about 80 percent of a putative ceiling consisting of those who reported that they preferred democracy in principle. As things stood in 2005, only a slightly larger percentage of citizens across eleven states expressed general satisfaction with the state of democracy in their countries, with Ghana again the highest and Cape Verde the lowest.

What might explain this apparent less-than-overwhelming satisfaction with, and commitment to, democracy—even in some of the countries that other surveys have shown to have achieved above average levels of democratic performance? Admittedly, the extent to which these data support a cup half full or one half empty requires more systematic longitudinal and comparative analysis beyond the scope of this chapter. One clue, however, may be found in the level of satisfaction with the *efficacy* of democratic elections, as distinct from the freeness and fairness of elections that Freedom House and the other surveys estimate. Table 5.8 portrays Afrobarometer surveys in these relatively high-performing sub-Saharan African democracies, indicating that only about 40 percent found elections to be efficacious in terms of addressing citizen interests and needs.

TABLE 5.7 African citizens' support for democracy principle

	Botswana	Cape Verde	Ghana	Kenya	Lesotho	Malawi	Mali	Mozambique	Namibia	Nigeria	Senegal	South Africa	Tanzania	Uganda	Zambia	Avg
No military rule	79	75	83	92	85	84	65	53	51	69	76	77	86	85	95	77
No pres rule alone	85	67	82	90	82	78	66	41	58	72	77	73	86	90	90	76
No one-party rule	68	79	79	75	61	66	71	42	55	80	76	67	62	54	72	67
Demo preferred	75	66	82	80	50	64	71	54	54	68	75	57	65	75	70	64
No chief elder rule	50		69	59	49	49	34	29	46	61	45	63	72	48	72	53
Demo patience	43	39	79	83	51	34	68	43	63	58	59	54	54	54	62	56
Satisfied with demo	66	33	71	79	48	47	63	54	59	35	57	44	63	60	54	54
Demo probs minor	70	40	76	76	48	58	63	67	60	32	58	47	63	53	48	54
Demo preferred to alternatives	44	69	67	55	30	53	37	63	56	56	37	51	62	55	51	50
Choose leaders demo	76	73	87	89	66	78	82	75	82	82	78	81	76	83	75	79
Yes to term limits	71	75	75	80	85	76	77	43	63	86	71	68	73	80	86	74
Parliament makes laws	47	49	59	77	56	61	71	46	36	76	68	58	65	83	72	61
Parties needed	59	62	56	74	31	64	55	44	62	59	40	67	67	41	52	55
Average	64	61	74	78	57	62	63	50	57	64	63	62	69	66	69	63

Source: Afrobarometer, Round 2 surveys, at http://www.afrobarometer.org/.

Note:

Numbers = percentage of citizens supporting democracy principles
No military rule = opposition to military rule
No pres rule alone = opposition to one-person rule
No one-party rule = opposition to one-party democracy
No chief elder rule = disagreement with idea that chiefs and elders should rule in preference to democratically elected leader
Satisfied with demo = satisfied with democracy
Demo problems minor = problems with democracy minor rather than major
Demo preferred to alternatives = democracy preferred to all the alternatives
Choose leaders demo = support for choosing leaders by elections in preference to other methods
Yes to term limits = self-explanatory
Parliament makes laws = parliament should be the lawmaking body, not the president alone
Parties needed = self-explanatory

This figure contrasts noticeably with citizens' reported sense of their political empowerment in the Afrobarometer surveys. Two-thirds of the citizens in these countries reported a strong sense of their *entitlement* to rights of free expression and free association and to have government act lawfully in responding to their demands. Moreover, by somewhat smaller majorities, citizens demonstrated the requisite knowledge, sense of engagement, and willingness to accept political and societal risks of political engagement. Nevertheless, by quite wide margins, elections, though generally free and fair in these countries, have generally failed to satisfy citizens' sense of their own democratic political entitlement. Thus, there appears to be a gap between political entitlement and political efficacy even in these relatively more democratic African states.

This gap may bear some relationship to a similar gap between the degree to which citizens have been prepared to invest their states with legitimacy and the markedly lesser degree to which they find that their governments have acted to cultivate state legitimacy in democratic terms. On the one hand, approximately two-thirds of the citizens surveyed in the fifteen countries of the second-round surveys were prepared to say that they owed unquestioned obedience to the requirements of the courts, the police, and the tax collector, i.e., the coercive dimensions of state power. Furthermore, citizens tacitly acknowledged their governments' coercive power in their own lives, with 88 percent conceding that they would be likely to be caught if they sought to evade taxes or committed a major crime. These statistics certainly tend to confirm Crawford Young's thesis that the heavy-handed coerciveness of colonial political orders pervades citizens' perceptions of the postcolonial state.[14] However, the perceived efficacy gap also prompts speculation on the extent to which coercive capacity alone, absent broader dimensions of citizen consent on the basic rules of the game as well as electoral participation, has become a sufficient indicator of postcolonial state legitimacy.

On the other hand, another measure of the degree to which citizens believed state power to have acquired democratic legitimacy was that on average they thought that big officials would be likely to be caught in illegal acts only about 64 percent of the time. In essence, they estimated that one in three criminal acts by officials would go unpunished. Moreover, democratic legitimation of state coercive power appears to be subject to potential erosion, in that only about half of the citizenry believed their officials to be untainted by corruption. Levels of political trust ranged even lower, at 43 percent. These numbers invite inquiry into the degree to which, even in a relatively strong state, a state's everyday working possession of monopoly coercive power may need to be *earned* by governmental performance accountable to citizens so as to earn their *approbation*. Simply being blessed periodically by free and fair

TABLE 5.8 Voters' sense of democracy's efficacy in sub-Saharan Africa

	Benin	Botswana	Cape Verde	Ghana	Kenya	Lesotho	Madagascar	Malawi	Mali
MPs visit area	21	68	41	51	65	62	46	39	46
Local MPs listen	35	36	15	36	22	27	34	27	53
Natl MPs listen	17	30	13	26	13	17	17	23	27
No offered gifts	66	98	94	87	57	98	65	90	71
Elect. free/fair	75	84	56	77	79	79	78	43	64
Offer other voters gifts	15	42	16	17	5	47	34	29	15
Keep promises	3	17	13	15	6	12	10	6	12
Seek development	7	13	13	17	7	13	11	8	18
Average	30	49	33	42	32	44	37	33	38

Source: Afrobarometer, Round 3 surveys, at http://www.afrobarometer.org; Michael Bratton, Robert Mattes, and E. Gyimah-Boadi, *Public Opinion, Democracy and Market Reform in Africa* (New York: Cambridge University Press, 2004).

Note:
MPs visit area = politicians visit respondent's area at least once a year
Local MPs listen = believe elected local councilors try to listen to what people have to say always or often
Natl MPs listen = believe elected members of parliament try to listen to what people have to say often or always
No offered gifts = percentage reporting no experience of being offered gifts by politicians in return for votes in last national election

elections is an insufficient foundation for regime and, perhaps ultimately, state legitimacy.

In sum, this review of the quantitative data on African democratization establishes that a number of African countries have made notable, above average progress by global standards toward establishing democratic states. However, the progress of these states has been neither complete nor unproblematic. Nor is there any reason to assume that this progress is irreversible. Nevertheless, democratization in these relatively high-performing democratizers has been broadly based, extending well beyond progress in conducting free and fair national multiparty elections to include strong civil society activity, broadened political pluralism, and significantly freer political expression, along with the sustaining and possible strengthening of states, rather than their weakening.

The obvious utility of the foregoing quantitative information is as an aid in discerning a valid overview of the condition of democratic stateness in sub-Saharan Africa. Its obvious limitations, however, must not be overlooked or

Mozambique	Namibia	Nigeria	Senegal	South Africa	Tanzania	Uganda	Zambia	Zimbabwe	Av
44	68	44	37	47	59	52	41	45	48
32	44	21	31	20	68	40	15	27	32
28	46	16	19	22	53	19	10	21	23
87	91	72	91	94	92	65	76	83	82
77	77	32	78	75	79	57	29	36	66
33	51	15	14	40	43	15	6	17	26
34	38	22	12	25	12	16	8	8	15
29	38	19	15	26	13	17	10	8	15
46	57	30	37	44	52	36	24	31	38

Note: (continued)

Elect free/fair = elections completely free and fair with but minor problems

Offer other voters gifts = percentage believing politicians only rarely or never offered gifts to voters during election campaigns

Keep promises = percentage believing elected leaders keep their promises

Seek development = politicians often or always do their best to deliver development

forgotten. The evidence underlying each of these measures is based largely on the subjective perceptions of observers, however skilled and balanced their observations may be. The data points on which these assessments are built are conditioned by time and circumstance. Their validity hinges on the nature of the questions posed, on how they are interpreted by those who pose them and by those to whom they may be posed, and more generally, on the theoretical premises underlying the surveys and animating the surveyors. In some cases, the observers are likely to be participants, directly or indirectly, in the processes they are called upon to observe. Nonetheless, the available survey data suggest potentially important implications for prominent currents in the contemporary literature on democratization and state strengthening.

Theories abound concerning how democratic progress should occur and how it is *expected* to occur, but actual testing and tentative amendment of these theories on the basis of empirical evidence, elsewhere as well as in sub-Saharan Africa, has remained a scholarly and policy frontier. With more systematic testing of prevalent hypotheses about the relationship between democratization and the strengthening of weak states, one would expect that some of the evidence would lead to more empirically-grounded recommendations for modifying empirical theory in this area so that it better merits that designation.

The evidence pointing to important divergences in democratic accomplishment among sub-Saharan African countries does indeed shed light on the complex, fundamentally important issue of the interrelationships obtaining between democratization and state viability and strength. Beyond the empirical importance of this issue for sub-Saharan Africa lies a question of fundamental theoretical importance: How do state strength and democratization relate to one another? Sub-Saharan African countries are uniquely suitable arenas in which to discern how strategies, policies, and evolving political processes have been serving to undermine or strengthen positive reinforcement between advancing democratization and the strengthening of weak states.

The evidence presented in this chapter challenges at least some of the more pessimistic assumptions about the connection between successful democratization and at least state stability, if not state strengthening. It appears that a significant number of sub-Saharan African states have accomplished both in tandem, although the process is not yet complete, and progress could be reversed for any number of reasons.

At the same time, the nature of the relationship between these simultaneous processes has been clouded by underlying *a priori* assumptions about how stateness and state building, and democracy and democratization are to be conceptualized and defined. In much of the literature, the preoccupation with elections has obscured the role of other critically important democratic processes outside of electoral arenas in establishing both democracy itself and in contributing to state building. As a result, essential connections between the rule of law and wider democratic processes and the *facilitation* and *legitimation* of a state's monopoly of the means of coercion have remained under-examined.

Edward Mansfield and Jack Snyder, in two recent works, have argued that democratization endangers the peace and stability of weak states and even that of the neighborhoods in which they reside.[15] They contend that prior to initiating multiparty competitive *elections*, states must not only preside over a healthy economy but must embrace the rule of law and build a competent, impartial civil service. In claiming that democratization *per se*, rather than specifically democratic *elections*, undermines weak states, they have blurred their essential underlying contention, which is that states must acquire other elements of democracy before they embark on elections. Moreover, they have overlooked the importance of other democratic processes not centered specifically on elections. Implicitly, they have narrowed the working definition of democracy to mean elections by assigning other elements of democracy to stateness and by ignoring the possibility that nonelectoral manifestations of democratic processes may have a significant bearing upon the building and strengthening of states.

Thomas Carothers rightly challenges what he takes to be Mansfield and Snyder's underlying assumption that authoritarian rulers are likely to change their stripes *on their own initiative* by grafting requisite elements of democracy onto state structures.[16] In so doing, he has argued rightly that Mansfield and Snyder have bypassed the question of how weak states come to acquire those other elements of democratization if *not* through elections. Sheri Berman has added to this critique, arguing that European states became democratic after a great deal of conflict, thereby challenging what she takes to be an implicit assumption by Mansfield and Snyder that conflict engendered by democratization in the short term predicts long-term democratic failure and weakened states or worse.[17]

Carothers contends that much of the conflict that Mansfield and Snyder adduce as empirical evidence in support of their thesis has been attributable to state making rather than to democratization initiatives.[18] In so doing, however, he appears to rely implicitly upon the Weberian conception of the state as being *primarily or exclusively* about the acquisition of a monopoly of the means of coercion *per se* within territorially defined boundaries. This reasoning appears to dismiss the question of how the Weberian requirement of *legitimating* a monopoly of coercive power is to be attained, unless it is to say, in effect, that might makes right or by treating legitimacy as a *derivative* of a such a monopoly to be pursued *after* it has been acquired.

Carothers appears to choose the latter alternative, insisting that any such democratizing features can be acquired only *after* a state has acquired a monopoly of coercive power, implicitly through coercion itself. Francis Fukuyama asserts that this is inescapable, because such features imply *limits* on state power that are inconsistent with a state's pursuit of a *monopoly* of such power. This contention appears to draw a distinction between a *state* whose sovereign power domestically is unlimited and a *regime* whose *exercise* of such power may be limited in preventing abuses and trampling on the rights of citizens to act in certain respects.

This position leaves no place for the rule of law as it is conventionally understood in a democracy. Furthermore, it leaves no room for the rule of law to be part of the *definition* of a state, as democracy requires, or for citizens to have a significant role in instituting and legitimating it. At the same time, in omitting a distinction between regime and state, this position leaves no room for rules to be written into the definition of a state by and on behalf of citizens, such that the regime itself is subject to them as well as accountable to citizens. Or, alternatively, it treats the rule of law as a state/regime *dispensation after* it has acquired a monopoly of coercive power, in which case it is not clear how such a state/regime becomes answerable to laws of its own dispensation. Moreover, citizens are effectively excluded from any role in their authorship.

Finally, the contention that any role for democracy in state building can occur only *after* a state establishes a monopoly of coercive power seems to deny the findings of a rich and growing empirically grounded conflict management scholarship, which indicates that states may be successfully rebuilt through intense peacekeeping, peacemaking, and consultative activities.[19] That literature documents instances in which citizens, at least vicariously through their leaders as members of warring factions, have accomplished exactly that. Through their faction leaders and with the aid of third parties, citizens have been involved in reconstructing states by arriving at terms on which they can agree to live together under a common political roof. The empirical evidence outlined in this chapter has demonstrated that a number of sub-Saharan countries have made important progress, even by global standards, by doing just that.

However preliminary, modest, and potentially evanescent that evidence may prove to be, states such as Mozambique, Namibia, South Africa, and even Ghana have been reconstructed in just such fashion. More fundamentally, this evidence makes clear that these states have made substantial democratic progress beyond free and fair elections, extending to not only the exercise of associational rights and strengthened media, but also increased state stability, stronger support for the rule of law, and even improved, accountable democratic governance.

In short, the significant democratic progress made by sub-Saharan African states has contributed potentially important insights on the process of becoming a postcolonial democratic state. At the same time, the evidence gleaned from the sub-Saharan African experience promises to expand geographically the empirical foundation on which democratic state theory has been grounded.

NOTES

1. Edward D. Mansfield and Jack Snyder, *Electing to Fight: Why Emerging Democracies Go to War* (Cambridge, Mass: M.I.T. Press, 2005); see also Jack Snyder, *From Voting to Violence: Democratization and Nationalist Conflict* (New York: Norton, 2000).
2. See http://www.freedomhouse.org.
3. See http://www.cidcm.umd.edu/polity/.
4. See http://www.govindicators.org; and http://www.afrobarometer.org.

5. At this writing, Kenya's progress was in danger of being undone by blatantly rigged national elections held December 27, 2007, which resulted in unprecedented waves of violence throughout the country. Over a thousand died as of this writing; more than three hundred thousand people were displaced. The violence also threatened Kenya's recent economic progress and the economies of its neighbors, as well. The Kenya case illustrates the point that while free and fair democratic processes may serve to strengthen a state, fatally flawed, corrupted ones may expose and undermine an unreformed state, particularly when it rests on the foundation of profound economic inequality.

6. Andreas Schedler, ed., *Electoral Authoritarianism: The Dynamics of Unfree Competition* (Boulder: Lynne Rienner Publishers, 2006).

7. A measure of the depth of Ethiopia's brutal military dictatorship from 1974–1991 is that Freedom House judged that it survived on the lowest rung of partially free countries, notwithstanding the violence and the wholesale arrests in the aftermath of its May 2005 elections. John W. Harbeson, "Ethiopia's Extended Transition," *Journal of Democracy* 16, no. 4 (2005), pp. 144–158.

8. Ibid.

9. Center for International Development and Conflict Management, University of Maryland, http://www.cidcm.umd.edu/polity/.

10. Daniel Kaufmann, Aart Kraay, and Massimo Mastruzzi, *Governance Matters VI: Aggregate and Individual Governance Indicators, 1996–2006,* Policy Research Working Paper (Washington, D.C., World Bank, 2007), http://go.worldbank.org/ZMIT3RL2EO.

11. Mansfield and Snyder, *Electing to Fight.*

12. Ibid.

13. Michael Bratton, Robert Mattes, and E. Gyimah-Boadi, *Public Opinion, Democracy and Market Reform in Africa* (New York: Cambridge University Press, 2004). See also http://www.afrobarometer.org/.

14. Crawford Young, *The African Colonial State in Comparative Perspective* (New Haven: Yale University Press, 1994).

15. Mansfield and Snyder, *Electing to Fight*; Snyder, *From Voting to Violence.*

16. Thomas Carothers, "The 'Sequencing' Fallacy," *Journal of Democracy* 18, no. 1, pp. 12–18; and Thomas Carothers, "Misunderstanding Gradualism," *Journal of Democracy* 18, no. 3, pp. 18–23.

17. Sheri Berman, "How Democracies Emerge: Lessons from Europe," *Journal of Democracy* 18, no. 1, pp. 28–41.

18. Carothers, "The 'Sequencing' Fallacy," and "Misunderstanding Gradualism."

19. One important work among many in this vein is Barbara F. Walter, *Committing to Peace: The Successful Settlement of Civil Wars* (Princeton: Princeton University Press, 2002).

6

In Pursuit of Authority

Civil Society and Rights-Based Discourses in Africa

AILI MARI TRIPP

One of the most important transformations globally in the 1990s and especially after 2000 was the merger of development and human rights discourses to form new rights-based approaches. There was a convergence of thinking among United Nations agencies, international financial institutions, nongovernmental organizations (NGOs), international NGOs like Oxfam, Amnesty International, and CARE International, and social movements in Africa involved in a wide range of concerns from human rights to the environment, women's rights, and development.

This chapter examines the rise of rights-based approaches (RBAs) within Africa and their global and local dimensions. It discusses the significance of the new interest in these approaches, as well as some of the critiques and limitations of these approaches. The chapter explores a few examples of the kinds of legalistic and rights-based struggles that have animated the civil society landscape since the 1990s: presidential term limits, NGO regulatory legislation, struggles for media autonomy, environmental concerns, women's rights, and, in particular, challenges to customary laws and practices. The new emphasis on RBAs has not only catalyzed new forces demanding rights, but also set various civil society groups onto a collision course by animating contradictory claims.

In recent years, debates over civil society in Africa have questioned the meaning and roles of civil society in sub-Saharan Africa and other non-European contexts. Some have questioned how well the concept travels. Others have dismissed civil society as a weak, donor-dependent sector of society that excludes much of society. Some authors have been critical of the liberal discourse that has emphasized how civil society is good for democratization and development. They have argued that civil society in Africa is fraught with ethnic divisions, patronage, corruption, donor dependence, and its elite nature, thus making it a problematic source for political transformation (Dicklitch 1998; Kasfir 1998; Kelsall 1992; Gibbon and Bangura 1992; Mercer 2003). Others have argued that NGOs are unlikely to have much impact on political reform because governments have become adept at constraining and dividing civil society. NGOs themselves are faulted for not having developed a notion of citizenship that would link state and society to promote democratization (Fowler 1993, 1995). And finally, some see donor funding of NGOs as responsible for depoliticizing NGOs, depriving them of legitimacy and autonomy, and diverting them from concerns that have to do with institution building and advocacy (Edwards and Hulme 1995).

From an anthropological perspective, Jean and John Comaroff (1999) have been critical of the way in which the idea of civil society has focused on Western-oriented intellectuals, lawyers, businesspeople, and Christian leaders, portraying them as untainted by identity politics, parochial loyalties, or intrusive governments. They assert that the parts of society that fall outside a liberal notion of civil society have essentially been erased. Globalization, they argue, rather than creating a homogenized, universal civil society has instead fragmented society. Their critique is a useful one, especially since there certainly are discourses, codes of conduct, collective rituals, and ways of interacting with the state that do not fall within the rights-based approaches discussed in this chapter. It would be absurd to claim that RBAs are the only conceptual framework at play in Africa. However, this chapter highlights how RBAs are becoming increasingly important not only as a result of globalizing influences but also because of the way they have resonated with important political battles and dynamics on the ground.

THE SPREAD OF RIGHTS-BASED APPROACHES

The new RBAs represented a nexus of international development and human rights concerns, bringing liberal thinking about rights together with African and other global realities, rooted in economic and social concerns. The marriage between these diverse approaches, as this chapter shows, is not without problems or tensions.

This expansion of rights-based approaches took place with the end of the Cold War, with the reconnecting of the two strands of human rights that had been enshrined in the 1948 Universal Declaration of Human Rights as indivisible, inalienable, and universal: civil and political rights *and* economic, social, and cultural rights pertaining to food, water, health, education, housing, and employment. In 1966, these two sets of rights were recognized in two separate treaties that were ratified, one as the International Covenant on Civil and Political Rights and the other as the International Covenant on Economic, Social and Cultural Rights. Western countries focused on civil and political rights, whereas the Soviet bloc and many developing countries emphasized economic and social rights. By the 1990s, the ideological barriers that had led to these distinctions had been removed, with the spread of democracy and political liberalization in Latin America, Eastern Europe, and parts of the former Soviet Union, Asia, and Africa (Manzo 2003, 446).

Rights-based approaches came to be adopted by United Nations agencies, bilateral donors, and even international financial institutions involved in the development enterprise. They were inspired by the late Senegalese jurist and legal scholar Kéba Mbaye's notion of development as a human right (Manzo 2003, 439),[1] as well as work on entitlements and human capabilities by Amartya Sen (1999) and Martha Nussbaum (2000). The adoption of the 1986 UN Declaration on the Right to Development (UNDRD) was a watershed for UN agencies in linking rights and development conceptually and programmatically. The United States was the only country in the General Assembly that voted against approving the UNDRD, with eight other countries abstaining. Agencies like the United Nations Development Programme (UNDP) and the United Nations Children's Fund (UNICEF) started using human rights measures as benchmarks to evaluate progress toward their objectives. By 1998, UN Secretary General Kofi Annan had vowed to mainstream human rights through all UN agencies, and the World Bank had incorporated the promotion and protection of human rights as one of its goals (Manzo 2003, 439). Among bilateral donors, the British Department for International Development (DfID) was one of the first to adopt such a rights-based approach in 2000 (Manzo 2003, 437–439).

African discourses on rights explored in this paper both informed and were informed by these changing international norms and debates around rights. The language of rights became ubiquitous as political liberalization was advanced in Africa. Rights-based approaches were adopted by a wide range of movements: groups of and for people with disabilities, women, children, the landless, and many other marginalized people; social movements of environmentalists, antipoverty groups, human rights, and other such activists; lawyers fighting to maintain the independence of the judiciary; church leaders fighting against poverty and debt; pastoralists pursuing land rights; media workers defending press freedom; and NGO activists seeking to preserve their autonomy. The language of rights was also appropriated by traditional authorities in South Africa seeking to protect customary rights, Maasai organizations in Kenya and Tanzania who have reinvented themselves as "indigenous peoples" in order to preserve their cultural rights; religious leaders hoping to advance the uniqueness of their religious practices and beliefs; and others promoting monarchism or the authority of chiefs, clan elders, and other traditional leaders.

The discourses on rights in Africa draw on a variety of sources of authority depending on the context. These include international treaties, conventions, and declarations and regional and subregional treaties and agreements like the African Union Charter on Human and People's Rights and the African Union Protocol on Rights of Women. They also draw on national legislation and national constitutions. Since 1990, thirty-eight African constitutions have been rewritten and eight had major revisions. Many of the changes have to do with basic individual rights and liberties, the rights of traditional authorities, the protection of customary rights, issues of land rights, and the rights of women.

Many of these discourses on rights are not new. In Africa the struggles for independence and national liberation were framed in terms of demands for the right to self-rule, self-determination, and the right to citizenship. They formed the basis for struggles against colonial injustice (Cornwall and Nyamu-Musembi 2006). In the 1970s, they were encompassed in the UN's New International Economic Order and into popular notions of sustainable development, "economics as if people mattered," and alternative technologies (Schumacher 1973), and later still into "people-centered development" (Korten 1995).

What we are seeing today are multiple debates around rights, drawing on different sources of authority. Many of these approaches are incompatible with one another, as we see in some of the debates between advocates for women's rights and those for cultural or group rights. Also advocates of similar approaches do not always see eye to eye when it comes to framing their objectives or in the tactics and strategies they adopt.

RBAs represent a paradigmatic shift in thinking—from seeing development as a need, to seeing development as a right. Accordingly, development assistance now has an obligation to help people fulfill their individual entitlements. Development as a right can be measured by the degree to which countries adhere to international human rights treaties and by the extent to which states promote their citizens' economic and social rights, including food, shelter, education, and health care. This shift in thinking has also challenged the neoliberal market-based views of development and growth that became prevalent in the 1980s and is a response to the failures of that approach (Manzo 2003,

438). It has allowed the use of human rights treaties to hold not only governments but also wealthy nations accountable (Nelson and Dorsey 2003).

The approach has fostered new synergies among organizations focused on development, human rights, and environmental issues, resulting in broad coalitions that link economic and social rights with more individually oriented civil and political rights. African NGOs, such as Nobel Prize–winner Wangari Maathai's Greenbelt Movement in Kenya, pioneered the links among development, democracy, the environment, and human rights and were making these connections as early as the 1980s. In fact, movements like the Greenbelt Movement have helped to shape more general thinking along these lines globally. They have also helped to dispel the onetime popular notion that human rights and women's rights were foreign neocolonial imports. As homegrown democrats, human rights activists, and feminists emerged, efforts to discredit these movements as representing foreign values became more difficult to justify and sustain.

National NGOs have sometimes linked up with international NGOs to advance various campaigns. World Vision, Amnesty International, and other international NGOs targeting corporations in Africa have produced the Clean Diamonds campaign to restrict the extent to which military and political leaders have access to profits from diamond exports, which have been seen as fueling conflict and massive human rights violations in the context of civil war. Others have challenged the privatization of public goods, adopting a human rights approach to access to water, for example, the Ghana National Coalition Against the Privatisation of Water. Other organizations link human rights to health concerns, like the campaign for access to essential medicines or the many organizations working on HIV/AIDS issues (Nelson and Dorsey 2003).

One sees a clear convergence of global discourses and local concerns in the fervent adoption of RBAs in post-conflict countries, where the presence of international peacekeepers and UN agencies like United Nations Development Fund, UNESCO, UNICEF, UNIFEM, and others are especially visible and influential. In a post-conflict country like Liberia, the discourses around human rights, and in particular the rights of the disabled, children, and women, are pervasive in the newspapers, on the radio, and on posters and fliers. Although women's rights activists, for example, admit that they were first exposed to these discourses through regional or international conferences or through their interaction with UN agencies or international NGOs, they insist that their interest in taking up these issues arose out of their own experiences during and after years of civil war. In other words, many of these rights discourses would not resonate if there were not a basis for them within society. Women's organizations, regardless of whether they receive support from donors, draw on discourses of rights in carrying out their work to address the problems women confront as a result of the war, especially pertaining to violence against women.

CRITIQUES OF RIGHTS-BASED APPROACHES

Rights-based approaches have not been adopted uncritically, even by their advocates. There are multiple and often competing discourses around approaches to rights. Many of the most active debates are within civil society itself. The language of rights generally draws from Western liberal rights frameworks, which incorporate notions of legal pluralism. However, not all rights are compatible with each another; for example, religious freedom and cultural rights for ethnic groups frequently clash with women's rights and children's rights. These rights are all protected within various United Nations treaties, yet they cannot always be easily harmonized.

The lack of state capacity and willingness to enforce rights, while not obviating the necessity of the rights themselves, often challenges the utility of holding out the promise of justice if the rights themselves cannot be realized. States are pivotal to the notion of rights. Some argue that the very international financial institutions that were responsible for limiting the scope of state activity are now advocating greater state involvement in enhancing new forms of accountability and conditionality with the new RBA (Manzo 2003, 438).

Some, like Peter Uvin (2002), have characterized the World Bank's motives in promoting RBAs as a somewhat cynical attempt to benefit from the moral authority and political appeal of the human rights discourse. For him, the development community is in constant need of regaining the moral high ground in order to fend off criticism and mobilize resources. It has for this reason hitched itself to the human rights bandwagon. Thus, the Millennium Development Goals and debt relief initiatives remain programs of economic liberalization under the guise of addressing poverty and human rights. According to critics like Uvin and Dzodzi Tsikata, the World Bank draws on the language of rights, while promoting the privatization of essential services like water and national banks. Land reform is ultimately advanced in order to benefit multinational corporations (Tsikata, n.d.).

Rights advocates in Africa have sought to limit the reach of the state when it has tried to restrict or control freedom of the media, freedom of association, or freedom of religion, but they have also sought to get the state to become a source of rights and protector of rights, which has often proven challenging. Over the years, declarations like the 1966 International Covenant on Economic, Social and Cultural Rights, the 1986 UN Declaration on the Right to

Development, and declarations on the right to food have added to the state's mandate the obligation to promote positive rights. Whether the state can realistically deliver is a very different matter and one that has caused considerable debate.

People's unequal access in exercising their rights due to resource inequality and power differentials creates additional challenges. Expensive lawyers, lack of access to legal aid services, illiteracy or lack of education, use of bribes by wealthier litigants, and other such factors can affect the ability of more marginalized sectors of society to bring their claims to court.

Another concern has to do with the state's slowness in passing laws to protect individuals from violations of their rights by other nonstate actors, for example, violence against women and children in the home. This exposes the limits of legal and state-based frameworks. Moreover, extralegal action taken by authoritarian or semi-authoritarian states and the lack of judicial independence create a situation where the legal system's credibility and utility are in question.

Because legal pluralism is prevalent in Africa, statutory law is often overridden by customary law either by design or by default, leaving women with weak protection of their property rights. They may be subject to discrimination in the area of personal law in countries like Benin, Lesotho, Kenya, Niger, Swaziland, Zambia, and Zimbabwe. As Celestine Nyamu-Musembi has pointed out, the granting of land titles and the reform of property rights do little to empower women if they do not have the means with which to exercise those rights. By the same token, the legal recognition of customary systems of land tenure in new land legislation in countries like Ghana (1999) and Tanzania (1999) does not necessarily ensure women's access to land (Nyamu-Musembi 2006, 1205).

Informal or customary legal institutions are often under the control of local male elders and political leaders, who may be more easily swayed by popular sentiments, bribes, and friendships in ways that may not serve justice. How laws are framed, and the normative contexts within which they emerge and exist, can also place limits on people's capacity to exercise their rights. Local courts may be driven by archaic and exclusionist ideas about justice, without reference to the law or due process, as Joe Oloka-Onyango found to be the case in Uganda. Adjudicators may lack adequate training, or they may act outside of their legal jurisdiction—arbitrarily and capriciously—without reference to broader concerns regarding the status of women and individual rights.

In Uganda, for example, Lynn Khadiagala found that although Kigezi women could take their disputes to locally elected courts of the Local Councils, they tended to prefer the magistrate courts that were stationed at the county and subcounty level. Women preferred these courts because they were often cheaper than local councils, where officials often extracted excessive unofficial payments. Moreover, women often perceived the Local Council courts to be biased against them (Khadiagala 2001).

Finally, not all proponents of rights share the same objectives, frameworks, and strategies, and they may even work at cross-purposes within the same general movement. These are all limitations of RBAs that need to be accounted for, while recognizing the emergence of these new sources of authority.

RIGHTS-BASED STRUGGLES

Rights-based struggles, appealing to a variety of sources of authority, have emerged around a host of issues. Movements to limit presidential terms were often based in legalistic appeals to constitutionalism. Women's rights movements around land concerns, environmental movements, struggles for NGO autonomy, and media freedom frequently drew on international conventions as well as legislative and constitutional bases. What follows are a few examples of the kinds of rights-based struggles that have animated the civil society landscape since the 1990s. They are based on an understanding of the indivisibility of rights, in which environmental or land rights are seen as inherently human rights, and in which the rule of law, constitutionalism, and the defense of political and civil liberties are essential to economic development.

Movements for Presidential Term Limits

There were only a few instances in the pre-multiparty period when presidents stepped down voluntarily, and then it was usually only after they had held office for over twenty years. One could count them on one hand: General Olusegun Obasanjo in Nigeria (1979), Ahmadou Ahidjo in Cameroon (1982), Julius Nyerere in Tanzania (1985), and Léopold Senghor in Senegal (1980). With the introduction of multipartyism, civilian rule, and the rewriting of constitutions in the 1990s, presidential terms were generally limited to two terms. The era of presidents-for-life seemed to be over with a few exceptions, for example, Guinea's Lansana Conté and Omar Bongo of Gabon. However, it did not take long for presidents to begin tinkering with the term limits imposed by these new constitutions.

The practice of prolonging the presidential term began in Namibia in 1998 when the Namibian constitution was amended to allow Sam Nujoma to have a third term. Term limits were also scrapped in Togo, Burkina Faso, Gabon, Guinea, Chad, Tunisia, and Uganda, in spite of opposition by legislatures and civil society. A few other heads of state toyed with the idea of extending their terms but ultimately stepped down, including Benin's Mathieu Kérékou, Kenya's Daniel arap Moi, Mozambique's Joaquim Chissano, Botswana's Festus Mogae and Ghana's Jerry Rawlings.

However, attempts to extend presidential terms were vigorously thwarted by civil society in several countries. In Malawi, where Hastings Banda had once declared himself president for life, civil society organizations and coalitions, including the Forum for the Defence of the Constitution, mobilized to resist efforts by President Bakili Muluzi to abolish term limits. In 2002, parliament voted down a bill that would abolish term limits. Similarly, Nigerian President Obasanjo's attempt to run for a third term in 2007, using a constitutional amendment bill, was blocked by the Senate Chamber and subsequently by the House of Representatives.

In Zambia, the Law Association of Zambia, in conjunction with key church coalitions, women's organizations, NGOs, and opposition parties, successfully resisted President Frederick Chiluba's bid for a third term in 2001. Lawyers spearheaded the opposition, drawing on liberal principles of individual liberty, inalienable rights, and human equality to make their case. According to Jeremy Gould (2005) their appeals were based not so much on a political discourse, but rather on a legalistic one drawing on the notion of the rule of law. A coalition of opponents of extending presidential term limits met in the Oasis Restaurant in 2001 and drafted what came to be known as the Oasis Declaration, laying out the legal basis for maintaining term limits. The declaration, which is heavily laden with references to the constitution, has been described by Gould as a "lawyerly" imagining of the state, with a liberal "legalist" mode of authority, of politics, and political morality.

According to Gould, the three societal groups that were most outspoken in Zambia on the issue of term limits were human rights and women's organizations and other advocacy groups; the churches (Catholic, Protestant, and Evangelical), with the Catholics in the forefront; and finally, the Law Association, which came in slightly later in 2001 to challenge the legal and ethical implications of extending term limits. Similar patterns of activism and actors can be found in other countries as well. In some cases, the press is also a contributing factor in these developments.

The new democrats are pressing for term limits and adherence to the constitution to avoid the past authoritarian practices in which leaders would monopolize power for extended periods of time, essentially barring other aspirants to power from seeking office. In other cases, proponents of term limits may have specific grievances against a head of state and wish to see a process in place that would allow for a change in leadership.

In almost all cases, the movements to limit presidential terms came from societal coalitions. However, they required legislative support, which is indicative not only of changing relationships between society and the legislature but also of the strengthening of legislatures. It suggests a growing sense of responsiveness of the legislature to popular pressures. While it would be an overstatement to suggest that there are close working relationships between civil society actors and parliamentarians, legislators are paying greater attention to what civil society actors are thinking and advocating. In the past, under single-party rule, parliament was simply a rubber-stamp extension of the executive branch. This is rapidly changing, as legislative independence has expanded in Namibia, Mauritius, Ghana, Benin, Botswana, Lesotho, Liberia, Senegal, Mozambique, and South Africa.

Similarly, judiciaries are also beginning to assert greater independence and are seeking support from lawyers and their associations. Today, lawyers and judges are increasingly coming to the defense of judicial independence in the face of the most flagrant violations by the executive. In November 2005, in Uganda, the key opposition leader, Kizza Besigye of the Forum for Democratic Change (FDC), was arrested on charges of treason and rape. The day he was to be brought to the High Court to be released on bail, a Black Mamba armed security squad had been deployed at the court to re-arrest him in an extralegal action by the president's office. This prompted protests from the High Court judges, the Chief Justice Odoki (who had been the head of the Constitutional Commission), the Inspector General of Government, leaders of the Uganda Law Society, the government's Human Rights Commission, and hundreds of lawyers, who condemned the siege of the courts as undermining the rule of law. Over three hundred lawyers went on strike to protest military interference in the independence of the judiciary. This would have been unthinkable even a few years earlier. Such examples of the assertion of judicial independence have become increasingly common in Africa.

NGO Regulatory Legislation

As many NGOs began to explicitly link human rights to developmental concerns, they increasingly drew criticism from regimes in sub-Saharan Africa. In the late 1980s and 1990s, NGOs found themselves fighting for the right to autonomy, while opposing governmental efforts to monitor and control NGO activities in Tanzania, Botswana, Ghana, Kenya, Malawi, Zambia, Zimbabwe, Uganda, and other countries (Gyimah-Boadi 1998, 22; Ndegwa 1996; Bratton 1989, 577). In the mid-2000s, governmental efforts to regulate NGOs, which had largely stalled in the previous decade, were revived.

Human rights advocates, women's groups, lawyers, environmental organizations, and other groups opposed efforts to pass such regulatory legislation. Although NGOs generally recognize the need for an administrative and regulatory framework, they have resisted what they consider heavy-handed infringement of their freedom to operate, even in countries calling themselves democracies. Bills regulating NGOs were drafted without sufficient transparency and without consulting NGOs, or only those closest to the government were consulted. In the case of Uganda, a regulatory bill was hurriedly pushed through parliament without adequate time for consultation with NGOs.

NGOs fear that these regulatory bodies will suppress civil society organizations that are deemed too political, especially if they adopt positions that challenge or differ from the government's stance, regardless of how benign the issue. In most of these struggles, NGOs have complained that the legislation assumed they were acting as opposition political parties, when in fact NGOs considered themselves nonpartisan. NGOs focused on development, in particular, resent the fact that they are seen as political groups. And although there are occasions when NGOs ally themselves with political parties to accomplish specific objectives, these groups argue that this does not warrant identifying them as political party organs and subjecting them to the same restrictions that parties face.

Because of government suspicions of the political nature of NGOs, especially those involved in advocacy, NGOs themselves are hesitant to attach the term "political" to their activities. Nevertheless, as Ghanaian Hamida Harrison argues, being political is unavoidable for women activists, given the nature of advocacy around women's rights:

> NGOs are supposed to be politically neutral, non-partisan and so on. And I think that many NGOs are afraid of the word "political," many of them actually say, "we are not political," while we in the women's movement are saying, "This is politics." The minute you start talking about power and resources and so on, it is politics. This is something that makes people within the NGO setting very uncomfortable. (Mama 2005, 129)

The NGO stance of claiming to be apolitical is understandable given the way they are often treated. The 2003 Tanzanian NGO Act provides for criminal sanctions against NGOs that do not register with the government. It also requires NGOs to align their activities with government plans and bans national NGO networks and coalitions. Tanzanian NGOs have strongly resisted these provisions, arguing that they contravene the Tanzanian constitution, the UN Declaration on Human Rights, and the International Covenant on Civil and Political Rights.

The deregistration of NGOs, for questionable reasons, in countries such as Zambia and Uganda caused many organizations to worry. In a more extreme case, Zimbabwe's 2005 NGO Act banned NGOs from receiving foreign funding for governance programs. NGOs appealed to the government on rights-based grounds, and Bob Muchabaiwa, of the National Association of Non-Governmental Organisations (NANGO) petitioned President Robert Mugabe, asking him not to sign the bill into law. Reflecting the rights-based approach that links development to human rights, the petition read: "Your Excellency, we appeal to you not to give assent to the NGO Bill because of its devastating effects on ordinary citizens, the economy and the country. All the work that NGOs do is human rights work whether it is access to water, land, information, education, treatment or promoting the rights of people with disabilities or living with HIV and AIDS."[2] Although Zimbabwe's legislation can be seen as extreme, most NGO regulatory bodies in other countries cite the oversight of foreign funding as one of their major functions.

Other activists have appealed NGO regulatory legislation on constitutional grounds. In some countries, they were able to stall the process for many years. In Zambia, for example, it took nine years before regulatory legislation was passed. In Uganda, NGOs fought heavy-handed legislative restrictions for five years. They opposed the domination of the NGO board by government officials and security agents, the bill's stipulation that NGOs register on an annual basis, and the board's power to de-register an NGO for violating any law. They argued that the board could use its power for political purposes and could undermine associational autonomy. In the end, the Ugandan parliament ignored strong protests from NGOs and donor countries and passed a restrictive registration bill in 2006.

As leader of the NGO coalition Development Network of Indigenous Voluntary Associations (DENIVA), Jassy Kwesiga (2001) reflected on one of the core concerns of NGO activists not only in Uganda but also throughout Africa: "As for denial of registration on the basis of incompatibility with Government policy, plans and public interest, what if the NGOs are expressing the will of the people that may be at odds with Government policy and Government definition of public interest? History in Uganda and elsewhere is full of many state inspired undemocratic misfortunes in the name of public interest." Rather, state and society need to respect the "independence, rights and obligations of the other," according to Kwesiga.

What is emerging from these struggles is an understanding that it may be desirable to register and monitor NGOs to prevent duplication of activities and facilitate collaboration between NGOs, or between NGOs and government. There are, on occasion, NGOs that are set up for unscrupulous purposes. However, regulation in order to suppress advocacy that challenges government policy is incompatible with democracy and is a holdover from the past thinking and practice of one-party states. Attempts to characterize normal NGO advocacy or watchdog activities as anti-government and therefore subject to controls have been resisted, as have efforts to curtail the autonomy of civil society more generally. Placing security personnel on NGO regulatory boards, for example, suggests that NGOs might pose a security risk of some kind.

Civil society activists are pointing to alternative ways of thinking about state-society relations. Many feel there needs to be more mutual trust built between governments and NGOs, with the understanding that a healthy democracy is built on productive synergies between the state and civil society. There needs to be room for societal activities that can help shape government policy through pressure and advocacy, serve as a check on corruption, and promote transparency. Civil society can also be an important resource for government, providing information, research, data, and other forms of knowledge to support activities of government. Moreover, it can provide powerful backing for policies and mobilize people to participate in initiatives and campaigns.

The Ministry of Gender and Development in Liberia, to take one example, relies almost entirely on women's organizations throughout the country, which since 2006 have enthusiastically and actively taken up their campaign to lessen violence against women. These types of productive synergies are only possible if they can be built in an atmosphere of trust and cooperation. It also requires that civil and political liberties more generally be ensured. Since Ellen Johnson-Sirleaf took over as president of Liberia in 2006, the human rights situation has improved dramatically; the press operates with almost complete freedom, as do NGOs and political parties; and a zero-tolerance policy for corruption is in place and enforced. The legislature and judiciary enjoy a level of independence rarely seen in Africa. NGOs have the confidence to operate freely because they know their advocacy will not be seen as antigovernmental activity, and they in turn do their best to support government when there is a need to assist.

Struggles for Media Autonomy

In the early 1990s, as winds of political liberalization swept Africa, and the those in the media began to assert themselves, various governments began to introduce new legislation to create regulatory councils to control media workers and their associations. The proposed legislation galvanized media workers to protect their professional interests as well as their freedom of speech (Lingo and Lobe 2001; Odhiambo 2001; Alabi 2001).

These struggles over media autonomy and freedom of the press have often placed media workers at the forefront of the civil-society struggles for autonomy from government control and freedom of expression. Media workers in Angola, Botswana, Chad, Kenya, Gambia, Nigeria, South Africa, Uganda, and Zambia have debated existing or proposed bills regulating the media over the past several years. These bills, which sought to regulate and discipline journalists and media workers and oversee their registration, were widely rejected on the grounds that they restricted the freedom of speech.

In Kenya, for example, the Kenya Mass Media Commission Bill (1995) and Press Council Bill (1995) were successfully stalled by media organizations. As M'inoti and Maina (1996) observed, "both bills propose to regulate speech as if it were some nuisance, a noxious thing or some other unlawful conduct. . . . The inarticulate [*sic*] premise in both bills is that the mass media and the craft of journalism are essentially venal and hence the need for a great deal of benevolent vigilance from the government." The battle between the government and the media came to a head in 2008. In 2007 the government had tabled the Media Act, which was passed, and an independent Media Council was created. However, in the wake of violence that erupted in 2008 following the presidential elections in Kenya, the president placed restrictions on the media, and, in response, the Media Institute and Kenya Editors Guild filed a lawsuit against the government to halt a broadcasting ban. The Media Council also decided to carry out an audit of media coverage of the elections. The government simultaneously announced that it would also audit media coverage of the elections and would establish its own Statutory Media Council, threatening to disband the independent Media Council of Kenya.

Some of the worst infringements of the freedom of the press have occurred in Zimbabwe, where the independent media has been effectively silenced with the vigorous application of such legislation, including the Access to Information and Protection of Privacy Act (AIPPA) and the Public Order and Security Act (POSA) passed in 2002. And even in democratic South Africa, government legislation in the form of a Film and Publication Amendment Bill was proposed in 2006 and is to be tabled in 2008. It requires newspaper editors to submit their entire paper to regulators prior to publication, seriously curtailing press freedom. As one lawyer put it, the bill would have a "chilling effect on the sociopolitical debates central to any functional democracy." The continued battles over media bills throughout Africa suggest that governments have yet to relinquish their attempts to restrict media freedom.

Women's Rights Movements

The 1990s saw the emergence of new women's movements, which served as catalysts for many of the new constitutional and legal challenges in women's rights that are occurring today in Africa. These movements had new priorities, new leaders, and new sources of funding independent of the state patronage networks that women's organizations had depended on in the past.

Women's rights organizations have drawn on international and pan-African treaties to advance their rights, especially the Convention on the Elimination of All Forms of Discrimination Against Women. Many of the new policies draw on the Platform for Action that emerged from the 1995 United Nations Conference on Women held in Beijing, which encouraged women to seek equal gender representation in political and other institutions, including legislatures, executives, judiciaries, nongovernmental associations, religious institutions, and other bodies.

Women activists have been advocating for greater representation in legislatures through regional organizations like the Economic Community of West African States (ECOWAS) and the Southern African Development Community (SADC). In 1987, SADC set a goal of 30 percent female-held legislative seats by 2005. In 2005, SADC a set a new goal for its member countries: 50 percent female representation in their legislatures by 2015. In early 2008 (the time of this writing), women held on average 21 percent of parliamentary seats in SADC countries. As a result of regional pressures, non-SADC countries in Africa have made progress as well, with an average of 12 percent of legislative seats being held by women.

Other women's rights issues have similarly generated regional attention. In 2005, an African Parliamentary Conference held in Dakar focused on female genital cutting, and speakers and members of twenty African national parliamentary assemblies unanimously adopted a declaration calling for an end to the practice, arguing that "culture is not immutable and that it is subject to perpetual change, adaptations and reforms" ("Final Declaration" 2005). Members pledged to work with civil society, traditional chiefs, religious leaders, women's and youth movements, and governments to adopt strategies to end the practice, drawing on a human rights framework by taking into consideration the education, health, development, and poverty dimensions of the problem.

Some of the pressures to end the practice are quite extraordinary. A group of distinguished Islamic scholars met at Al-Azhar University in Cairo and issued a statement calling female genital mutilation "a deplorable, inherited custom, which is practiced in some societies and is copied by some Muslims in several countries."[3] They concluded that "there are no written grounds for this custom in the Qur'an with regard to an authentic tradition of the Prophet" and acknowledged that "female genital circumcision practiced today harms women psychologically and physically." They insisted that the practice be stopped and called for the practice to be criminalized.

Since the 1990s, women's organizations have been pushing and often succeeding in getting constitutional reforms and legislative changes to protect their rights in ways that override customary laws and practices that violate women's rights, discriminate against women, or violate bill-of-rights provisions regarding gender equality. These are extremely profound challenges. They are, in effect, attempts to legitimize new legal-based sources of authority for rights governing relations between men and women, family relations, and women themselves. In the past, even when laws existed to regulate marriage, inheritance, custody, and other such practices, customary laws and practices coexisted and generally took precedence when it came to family and clan concerns. Today, women's movements are challenging these norms through constitutional and legislative changes—an approach not seen in the past. These reforms represent a new generation of policy measures to address women's status, distinct from the earlier legislation around marriage and inheritance, maternity leave, employment practices, and the taxation of women.

Since 1990, new constitutions in Namibia (1990), Ethiopia (1995), Malawi (1994), Uganda (1995), South Africa (1996), Rwanda (2003), Burundi (2005), and Swaziland (2006) have included nondiscrimination or equality provisions, prohibiting customary practices if they undermine the dignity, welfare, or status of women. These are significant new developments in African constitution-making that contrast sharply with constitutions approved prior to 1990, in which customary law generally was not subject to any gender-related provisions. Women's movements played an important role in ensuring that these clauses were included.

In terms of legislative change, women's movements have been very engaged in strengthening women's property rights. One of the most dramatic changes in land tenure reform today is that, for the first time since the precolonial period, states are granting legal recognition to existing customary tenure regimes, which are being treated as legitimate land tenure systems on a par with the freehold/leasehold systems rather than obsolete systems to be eradicated or phased out. This change came in response to clan leaders' concerns about increasing land scarcity and the growing commercialization of land. However, the clan system they are seeking to preserve places even greater constraints on women's access to land instead of affording women the support it is said to have guaranteed. Ironically, at the very time that these gains are being won in the name of the rural poor, pastoralists, and the landless, African women have mounted a new collective movement to eradicate customary land tenure practices, pushing instead for a system that would allow women to inherit, purchase, and own land in their own name.

Feminist lawyers working with these movements have argued that customary law in the present-day context has been used to selectively preserve practices that subordinate women. The bases of customary ownership have been eroded since the time of colonialism, making women's access to land significantly more precarious as the protections traditionally ensured by the clan system have been peeled away. Rather than seeing customary land practices as a basis for improving women's access to land, they are now advocating for a rights-based system that would guarantee a woman's right to buy, own, and sell land and to obtain title to that land.

Women have also adopted individual strategies of purchasing land and taking their land disputes to court. For example, in Uganda, women of all classes have been purchasing and selling land throughout the country. Several studies by the Makerere Institute for Social Research, carried out in 1995 and 2000 in Lira, Mpigi, Mbale, Kamuli, Mbarara, Nebbi, Mubende, and Kabarole districts show that 15–20 percent of women own land in these districts, which are located throughout Uganda. A study of Mukono in 2002 showed that 45 percent of women owned land. Women's main concern in all these studies was their difficulty in accessing land, meaning they had to rely on their husbands, which was not a viable strategy (Sebina-Zziwa, Kibombo, et al. 2002). Purchasing land has, in effect, become a way of circumventing the traditional authorities.

Women have been active in a variety of land alliances and coalitions throughout Africa, many of which have arisen in response to legislative and constitutional changes in tenure laws. New land laws were enacted in Uganda, Tanzania, Zanzibar, Mozambique, Zambia, Eritrea, Namibia, and South Africa in the 1990s. Rwanda, Malawi, Lesotho, Zimbabwe, and Swaziland adopted new land policies and Kenya is drafting a land bill. Women have been at the forefront of organizations like the Uganda Land Alliance, the National Land Forum in Tanzania, the Zambia National Land Alliance, National Land Committee in South Africa, Kenya Land Alliance, Rwanda Land Alliance, and the Namibian NGO Forum (NANGOF)—all of which have fought for the land rights of women, pastoralists, the landless, and other marginalized people. Regional organizations like Landnet in East Africa have also formed to network with other countries. At the same time, key women's organizations have been actively engaged in land issues in all these countries and have often played a leading role in forming the broader land alliances. In East and Southern Africa, Women in Law and Development in Africa (WiLDAF) has been active since the early 1990s in land and other issues, as has Women and Law in Southern Africa (WLSA) in seven southern African countries (Tripp 2004).

The new movements have been galvanized by mounting land pressures and the placement of constraints on women, who generally do not have sufficient access to and control over land. While the focus of the women's movements has been customary land practices, they have also been concerned with the negative effects of the privatization of land and land grabbing, as governments have increasingly sought foreign investment through tourism, mining, and other businesses. Women have joined forces with pastoralists, who have often found themselves shut out of vast grazing lands in many parts of East Africa, Botswana, and Namibia as a result of large land sales (Palmer 1998).

The movements have taken up a variety of concerns, including the following:

- Ugandan women's rights advocates have long fought to expand women's land rights. After facing numerous setbacks, advocates from Law and Advocacy for Women in Uganda finally got the constitutional court to strike down key provisions of the Succession Act concerning women's right to inherit property. The law did not allow women to inherit the property of a deceased person, including that of a husband, and was found to be discriminatory and unconstitutional.[4] It provided only for male intestacy, assuming that women who died intestate had nothing to bequeath; allowed for 15 percent of the estate to go to the widow, and 100 percent to go to the widower; and provided for the appointment of a guardian of the children even though the widow could be appointed as guardian. The Ugandan parliament was charged with enacting new laws to replace these unconstitutional provisions.
- Women's organizations were active in Tanzania, where they won the right to acquire, hold, use, and transfer land in the Land Act 1999 and Village Land Act 1999. These laws also ensure that women are represented in land administration and adjudication bodies. The Land Act overrides customary law if it denies women their right to use, transfer, and own land. Women's rights of co-occupancy are also protected.
- Women's organizations played a leading role in the passage of Mozambique's new land law in 1997. They were active in and led the Land Forum, a coalition of 200 organizations that participated in discussions leading up to the passage of the land bill. The law not only protects customary tenure arrangements but also includes provisions that allow women to own land and protections that give them greater access to and control over land. Women still face enormous resource and social constraints in accessing land, but with this legislation many of the legal constraints have been removed.

Environmental Movements

Since 2000, NGOs have responded to a series of environmental challenges on a scale not seen in the 1990s.

- When the Ugandan government considered a request by the Mehta Group's Sugar Cooperation of Uganda to take over 7,100 hectares of Mabira forest to expand its sugarcane plantation and double sugar production, a broad coalition of NGOs protested the move. They forced the cabinet to halt the proposed giveaway of the forest until a policy is developed to determine the use of such land. Mabira is the largest natural forest in the country and serves as a significant water catchment area for Lake Victoria. A broad range of environmental, religious, developmental, and human rights groups protested the move, arguing that it was a breach of the constitution to degrade the forest reserve.[5]

- In Sudan, a movement led by the Hamdab Dam Affected People has organized to stop the construction of the Chinese-built Merowe Dam that will displace several communities of 60,000 people and archeological sites in proximity to the Nile River within an area of 175 by 4 kilometers. The project is intended to double Sudan's power production.
- Protests broke out in Côte d'Ivoire with the news that a tanker ship of the Dutch company Trafigura Beheer BV had dumped around 528,000 liters of liquid chemical waste in Abidjan in 2006, causing 77,000 Abidjan residents to seek medical treatment. At least ten were known to have died from the chemical dumping. The Ivorian Human Rights League (Lidho) and associations of toxic waste victims sought compensation for the victims from the company. They have been pressing for and exploring changes in international legislation and monitoring mechanisms in order to avoid the recurrence of such environmental catastrophes in Africa.
- In one of the better-publicized struggles—especially after the execution of environmental activist Ken Saro-Wiwa in 1995—the Movement for the Survival of the Ogoni People (MOSOP) has been seeking redress for environmental degradation as a result of oil drilling in the Niger Delta by multinational oil companies such as Royal Dutch Shell and Exxon Mobil. Over the past fifty years, more than 1.5 million tons of crude oil has been spilled in the area, threatening rare species of birds and animals and threatening the livelihood and health of 20 million residents. The Niger Delta has been identified as one of the five most polluted spots in the world. This has in turn fueled violence in the region.
- The Kimarer-Sugutek Rights Group and other groups have protested pollution by Kenya Fluorspar Company as calcium fluoride was found to have been transported by the Kerio River into the gorges of the Kerio Valley, Rift Valley Province, making the water undrinkable for humans and animals.
- Earthlife Namibia, the National Society for Human Rights, and Germany's Oeko Institute raised concerns in 2005 about the new Langer Heinrich uranium mine, which is located in the environmentally vulnerable Namib-Naukluft Park. The groups are concerned about groundwater and surface water pollution, the human health impacts from emissions of radioactive dust, and the ecological impacts on plants and animals in the park.

These are just a few of the many environmental movements that have sprung up across the continent. The large and growing number of environmental crises in sub-Saharan Africa has led to the creation of linkages among various rights-based organizations.

CLASH OF RIGHTS

The new emphasis on RBAs has not only catalyzed new forces demanding rights but also set various civil society groups onto a collision course by animating contradictory claims. With the new 1996 constitution in South Africa, women's organizations were able to lobby for and obtain key provisions ensuring the protection of women's rights. They also gained greater representation at higher levels of government and in the legislature. Many women thought that with the end of apartheid and with the new constitution they would be free of discriminatory customary practices. However, the constitution also provided for the rights of traditional authorities, who are now threatening women's bid for a new allocation of resources, the most important of which is land. Both women and traditional authorities draw on the 1996 constitution to make claims for their rights, but in ways that potentially clash. In other parts of Africa, similar conflicts exist between those claiming rights to religious and cultural freedom and women's rights advocates pressing for reforms in the areas of family codes, polygamy, child marriage, and female genital cutting.

The political opening and democratization of South Africa not only provided space for women's mobilization; it also energized the traditional authorities. In the case of chieftaincies in southern Africa, to take one example, the weakness or inaccessibility of the state or local government has led populations to seek more accessible traditional authorities. After 1994, a strong lobby of chiefs emerged, seeking legal recognition and protection. Rather than disappearing, traditional authorities (clan formations, elders councils like the *kgotla* in Botswana, the monarchical parliament in Buganda, hometown associations, women's and men's councils in eastern Nigeria, to name a few) have become invigorated with political liberalization throughout Africa. These institutions exist side by side and interact with modern parliaments and local governments.

In Nigeria, there are tensions between advocates for children's rights, who want to raise the age of marriage under the Child Rights Act of 2003, and the Supreme Council for Shari'a in Nigeria, which appeals to Islamic law for its authority. Federal laws that are passed at the national level are required to be passed within the State Houses of Assembly. By 2007, ten of the thirty-six state assemblies had adopted the Child Rights Act, but the Islamic Supreme Council has said that if the act is passed, it will destroy the very basis and essence of the Sharia and Muslim culture. The controversial sections of the Child Rights Act include provisions that make it illegal for parents to marry off their daughter if she is younger than eighteen or to consummate a marriage with a child under eighteen years of age. Proponents of the law see the age limit as a way of ensuring that girls complete their schooling, which has implications for women's economic status and for development in the country more generally. The law also gives both boys and girls equal inheritance rights.

In other contexts, there are tensions between those who share a common agenda. At the end of military rule in 1999, women's groups in Nigeria found themselves with competing notions of rights and competing bases for advocating for women's rights. Some groups saw women's empowerment in terms of promoting family welfare, whereas feminists (for example, Women in Nigeria) saw women's rights advancement as linked to equality and opposition to discrimination. For some Islamic women's groups, women's empowerment was tied to educating people and building awareness among women of their rights under the Sharia. Still other Muslim women's organizations wanted to improve the rights of women and girls by appealing to Islamic law itself. The Federation of Muslim Women Associations of Nigeria (FOMWAN) sees Islamic family law as historically constituted with well-defined notions of rights that can be reformed, but only within the Islamic legal system (Toyo 2006).

CONCLUSIONS

Rights-based approaches have acquired new salience in much of Africa with the convergence of local and global discourses around human rights, including the rights of children, the rights of women, and the rights of the disabled, as well as environmental, economic, civil, and other rights. Certainly these are not the only discourses within society, but they are increasingly prevalent within civil society and have become an important frame for debates with the state in carving out greater autonomy for NGOs and the media, in limiting executive power, and in struggles for greater judicial and legislative independence. Emerging out of these debates are new norms and conceptions of state-society synergies and ways in which state and society can productively interact to advance both development and human rights broadly defined.

As we move into an era where RBAs increasingly prevail, it is also worth paying attention to the many and often competing definitions and sources of authority for rights and the politics of how rights come to be defined, and to how civil society employs these notions and to what end. While there may be agreement on the adoption of RBAs, there are clearly different understandings of what they mean. Semi-authoritarian and authoritarian states have relied on legislative and constitutional sources of authority to rein in and control civil society and the media, while civil society has sought protection and autonomy using the same instruments. Land alliances and property laws have been embraced to protect the rights of marginalized groups, while unleashing the forces of the market, creating possible collision courses. New democratizing constitutions invigorated not only women's and children's rights activists but also traditional authorities and religious activists, who worked at cross-purposes when it came to women's land rights and such issues of personal law as child marriage and polygamy. Thus, when looking at the rise of rights-based approaches, it is important to examine not only the reasons why and ways in which rights discourses are being appropriated by different societal actors but also the competing claims between them.

NOTES

1. Mbaye was author of *The Realities of the Black World and Human Rights, Family Law in Black Africa and Madagascar*, and *Human Rights in Africa*. Mbaye served as Vice President of the International Court of Justice and was a long-time member of the International Commission of Jurists (1972–1987), serving as its president in 1977–1985. He also served on the International Olympic Committee (1973–2002).

2. "Mugabe Urged to Ditch NGOs Bill," *Zimbabwe Standard*, April 3, 2005.

3. Available at http://www.target-human-rights.com/HP-00_aktuelles/alAzhar Konferenz/index.php?p=beschluss&lang=en (accessed December 16, 2006).

4. "Implication of the Ruling on Adultery." *New Vision* (Uganda), April 8, 2007.

5. These included the Uganda Joint Christian Council, National Foundation for Democracy and Human Rights in Uganda, Uganda Land Alliance, Environmental Action Network, Advocates Coalition for Environment and Development, Uganda Forestry Association, the Advocacy Coalition for Development and Environment, Greenwatch, the Environmental Action Network, Environmental Alert, and the Anti-Corruption Coalition.

REFERENCES

Alabi, N. (2001). *The Windhoek Seminar: Ten Years On: Assessment, Challenges, and Prospects.* Western African Regional Perspectives, Summary Review. Windhoek, Namibia, May 3–5.

Bratton, M. (1989). "The Politics of Government-NGO Relations in Africa." *World Development* 17 (4): 569–587.

Comaroff, J., and Comaroff. J., eds. (1999). *Civil Society and the Political Imagination in Africa.* Chicago and London: University of Chicago Press.

Cornwall, A., and C. Nyamu-Musembi (2006). "Putting the 'Rights-Based Approach' to Development into Perspective." *Third World Quarterly* 27 (7): 1415–1437.

Dicklitch, S. (1998). *The Elusive Promise of NGOs in Africa: Lessons from Uganda.* London: Macmillan.

Edwards, M., and D. Hulme, eds. (1995). *Beyond the Magic Bullet: NGO Performance and Accountability in the Post–Cold War World.* London: Earthscan; and West Hartford, Conn.: Kumarian Press.

"Final Declaration." (2005). Paper presented at the African Parliamentary Conference Violence Against Women, Abandoning Female Genital Mutilation: The Role of National Parliaments, Dakar, Senegal, December 4–5.

Fowler, A. (1993). "NGOs as Agents of Democratization: An African Perspective." *Journal of International Development* 5 (3): 325–339.

_______. (1995). "Assessing NGO Performance: Difficulties, Dilemmas, and a Way Ahead." In M. Edwards and D. Hulme, eds., *Beyond the Magic Bullet: NGO Performance and Accountability in the Post–Cold War World.* London: Earthscan; and West Hartford, Conn.: Kumarian Press.

Gibbon, P., and Y. Bangura (1992). "Adjustment, Authoritarianism, and Democracy: An Introduction to Some Conceptual and Empirical Issues." In P. Gibbon, Y. Bangura, and A. Ofstad, eds., *Authoritarianism, Democracy and Adjustment: The Politics of Economic Reform in Africa.* Uppsala: Nordiska Afrikainstitutet.

Gould, J. (2006). "Strong Bar, Weak State? Lawyers, Liberalism and State Formation in Zambia." *Development and Change* 37 (4): 921–941.

Gyimah-Boadi, E. (1998). "The Rebirth of African Liberalism." *Journal of Democracy* 9 (2): 18–31.

Kasfir, N., ed. (1998). *Civil Society and Democratisation in Africa.* Ilford, Essex, U.K.: Frank Cass Publishers.

Kelsall, T. (2002). "Donors, NGOs, and the State: Governance and 'Civil Society' in Tanzania." In O. Barrow and M. Jennings, eds., *The Charitable Impulse: NGOs and Development in East and North East Africa.* Oxford: James Currey: 133–149.

Khadiagala, L. S. (2001). "The Failure of Popular Justice in Uganda: Local Councils and Women's Property Rights." *Development and Change* 32 (1): 55–76.

Korten, D. (1995). *When Corporations Rule the World.* West Hartford, Conn.: Kumarian Press.

Kwesiga, J. (2001). "NGOs Call for Change." *Monitor* (Kampala), March 6.

Lingo, C., and S. K. Lobe (2001). *The Windhoek Seminar: Ten Years On: Assessment, Challenges, and Prospects.* Central African Regional Perspectives, Summary Review. Windhoek, Namibia, May 3–5.

Linscott, J. (2007). "Clear danger in vague phrases," *Business Day* (South Africa) 28, May 28.

Mama, A. (2005). "The Ghanaian Women's Manifesto Movement: Amina Mama Speaks with Dzodzi Tsikata, Rose Mensah-Kutin, and Hamida Harrison." *Feminist Africa* 4: 124–138.

Manzo, K. (2003). "Africa in the Rise of Rights-based Development." *Geoforum* 34: 437–456.

Mercer, C. (2003). "Performing Partnership: Civil Society and the Illusions of Good Governance in Tanzania." *Political Geography* 22 (7): 741–763.

M'inoti, K., and W. Maina (1996). "The Press Council of Kenya Bill and the Kenya Mass Media Commission Bill: A Critical and Comparative Review." *Nairobi Law Monthly* 60: 15–17.

Ndegwa, S. (1996). *The Two Faces of Civil Society: NGOs and Politics in Africa.* West Hartford, Conn.: Kumarian Press.

Nelson, P. J., and E. Dorsey (2003). "At the Nexus of Human Rights and Development: New Methods and Strategies of Global NGOs." *World Development* 31 (12): 2013–2026.

Nussbaum, M. (2000). *Women and Human Development: The Capabilities Approach.* Cambridge: Cambridge University Press.

Nyamu-Musembi, C. (2006). "Ruling Out Gender Equality? The Post–Cold War Rule of Law Agenda in Sub-Saharan Africa." *Third World Quarterly* 27 (7): 1193–1207.

Odhiambo, L. O. (2001). *The Windhoek Seminar: Ten Years On: Assessment, Challenges, and Prospects.* Eastern African Regional Perspectives, Summary Review. Windhoek, Namibia, May 3–5.

Oloka-Onyango, J. (n.d.). "'Popular Justice,' Resistance Committee Courts and the Judicial Process in Uganda (1988–1992)."

Palmer, R. (1998). *Oxfam GB's Land Advocacy Work in Tanzania and Uganda: The End of an Era?* Oxford: Oxfam.

Schumacher, E. F. (1973). *Small Is Beautiful.* Vancouver, B.C.: Hartley & Marks Publishers.

Sebina-Zziwa, A., R. Kibombo, et al. (2002). *Patterns and Trends of Women's Participation in Land Markets in Uganda.* Eighth International Interdisciplinary Congress on Women, Kampala, Uganda, Makerere Institute of Social Research, Makerere University.

Sen, A. K. (1999). *Development as Freedom.* Oxford: Oxford University Press.

Toyo, N. (2006). "Revisiting Equality as a Right: The Minimum Age of Marriage Clause in the Nigerial Child Rights Act, 2003." *Third World Quarterly* 27 (7): 1299–1312.

Tripp, A. M. (2004). "Women's Movements, Customary Law, and Land Rights in Africa: The Case of Uganda." *African Studies Quarterly* 7 (4).

Tsikata, D. (n.d.). "The Rights-Based Approach to Development: Potential for Change or More of the Same?" Working Paper, Center for Developmental Practice.

Uvin, P. (2002). "On High Moral Ground: The Incorporation of Human Rights by the Development Enterprise." *PRAXIS The Fletcher Journal of Development Studies* 17: 1–11.

7

The AIDS Crisis

International Relations and Governance in Africa

Alan Whiteside and Anokhi Parikh

INTRODUCTION

It is just over fifty years since the first African countries gained independence. In 2008, the continent is faced with very different problems from those experienced at independence. In global terms, Africa has not done well; its development has been faltering and unequal. In addition to the "normal" challenges of economic growth, equitable development, democratization, and representation, leaders and citizens of Africa must confront the challenges of global climate change and the AIDS epidemic. Both were first recognized in the early 1980s and have been exhaustively studied. This chapter focuses on AIDS, a disease that has become practically synonymous with Africa in the world's imagination.

AIDS kills more than 4,000 persons a day in sub-Saharan Africa, many more than any civil conflict on the continent.[1] Losses of such magnitude have serious implications for African society. It is no surprise then that AIDS was identified as a security threat in 2000 by the UN Security Council. Although the "securitization" of the AIDS threat may be vastly overstated (a subject discussed later in the chapter), its significant implications for human security are unquestionable. As Lindy Heinecken has observed, it is "the collective impact of the disease on the structure of society and on the state strength that creates the problem."[2]

It is thus appropriate that a chapter on AIDS is included in a book on African politics in the post-9/11 world. This is a time when increased attention is being paid to human security and poverty, through the Millennium Development Goals, the Blair Commission, and other regional and international initiatives. AIDS has become an area of intensified engagement between the African continent and the rest of the world. What is of great concern, however, is the type of global engagement, as well as the lack of engagement by many Africans, especially those in leadership positions.

This chapter provides an overview of the AIDS epidemic in Africa, and its various social, economic, and political impacts. We discuss the way in which the African and international communities have engaged with and responded to the disease.

THE EPIDEMIC

At the end of 2005, UNAIDS estimated that there were 38.6 million people living with HIV (human immunodeficiency virus) or AIDS (acquired immunodeficiency syndrome), of whom approximately 24.5 million were in sub-Saharan Africa.[3] However, the epidemic within the continent is heterogeneous—with significant differences in its size and trajectory. Southern and Eastern Africa have generalized epidemics—where the epidemic is not restricted to any one sub-population—that accounted for 17.3 million infections, or about 70 percent of Africa's total HIV infections and 45 percent of global infections. The Southern African Development Community (SADC) countries alone had an estimated 14.9 million infections.[4] North and West Africa have concentrated epidemics, where the epidemic is confined to groups that are "high risk," such as sex workers. Figure 7.1 shows the adult HIV prevalence rates in 2005.

In most of Africa, the only reliable information gathered on the epidemic is on HIV prevalence rates. This figure is the number of people infected as a percentage of the sampled population. The most common surveys on which prevalence data are based are taken from pregnant women attending state antenatal clinics. The blood taken routinely from these women for other tests can also be used for HIV testing. The sample can be anonymous and unlinked; i.e., the HIV status of a particular woman will not be known. Since 2000, there have also been an increasing number of population surveys where a random sample of the population is tested.[5] This method has provided more comprehensive data, but it is expensive, and in most countries only one or two such surveys have been conducted, meaning there is as yet no longitudinal data.

FIGURE 7.1 HIV prevalence in adults in Africa, 2005

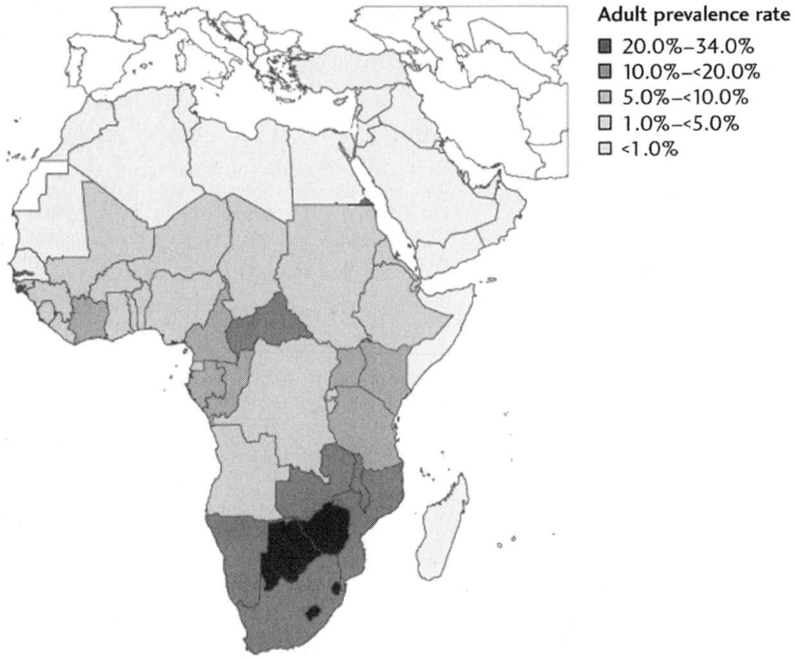

Source: UNAIDS, *Report on the Global AIDS Epidemic, 2006* (Geneva: UNAIDS, 2006), p. 14.

The total number of infections, projected demand for health care, number of deaths, and number of orphans are often modeled using these survey results.

It is important to remember that all HIV data originate from the countries themselves, and each nation's data are only as good as their surveys. There is, probably, no longer distortion of data for political reasons: famously, in the early years of the epidemic, Kenya denied the existence of HIV in its population, fearing negative impacts on its tourist industry, and in the late 1980s, Zimbabwe altered the number of reported AIDS cases to have just one fewer than South Africa's.[6]

The epidemic has a number of unique features.

- It is spread through intimate contact.
- Most cases in Africa are transmitted through heterosexual intercourse.
- A significant number of infants are infected through mother to child transmission.

- Some people may be infected by contaminated medical (Western or traditional) equipment; and sharing of injection drug using equipment is very risky.
- Because of the way it is transmitted, infections tend to occur primarily among young adults, people who are sexually active, and in many cases, people who have begun working and having children.
- The epidemic is a 'long-wave event,' a point we shall return to in the next section.

North Africa has had few infections, and the numbers are growing very slowly. There, sexual intercourse is the dominant form of transmission, although there are some signs of spread among drug users. AIDS is stigmatized, which means that the relatively few people who are infected are reluctant to come forward and seek treatment, and prevention campaigns face additional challenges in reaching target populations. In West Africa, HIV has not spread widely.[7] The highest prevalence has been in Côte d'Ivoire at 7.1 percent in 2005. The mainly Islamic countries have low prevalence. Senegal has been held up as a model for successful prevention; adult HIV prevalence was below 1 percent throughout the 1980s and 1990s, increasing slightly to 1.1 percent in 2002, and then falling back to 0.9 percent in 2005. Observers have suggested that this is due to strong leadership and openness about HIV/AIDS; legalized and regulated sex work; and male circumcision.[8] In terms of numbers, the worst epidemic in West Africa has been in Nigeria, where there were an estimated 2.9 million people living with HIV, equivalent to an adult prevalence of 3.9 percent.

The relatively low reported prevalence in Sierra Leone and Liberia (and further south in Angola) suggests that periods of conflict may mean less HIV is transmitted as a result of circumscribed travel. This makes proactive action during the post-conflict period even more critical. There is also the potential for increased gender violence as people return to their home villages and try to pick up their lives. This is the time when HIV/AIDS interventions should be occurring.

In East Africa, prevalence has peaked and has been declining. Behavioral data show this decline to be due to increased condom use in casual relationships, reduction in numbers of partners, and delayed sexual debut. The greatest reduction has been in Uganda, which, in the 1980s, was the global epicenter of the epidemic. At the peak in 1990, HIV prevalence may have been 31 percent among pregnant women. By 2002, it was estimated to be just 4.7 percent in this group. There have been some indications to suggest that prevalence has since risen slightly, showing that prevention efforts need to be maintained. Kenya, Tanzania, Rwanda, and Burundi all have had adult prevalence rates of 7 percent or lower which seem to be falling.

In 2002, Ethiopia was identified as one of the five "next-wave" countries by the U.S. National Intelligence Council.[9] It was estimated that there were between 4 and 6 million Ethiopians infected with HIV in 2002 and that this number would grow substantially. However, the 2006 UNAIDS country report for Ethiopia estimated that there were only between 420,000 and 1,300,000 people living with HIV.[10] Ethiopia has been one of the countries where the data have remained politically influenced. The government has not allowed UNAIDS to make specific estimates; they were only able to publish a range.

Southern Africa has had the worst epidemic in the world. In Mozambique, the adult HIV prevalence rate in 2005 was estimated at 16.1 percent and rising; in Malawi, it was estimated that the rate had stabilized at about 14 percent. Swaziland has had the world's highest prevalence rate. In 2004, this figure stood at 42.5 percent of antenatal clinic attendees, although the latest survey, in 2006, found a slight decline to 39.2 percent. South Africa's antenatal clinic survey recorded an slightly increased prevalence from 29.5 percent in 2004 to 30.2 percent in 2005 and then a small decline to 29.1 percent in 2006. Similar prevalence rates are seen in Botswana and Lesotho, while Namibia has a prevalence of just under 20 percent. But there are also hopeful signs: Data from Zimbabwe and Zambia have suggested a fall in prevalence in those countries. In Zimbabwe, HIV prevalence in pregnant women fell from 26 percent in 2002 to 21 percent in 2004. In the southernmost countries, one notable feature of the epidemic is its homogeneity. There have not been large differences in prevalence rates across countries or between rural and urban areas.

THE IMPACTS OF AIDS

The scale of the epidemic determines the impact that it will have. It is not surprising then that different parts of Africa have received different amounts of attention. For instance, Eastern and Southern Africa have been the focus of international efforts and resources, in keeping with their large generalized epidemics.

Before delving further into the specifics of the impact of AIDS, it is important to understand that AIDS is a long-wave event. Its impacts will be experienced for many years to come. HIV is a *lentivirus*, or a slow-acting virus, that leads to symptomatic illnesses only six to ten years after infection. If untreated, the infected person will experience episodes of illness that increase in frequency, duration, and severity and that end in death. There is currently no cure for AIDS, but there are antiretroviral (ARV) drugs available that will keep people alive and able to function normally for as long as ten to twelve years. These drugs are expensive by African standards. In June 2007, the cost of the cheapest drugs available was $94 per patient per year, which excluded all ancillary costs.[11] The fact that the drugs have to be taken for life means that ARV provision will be a huge cost burden on these countries for decades.

Given the epidemic's long-wave nature, the impact is seen by different categories of people in different ways. Medical staff dealing with symptoms presented are the first to be aware of the developing epidemic (although they generally do not appreciate the magnitude of what is to come). Researchers, on the other hand, often look at what has taken place already and have difficulty in picking up current and future challenges. (The parallels with climate change are striking.) The evolution of the disease over time is illustrated by the three curves in Figure 7.2. During the first stage, HIV spreads. This is followed by climbing numbers of AIDS-related illnesses and deaths. The number of deaths will increasingly depend on the availability of ARV treatment. The third curve shows the impact, including such consequences as rising numbers of orphans, reduced rural production, and increased impoverishment. Evidence from Uganda has suggested that the number of orphans is highest some fifteen years after HIV prevalence has peaked. This means that even if the indications are that HIV prevalence has started falling in South Africa and Swaziland, the number of orphans will continue to rise until 2020. AIDS will be a part of the sociopolitical reality of parts of Africa for decades to come.

FIGURE 7.2 AIDS as a long-wave event: The three epidemiological curves

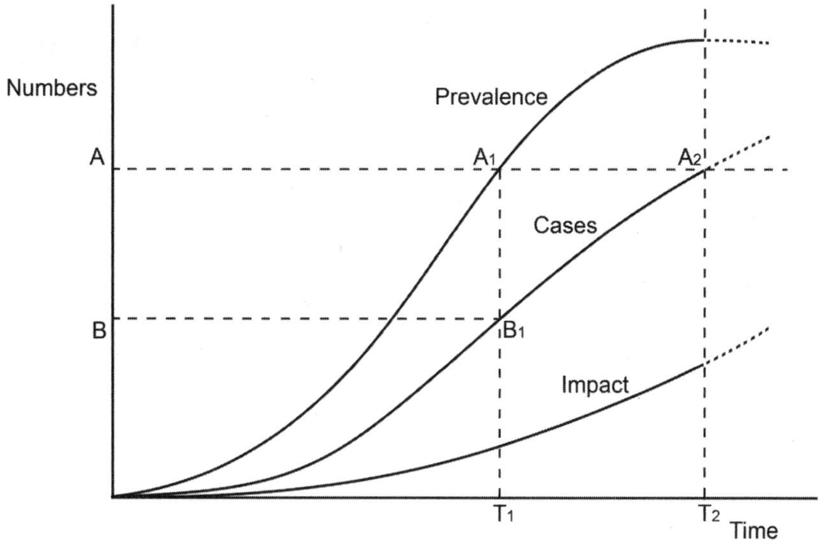

Source: Alan Whiteside, *HIV/AIDS: A Very Short Introduction* (Oxford: Oxford University Press, 2008), p. 5.

That being said, many impacts are already being felt. The following sections consider the effects that are particularly relevant for human security and governance.

Demographic Impact

The demographic consequences of AIDS include increased mortality rates; rising infant and child mortality; falling life expectancy; changes in population size, growth, and structure; and a growth in the number of orphans. The high levels of mortality, particularly in generalized epidemics—defined as those countries with adult prevalence rates over 5 percent—have resulted in substantial demographic effects.

AIDS disproportionately affects young persons; the peak of infection is in the twenty- to forty-year age group. Most deaths occur about five to fifteen years after infection, which results in an increased number of deaths among those who would typically have the lowest mortality rates and who are an economically active segment of the population. AIDS has been identified as a major cause of death among fifteen- to forty-nine-year-olds in countries as far apart as Tanzania[12] and Cote d'Ivoire.[13]AIDS is the primary cause of death in sub-Saharan Africa. Recent data from Swaziland indicate that the crude death rate has steadily increased since 1995 (see Figure 7.3). South African mortality data are shown in Figure 7.4, which depicts both the increase in deaths over time as well as the increase in deaths of young persons (cause is not ascribed).

The pattern of mortality shown in Figure 7.4 is found across high-prevalence countries. These increased death rates have severe consequences for society. Those who die have received education and training and would have been generally economically productive; many would be in the middle ranks of employment, gaining experience and skills of value to their country's economy.

In an AIDS epidemic, infant and child mortality rises for two reasons. First, children born to infected mothers have, in the absence of intervention, about a 30 percent chance of being infected, and if they are HIV-positive, they have poor life expectancy. The second reason is that losing a mother, for any reason, has an adverse impact on child survival, irrespective of child's HIV status. The chance of a child dying increases threefold in the year before the mother's death and fivefold in the year after.

The U.S. Bureau of the Census issued a report in 2004 on the impact of AIDS on global population, which includes demographic projections both for actual population and for population in the absence of the epidemic—that is, "with AIDS" and "without AIDS." In Botswana, the crude death rate in 2002 was estimated to be 28.6 per 1,000; without AIDS, it would have been a mere 4.8 per 1,000. For Tanzania, the 2002 figures were 17.3 per 1,000 with AIDS,

FIGURE 7.3 Crude death rate in Swaziland, 1990–2005

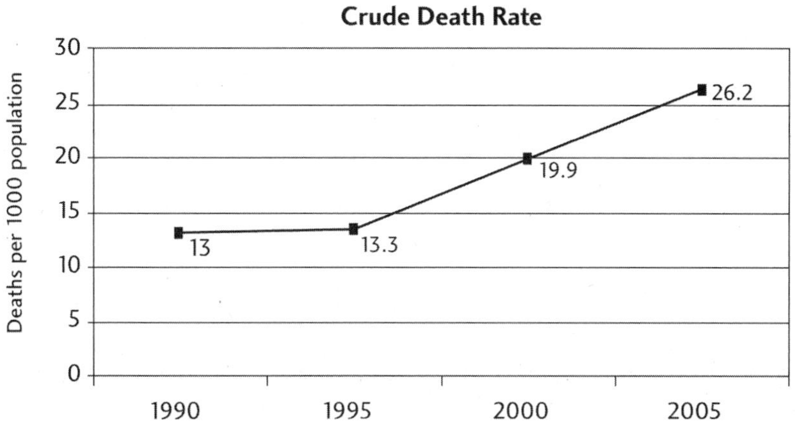

Source: Amy Whalley, "Reviewing Emergencies: Shifting the Paradigm for a New Era," paper prepared for HEARD, Durban, South Africa, September 2007, p. 18.

FIGURE 7.4 Mortality by age group in South Africa, 1997–2004

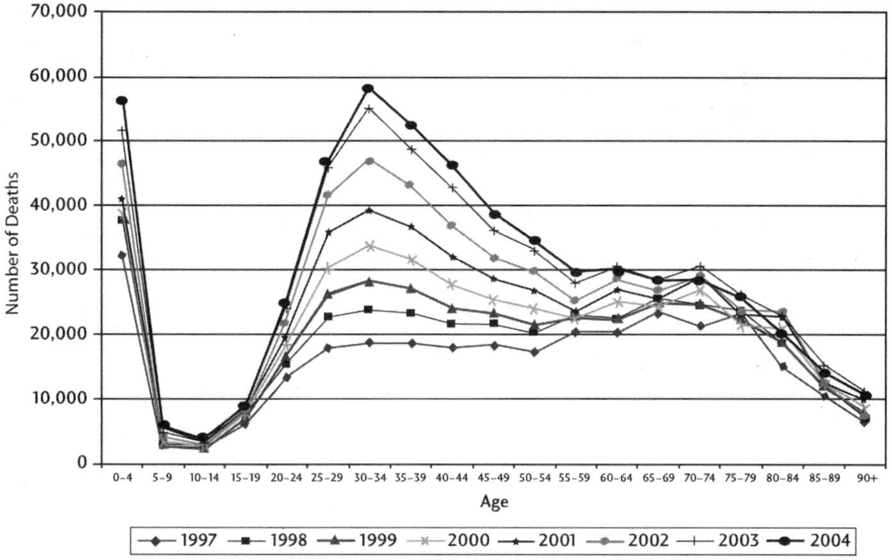

Source: Mortality and Causes of Death in South Africa, 2003 and 2004: Findings from Death Notification (Pretoria: Statistics South Africa, 2006), p. 11.

and 12.1 without AIDS. The child mortality rates are even more severely affected. The greatest increase in mortality was in Botswana, where the rate was estimated to be 107.1 per 1,000 in 2002. Without AIDS, it would have been a much lower 30.6.[14] Another study found that, at 2004 mortality rates in Swaziland, the probability that a young Swazi aged fifteen would reach age fifty was 28 percent for males and 22 percent for females, compared to 94 percent and 97 percent in a scenario excluding the impact of HIV/AIDS.[15]

AIDS is knocking years off life expectancy, especially in Africa. Table 7.1 shows that this impact will be felt most strongly during 2010–2015. A sustained and expanded rollout of treatment would change this. The data for the African countries in Table 7.1 is aggregated, and therefore the numbers do not fully reflect just how seriously some countries have been affected. According to the UNDP, in 2006, life expectancy at birth was just 33 years in Swaziland, 36.6 in Botswana, and 37.2 in Zimbabwe. In Kenya, it was 47, and in Senegal 55.6.[16]

Population growth rates have already begun to fall as a consequence of AIDS. UNAIDS estimated in 2006 that South Africa had 320,000 deaths from AIDS; Nigeria had 220,000, and Zimbabwe had 180,000.[17] It is expected that by 2015, close to 6 million South Africans—or 13 percent of the population—will have died of AIDS. Mortality from AIDS is leading to an extreme change in Africa's population structure. Figure 7.5 shows Botswana's projected population for 2020. The inner bars show the expected future shape and size of the population, and the outer bars show what it would have looked like without AIDS. By 2020, instead of just over 80,000 women in the 40–45 age group, there will be only about 18,000.

As a result of changes in the population structure, the dependency rate—the ratio of working-age adults to children and elderly—will change. Higher dependency places greater demands on government and society to provide education, health care, and social services. This could adversely affect economic growth by depressing the national savings rate and reducing resources for investment. Conventional dependency ratio calculations assume most adults are productive. In AIDS epidemics, a significant number of people are chronically sick and therefore should be counted in the "dependents" category.

Economic Impact

Early in the epidemic, people believed that AIDS would slow economic growth. In the late 1980s, economists were concerned with the following questions:

- Would national output grow more slowly or even decline because of AIDS?
- What would be the effect on per capita incomes?

TABLE 7.1 Impact of HIV/AIDS on mortality

Life expectancy at birth (years)	All 53 countries			38 African Countries			7 countries with prevalence of 20% or more		
	1995–2000	2010–2015	2020–2025	1995–2000	2010–2015	2020–2025	1995–2000	2010–2015	2020–2025
Without AIDS	63.9	68.4	70.8	52.7	58.3	62.1	62.3	67.0	69.6
With AIDS	62.4	64.2	65.9	47	47.1	51.3	50.2	37.6	41
Absolute difference	1.5	4.1	4.9	5.7	11.3	10.8	12	29.4	28.6
Percentage difference	2.4	6.1	6.9	10.9	19.3	17.4	19.3	43.9	41.1

Source: United Nations Department of Economic and Social Affairs, Population Division, *World Population Prospects: The 2002 Revision*, CD-ROM (New York: United Nations Department of Economic and Social Affairs/Population Division, 2002).

Note: The 53 countries include 38 African, 5 Asian, 8 Latin American and Caribbean countries, the Russian Federation, and the United States.

FIGURE 7.5 Altered population structure due to HIV/AIDS, Botswana

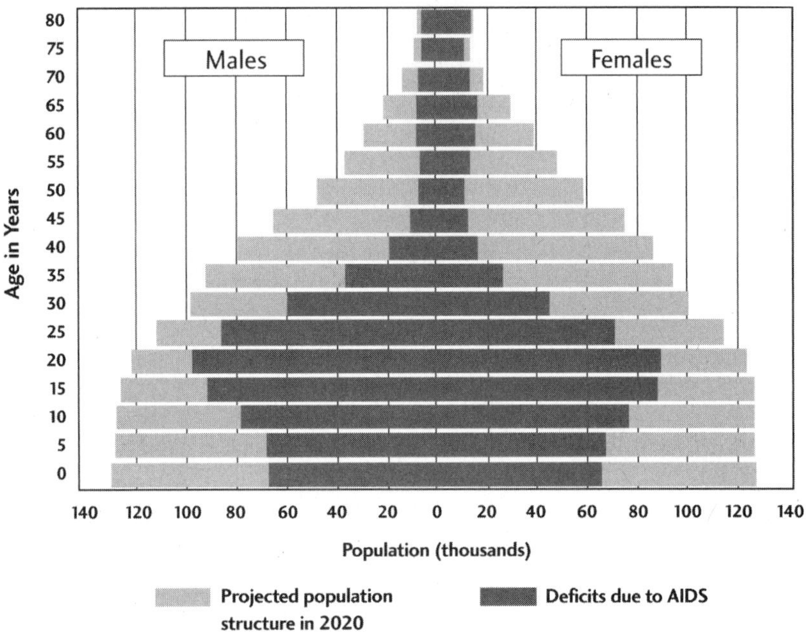

Source: United Nations Joint Program on HIV/AIDS, *Report* (Geneva, 2000), p. 22.

In 1992, the World Bank published a model looking at how AIDS affected economic growth in thirty African countries through its effect on the labor force, capital accumulation, and other factors.[18] The study concluded that economic growth rates would be 0.56–1.47 percent lower as a consequence of the AIDS epidemic. Subsequent models came up with similar figures. In 2000, Bonnel estimated that AIDS had reduced Africa's economic growth by 0.8 percent in the 1990s.[19]

There have been two groups of country-specific studies: the first in the early to mid-1990s, followed by a flurry of studies early in the new century.[20] As it turned out, the results have not varied much in these studies; they show that GDP grew more slowly with AIDS than it did without AIDS, and the effect on per capita income was sensitive to varied assumptions—that is, it could rise or fall. The macroeconomic impact of AIDS was likely to be negative but small, even over a twenty-five-year period.

Set against this are data from individual African countries. Uganda had the worst epidemic in the world, yet it experienced consistent economic growth throughout the 1990s, estimated at 6.5 percent per annum from 1991 to 2002. Botswana's growth rate over the same period was 5.6 percent. South Africa has seen steady growth and posted its forty-seventh month of consecutive growth in March 2006, with an estimated growth rate of 4.4 percent. In 2007, after spending twenty years of watching the epidemic develop and the impacts that have resulted, we are forced to conclude that macroeconomic impacts are hard to find and that indeed this is not the place we should even be looking. The reasons lie in global economic trends, the time scale, and the ability of companies to respond. Labor is no longer the key constraint in productivity; indeed in many countries there are surplus unskilled workers. It is possible that economies will, in the long term, be adversely affected by social changes and pressures, but this will take time. Finally, we have found that companies, both large and small, adapt to the epidemic and develop coping mechanisms. Few studies have been able to isolate the impact of HIV/AIDS from other factors affecting economic development in Africa. A study of tea plantation workers in Kenya showed that pluckers who died of AIDS were absent twice as often as other workers in their last years of life and that their output fell three years prior to their death.[21] This is one of the few examples of research that managed to isolate the impact of AIDS, and it showed a significant effect.

Although the impact of AIDS on growth and the macroeconomy may be minimal or yet to be fully experienced, households are impacted immediately, and the death of a breadwinner at this level is devastating. This has been documented throughout the continent. Several studies have shown the link between HIV/AIDS-affected households and their subsequent impoverishment through loss of employment due to illness, death of a breadwinner, and increased medical and funeral expenses.[22] A detailed case study in Malawi (adult prevalence 14.1 percent) has shown that many AIDS-affected households suffer from chronic illness and are unable to provide the labor needed for even low-productivity subsistence agriculture. In the central region, it was found that between 22 and 64 percent of households suffered from chronic sickness. The consequences were that 45 percent of these households delayed agricultural operations, 23 percent left land fallow, and 26 percent changed the crop mix. Female-headed households have been the worst affected, since women do much of the agricultural work, in addition to childrearing.[23] HIV/AIDS is thus contributing to the steady impoverishment of households all over the continent.

Security and Politics

By early 2000, HIV/AIDS was regarded as a threat to security. On January 10, 2000, then U.S. Vice President Al Gore identified HIV as a global security threat in a statement to the UN Security Council: "It [HIV] threatens not just individual citizens, but the very institutions that define and defend the character of a society. This disease weakens workforces and saps economic strength. AIDS strikes at teachers, and denies education to their students. It strikes at the military, and subverts the forces of order and peacekeeping."[24] Six months later, the Security Council passed Resolution 1308, which stated: "The HIV/AIDS pandemic, if unchecked, may pose a risk to stability and security."[25] In June 2001, the UN General Assembly held a special session on HIV/AIDS, which called for an urgent and sustained response to the epidemic partly on security grounds.

We believe that the "securitization" of HIV/AIDS has been overstated. There may have been some practical and strategic reasons for this, however, as Gwin Prins noted in 2004:

> During the last twenty years, there has often been an uneasy relationship between the claim that an issue is important and that it is a security issue. That is because the political stakes of so doing are high, but so too are the costs. If an issue can be "securitized," it is the equivalent of playing a trump at cards, for at once it leap-frogs other issues in priority. But the unavoidable cost of this is first, that to obtain that priority, people must be persuaded to be afraid of the threat, and to see it as a "real and present danger." Secondly, it throws the solution into the hands of the state—or state-derived and mediated structures, for they alone command the resources to satisfy the scale and urgency of the securitised threat once accepted as such.[26]

One area that deserves particular debunking is the notion of the military, typically staffed with young sexually active men, as a source of infection. An assessment of the risks of infection in militaries has shown that those populations do not necessarily, at the aggregate level, have a higher prevalence of HIV than male civilian populations.[27] Armed forces are primarily made up of young men, but male HIV prevalence rises with age. Most militaries test recruits and exclude those who are HIV positive.

There is no evidence that HIV/AIDS is a war starter or a war stopper. It is possible that the Ugandan army in the late 1980s and early 1990s was affected by the disease, and there have been anecdotal reports of some African countries having difficulty in putting together units for peacekeeping operations due to HIV in their ranks.[28] Most analyses of the relationship between AIDS and national security have consisted of a catalogue of reasons why the epidemic may lead to all kinds of security crises, but there is no evidence that it has done so. Laurie Garrett of the Council on Foreign Relations suggests that periods of conflict actually lower HIV spread.[29] Tony Barnett and Gwyn Prins of the London School of Economics point to the use of "factoids"—frequently repeated information which is then held to prove a point—in the discussion of this issue.[30]

Nevertheless, the epidemic has been implicated in the disintegration of Zimbabwe. Andrew Price-Smith and John Daly argue that because AIDS operates simultaneously across various domains, it can destabilize states and threaten their national security. Zimbabwe faces many crises—economic contraction, political corruption, failed land reform and collapse of agricultural production, environmental change, and runaway inflation. AIDS is a powerful stressor with an additional negative impact.[31] For countries like Malawi and Swaziland, AIDS may have a similar impact. State failure might happen as the public sector becomes less and less efficient. Civil servants are not as well paid as people in the private sector, but they expect greater security and benefits, making it harder for the public sector to adapt to increased rates of illness and death. Economic growth and especially subsistence agriculture are adversely affected, as well. Moreover, as the role of donors increases, the ability of governments to make independent decisions is reduced.

AIDS, AFRICA, AND THE WORLD

The magnitude of the pandemic has resulted in a significant international response. A large proportion of resources expended on HIV/AIDS programs has come from donors, not national budgets. Most treatment programs would not be possible without such financial assistance. As with other aid, however, this poses challenges in governance, with the power to dictate domestic policy being tipped toward the donors. This section examines the way in which African countries are affected by and negotiate international responses in terms of policy.

AIDS, Aid, and African Governance

Subsequent to UN Resolution 1308 there were three new major initiatives specific to HIV/AIDS. In 2001, the Global Fund to Fight AIDS, Tuberculosis, and Malaria (GFATM) was established. In January 2003, President Bush established the $15 billion President's Emergency Plan for AIDS Relief (PEPFAR) to fund programs in fifteen countries. The third was the announcement by World Health Organization (WHO) Director-General Lee Jong-wook that HIV/AIDS would be his top priority. To that end, he unveiled a new plan on December 1 (World AIDS Day), 2003, with the goal of treating 3 million people in poor countries by the end of 2005. This ambitious plan, to be administered with UNAIDS, was dubbed "3 by 5."

For many African countries, these initiatives led to a marked increase in funds for HIV/AIDS treatment and prevention. Figures 7.6 and 7.7 show trends for select countries. Two key points are illustrated by these figures: first, between 2000 and 2004, there were substantial increases in external funding (1,100 percent in the case of Lesotho); second, in some countries, that funding was not sustained. As shown on Figure 7.6, Mozambique, Lesotho, and Swaziland all saw funding reductions, while in Malawi, funding remained unchanged.

Although such funding has been critically important in the fight against AIDS—and indeed even more funding is needed to address the magnitude of the problem—there are nonetheless institutional concerns associated with external funding. Aid dependency may weaken a government's capacity to generate domestic resources and may distort incentives for raising revenue. We say "may" because we do not yet have data to show this is the case. Large amounts of aid undermine the local democratic process, in that donors often dictate policy (how much of the aid is spent on treatment versus prevention, and so on).[32] Donor-dictated policy has tended to favor investment in "vertical public health programs" geared toward attacking specific diseases, instead of improving the health system at large and institution building.[33] In addition, aid is often associated with attempts to reform institutions, which may or may not be desirable. And finally, the sharp rise in funding over a short period of time may induce corruption and rent seeking and may shift accountability toward donors instead of citizens.[34] There is evidence of corruption associated with AIDS funding in Uganda (though one cannot ascribe causality). The Global Fund suspended its grants to Uganda in 2005 after finding that the health ministry seriously mismanaged money. In 2007, President Yoweri Museveni ordered the arrest and prosecution of former Health Minister Jim Muhwezi and his two deputy ministers for mismanaging assistance funding from the Global Fund.[35]

Ann Swidler has observed that AIDS has generated an organizational response that may alter the patterns of governance across Africa.[36] A large number of international organizations are tracking and "managing" African responses to HIV/AIDS, including GFATM, PEPFAR, United Nations Population Fund (UNFPA), WHO, Swedish International Development Agency (SIDA), Danish International Development Assistance (DANIDA), and Department for International Development (DFID). Many other types of organizations have joined the fight against HIV/AIDS, ranging from universities, to consortia, to freelancers. African governance around HIV/AIDS and health is thus heavily influenced and controlled by these organizations. This has been

FIGURE 7.6 Trends in external funding commitments for HIV/AIDS for selected African countries, 2000–2004

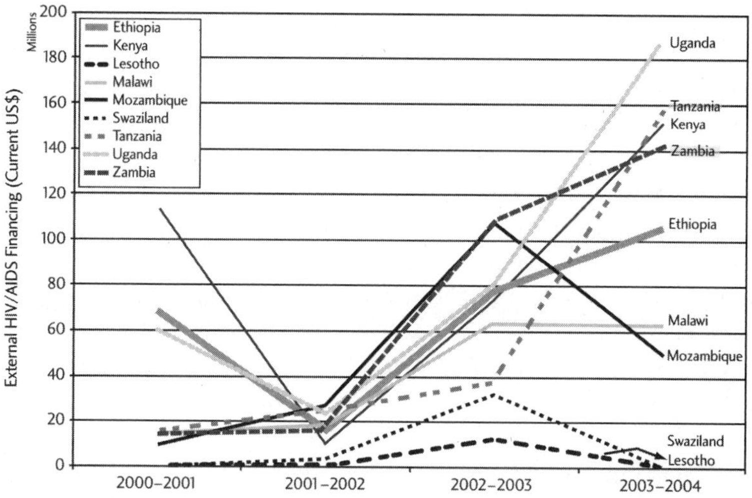

Source: M. Lewis, *Addressing the Challenge of HIV/AIDS: Macroeconomic, Fiscal and Institutional Issues,* Working Paper 58 (Washington, D.C.: Center for Global Development, 2005), p. 7.

FIGURE 7.7 Changes in external funding for HIV/AIDS for selected African countries, 2000–2004

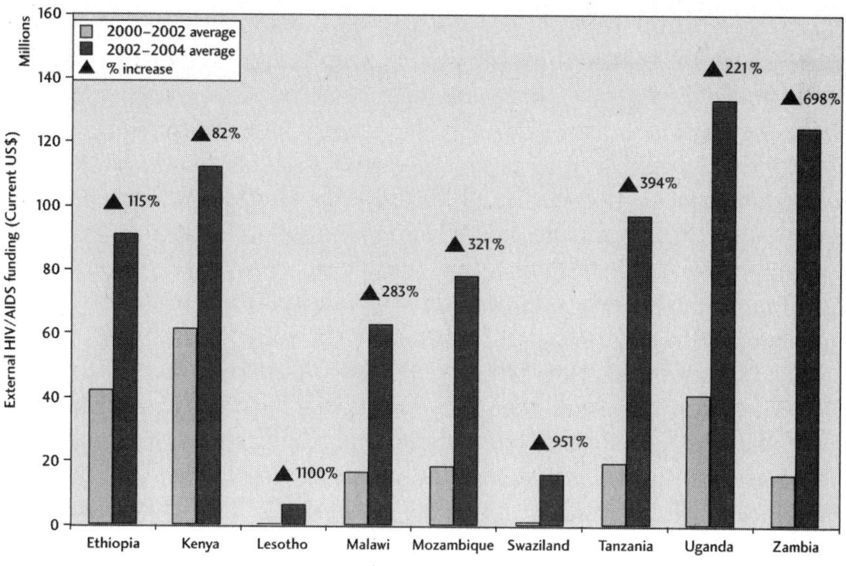

Source: M. Lewis, *Addressing the Challenge of HIV/AIDS: Macroeconomic, Fiscal and Institutional Issues,* Working Paper 58 (Washington, D.C.: Center for Global Development, 2005), p. 8.

most clearly seen in South Africa with the Treatment Action Campaign, which in 2001 took the government to court and forced it to provide nevirapine to prevent mother-to-child transmission.[37] Médecins Sans Frontières (MSF), an international humanitarian aid organization, has been influential in pushing antiretroviral treatment in many African locations, from Khayelitsha outside Cape Town to the northeastern Amhara region of Ethiopia. In many cases, this has forced governments to roll out treatment themselves.

These many actors, both local and international, are influential. Swidler found that an internal report on decentralization in Uganda began with a long list of acronyms and abbreviations, including those of many international organizations. The high levels of international funding mean that governments may not even be able to discuss governance structures without referring to the many international organizations with which they interact.

Moreover, the various funding bodies have stringent monitoring and evaluation requirements (for example, PEPFAR). Capacity-constrained countries have had to mobilize human resources to keep up with organizational procedures required by donors. A brief look at the proportion of the health budget that is provided by donors versus that contributed by government (see Figure 7.8) gives a good indication of the level to which governance could be affected by the will and desires of international organizations.

Negotiating the U.S. Response

PEPFAR has established the goal of preventing 7 million new infections and putting 2 million people on treatment by 2008. Some have argued that the Bush administration placed HIV/AIDS at the fore of its international agenda largely due to pressure from its conservative Christian base, who felt a moral obligation to take action against HIV/AIDS.[38] The United States now provides over half the global foreign aid dedicated to fighting HIV/AIDS. With the money, however, came a number of moral and policy negotiations for African governments. When the Bush administration pledged the funds, its conservative base naturally played a part in shaping AIDS policy. This has been particularly problematic with respect to prevention. One-third of all U.S. funds devoted to prevention has gone to programs that focus solely on abstinence until marriage (although there are signs of this changing), even though condoms have been shown to be effective when used properly and consistently. Thus, the moral imperative espoused in the Bush AIDS policy conflicts with what is understood as best practice in medicine.[39] Researchers who have evaluated both comprehensive sex education and abstinence-only programs have found the former to be far more effective.[40] The abstinence-only approach

FIGURE 7.8 Trends in domestic health funding and external financing for HIV/AIDS, 2000–2004

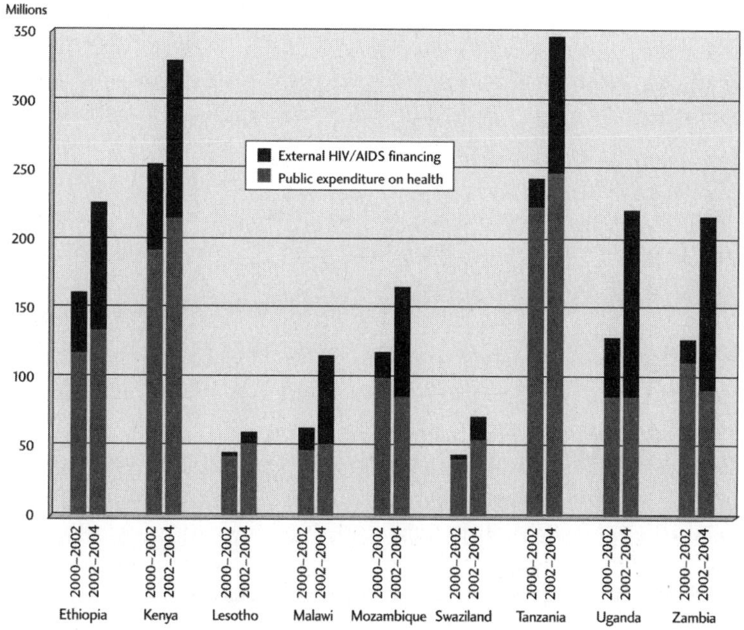

Source: M. Lewis, *Addressing the Challenge of HIV/AIDS: Macroeconomic, Fiscal and Institutional Issues,* Working Paper 58 (Washington, D.C.: Center for Global Development, 2005), p. 12.

fails to consider the social realities under which people have sex, particularly in marginalized communities. Indeed, the Bush policy came under great attack at the 2006 International AIDS Conference held in Toronto.

One example of the direct impact of PEPFAR's policies on domestic policy comes from Uganda. Uganda has received a lot of recognition for undertaking a hugely successful prevention campaign and bringing down new infection and overall prevalence rates. The extent to which abstinence, versus condom use, has been responsible for the success has been debated. Since PEPFAR started funding Uganda, there have been some shifts in prevention policy, with an increase in abstinence-only programs and a decrease in support for condom use. In 2005, 32 million condoms were impounded in government warehouses.[41] Such shifts in policy will have drastic implications for prevention and transmission of the virus. Although the president of Uganda and his wife, in particular, have supported this shift in policy, it is clear that in many instances national HIV policies have been altered due to pressure from foreign donors, driven by a moral agenda. The use of condoms to control HIV has had a controversial history in Uganda; their use was promoted in the 1990s, and they were made widely available. Helen Epstein, in her book *The Invisible Cure: Africa, the West, and the Fight Against AIDS*, describes how policy later shifted in Uganda: "Shortly after Mrs. Museveni returned from Washington in 2003, where she helped the Republicans lobby for the $1 billion appropriated for abstinence campaigns, Ugandan officials resumed denouncing condoms after a ten-year hiatus."[42]

Our Common Interest: Report of the Commission for Africa

The Commission for Africa was established by British Prime Minister Tony Blair in early 2004. In its report issued in March 2005, the commission proposed a "coherent package" to address Africa's interrelated development problems, which included poor governance, lack of growth, environmental degradation, adverse terms of trade, and debt.[43] It argued that these challenges had to be met through a new kind of partnership for development, based on mutual respect and solidarity between donors and recipients, and an analysis of "what works." One solution proposed by the commission was to significantly increase foreign assistance, specifically, by an additional $25 billion per year by 2010, and a further $25 billion per year by 2015. Other actions envisaged included the following:

- investing in African capacity;
- supporting accountable budgetary processes and anti-corruption measures;
- supporting conflict-management structures and processes;
- funding educational and health-care services;
- supporting economic growth and poverty reduction strategies; and
- promoting more and fairer trade.

Although the commission's report had just one subsection on HIV/AIDS (in the chapter titled "Leaving No One Out: Investing in People"), AIDS is considered a cross-cutting issue by the authors. For example, mortality is identified as a cause of teacher shortages in Africa. In the chapter titled "Growing for Growth and Poverty Reduction," the economic impact of HIV and AIDS is identified as a key challenge to growth: "Top priority must be given to scaling up services needed to deal with the catastrophe of HIV and AIDS. . . . But this must be done through existing systems, rather than parallel new ones. Governments should also be supported to protect orphans and vulnerable children and other groups who would otherwise be left out of the growth story."[44]

Overall the recommendations concerning the AIDS epidemic were unexceptional. The two innovative ideas were that the HIV and AIDS response should be "mainstreamed" and that UNAIDS should develop an accreditation system for international agencies, businesses, and nations to assess their HIV and AIDS competency. It is not clear what was meant by mainstreaming. Other suggestions were more predictable: The international community should reach global agreement by 2005 to harmonize "the current disparate response to HIV and AIDS," and "donors should meet immediate needs and increase their contribution to $10 billion within five years in line with the goals of the United Nations General Assembly Special Session (UNGASS) agreement."[45]

The Gleneagles Summit and Subsequent G8 Meetings

At the Gleneagles summit (Scotland, July 2005), G8 leaders, the presidents and prime ministers of Brazil, China, India, Mexico, and South Africa and the heads of the major international organizations met to discuss a range of issues, including development in Africa and how to accelerate progress toward the Millennium Goals. The G8 leaders agreed to a comprehensive approach to support these objectives, including the provision of substantial additional resources, some for "investment in health and education, and to take action to combat HIV/AIDS, malaria, TB and other killer diseases."[46]

They agreed that aid for Africa should be doubled by 2010 (from $25 billion to $50 billion a year) and that it should be accompanied by innovative mechanisms to deliver and bring forward this financing. (The World Bank would have a key coordinating role.) The G8 also agreed to cancel all debts owed by eligible heavily indebted poor countries to the World Bank's International Development Association, the International Monetary Fund, and the African Development Fund. With respect to HIV/AIDS, the G8 pledged to "do everything in its power to achieve universal access to treatment for those who need it."[47] Like the Blair commission, however, the summit did not make any exceptional recommendations.

Former UN Special Envoy for HIV/AIDS Mr. Stephen Lewis has scathingly criticized the G8 for underdelivering on promises made at Gleneagles. Just two months after the summit, the G8 countries had already fallen several billion dollars short of their commitment to the GFATM. Moreover, the Development Assistance Committee of the OECD noted that between 2005 and 2006, Official Development Assistance had stagnated for Africa. These aid flows are critical for treating those infected with HIV/AIDS; the lack of commitment on the part of the G8 countries, with respect to AIDS, could condemn millions to death.

WTO, Intellectual Property, and Access to Medicines

In addition to funding, there is another issue that African countries must negotiate with the world when it comes to HIV/AIDS: access to affordable medicines and intellectual property rights. The past decade has seen ongoing battles between drug companies, who desire to get a return on their investment in new drugs, and public health activists, governments, and patients, who seek affordable medicines. At the 2001 Doha round of the WTO ministerial conference, trade ministers agreed that public health should be promoted by increasing access to affordable medicine. To that end, least-developed countries were granted exemptions on pharmaceutical patent protections until 2016.[48] African countries have benefited greatly from this; prices of ARVs have declined rapidly in the past few years, allowing governments to treat more persons without increasing budgets. However, this process of innovation and lowering prices will have to be continuous, as those who are on ARVs today develop resistance and seek new drugs.

The way in which African health ministries can respond effectively to the challenge of treatment depends not only on their position and bargaining power within the WTO but also upon the patent policies of other countries. For example, India is the primary source of cheap generic ARVs to the developing world.[49] Its domestic policies and patent laws thus have an impact on the availability of affordable medicines in Africa. Before India signed the agreement on Trade Related Aspects of Intellectual Property Rights (TRIPS) in 2005, its patent laws allowed other companies to compete with patent holders, which resulted in cheap generic drugs for the world. However, under the new patent law, companies will no longer be allowed to produce cheaper, generic versions of new drugs.[50] India's decision to sign the TRIPS agreement will have enormous implications for the supply of affordable medicines and access to treatment for Africans and illustrates how Africa's ability to provide treatment for its people is affected by international players.

CONCLUSION

More than twenty-five years into the HIV epidemic, it is clear that there are significant regional differences in the way the disease has impacted African populations. There is not a serious epidemic in North Africa or in most of

West Africa. In central and eastern Africa, prevalence seems to have peaked among adults at less than 20 percent and is now falling. "Ground zero" in terms of HIV is southern Africa. Here, prevalence has reached unprecedented heights. However, this part of the world is only at the beginning of the AIDS epidemic. Mortality will rise, and the number of orphans will grow.

The impact is more complex than often appreciated. It seems that at the national level, AIDS is not currently having a significant macroeconomic impact. Economies are more resilient than anticipated, and the importance of labor as a factor of production is decreasing. However, it is very clear that the epidemic has great effects at the level of individuals and households. AIDS is impoverishing and probably widens the gap between the rich and the poor.

For the international community and its engagement with Africa, AIDS poses some significant questions around national sovereignty and commitment. If African nations are receiving substantial amounts of foreign funding for the treatment and prevention of HIV/AIDS, then there is the inevitable question, Can African governments own or control the problem? The evidence suggests that the answer is no. HIV/AIDS is not high on national agendas, and the ministries of health remain dependent on donor resources.

One of the big questions asked about AIDS is: why have leaders not been more engaged with the issue? President Mbeki of South Africa and his minister of health, Dr. Manto Tsabalala-Msimang, are the most flamboyant examples of a lack of engagement. Similarly, in Swaziland, the king continues to take a new wife every year. In Zambia, the Africa AIDS conference in 1999 was supposed to provide leaders with a chance to put their weight behind responding to the epidemic, yet not a single leader, including the Zambian president, showed up. Why has there been outright denial of AIDS in some countries, most notably in South Africa up to 2007? One answer concerns the time frame. As was shown in Figure 7.2, most of the impact is still in the future, and it is difficult to predict accurately. It is said that politicians look to the next election, whereas statesmen look to the next generation. There have been too few statesmen (and women) involved in the response to the disease. Equally, those of us working in the field have been unable to find the right messages and media to convince the leadership of the importance of tackling this disease. Another possible reason is that the international attention means African governments do not feel that they have ownership of the issue.

That being said, it is largely due to the efforts of the international community that, as of December 2006, an estimated 1.3 million people in sub-Saharan Africa were receiving antiretroviral treatment, with coverage of 28 percent (24–33 percent). In 2003, only 100,000 were on treatment, and coverage was only 2 percent. The median cost of drugs in 2006 was $94 per patient per year.[51]

But if donors are to make the commitment to put a person on treatment, then that commitment has to be for the life of the person. Correctly, the world has moved to provide treatment, but the long-term nature of this has not been appreciated.

In countries with serious epidemics, the situation is dire. In June 2007, the head of Swaziland's National Emergency Response Council on HIV/AIDS, Dr. Derek von Wissell, published an open letter in the local newspaper, in which he described the situation in that country. He talked about the 70,000 orphans in Swaziland and the fact that soon 10 percent of the population would be orphaned children. He then went on to ask:

> What will our society look like in 10 years time if we continue to treat this shocking situation as normal? . . . Swazi society has transformed. We have the highest HIV rate in the world. An estimated 16,000 people die as a result of HIV each year—that is 45 people each day. Life expectancy has dropped from nearly 60 years old in the 1990s to just over 30 years today. Each weekend people are buried. Too many households care for someone who is sick.
>
> All of this is accepted as normal, as if these same things are also happening in the rest of the world? They are not. . . . People live in extreme poverty and silently accept that this should be so—normal. . . . Violence associated with sex has become a norm . . . sexual abuse and violence continues unabated as though normal. . . . Systematic corruption and plundering of public funds and the abuse of privilege is quietly accepted. Nothing can be done; it is the way it is. . . . These abnormal situations now seem normal. We have come to accept the unacceptable. Society has been turned on its head. How will our children know right from wrong when nothing is as it should be? We are no longer a normal society. The time has come for us to do abnormal things to turn our society back to a normal one. We must think about the children and their future.[52]

In the post-9/11 world, normality has changed for us all. In Africa, AIDS has changed what is normal. Concerted international engagement with African states and their citizens will be needed for a number of years as the impacts of the epidemic fully manifest themselves.

NOTES

1. World Health Organization Regional Office for South-East Asia, HIV/AIDS: facts and figures, 2005 http://w3.whosea.org/EN/Section10/Section18/Section348.htm, accessed May 2005.

2. L. Heinecken, "Facing a Merciless Enemy: HIV/AIDS in South African Armed Forces," *Armed Forces and Society* 29 (2003), p. 296.

3. UNAIDS, is the Joint United Nations Programme on HIV/AIDS, bringing together the efforts and resources of ten UN cosponsors including UNHCR, UNICEF, WFP, UNDP, UNFPA, UNODC, ILO, UNESCO, WHO, and the World Bank.

4. The SADC member states are Angola, Botswana, the Democratic Republic of Congo, Lesotho, Madagascar, Malawi, Mauritius, Mozambique, Namibia, South Africa, Swaziland, United Republic of Tanzania, Zambia, and Zimbabwe.

5. See HIV/AIDS survey data at Demographic and Health Surveys, at http://www.measuredhs.com/hivdata/.

6. T. Barnett and A. Whiteside, *AIDS in the Twenty-First Century: Disease and Globalization*, 2nd ed. (Basingstoke: Palgrave Macmillan, 2006).

7. The data cited in this section come from UNAIDS, *2006 Report on the Global AIDS Epidemic*, at http://www.who.int/hiv/mediacentre/news60/en/index.html.

8. Barnett and Whiteside, *AIDS in the Twenty-First Century*.

9. National Intelligence Council, *The Next Wave of HIV/AIDS: Nigeria, Ethiopia, Russia, India, and China*, ICA 2002–04D, September 2002, prepared under the auspices of David F. Gordon, at http://fas.org/irp/nic/hiv-aids.html.

10. UNAIDS, *2006 Report on the Global AIDS Epidemic*, at http://www.unaids.org/en/Regions_Countries/Countries/ethiopia.asp.

11. World Health Organization, Global Price Reporting Mechanism, 2006, at http://www.who.int/3by5/amds/en/.

12. T. J. Boerma, J. Ngalula, R. Isingo, M. Urassa, K. Senkoro, R. Gabone et al., *Levels and Causes of Adult Mortality in Rural Tanzania with Special Reference to HIV/AIDS*. The Socio-Economic Impact of AIDS in Africa Conference, 1997. International Union for the Scientific Study of Population and the University of Natal, Durban.

13. J. A. Adentunji, *Assessing the Mortality Impact of HIV/AIDS Relative to Other Causes of Adult Deaths in Sub Saharan Africa*, the Socio-Demographic Impact of AIDS in Africa Conference, 1997, International Union for the Scientific Study of Population and the University of Natal, Durban.

14. U.S. Census Bureau, "The AIDS Pandemic in the 21st Century," *International Population Reports*, WP/02–2 (Washington D.C.: U.S. Government Printing Office, 2004).

15. M. Haacker, *The Macroeconomics of HIV/AIDS* (Washington, D.C.: International Monetary Fund).

16. UNDP, *Human Development Report*, 2006, at http://hdr.undp.org/hdr2006/statistics/indicators/89.htm.

17. UNAIDS, *2006 Report on the Global AIDS Epidemic*, at http://www.who.int/hiv/mediacentre/news60/en/index.html.

18. M. Over, *Macroeconomic Impact of AIDS in Sub-Saharan Africa* (Washington D.C.: World Bank, Africa Technical Department, Population, Health, and Nutritional Division, 1992).

19. R. Bonnel, "HIV/AIDs and Economic Growth: A Global Perspective," *Journal of South African Economics* 68 (2000), pp. 820–855.

20. The studies are summarized in Table 11.5 of Barnett and Whiteside, *AIDS in the Twenty-First Century*.

21. M. Fox, S. Rosen, W. MacLeod, M. Wasunna, M. Bii, G. Foglia et al., "The Impact of HIV/AIDS on Labour Productivity in Kenya," *Tropical Medicine and International Health* 9 (2004), pp. 318–324.

22. For example, see M. Bachmann and F. Booysen, "Health and Economic Impact of HIV/AIDS on South African Households: A Cohort Study," *BMC Public Health* 3, no. 14 (2003); and T. Yamano and T. S. Jayne, "Measuring the Impact of Working-Age Adult Mortality on Small-Scale Farm Households in Kenya," *World Development* 32, no. 1 (2004), pp. 91–119.

23. A. C. Conroy, M. J. Blackie, A. Whiteside, J. C. Malewezi, and J. Sachs, *Poverty, AIDS and Hunger: Breaking the Poverty Trap in Malawi* (Basingstoke: Palgrave Macmillan, 2006).

24. Remarks as Prepared for Delivery by Vice President Al Gore, U.N. Security Council Session on AIDS in Africa, January 10, 2000, archived at U.S. Department of State, at http://www.state.gov/www/global/oes/health/000110_gore_hiv-aids.html.

25. UN Security Council Resolution 1308, On the Responsibility of the Security Council in the Maintenance of International Peace and Security: HIV/AIDS and International Peace-Keeping Operations, July 2000, at http://www.unmis.org/english/documents/resolutions/res1308.pdf.

26. Gwyn Prins, "AIDS and Global Security," *International Affairs* 80, no. 5 (2004), pp. 931–952.

27. A. Whiteside, A. deWaal, and T. Gebre-Tensae, "AIDS, Security, and the Military in Africa: A Sober Appraisal," *African Affairs* 105 (2006), pp. 201–218.

28. Ibid.

29. L. Garrett, *HIV and National Security: Where Are the Links?* (New York: Council on Foreign Relations, 2005).

30. T. Barnett and G. Prins, "HIV/AIDS and Security Fact, Fiction & Evidence—A Report to UNAIDS." *International Affairs* 82 (2005), pp. 359–368.

31. A. T. Price-Smith and J. L. Daly, "Downward Spiral: HIV/AIDS, State Capacity, and Political Conflict in Zimbabwe," *Peaceworks 53* (2004), pp. 1–52.

32. D. Bevan, "An Analytical Overview of Aid Absorption: Recognizing and Avoiding Macroeconomic Hazards." Seminar on Foreign Aid and Macroeconomic Management, Maputo, Mozambique, 2005.

33. M. Lewis, "Addressing the Challenge of HIV/AIDS: Macroeconomic, Fiscal and Institutional Issues." Working Paper 58 (Washington D.C.: Center for Global Development, 2005).

34. Bevan, "An Analytical Overview of Aid Absorption."

35. "Arrest Call over Uganda AIDS Fund," *BBC News*, May 1, 2007, at http://news.bbc.co.uk/1/hi/world/africa/6613071.stm.

36. A. Swidler, "Syncretism and Subversion in AIDS Governance: How Locals Cope with Global Demands," *International Affairs* 82, no. 2 (2006), pp. 269–284.

37. Nicoli Nattrass, *Mortal Combat: AIDS Denialism and the Struggle for Antiretrovirals in South Africa* (Pietermartizburg: University of KwaZulu-Natal Press, 2007).

38. H. Burkhalter, "The Politics of AIDS: Engaging Conservative Activists," *Foreign Affairs* 83, no. 1 (2004), pp. 8–14.

39. Ibid.

40. D. Altman, "Taboos and Denial in Government Responses," *International Affairs* 82 (2006), pp. 257–268.

41. "Health GAP Report: Between the Lines," 2005, http://www.healthgap.org/camp/pepfar.html.

42. Helen Epstein, *The Invisible Cure: Africa, the West, and the Fight Against AIDS* (New York: Farrar, Straus and Giroux, 2007), p. 194.

43. Commission for Africa, *Our Common Interest: Report of the Commission for Africa*, 2005, at http://www.commissionforafrica.org.

44. Ibid., p. 15.

45. Ibid., p. 72.

46. Summit Documents, Gleneagles Summit, July 8, 2005, at http://www.g8.gov.uk.

47. S. Lewis, RESULTS Educational Fund Annual Conference, June 12, 2007, Washington, D.C.

48. Y. Beigbeder, "HIV/AIDS and Global Regimes: WTO and the Pharmaceutical Industry," in N. Poku, A. Whiteside, and B. Sankjaer, eds., *AIDS and Governance* (Hampshire: Ashgate, 2007).

49. Médecins Sans Frontières, Campaign for Access to Essential Medicines, "Examples of the Importance of India as the 'Pharmacy for the Developing World,'" 2007, at http://www.accessmed-msf.org/prod/publications.asp?scntid=29120071111256&contenttype=PARA&.

50. Médecins Sans Frontières, Campaign for Access to Essential Medicines, "A Key Source of Affordable Medicines Is at Risk of Drying Up: The Case of Novartis's Challenge Against the Indian Government," 2006, at http://www.accessmed-msf.org/prod/publications.asp?scntid=201220061142378&contenttype=PARA&.

51. World Health Organization and UNAIDS, *Towards Universal Access*, April 2007, at http://www.who.int/hiv/mediacentre/universal_access_progress_report_en.pdf.

52. Derek Von Wissel, *Swazi Observer*, June 19, 2007.

8

The Privatization of Africa's International Relations

WILLIAM RENO

This chapter explores growing private actor involvement in the conduct of international relations in Africa. This trend is manifest in the rising importance of foreign energy sector firms in the conduct of these interstate relations. Moreover, nongovernmental organizations (NGOs) continue to proliferate worldwide and seek direct contacts with counterparts in other countries. Since the late 1990s, NGOs have taken on an enhanced importance in the programs that international financial institutions (IFIs) such as the World Bank and the International Monetary Fund (IMF) negotiate with African officials. Multilateral debt forgiveness and post-conflict reconstruction programs reserve ever larger roles for African and non-African NGOs too. Even the conduct of formal diplomacy falls within the scope of privatization. The not-for-profit firm Independent Diplomat, for example, works on behalf of unrecognized states such as the Republic of Somaliland and the Saharawi Arab Democratic Republic.[1]

Many scholars view privatization in Africa of what are commonly thought of as state functions as a step in the failure of states. The privatization of security, for example, is linked to the advent of warlords and mercenary armies.[2] The integration of officials in some African states into global illicit economies, where they manipulate the prerogatives of their offices for personal gain, reinforces this analysis. It points to the "criminalization of the state" that pits private uses of state institutions against the preservation of state capacity.[3] Some identify neoliberal economic policies at the behest of IFIs and foreign governments as responsible for declining state capacities, especially as governments are directed to cut civil service employment and contract more tasks to private sector firms.[4] More generally, the growth in private transactions plays a major role in fueling turmoil in Congo, in persisting factional struggle in Somalia after the collapse of its central government in 1991, and in protracted political instability and violence elsewhere.

An alternative analysis identifies the private conduct of international commercial and financial relations as central to prosperity and increased state capacity. Some IFI analysts regard privatization as the foundation of sub-Saharan Africa's recent economic out-performance of all major regions of the world, except for East Asia. They point to the increasing intensity of private international contacts as responsible for sub-Saharan Africa's 5.7 percent growth in 2006 and expected 6.8 percent growth in 2007, the highest since the early 1970s.[5] For them, privatized international relations makes African states stronger, since this activity generates increased revenues for state administration and bolsters the legitimacy of governments.

The privatization of African international relations therefore is a major element in contentious readings of Africa's future. The argument in this chapter about the privatization of Africa's international relations charts its own course. As I explain below, it is a key to understanding Africa's increasingly differentiated but generally intensified integration into the global economy and its shifting positions in international politics. The core of the argument in the next section is that these trajectories reflect the intersecting interests of African and non-African actors. This chapter is very much about how these interests drive the privatization of Africa's international relations. The subsequent section examines the major channels of this privatization through businesses, NGOs, IFI links, and so forth. The section that follows then focuses on the interests of these different actors. These interactions shape the different political configurations of the privatization of Africa's international relations. I then consider elements of the privatization of Africa's international relations that undermine efforts to strengthen African states. The overall argument, however, is that the privatization of international relations is not only compatible with states. It is fundamental to the shared global elite project of redesigning African states to play more active roles in integrating the continent into the global political economy. Ironically, this leads to greater bureaucratic autonomy for states, or at least for regimes that address the interests of powerful outsiders. Corruption and nepotism continue, but now in a more centralized context that bolsters state power. This sustains the delivery of goods and services, which regime elites and powerful outsiders agree are necessary, but offers little to bolster democratic processes.

THE ARGUMENT

The argument in this chapter accepts the analysis that some types of privatization lead to greater involvement of state officials in illicit activities at the expense of state administrative capacity. Privatization of this type promotes disorder and is associated with state failure and conflicts in places like Liberia, Sierra Leone, Congo, and Somalia since the end of the Cold War. Liberia's President Charles Taylor (1997–2003) exemplified this kind of privatization. During 2000 and 2001, he used his state office to manage personal business ventures that produced about $500 million in revenues for his own enrichment and to sustain his political network. This occurred against the Government of Liberia's annual revenues of only about $60 million at that time.[6]

At the same time, the proliferation of private channels of international relations brings new resources to African regimes in ways that do not entirely replace state institutions. These diverse links beyond Africa's frontiers constitute part of what Christopher Clapham calls the "politics of state survival." Many regimes use links to overseas nonstate actors to enhance their domestic control when rulers lack the institutional or material resources to do this for themselves.[7] Private foreign investors can help regimes control territory in ways that ultimately promote an international image of the state as able to assert domestic sovereignty. Foreign NGOs provide services to citizens and in the process help state officials to manage internal disorder and sustain the construction of indigenous institutions that claim credit for the delivery of social services that outsiders provide. In Uganda, for example, donor support of more than $800 million annually finances over half of the state budget and 80 percent of development spending.[8] Outsiders underwrite this mutually beneficial arrangement. They help improve conditions in local people's lives and enlist the government as the main partner in maintaining order and predictability in a country bordering three others that have seen major conflicts in recent years. This in turn helps increase the control and durability of the regime as it plays a key role in channeling these outside resources.

This sort of privatization of international relations for the benefit of domestic regimes is not new in Africa. The remarkable rise of King Ja Ja of Opobo in the nineteenth-century Niger Delta occurred as European government suppressed the old slave trading basis of the local economy in favor of commerce in palm oil and other industrial commodities. The shift in policy enabled this enterprising son of slaves to translate his personal connections to Liverpool traders to build his own politico-commercial empire.[9] Closer to our own times, the activities in the 1980s of Roland "Tiny" Rowland, the head of Lonrho Corporation, provided another example of how state officials and private foreign actors could pursue related interests together. Rowland provided his personal diplomatic skills and private jet to bring together insurgent leaders and heads of state to negotiate peace as he built the relationships with incumbent and future rulers that enhanced the profitability of his business ventures. But these earlier versions of privatization did not reinforce the external image of statehood or reshape domestic institutions as systematically as important forms of privatization do today.

A key point of this analysis is that the current privatization of Africa's international relations actually is part of the large process of the homogenization and standardization of the organization of African states on a Western model. As the contemporary version of privatization has taken over many of the tasks of state-to-state and multilateral aid of the 1960s and 1970s, its designers now seek to build African states in a new image. The establishment of new institutions such as Ministry of Gender and Development and the reform of others turn them into useful focal points for foreign NGO aid and "public-private partnerships" that utilize corporate contributions to force shifts in the domestic politics of African states and the priorities of African officials. In more extreme instances, private firms simply take over state institutions; for example, some governments contract with the British firm Crown Agents to collect tariffs and other fees. In doing so, they aim to shape institutions in the image of successful modern Western states. This creates conditions in which the universality of the state, and in particular the model of efficient bureaucracies driven by the discipline of global markets, is secured as the principal basis for political order in Africa.

At first glance, African officials seem to have little leverage in their relations with non-African states, creditor institutions, foreign NGOs, and private firms. Africa's shrinking share of global exports from about 7.2 percent in 1948 to 1.8 percent in 2004 and the near total absence of African private investment outside the continent (except from South Africa) underlines this peripheral status.[10] But external priorities still offer potential political tools to those who run states. Officials in some African states find that intensified private international relations increase the value of controlling the prerogatives of state sovereignty. Individual officials also find that their relations with new private actors can be used to promote the fortunes of their own faction. This informal aspect of international relations reflects shared interests and the overlapping strategic calculations of different elite groups that previously had less contact. On one level, this interaction promotes global networking among African and foreign officials and a variety of NGOs and commercial groups. They may come to a common understanding of the relationship between private markets and governance and, in particular, the disciplining effect that the efficiency of global markets has on domestic economic policies and bureaucratic function. But this interaction also gives officials in particular African states leverage to call bluffs and to exploit the vulnerabilities and anxieties of their more powerful partners. The appearance of private participants in the relations between states gives officials in less powerful African states entrée into the domestic politics of powerful states. African officials then call upon their partners to pressure democratic governments to heed the shared interests of African officials and their private foreign partners.

Thus a second key element of this analysis is that these relationships between African and non-African actors contain surprisingly high degrees of reciprocity that measures of material inequalities miss. African officials and non-African officials, for example, share a strong interest in making African states more capable. Most non-African private actors in this relationship also desire stronger states. But motivations for this preference vary. African officials see opportunities to expand the power and security of their regime or a particular faction. Foreign businesses desire greater security for current investments, access to new commercial opportunities, and protection from unruly populations that predictable and stable strong states offer. Many non-African officials want to change the priorities of African states through privatized international relations, whether through greater NGO engagement or commercial expansion to tilt African governments toward more accommodating positions on global commercial and political norms. Their belief is that this will create more capable African states as they become more integrated into global commercial networks. Then officials there will become more able and interested in monitoring citizens and controlling borders. Ultimately, shared interests are critical to this relationship, as engineering such a change in the design of African states would be beyond the material or political capacity of non-African states to orchestrate through direct pressure.

Integrating public and private international relations has become more urgent for European and American officials after the September 11, 2001, al-Qaeda attacks on New York and Washington. President Bush declared: "The events of September 11, 2001, taught us that weak states, like Afghanistan, can pose as great a danger to our national interests as strong states . . . poverty, weak institutions, and corruption can make weak states vulnerable to terrorist networks and drug cartels within their borders."[11] Britain's Foreign Secretary Jack Straw also linked weak states to a growing security threat: "After the mass murder in the heart of Manhattan, no one can doubt that a primary threat to our security is now posed by groups acting outside formal states, or from places where no state functions at all. It is no longer possible to ignore misgoverned parts of a world without borders, where chaos is a potential neighbour anywhere from Africa to Afghanistan."[12] Privatized international relations play a major role in the security policies of these two countries. "Trade is seen as an important element of drawing countries more deeply into a global web of capitalism and democracy," wrote U.S. foreign policy advisors, "without which the international community, and the West and the U.S. in particular, run the risk of alienation and radicalism and their effects."[13]

Strategic concerns about access to oil also link African regimes to non-African states and private actors. Since 2000, U.S. competition with China for access to Africa's oil has emerged as a major new strategic issue. "To compete more effectively with China," wrote a Council on Foreign Relations Task Force, "the United States must . . . develop more innovative means for U.S. companies to compete" and must emphasize "public–private partnerships."[14] Likewise, the emergence of Angola in 2006 as China's largest foreign supplier of oil raises the stakes of "energy international relations" in Africa for Chinese officials too.

This inclusion of private actors into the strategic policies of non-African states creates new points of leverage for African officials. Chinese loans of nearly $2 billion to Angola for construction projects, for example, enable Angola's government to resist IMF demands that it reform its economic regulations. Anxieties of non-African states to maintain access to African oil or to bolster African efforts to resist terrorist infiltration can be used to renegotiate or ignore earlier agreements. NGOs that are drawn in to promote "good governance" alongside investments in oil production can be used to help pacify local populations. The appearance of local NGO partners, with some political backing, also may convince outside actors that the regime is committed to more open politics and anti-corruption surveillance.

Ultimately, Africa's privatized international relations strengthen the hands of officials in African states, but only if they accept the broad requirement to participate in global markets and at least pay lip service to pluralist politics at home. It reinforces sovereignty, since much of this new activity is focused on bolstering Africa's existing states to the disadvantage of regime critics and those who would want to reorganize the continent's politics on a different basis. But this chapter also shows how the privatization of Africa's international relations provides African officials with considerable leeway to reshape domestic politics to their own benefit. In this sense, the privatization of Africa's international relations, an important feature of what is commonly called "globalization," is neither radical nor overpowering. Instead it supports existing states by design and existing regimes by practice. It is firmly hitched to a hegemonic effort to quell ideological challenges and security threats that menace the status quo. Thus, it is deeply conservative. The expansion and intensity of international relations through these new channels is novel, however, and is the subject of the next section. In this regard, it marks a new phase in the development of Africa's state system.

THE CHANNELS OF AFRICA'S PRIVATIZED INTERNATIONAL RELATIONS

The energy sector has become a major arena of privatized international relations. By the end of 2006, Africa had surpassed the Middle East region as the largest foreign supplier of oil to the United States and was predicted to supply 25 percent of American oil imports by 2015 (a degree of regional dependence that China reached in 2006).[15] The involvement of the foreign policy establishments of these two countries in the African oil sector overshadows the efforts of other countries. This was not true in the fairly recent past. Until the 1990s, French officials pursued vigorous privatized international relations in Africa through *la Francafrique*, a network linking French government officials, military officers and weapons, and oil firms to African elites. This led to the Elf scandal of the 1990s, in which executives of the recently privatized oil firm skimmed nearly $350 million for personal use and to buy political favors from officials in Angola, Cameroon, and Congo-Brazzaville. Then the advance of World Trade Organization standards for commercial relations helped to undo France's privileged relations with African client states and exposed the continent to growing U.S. and Chinese competition.[16]

The American and Chinese search for African oil exports brings private capital and state officials into a new set of tight relationships. The use of state-owned oil exploration and drilling companies makes the relationship more direct in the case of China. Sinopec produces oil in Sudan and Angola, for example, as part of an official Chinese policy to diversify sources of energy. But private investment also plays a big role in Chinese relations with African states. China's Ministry of Commerce maintains an extensive network of officials in Africa to promote commercial relations with individual countries, organize trade exhibitions, and arrange visits for officials.[17] This has been particularly successful in Angola, where large-scale Chinese oil-field investments and the $2 billion soft loan create opportunities for Chinese construction firms to play a major role in building that country's infrastructure.

Although private firms loom larger in U.S. commercial relations, U.S. practice bears some resemblance to the Chinese practice. U.S. government agencies, such as the Overseas Private Investment Corporation and the Export-Import Bank, help to "mobilize the U.S. private sector to advance U.S. foreign policy and development initiatives."[18] The private-sector U.S.-Angola Chamber of Commerce also helps to coordinate deals in a manner that demonstrates the difficulty of establishing firm boundaries between public and private spheres. For example, the head of the private organization was a special U.S. government envoy to Angola who helped to negotiate the country's 1994 peace agreement. The migration of personnel between these public and private roles helps to coordinate trade and investment missions with the activities and interests of a variety of U.S. agencies. Officials in Angola recognize the importance of this private-sector relationship. Their initiation in 2000 of thrice weekly, direct Luanda–Houston air service underlined the importance of this relationship to Angola's government,[19] as did their hiring of former U.S. officials as lobbyists to represent their interests in Washington.

The U.S. interest in oil has led to other "public–private partnerships" that have tapped corporate donations to supplement official U.S. bilateral aid to Angola, thereby effectively increasing the bilateral assistance budget by 20 percent. This includes a March 2007 launch of a five-year, $5.5 million partnership between USAID and the Chevron Corporation focused on agricultural development projects.[20] This partnership fit the criteria of USAID's Global Development Alliance (GDA) program, which was devised in 2001 by the Bush administration to leverage corporate and private foundation material support for projects that also receive U.S. government funding.[21] These projects stress the leadership of the private sector, as GDA guidelines stipulate a maximum U.S. government financial stake of 50 percent.

Multinational corporations develop their own versions of "public–private partnerships." While U.S. and other non-African government officials are more concerned with leveraging their finances, corporate concerns focus on managing political risk. Oil producers in Nigeria's Niger Delta, for example, face considerable local opposition to their activities. Allegations that Shell's Nigerian subsidiary supplied material support to the Nigerian government's repression of local political activists in the 1990s created a serious public relations crisis for Shell in Nigeria and abroad and threatened the viability of its operations in Nigeria. The December 1998 Kaiama Declaration of Ijaw Youths asking foreign oil producers to leave the Delta highlighted the threat of local opposition. Opposition eventually produced an armed insurgency, Movement for the Emancipation of the Niger Delta, which kidnaps oil-field employees and attacks oil production facilities.

Frustrated with corrupt Nigerian authorities who fail to use oil revenues for the benefit of citizens, Shell and other foreign corporations have tried to directly manage their private international relations with local Delta communities. This has taken the form of payouts to "community leaders," some of whom demand payments in return for promises not to attack corporate targets.[22] The problem for these oil companies is that Nigeria's government is not an effective protector of property or manager of the country's domestic politics. This problem prompted a corporate shift to more comprehensive "corporate partnerships" with local and regional Nigerian authorities and NGOs. Their hope was to put local governments and NGOs in place of the national government as providers of basic services. This, they hoped, would shift public ire for poor community conditions to local government officials instead of the foreign corporations that produce the country's main source of wealth. Shell and its local subsidiary already had spent $336 million on community development projects between 1997 and 2003, some in partnership with international organizations and foreign NGOs.[23]

Corporate spending on development projects in the Niger Delta intersects with USAID's GDA program. Citing the strategic importance of Nigerian stability and its role as a major supplier of oil to the United States, USAID partnered with Chevron to finance a Youth Education and Self-Reliance Project, one of several such collaborations.[24] These programs serve multiple purposes. They help private corporations divorce themselves as much as possible from corrupt officials with whom they have been associated in the eyes of the public. They bring American aid officials directly into the micro-politics of often violent relations with local communities. Oil producers then can find help from American embassy and Washington-based officials to force Nigeria's government to address problems of corruption and to assert more effective control over the Niger Delta. The relationship also more solidly ties the issue of corporate access to oil and local political stability to national security concerns. From the point of view of corporate interests, privatized international relations that bring in NGOs and non-African government officials are an effective way of reducing political risk. Ironically, privatized international relations enable corporations to get American officials to effectively nationalize an important element of commercial risk that has hindered investment in parts of Africa.

Foreign NGOs also play growing roles in policymaking and budget priorities in Nigeria as a whole. A condition of the 2005 G8 summit decision to cancel $31 billion of Nigeria's $36 billion foreign debt included the creation of a monitoring body to track expenditures of revenues that now will not have to go toward debt payments. Nigeria's government created the Virtual Poverty Fund and included Nigerian associates of Oxfam and Action Aid as an oversight body to track its $1 billion annual expenditures. Uganda's Poverty Action Fund, also linked to debt relief, includes local NGO monitors too. A principal monitor, the Poverty Action Fund Monitoring Committee, includes local NGOs funded through Oxfam, the Washington-based International Budget Project, and Scandinavian government aid agencies.[25]

Negotiating this new set of international relations requires cross-national compatibilities in bureaucratic management and capacity. In preparation for Nigeria's negotiations for debt relief, Britain's Department for International

Development (DfID) engaged the private British consultancy Crown Agents to help Nigerian officials redesign their institutions and change their operating procedures to even begin to negotiate this deal. This essentially involved tallying the financial commitments that numerous Nigerian official agencies had incurred and standardizing data reporting. In Angola, Crown Agents helped Angola's government restructure its customs and tax collection system and prepare a Consolidated Customs Code to meet the standards of international organizations such as the World Customs Organization and the WTO. Crown Agents also ran Mozambique's customs service for a decade up to 2006, and in the words of the country's finance minister, leaving "a modern customs service that has been permanently adapted to international trade and security demands."[26]

Crown Agents and other consultants and "public–private partnerships" essentially stand in for government agencies when smooth international relations require standardized practice and function and are thus powerful "enablers" of globalization on the terms of the world's rich countries.[27] Non-African governments and multilateral institutions hire Crown Agents and other private consultancies to reform or even outright create the kinds of African government institutions that these outsiders need in order to begin to engage in the kinds of state-to-state relations and thereby enable African participation in the multilateral agreements that they require. For example, the UN's Millennium Development Goals poverty reduction program has spawned official aid initiatives, such as the U.S. government's Millennium Challenge Account. All such programs require uniform data collection, reporting, and procurement procedures as part of their operating procedures, much less the larger goals of promoting government reform and boosting government efficiency in poor countries. Sometimes this can take the form of outright policy execution, as in Crown Agents' health services delivery program in Nigeria in partnership with DfID and a Nigerian NGO consortium.

A more institutionalized example of public–private relationships appears in arrangements surrounding the construction of the Chad-Cameroon oil pipeline. Fearing involvement in the kinds of problems of local corruption and violence that had been plaguing them in Nigeria, Shell and Elf withdrew in 1999 from the consortium organized to build the pipeline. In response to the continuing threat that political risks posed to this project, World Bank officials devised a Petroleum Revenue Management Program and made its support for the $3.7 billion project contingent on Chad's acceptance of this proposal. This plan made World Bank funding for the project, and thus the Chad government revenues from oil, contingent upon a promise that it would allocate 72 percent of oil receipts to social services, 4.5 percent to local pipeline communities, and 10 percent to a trust fund for the post-oil era, leaving 13.5 percent for general revenues. The agreement created the Collège de Contrôle et de Surveillance de la Gestation des Ressources Pétrolières, which included local NGO members to approve Chad's government expenditures of oil revenues.

Chad's president, Idriss Déby, soon defied consortium efforts to control his government's spending. He himself came to power in a coup in 1990. In 2005, Déby faced a growing rebellion. Rebels included members of the military and even some of his family after Déby changed the constitution to run for election to a third term. Facing a serious threat to this regime, in January 2006, Déby abolished the trust fund and used the money to buy weapons. This move, along with French military intervention, helped him to weather the April 2006 rebel invasion of his capital, which resulted in 400 deaths. World Bank officials cut off loans, but after Déby threatened to halt oil production, the Bank restored them without requiring Déby to retreat from his position. At the same time, Chad's government opened negotiations with Beijing to recognize mainland China in place of Taiwan.

These "public–private partnerships" represent a major advance in the privatization of Africa's international relations, particularly when it concerns African relations to non-African actors. Non-African state officials and officials of multilateral organizations use private firms and NGOs to leverage the impact of their policies and expenditures in Africa. At first glance, this appears to intensify an already drastically unequal relationship. African officials' struggles to get debts canceled and to do business with the rest of the world bring with them ever higher degrees of foreign intervention in the inner workings of their own governments. It brings direct foreign government contact with NGOs within African countries to change the behavior of African governments. This has been branded as a new form of colonialism in media in Africa and abroad. It raises suspicions in some quarters, in the wake of "color revolutions" in Ukraine, Georgia, Kyrgyzstan, and Lebanon, that involved NGOs and private groups within these countries had close contacts with foreign NGOs and governments.[28]

The politics of the privatization of Africa's international relations shows that these relationships are not quite so one-sided. They offer selective leverage to African officials that they did not possess under a more exclusively state-to-state international relations. They boost both the façade and the material substance of state sovereignty insofar as they bolster the capacity of governments to monitor people and manage transactions. This outcome reflects a broadly shared agenda on the part of African and non-African officials. As the evidence and argument in the next section show, these relationships have a tendency to strengthen the role of executives in African governments. They bypass formal government institutions of deliberation, albeit often dysfunctional ones, in favor of more decisive and predictable "partnerships" that can more easily deliver desired policy outcomes. At the same time, these "partnerships" also strengthened the position of incumbent factions in power and redirected policies toward domestic and foreign actors who may be more easily manipulated than a leader's own domestic political opposition.

AFRICAN REGIME STRATEGIES AND PRIVATIZED INTERNATIONAL RELATIONS

There is a high degree of mutuality of interests in Africa's privatized international relations among African and non-African actors, regardless of whether they are holding offices in states or not. This is because most of them have compelling interests in maintaining the present state-centric structure of the international system. To this end, they strive to increase the capacity of Africa's states to monitor citizens, control territory, promote commerce, and provide basic services for citizens to bring them into closer contact with markets. These tasks require adopting uniform practice and standardized institutions. Thus, the privatization of Africa's international relations represents the latest stage of the Westernization of African states, following in the wake of the failure of the post–World War II modernist vision of state-led development.

Most African elites share this state-centric focus, since so many of them depend upon their association with a particular state to maintain this status. Alongside this, they have interests related to the maintenance of regimes and personal access to power. Greater private sector participation in the conduct of international relations provides them with more points of leverage to pursue those particular interests. This is especially true when non-Africans' interest in state maintenance coincides with regime maintenance, as it often does. This in turn generates more flexibility for African officials to strengthen their positions in domestic politics, provided they succeed in presenting a convincing external image of reform to their foreign interlocutors.

The current state of affairs bears some resemblance to Cold War–era international relations. During the Cold War, African leaders could use their positions as heads of sovereign states to bargain with much more powerful superpower patrons. They maximized their international and domestic freedom of action through trading diplomatic alignment for resources to build their domestic power bases and confront their rivals.[29] The overarching strength of the particular foreign patron did not preclude leverage on the part of the weaker client. Threats of withdrawal of aid were met with hints of switching alignments and exploiting patron fears that other clients might judge them to be unreliable or ungenerous patrons.

Much of this flexibility on the part of weaker client states seemed to disappear as the Cold War ended. The nearly simultaneous declarations in 1990–1991 of transitions to multiparty electoral systems across the continent followed internal, and now sudden external, pressures on regimes to give up their monopolies on power. Since then, the increasing privatization of Africa's international relations seems to reinforce this external capacity to determine internal political arrangements, and as creditors gained the upper hand, the internal economic policies of Africa's states as well. However, this ambitious project of reforming African states presents targeted officials with opportunities reminiscent of their Cold War–era counterparts. Recall the situation of Chad's President Déby in 2005–2006 noted above. His creditors imposed tight controls over how he could spend revenues from oil production in return for encouraging the private foreign investment in this industry that made his windfall possible. But when faced with domestic challenges to his rule, Déby violated his agreement and used this money to buy guns instead.

The intensification of private interests in Africa's international relations handed Déby new levers of negotiation with his foreign partners. Once foreign private oil producers had invested in Chad's production, they were loathe to abandon their fixed assets. Officials in Western states, particularly in the United States, were anxious to keep Chad's oil on global markets. Déby's confrontation coincided with the intensification of the insurgency in Iraq and the realization that Iraqi oil production would not rise in the near future. Alongside troubles in a minor oil producer like Chad, attacks on Nigerian oil installations and low Iraqi production posed threats to the economies of rich countries. Moreover, such problems were likely to have an impact on the looming November 2006 congressional elections in the United States. Déby's own situation perhaps provided him with his strongest point of leverage. World Bank President Paul Wolfowitz, "concerned about causing the collapse of Chad's government, which would risk turning the country into a failed state and a haven for terrorists,"[30] ended sanctions against Chad and accepted Déby's alteration of the original agreement. Although Chad's government agreed to reinstate controls on expenditures in 2006, rebel attacks on the capital in late 2007 again caused its foreign partners to grow concerned that the overthrow of this regime would bring chaos in its place.

Angola's government also has leveraged outsiders' conditions through negotiating with Chinese firms to boost oil production. Following the Chinese government's $2 billion soft loan in March 2004 and the 2005 visit of the Chinese leader to Angola, Chinese firms agreed to invest about $1 billion in infrastructure projects. Then in May 2006, Chinese and Angolan officials agreed to a $2.2 billion joint venture to develop new offshore oil fields. Meanwhile,

Angolan officials informed the IMF that they would not continue to negotiate to reschedule the country's debt or ask for IMF-monitored loans. This choice of external partners enabled Angolan officials to run the country's oil industry as they see fit, which has included continuing to skim off oil revenues to redistribute on the basis of domestic political criteria, to buy the political support of members of the country's elite, and to purchase weapons. A Human Rights Watch report estimated that these diversions exceeded $4 billion between 1997 and 2002, a practice that IMF oversight would threaten.[31] Moreover, engagement with Chinese businesses permitted the regime to begin major infrastructure projects in transportation and communication, which will expand citizens' capacity to engage in commerce. They also translate into tools to shape domestic politics to the extent that they enhance the regime's capacity to control and monitor territory and citizens, a pressing concern after the 2002 conclusion of Angola's twenty-seven-year civil war.

Angola's poor relations with the IMF do not appear to have damaged the country's private international relations with oil firms in the United States or elsewhere. These "public–private partnerships" with oil companies and bilateral aid agencies provide the country's officials with new channels of contact and influence overseas. Because Angola is a major oil producer, its officials have the capacity to play contending interests in foreign countries against one another to its advantage. If forced to choose between backing IMF demands for fiscal probity and maintaining good commercial relations with this major oil producer, governments in most oil-consuming countries would consider the second quite seriously. The Angolan government's pursuit of its own private international relations helps to reinforce this choice. In the United States, for example, Angola's government employs C/R International, a major Washington lobbyist, to help represent its interests in Washington and to participate in organizing U.S.-Angola Chamber of Commerce events.[32]

The recruitment of private firms to run state agencies also creates new options in domestic politics for state officials. Contracting the Houston firm OIC Services to oversee Angola's shipping certification and fee collection removes a key task from the hands of untrustworthy state agencies and puts it under the control of a foreign firm with no incentive to challenge the political position of the government that pays its fees.[33] This exercises sovereign prerogatives of the state to regulate external relations more decisively in the interests of the country's regime, much as the use of firms like Crown Agents in Angola and in other countries channels revenues more directly to the top of domestic political hierarchies.

Foreign firms' engagement in tasks customarily reserved for states serves two interests: The first is to assuage the anxiety of foreigners by ensuring that the corrupt and incompetent bureaucracies of a weak state will no longer be charged with handling resources. The second interest is that of the country's leadership. Foreign firms collect these revenues on behalf of the state that employs them. The state, in this view of interests, is coterminous with the regime. Moreover, effective collection and delivery of these revenues enhances the standing of the regime in international circles. Just as politicians in recent elections in France and the United States have discovered that voters approve of them more highly when they run against their own establishments, African presidents win support from foreigners when they campaign against their own state bureaucracies. This also can help leaders shed patronage obligations, which presents an image of reform overseas while it centralizes power at home.

Thus, institutions with foreign NGO or foreign-backed local NGO monitors, such as Nigeria's Virtual Poverty Fund and Uganda's Poverty Action Fund, cut out layers of corrupt bureaucracy and simplify the process of allocating resources to social services. The intersection of interests can be considerable. Foreign firms that produce domestic revenues benefit from bringing a new agency responsible for state spending between them and corrupt politicians. This helps insulate firms from popular complaints of government corruption that lead to citizen demands on firms to hand over income directly to them for the local resources that the firm exploits. These arrangements may even result in more effective deliveries of service and enhance the popularity of rulers.

This intersection of interests creates a powerful coalition that pushes for greater integration of African states into the global political economy. It recalls Fareed Zakaria's admonition that developing countries should expand the rights of individuals to conduct commerce and to protect their property, and to provide effective administration, even if only as "liberal semi-democracies."[34] Such reforms rest upon intensified reliance of African governments on private technocratic experts, in the form of consultants like those who work for firms like Crown Agents, or NGO policy experts, in organizations like Oxfam or Action Aid. The popular legitimacy for these policies or these foreigners engaged in domestic politics is not about responding to popular will. Instead, it is about eventually getting enough citizens to see that the new policies are the correct ones, and that they are better than the old ones. In Zakaria's analysis, successful economies in places like Singapore and Chile came about only because "benign despotisms and dictatorships" undertook reforms that no elected politician would dare attempt.[35] Likewise, in Africa these elements of privatized international relations provide the global alliances and domestic conditions to force forward the process of reform.

Although the incorporation of privatized international elements into domestic political affairs may lack popular legitimacy, it creates opportunities to attack their own government, as in Nigeria, for example, where thirty-one of Nigeria's thirty-six governors were indicted on charges of corruption in 2007. In the months before the 2007 elections, five political opponents of the president were impeached for violating constitutional procedures. The appearance of decisive action against corrupt officials garnered short-term benefit for the president to address a significant drop in popular trust in the electoral process and in the nation's democratic institutions.[36] For example, 70 percent of people living in the oil producing regime who were surveyed in 2000 expressed trust in the one-year-old electoral process that had just replaced a military dictatorship. By 2003, only 9 percent did so. Likewise, nation-wide surveys indicated that state institutions and officials were held in low regard for their inefficiency and corruption, even if democracy as an ideal remained popular. Economic reforms also were held in low regard by a significant portion of Nigerians. Efforts to increase the value added tax and cut fuel subsidies, one of the few concrete benefits that Nigerians have seen of their country's oil wealth, provoked a general strike in June 2007.

Thus in spite of the unpopularity of many reforms, the tendency for new foreign actors to take over elements of state function can help presidents carry out contentious reforms, while adopting a populist stance and bolstering their own political positions. These privately assisted reforms in turn bind national governments to a wide array of practices, standards, and specific economic policies that expose their national economies and government bureaucracies to the discipline of the global markets.

DISRUPTIVE EXCEPTIONS

Some NGOs target specific regimes to ostracize them. This behavior defies the proposition that Africa's privatized international relations reinforce state capacity and regime security in tandem. For example, Global Witness played a significant role in the British government's campaign in favor of UN sanctions against Charles Taylor's regime (1997–2003) in Liberia that contributed to his removal from power. Global Witness detailed how Liberian officials were involved in the illicit trade in diamonds to support insurgencies in neighboring countries.[37] Likewise, the International Crisis Group conducts research detailing how corrupt officials in some countries engage in the weapons trade with combatants in war zones. The Sudan government's violations of human rights in Darfur have also drawn NGO attention. Many campaign for international intervention, including military, against the domestic policies of Sudan's government.

This involvement highlights two main points. First, NGOs are most threatening to regimes whose behavior diverges most from evolving international standards. Thus, governments such as those in Zimbabwe and Sudan have become targets of NGO campaigns to ostracize them, cut off their resources, and provoke a transition. Second, most NGOs contribute to the reinforcement of uniform standards of internal governance in Africa. Ironically, the Zimbabwe government's legalization of opposition parties and its conduct of competitive multiparty elections, albeit rigged ones, demonstrate the extent to which uniformity and standardization have become imperatives—even in that state. But Zimbabwe's Mugabe regime is still an anachronism. Such conduct twenty-five years earlier in that region would have marked Zimbabwe as one of its most democratic states. But now virtually all governments in Africa conduct regularly scheduled multiparty elections, even if these are not always accepted as fair. The trade of local resources for illicit purposes—for example, government involvement in sales of "conflict diamonds" to fund weapons for insurgents—which has become a growing concern since the 1990s, has become an area of aggressive NGO concern.

The NGO practice of distinguishing between regime and state creates for them a distinct sphere of privatized international relations that differs from that of private commerce. Most NGOs are "private" in the sense that they conceive of their activities as taking place against repressive state authority. Ideally, in a liberal political context, this NGO activity contributes to the legitimacy of states and regimes. This activity compels state officials to consider societal needs and interests, and can become the basis of mutually supportive relations in a political system that tolerates the engagement of plural interests. This is one of the reasons why both indigenous and foreign NGOs are popular with foreign creditors and donors. They make governments behave better or, in the case of ostracized regimes, apply pressure to force fundamental changes in regime practice or to remove them altogether.

Firms, however, depend upon the consent of regimes to allow them access to the territory of a particular state to exploit domestic commercial opportunities. They need to convince regimes to exercise other prerogatives of sovereignty on their behalf too. Firms need to produce official documents that explain their operations for investors and regulators in other countries, for example. Firms can collude with African officials to produce fraudulent documents and other services that officials can provide by virtue of their sovereign status. But it is rare for firms to actively conspire to remove a regime or do business directly with regime enemies such as rebels. The few that attempt this usually find themselves in court. For example, in the early 1990s Firestone Tire & Rubber allegedly paid protection payments to a rebel group that controlled their Liberian rubber plantation, which later incurred the wrath of the Liberian government in U.S. District Courts.[38] More recently, in 2004 a syndicate of British and South African businessmen attempted to overthrow the government of Equatorial Guinea to install a compliant successor regime that would then sign lucrative contracts for oil field services. Various participants ended up in criminal and civil courts in several countries, targets of the Equatorial Guinea government's legitimate ire.[39] Access to foreign courts emerges as yet another prerogative of sovereignty accessible even to the very weakest states. Most firms can sue governments, but firms that try to overthrow governments or do deals with rebels lose legal standing, whereas NGOs that try to eliminate governments that are widely considered to be odious may even receive support from overseas officials, as happened when Global Witness targeted Liberia's President Taylor.

NGOs generally enjoy more autonomy than firms in their relations with Africans. At their most threatening, some foreign NGOs have helped their armed enemies. For example, when remnants of Rwanda's genocidal regime fled and settled in refugee camps in Congo, "hundreds of NGOs" arrived in the camps and spent $1.4 billion for aid in eight months in 1994. Former government officials and activists from Rwanda skimmed off part of this aid. "The chaotic situation and abundant aid provided a windfall for the militants, who used it to support their planned invasion of Rwanda."[40] Some scholars claim that NGOs willingly aid militants, viewing this as an unfortunate necessity to reach those in need or simply to ignore the problem to avoid upsetting contributors.[41]

Some regimes defend themselves from what they consider to be threatening activities of foreign and indigenous NGOs with government-operated NGOs (GONGOs), which pose as NGOs but act as vehicles for state interests. GONGOs in Africa attract overseas aid partners.[42] Notable examples include the "private" Angolan Eduardo dos Santos Foundation, named after the country's president. This GONGO accepts donations from foreign oil producers and distributes the proceeds under the president's direction as a private individual.[43] Likewise, the Ecological Youth of Angola is under presidential direction, while receiving sponsorship from corporations and UN agencies. Nigeria's military governments in the 1980s and 1990s maintained GONGOs under the direction of the president's wife. Maryam Babangida's Better Life for Rural Women and Maryam Abacha's Family Economic Advancement Programme presented an international image of responsiveness to societal concerns, while allowing benefits to be channeled according to the political interests of the regime.

A SUSTAINABLE CHANGE?

The privatization of Africa's international relations occurs alongside what is commonly known as globalization. More than the intensification of global commercial transactions, it reflects the standardization of a model of states based on market economies and competitive domestic politics. The result has been to diminish the relative exclusivity of officials of states in the conduct of relations with foreigners and has produced much greater uniformity in policies. Except in Zimbabwe, inflation and exchange controls that were once common across the continent have disappeared. Markets are crowded with foreign goods. The rhetorical commitment to competitive elections is nearly universal. Governments sign protocols on a bewildering array of issues, from security to trade to environmental protection and much else besides. As a Sierra Leone government official commented, "it is too much for a small country to even keep track, much less meaningfully comply."[44] Thus, the state has become less exclusive as a political actor, yet more important as a coordinator and monitor of this new activity. Since the mid-1990s, major agreements on food standards, shipping inspection certificates, air traffic control, commercial arbitration, and a multitude of other activities have become important elements in the domestic policies and national interests of the world's most powerful countries. Participation in this evolving global system thus now requires performance of these tasks as well.

The privatization of Africa's international relations plays a critical role in bolstering the capacities of many African states. Privatized international relations challenge the exclusivity of sovereignty but need not threaten officials in targeted states. There is nothing new in this. Stephen Krasner observed that sovereignty has always been challenged. Nineteenth-century European Great Powers, for example, intervened massively in the affairs of new states in the Balkans. They appointed government ministers, commanded national armies, installed comptrollers in finance ministries and banks, and wrote their constitutions to ensure that local people built their states according to the proper model.[45] Africa's proliferating privatized foreign relations with the rest of the world represents much the same process of standardization, or what used to be called modernization and Westernization.

Stronger states have been the result in Africa in the sense of states acquiring greater capabilities to control their domestic realms and to conduct their relations with outsiders. Although "Afro-pessimists" enjoy a vogue in some intellectual circles, this process has contributed to a significant shift in Africa's position in the world's political economy. As noted above, Africa's oil attracts intense outside interest. Significantly, since 1995, sub-Saharan African economies have enjoyed their fastest decade of economic growth since the early 1970s. Economic growth reached 5 percent in the decade prior to 2006. This surge in growth is largely a consequence of a boom in Africa's natural resource commodity exports. Moreover, Africa's global economic focus has begun to shift. Intensified economic relations with the United States and China have contributed to a 50 percent decline in the European Union's share of African exports.[46] This shift is important for the role it plays in determining which powerful country's standards become the model for building effective states in Africa.

These changes may give poor people in Africa more of a stake in the contemporary market-driven global system. This seems possible even in some of Africa's major non-oil-producing countries. For example, between 2000 and 2006, Ghana experienced a growth rate of 5.5 percent; Uganda, 5.9 percent; and Tanzania, 6.7 percent.[47] Taking account of population growth, the per capita income of Tanzanians is projected to double in fifteen years. Ghana's economy shows some signs of a transition toward the path that has benefited people in places like India and Southeast Asia. Metropolitan Accra is experiencing a building boom, as expatriate Ghanaians return to invest in their home country with capital they earned overseas. Offshore data processing and calling centers exploit Ghana's deregulated telecommunications, improved electricity delivery (in part a result of new power stations built by U.S. engineering companies with support from USAID), and widespread English fluency.

The long-run threat to this model, however, lies in the new proximity to the global economic networks that deliver the benefits that Africa's privatized international relations bring to the continent. These new links between African officials and a wide array of private foreign actors leave African governments with coordinated policies that tie their institutions and national economies to the discipline of global markets. This common tie is reflected in a shared global elite identity, as South African presidents and Nigerian finance ministers rub shoulders with their creditors, benefactors, and movie stars at annual meetings of the Global Economic Forum in Davos, Switzerland, for example.

These connections leave even the most democratic African governments ill prepared to respond to popular discontent, regardless of political openness and respect for civil liberties. This imparts brittleness to the arrangements that Africa's privatized international relations create. This would especially be the case if they were to face the stress of a recession in the world's major economies, since these connections are created in part to insulate policies from domestic politics. These diverse private links between the global economy, African governments, and their private partners would speed the transmission of the effects of a recession. The result would be a risk of an anti-modern, anti-Western backlash, since the criticism of this privatized model of state-building would be an attractive target for populist challengers. Ultimately, the delivery of goods and services to African people is predicated on buffering African officials from citizen demands. This undemocratic element of the arrangement would become a much larger issue if the material end of the bargain were to go unmet. Yet African governments have little alternative to the privatization of international relations. At present, the fate of alternatives—Zimbabwe, for example—is simply to become isolated anachronisms in a global community of increasingly standardized and interlinked states.

NOTES

1. See Independent Diplomat, at http://www.independentdiplomat.com/index.htm.

2. For example, Abdel-Fatah Musah, "Anatomies of Failure and Collapse: Privatization of Security, Arms Proliferation, and the Process of State Collapse in Africa," *Development and Change* 33, no. 5 (2002), pp. 911–933.

3. Jean-François Bayart, Stepehen Ellis, Béatrice Hibou, *The Criminalization of the State in Africa* (Oxford: James Currey, 1999).

4. Arthur Goldsmith, "Africa's Overgrown State Reconsidered: Bureaucracy and Economic Growth," *World Politics* 51, no. 3 (1999), pp. 520–546.

5. World Economic Forum, *Africa Competitiveness Report 2007* (Washington, D.C.: World Bank, 2007), p. 3.

6. Taylor's income: United Nations Security Council, *Report of the Panel of Experts Pursuant to Security Council Resolution 1395 (2002), paragraph 4, in Relation to Liberia* (New York: UN, April 11, 2002). Government revenues: International Monetary Fund, *Liberia: Selected Issues and Statistical Appendix,* February 25, 2003, pp. 7, 41–42.

7. Christopher Clapham, *Africa and the International System: The Politics of State Survival* (New York: Cambridge University Press, 1996).

8. Andrew Mwenda and Roger Tangri, "Patronage Politics, Donor Reforms, and Regime Consolidation in Uganda," *African Affairs* 104, no. 416 (2005), p. 453.

9. K. Onwuka Dike, *Trade and Politics in the Niger Delta, 1830–1885: An Introduction to the Economic and Political History of Nigeria* (Oxford: Clarendon Press, 1956).

10. Harry Broadman, *Africa's Silk Road: China and India's New Economic Frontier* (Washington, D.C.: World Bank, 2007), pp. 6–7.

11. George W. Bush, *The National Security Strategy of the United States of America,* at http://www.whitehouse.gov/nsc/nss.html.

12. Jack Straw, "Order out of Chaos: The Challenge of Failed States," in Mark Leonard, ed., *Re-Ordering the World: The Long-term Implications of September 11* (London: Foreign Policy Centre, 2002), p. 98.

13. National Intelligence Council, *External Relations and Africa* (Washington, D.C.: NIC 2020 Project, 2004), p. 3.

14. Special Task Force, *More Than Humanitarianism: A Strategic U.S. Approach Toward Africa* (New York: Council on Foreign Relations, 2005), p. 24.

15. Lauren Ploch, "Africa Command: U.S. Strategic Interests and the Role of the U.S. Military in Africa," Congressional Research Service, Report RL 34003, May 16, 2007, p. 12; National Intelligence Council, *Global Trends 2015* (Washington, D.C.: National Intelligence Council, 2000), p. 73.

16. J. C. Servant, "Le Chine à l'assaut du marché africain," *Le Monde Diplomatique*, May 2005, p. 3.

17. Ministry of Commerce, People's Republic of China, at http://english.mofcom.gov.cn/.

18. See OPIC Web site at http://www.opic.gov/about/index.asp.

19. Air service to Luanda is provided via the Angolan state-owned oil and gas industry's subsidiary Sonair Houston Express, at http://www.sonairsarl.com/houstonExpress_en.shtml.

20. Council on Foreign Relations, *Toward an Angola Strategy: Prioritizing U.S.-Angola Relations* (New York: CFR, 2007), pp. 33–34.

21. United States Agency for International Development (USAID), *The Global Development Alliance: Public-Private Alliances for Transformational Development* (Washington, D.C.: USAID, 2006), p. 20. German aid officials operate similar partnerships; see GTZ, Partnerships and Alliances, at http://www.gtz.de/en/unternehmen/1734.htm.

22. Dino Mahtani and Daniel Balint-Kurti, "Shell Uses Nigerian Companies Linked to Rebels," *Financial Times*, April 26, 2006, p. 1.

23. Uwem E. Ite, "Changing Times and Strategies: Shell's Contribution to Sustainable Community Development in the Niger Delta, Nigeria," *Sustainable Development*, 15, no. 1 (2007), p. 8.

24. USAID, *Strategic Framework for Africa*, February 24, 2006, at http://www.uneca.org/itca/youth/Documents/Strategic%20Framework%20for%20Africa_usaid_2006.pdf.

25. International Budget Project, at http://www.internationalbudget.org/about/staff.htm.

26. Crown Agents, *Crown Agents Annual Review 2006*, London, 2006, p. 8, at http://www.crownagents.com/uploads/public/documents/downloads/About%20Us/Crown%20Agents%20Annual%20Review%202006.pdf.

27. Brenda Chalfin, "Global Customs Regimes and the Traffic in Sovereignty," *Current Anthropology* 47, no. 2 (April 2006), pp. 243–276.

28. See, for example, Rotimi Sankore, "What Are the NGOs Doing?" *New African*, September 2005, pp. 12–15.

29. Steven David, *Choosing Sides: Alignment and Realignment in the Third World* (Baltimore: Johns Hopkins University Press, 1991).

30. Paul Blustein, "Chad, World Bank Settle Dispute Over Oil Money," *Washington Post*, July 15, 2006, p. D1.

31. Human Rights Watch, *Some Transparency, No Accountability* (New York: Human Rights Watch, Jan 2004), pp. 16–46.

32. U.S. Department of Justice, *Report of the Attorney General to the Congress of the United States on the Administration of the Foreign Agents Registration Act* (Washington, D.C.: U.S. Department of Justice, June 30, 2006), p. 3.

33. United States Department of Agriculture, "Angola Exporters Guide," Washington, D.C., June 3, 2006, p. 9.

34. Fareed Zakaria, *The Future of Freedom: Illiberal Democracy at Home and Abroad* (New York: W. W. Norton, 2003), pp. 89–118.

35. Ibid.

36. Peter Lewis, "Identity, Institutions, and Democracy in Nigeria," Michigan State University Department of Political Science, East Lansing, March 2007, pp. 14, 19.

37. Global Witness, *The Usual Suspects: Liberia's Weapons and Mercenaries in Côte d'Ivoire and Sierra Leone* (London: Global Witness, March 31, 2003).

38. Ministry of Finance, "Memorandum" [letter to Firestone Synthetic Rubber & Latex Company], Monrovia, Republic of Liberia, May 6, 1993.

39. Adam Roberts, *The Wonga Coup* (New York: Public Affairs, 2006).

40. Sarah Kenyon Lischer, *Dangerous Sanctuaries: Refugee Camps, Civil Wars, and the Dilemmas of Humanitarian Aid* (Ithaca: Cornell University Press, 2005), p. 90.

41. James Ron, "The NGO Scramble: Organizational Insecurity and the Political Economy of Transnational Action," *International Organization* 27, no. 1 (Summer 2002), pp. 5–39.

42. Moises Naim, "What Is a GONGO?" *Foreign Policy*, May–June 2007.

43. Christine Messiant, "The Eduardo dos Santos Foundation: Or, How Angola's Regime Is Taking Over Civil Society," *African Affairs* 100 (2001), pp. 287–309.

44. Personal communication, Sierra Leone government minister, July 4, 2005.

45. Stephen Krasner, "Abiding Sovereignty," *International Political Science Review* 22, no. 3 (2001), pp. 229–251.

46. Broadman, *Africa's Silk Road*, p. 15.

47. International Monetary Fund, *Regional Economic Outlook: Sub-Saharan Africa*, April 2007, Washington, D.C., p. 17.

9

Inter-African Negotiations and Reforming Political Order

I. William Zartman

Since independence, African states have been confronted with a dilemma (among others): As new state units, achieving the sovereignty and self-determination for which they struggled, should they take their place among others in the reigning system of world order (like children reaching adulthood and joining the family council), or as new units with a different political history, should they join the system of world order that they did not create and work to change it, just as they struggled to upset the colonial order (like new immigrants on the block with their own histories and customs)? The dilemma in the current context is half a century old and has taken many forms since 1956 and thereafter. It does not begin with nor is it peculiar to the new millennium or to the twenty-first century, but the end of the bipolar Cold War system of world order and the advent of the globalized balance of power sought by al-Qaeda do pose the question in a new form. The twenty-first-century form of the dilemma has a particular impact on Africa's foreign policies and negotiations with the external world, but it also has a defining impact on Africans' negotiations with themselves.

Order is created, and altered, by a limited number of means: force, fiat, negotiation, and trial and error.[1] For fiat to work, there must already be an order that gives it authority, and behind it generally stands some sort of force. Trial and error means that component parts take order-changing actions and get away with it. But the characteristic of the postcolonial era is that orders are established and changes created by negotiation, broadly in the world but more specifically in Africa, where force is almost irrelevant behind diplomatic exchanges. So negotiations are important, whether to set up and operate an all-African order, such as the African Union (AU), a regional order, such as the Southern African Development Community (SADC), or simply to define a bilateral order of relations, such as the end of the Eritrean-Ethiopian war. Moreover, they take place when force, if used at all, has reached an impasse and cannot impose its way (as in the latter case).

In inter-African relations, two is a conflict, three is company, and fifty-odd is a crowd of free riders jealous above all of their fragile sovereignty. African negotiations over conflict and cooperation are a highly developed exercise, with their own characteristics and patterns, strengths and limitations. In dealing with conflict, bilateral negotiations and broad multilateral negotiation tend to be ineffective in producing outcomes; in between, mediation is frequently needed to bring negotiations among conflicting parties to fruition. In cooperation, multilateral negotiations have a high record of success, although the impact of the outcome has its own limitations and characteristics. These qualities have not changed in their essence over the half-century of independence, and they have inhibited African states, individually and collectively, from playing the role they might in the world order and in the establishment of their own order. This chapter presents the characteristics of that process as practiced in Africa, with examples, and seeks explanations for those characteristics.

In assessing these results and in analyzing the process by which they are achieved, it should be remembered that conflict is an inevitable—and sometimes functional or even desirable—condition of interstate relations, and that negotiation is a means of limiting it; whereas cooperation—although desirable and sometimes functional—is by no means inevitable, and negotiation is the means of achieving it. As a result, the playing field has different slopes according to the subject, imparting different types of difficulties to the negotiation process. In Africa, the paucity of direct violent conflicts between states reduces the pressure to resolve interstate conflict and leaves negotiations at the lowest common denominator: the protection of each party's sovereignty; In intrastate conflict, the violence is often ferocious and durable, since the government defends its personalized sovereignty and the rebellions seek to grab hold of it, making negotiations equally protracted.

Across this distinction runs another, related to the size of the teams. At one end of a spectrum stand conflicts and cooperations that are highly personalized in the head of state, with little interest and involvement by society; at the other are conflicts and cooperations that are national causes, affecting society deeply and arousing deep popular sentiments, often making heads of state and other actors prisoners of larger dynamics.[2] This dichotomy has its impact on negotiations, although the distinction contains a large gray area between the two clear extremes. Personalist leaders speak in the name of their societies and mobilize societal interest behind their positions; yet states and societies do not negotiate—only people do.

BILATERAL CONFLICT NEGOTIATIONS

Direct bilateral negotiations are not an effective way of ending conflict in Africa. Nor are large-scale multilateral negotiations in regional or subregional organizations, although these organizations do play an important role in setting the norms and parameters for terminating conflicts—either by victory or by reconciliation. It is "trilateral" or mediated bilateral negotiations that are most effective.[3]

These characteristics call for an attempt at explanation. Four reasons suggest themselves. First, because of the engrossing nature of African conflicts and their often functional aspects, African states or leaders in conflict are so taken up with the unilateral pursuit of the dispute that they are unable to conceive of bilateral or multilateral solutions on their own; they need help. Whether the conflict is a personal dispute between heads of state or the result of a societal feeling of personal right or neighboring hostility, it becomes an emotional and political cause of high importance, leaving little leeway for creative thinking on alternative solutions. In the conflicts in central Africa in the late 1990s and early 2000s, the personal animosity between Zimbabwean and South African Presidents Robert Mugabe and Nelson Mandela, between Congolese and Ugandan Presidents Laurent Kabila and Yoweri Museveni, and between Kabila and Mandela, and between Congolese and Rwandan presidents Joseph Kabila and Paul Kagame intractably framed the dispute. This characteristic is reinforced by the absence of other elements that would serve to enlarge the space for the consideration of foreign policy issues: the small size of foreign policy establishments, the often impetuous nature of decisions, and the absence of a loyal opposition and of public political debate.

Second, until the 1990s, African conflicts were the occasion for a competitive race among external great powers for allies, first within the continent and then outside. Bilateral conflicts generally did not remain bilateral but engaged, first, factions within the continent and then European powers and superpowers. This characteristic prevented bilateral settlements but, paradoxically facilitated mediation.[4] After the Cold War ended, this characteristic was reversed. Simply, no one cared, until the anti-terrorist campaign returned the U.S.' interest to Africa and its conflicts (though U.S. interest would be revived with its post–9/11 war on terrorism). With less interest and influence from external parties, African states tended to find themselves locked in their conflicts, unable to reach for a solution. Thus, the post–Cold War conflicts in the Horn, central Africa, and the West coast all remained primarily African conflicts without much outside control, but they escalated to competing African coalitions that were impervious to effective mediation. While this may not be a durable feature, while it lasts, external disinterest in taking sides in a conflict has also been paralleled by a lowered interest and leverage in mediating as well.

Third, there is usually little incentive for African states to reduce, let alone resolve, their conflicts, just as there is little pressure to push them to bilateral accommodation. Conflicts, as noted, are popular and useful, particularly when kept at a low, less costly level; they can then be revived at any time for purposes of national gain and national unity. Somalia's, Libya's, Nigeria's, and Morocco's long irredentist claims on their neighbors are cases in point, extreme versions of the various other border disputes, structural rivalries, and recurrent involvements in neighboring politics which make up much of African conflict. There is little to gain for the parties in making peace and much face to save in pursuing conflict.[5]

Finally, since few unmediated bilateral negotiations had any significant effect on their conflict, precedent gives little incentive to negotiate. A few examples illustrate the problems. The border dispute that troubled relations between Morocco and Algeria since their independence was initially and occasionally the subject of direct negotiations.[6] As early as the three first years of the 1960s, the Moroccan kings met with the presidents of the Provisional Government of the Algerian Republic (GPRA) to discuss the problem, among others; when independence came to Algeria in 1962, the agreements to settle the problem between sovereign states were pushed aside since they were unwitnessed and were considered nonbinding. Instead, war broke out, and the dispute was taken up by the newly created Organization for African Unity (OAU). The war was ended through the good offices of Emperor Haile Selassie and Malian President Modibo Keita. After further mediation, King Hassan II and President Ahmed Ben Bella met at Saidia in April 1965 and renewed the GPRA's commitment. Ben Bella was overthrown by his army three months later, with the Saidia agreement cited as one of the specific grievances.

Once again, the OAU provided the framework for a reconciliation between King Hassan II and the new Algerian ruler, Col. Houari Boumedienne, in 1968—leading to bilateral summits in the following two years and then a final border treaty again in the context of the OAU, when Hassan II made his first trip to Algiers, prepared by the mediation of Tunisian President Habib Bourguiba. The implementation of the Rabat border agreement of 1972 was interrupted by the eruption of the Western Saharan issue, destroying all chances for effective bilateral negotiation. As the war moved beyond initial expectations of duration and toward an apparent stalemate and division of the territory, preparations began for a bilateral summit at the end of 1978. Boumedienne's death cancelled these plans; Hassan expected the new president to be more flexible, and the new president, Col. Chadli BenJedid, had to consolidate his own position before any of his purported flexibility could be shown.

It took another five years and a new stalemate more favorable to Morocco—with many intervening failed mediations—to produce a bilateral summit in February 1983. Despite high hopes and an agreement, the mutual understanding fell apart almost immediately, specifically because there was no third party present to "hold the bets" and witness the agreement. Instead, each party soon felt betrayed by the other. A second summit was held in May 1987 under the auspices of Saudi King Fahd, followed by multilateral summit meetings a year later in Algiers among the Arab heads of state and then in February 1989 in Marrakesh to inaugurate the regional Arab Maghrib Union (UMA). Whatever agreements emerged from these meetings have shown the necessity of witnesses and active mediation. The lesson from this lengthy conflict, still unended, is not that mediated and trilateral negotiations are ipso facto assured of success, but that bilateral negotiation is ipso facto assured of failure. As in other cases, the presence of one or more third parties to midwife and witness an agreement is the necessary but not sufficient condition of success.

There are many other examples in the negative. Conflicts between Angola and Zaire, Somalia and Ethiopia, Sudan and Ethiopia, Eritrea and Ethiopia, Mali and Burkina Faso, Nigeria and Cameroon, Senegal and Mauritania, among others, were not settled by their bilateral summits; when settlement or progress toward settlement was made, it was in meetings that included other parties than the principals. Even in internal wars, which in principle are particularly difficult to mediate, settlements, when reached, have been the result of third-party assistance, as in Angola in 1990 and 1994, Liberia between 1991 and 1996, Ethiopia in 1991, Mozambique in 1992, Rwanda in 1993, Sierra Leone in 1996, Burundi in 1998, Lesotho in 1994 and 1998, and so on. As bilateral failure is so pervasive, it is pointless to look for other necessary ingredients, but rather more productive to turn to mediation to find out what else is necessary to produce new order in Africa.

MEDIATION

Africa does not lack mediators. Whether it is from a continental cultural tradition or from a conscious interest in maintaining the African state system,[7] African heads of state do more than stand ready to be of assistance—they rush in, in numbers, often competing to bring good and even better offices to the resolution of their colleagues' conflicts, to the point where there is a confusion of marriage counselors trying to restore domestic tranquillity in the African family. At least this profusion of mediators permits some conclusions on the characteristics of success—both contextual and tactical.[8]

Mediators have their own interests supporting their activities; African mediators have an overriding interest in preserving the African state system and hence maintaining acceptance of the status quo. They therefore also have a framework within which to seek to place their mediated resolutions, reinforcing their efforts and facilitating their acceptance.[9] But they also have their own state interests, like any other mediators—interests in maintaining or improving relations with the conflicting states, in ending a conflict that strains relations in their region, and sometimes in achieving a particular outcome.

African mediators tend to come from neighboring states, from within the same subregion if not from contiguous states; indeed, contiguous states often have enough of their own problems with their immediate neighbor to be disqualified or at least handicapped in mediation. There is a major exception: When the conflict is an internal dispute between a government and an insurgency in which a neighboring state serves as the insurgents' sanctuary, the neighbor can be a useful mediator if it "delivers" the agreement of the insurgents.[10] Mediators also tend to come from states of the same colonial background as the disputants when both of the conflicting parties are French- or English-speaking, illustrating the importance of both personal political ties and communications.

Mediation is a personal affair, conducted personally by African heads of state among other heads of state. It does not lend itself easily to practice by lesser officials—a point that is crucial to understanding the stillbirth in 1964 of the OAU Commission of Mediation, Arbitration, and Conciliation, which mandated respected jurists and civil servants but not heads or former heads of state.[11] Even the respected Special Representative of the Secretaries-General (SRSG) of the OAU and the UN, Mohamed Sahnoun, allied himself with the president of Gabon in his mediations in Congo (Brazzaville) in 1993 and 1997, and with the Emperor of Ethiopia in his mediation in Sudan twenty years earlier.[12]

Of the three roles available to the mediator—communicator, formulator, manipulator—African heads of state operate primarily in the first two, overcoming obstacles to communications between the conflicting parties and helping them find and formulate mutually acceptable ways out of their conflict.[13] A function of the personal mediator is to reduce the risks and mistrust that impede the parties' agreement to reconciliation. Since the conflict not only bears on the issue at hand but also colors the whole tone of relations between the disputants, they do not trust each other's word and do not know how much risk is involved in their agreement; the mediator is needed as the agent of trust and the assessor of risk.

The condition for effective mediation to begin is the mutually hurting stalemate, which makes it possible for the mediator to be welcome in his offer of a way out.[14] Stalemate makes the mediation possible; the mediator makes the stalemate fruitful. Without the mutual hurting stalemate, the parties have no interest in being saved from their conflict by meddling outsiders. The first war in southern Sudan was successfully ended following a stalemate in 1972 by layers of mediation, beginning with the World Council of Churches and the All-African Council of Churches, backed by OAU Assistant Secretary General Sahnoun, with Emperor Haile Selassie acting as mediator of last resort at a crucial juncture. Since war broke out again when the Addis Ababa Agreement was dismantled ten years later by its author, President Jaafar Numeiri, with the connivance of the southern Sudanese tribal animosities, mediation became much more difficult, first, because of active support of the new Marxist government, Ethiopia had thrown its support behind the insurgent Sudanese People's Liberation Movement/Army (SPLM/A) in southern Sudan, and, second, after 1989, because the northern Sudanese government became intransigent when a Muslim fundamentalist military junta took over the government in Khartoum in 1989. The shift in fortunes blocked mediated resolution throughout the 1980s and 1990s, and turned the rebellion in the south from a movement to reform the entire Sudanese political system to a secessionist movement. Many mediators tried to resolve the conflict, but none succeeded; the stalemate never existed, and the situation was not ripe.

The situation was finally changed by foreign mediatory intervention, in the form of U.S. pressure on the Islamist government to come to terms with the southern rebels or face stiff economic sanctions. The SPLM/A was already in difficulty, so that the foreign pressure on the north, as a result of the antiterrorist campaign and the Christian activists' pressure in favor of the south in the U.S., created the hurting stalemate that the mediation needed. Mediation itself was carried out by the Kenyan government on behalf of the Intergovernmental Authority on Development (IGAD), and gradually brought about a Comprehensive Peace Agreement (CPA) at Naivasha in January 2005. A new order had been created in Sudan, providing immediately for a power-sharing government, and for a referendum to be held after a period of six years to decide whether the south would become fully independent. The new order is shaky, to be sure, and may even be coming apart and the referendum never take place, and the North-South conflict has broken out anew in Darfur to the west and Beja to the east, but these in turn have been subject to a negotiation process, stumbling in its turns because the necessary mutually hurting stalemate has not set in.

Similar characteristics appeared in the negotiation of the Eritrean conflict, which resisted repeated attempts at mediation throughout its thirty-year history, until it finally overthrew the Ethiopian government in 1991 and seceded. The Soviet Union, East Germany, the Italian communist party, and President Jimmy Carter of the Carter Center at Emory University all tried their hands at mediating between the Eritrean rebels and the Ethiopian government between 1978 and 1989, but the conflict was never ripe.[15] Instead, the new order was created by force in 1991, when the Eritrean and Ethiopian Tigrean forces combined to overthrow the Marxist government and provide for a two-state solution, accepted in referendum in 1993.

After Eritrea achieved independence, war broke out over the common border and other matters in mid-1998, the U.S. and Rwanda nearly succeeded in mediating an agreement, but subsequent attempts by the U.S. and by SRSG Sahnoun over the next twelve months were not able to close the gap. Although militarily stalemated, both sides still believed in victory and refused to see the cost. Again, as the tremendous cost of the war and the fact of the stalemate began to sink in, it took the personal intervention of the President of Algeria, Abdulaziz Bouteflika, to bring the sides, reluctantly, to a conflict management agreement that put the border in the hands of a boundary commission arbitration; although both sides agreed to the terms, Ethiopia rejected its decision to give the disputed border village of Badme to Eritrea. Agreement was finally reached in 2007, but the conflict continues by proxy in Somalia and by preparation for a further outburst. When negotiation fails, mediation and arbitration become necessary but they do not carry the direct ownership in the agreement that (successful) direct negotiation provides.

The mediation attempted by Zairean President Mobutu Sese Seko in the Angolan civil war at Gbadolite and some lesser venues in 1989 suffered from the absence of a mutually hurting stalemate (which only occurred a year later in the battle for Mavinga) and of a capable mediator (who only appeared two years later in Portugal). It was further muddied by Zambian and Zimbabwean Presidents Kenneth Kaunda's and Robert Mugabe's attempts to save the situation later in the same year at Lusaka as the Gbadolite démarche was collapsing. But the agreements signed at Bicesse in 1991 under Portuguese mediation after the Mavinga stalemate collapsed in the ensuing elections the following year, and the more careful agreements mediated by the U.S. and the UN in 1994 in Lusaka also broke down by 1998. The double lesson from Angola was: first, that hurting stalemate is a subjective, perceptional matter that Jonas Savimbi never allowed himself to feel; and therefore, second, that sometimes conflicts are beyond any negotiable formula and can be handled only by the assassination of one side's leader, as finally occurred in 2003.

Particularly striking is the War of the Zairean Succession and its regional extensions that began in 1996. In May 1997, as the Alliance of Democratic Forces for the Liberation of the Congo (AFDL), backed by Rwanda and Uganda, approached the gates of Kinshasa, South Africa, backed by the U.S., tried to mediate a cease-fire and smooth transition from Mobutu to Laurent Kabila. The effort was particularly ill-conceived, since there was no stalemate, and the last persons that each party wished to engage in negotiations was the other! A year later, in August 1998, many of the parties of AFDL, now alienated from Kabila, launched a new rebellion under the name of the Rally for a Democratic Congo (RDC) with the support of the same neighbors; Zimbabwe, Namibia, and Angola (and to a lesser extent, Chad, Libya, and Sudan) rushed to save the Kabila government. The Southern African Development Community (SADC), which backed the intervention by the three member states, also tried to mediate a cease-fire throughout the end of 1998 and early 1999, under the chairmanship of Zambian President Frederick Chiluba and then under former South African President Nelson Mandela, a charismatic and unrefusable personality of enormous stature. But both sides clung to the expectation of victory, the mediating body clung to its partisan involvement, and the Congolese government refused to meet the rebels. By July 1999, an agreement among Congo and its neighbors was signed at Lusaka, but it took another three months to bring in the rebel movements. New Congolese president Joseph Kabila then turned to direct negotiation with Rwanda and Uganda to make agreements in July and September 2002, respectively, but the internal parties needed the mediation of the new South African President Thabo Mbeki to sign agreements setting up a new Congolese order in Pretoria and Sun City in December 2002 and February 2003; in the process, through clever maneuvering, Kabila and his government moved from equal status with the rebel movements in the Lusaka agreement, to *primus inter pares* in the South African agreements, and finally to winner of the ensuing Congolese elections in July 2006. Powerful mediation and savvy, single-minded negotiating tactics were the prime methods in creating the new order.

The Mali-Burkinabe (Voltaic) border dispute, recurrent over a quarter-century after the countries' independence, was mediated by an OAU ad hoc commission composed of French-speaking states of the region, bringing a cease-fire in July 1975, and again by a series of mediators—Libya and Algeria, who failed at the end of 1985, and then Senegal and Ivory Coast within the framework of the French-speaking West African Economic Community (CEAO), who succeeded in January 1986.[16]

Mediators also abounded in the Horn of Africa, until conflict overtook the states themselves in the 1990s and defied all attempts to bring it under control.

President Ibrahim Abboud of Sudan stepped into the 1963–1964 border war between Somalia and Ethiopia to bring about a cease-fire and other conflict management measures. President Julius Nyerere of Tanzania attempted the same in the "bandit" war between Somalia and Kenya the following year but was hindered by his approach and his own problems with Kenya; he was succeeded by President Kenneth Kaunda of Zambia in 1967–1968 who was able to get the parties talking as a new stalemate weighed in on them. When the conflict management arrangements agreed to did not produce the next step of conflict resolution, Somalia invaded Ethiopia. No one was able to mediate, although the United States did successfully press the Soviet Union to guarantee that Ethiopia would not cross the border as it threw back the Somali invaders in 1978.[17] Eight years later, Somalia offered Ethiopia a new round of conflict management measures; the secretary-general of the Intergovernmental Authority on Drought and Development (IGADD) and Djibouti, the IGADD host, served as mediators to bring the two heads of state together in January 1986 and finally, in April 1988, to win Ethiopian agreement to the proposals. Ironically, withdrawal of Ethiopian support and control of Somali rebels left them free to overthrow their own government in 1990, at the same time as the Ethiopian government fell to its own ethnic rebellions. Many mediators—Egypt, Ethiopia, the UN SRSG, the United States, among others—have tried throughout the 1990s and 2000s to mediate the ensuing conflict in the collapsed state of Somalia, without avail.

The African mediator's primary weapon is persuasion, which reinforces the personal nature of the task and reflects the need for the perception of a mutually hurting stalemate. The mediator's main leverage lies in his ability to help his brothers out of the bind into which their conflict has led them. There are unfortunately not enough studies of the direct mediatory exchanges among heads of state to permit a detailed analysis of actual mediation behavior, but all available evidence indicates an exercise in pure persuasion.[18]

In internal conflicts—increasingly the predominant type of African conflict—the key to effective mediation seems to be the mediator's ability to guarantee fair treatment and a share in the new political system for all parties, rather than any tangible side payments. In Liberia, first the Liberian Council of Churches and then fellow members of the Economic Community of West African States (ECOWAS) tried again and again between 1990 and 1996 to mediate a cease-fire that would last between the factions, coming finally to agreements in August 1995 and in 1996 when the mediation was taken over by Nigerian dictator Gen. Sani Abacha, whose military contingents made up the bulk of the West African Military Observer Group (ECOMOG).[19] The Abuja agreements finally gave the remaining combatants a stake in the outcome and ended in the election of Charles Taylor as president in July 1997. Another three-year civil war, in Rwanda, was temporarily brought to a mediated agreement in August 1993 at Arusha under the auspices of the OAU and Tanzania, made possible by the introduction of a UN peacekeeping force. The Arusha agreement was then destroyed in the 1994 genocide by the Coalition for the Defense of the Republic (CDR) extremists excluded from Arusha.[20]

There are a few exceptions to the pure persuasion characteristic, none of them very clear, by the nature of the subject. King Fahd, host of the 1987 summit between King Hassan and President BenJedid, was operating as Morocco's past funding source and Algeria's potential funding source of the future, whether specific financial arrangements were mentioned or not.[21] When the World Council of Churches moved the government of Sudan and the Southern Sudanese Liberation Movement (SSLM) toward Addis Ababa, where an agreement to end the war was eventually signed in 1972, it threatened on occasion to withdraw from mediation and resume the provision of humanitarian supplies to the SSLM if its efforts were rejected.[22] After a complex stalemate, President Samora Machel of Mozambique, who served as one of the several mediators in the Lancaster House negotiations in 1979 leading to Zimbabwean independence, threatened to close down the Patriotic Front's bases in Mozambique if its leader, Robert Mugabe, did not go along with the settlement being negotiated.[23] Similarly, the Frontline States and particularly Angola threatened the South West African People's Organization (SWAPO) with loss of support and sanctuary if it did not stay in the Namibian negotiations.[24] Following a gradual stalemate reinforced by a drought, the October 1992 Mozambican peace settlement negotiated in Rome by the Sant'Egidio Community in the presence of a number of interested states contained a provision of $15 million for the Mozambican National Resistance (ReNaMo) to facilitate its transformation from a guerrilla group to a political organization.[25] There may be other examples.

In general, failed attempts at mediation did not benefit from the conditions and tactics which caused success—effective perception of stalemate on the part of all parties, skillful persuasion by the mediator, and a convincing formula for a way out that is minimally satisfactory to all. At best, one can conclude that the mediator can pull an agreement on a salient solution out of a propitious context—that is, accomplish a negotiation that overcommitment to the conflict prevents the parties from doing by themselves—but he cannot create a ripe moment and a winning solution out of thin air, among peers in Africa anymore than anywhere else.

MULTILATERAL CONFLICT NEGOTIATION

The OAU was the major multilateral African forum for the conduct of negotiations to deal with conflict,[26] and its poor record for nearly forty years was one of the reasons why the leaders of the continent felt that a new organization was necessary. The OAU increasingly shared its role with subregional organizations, the most active of which are the Inter-Governmental Agency for Development (IGAD) in the Horn of Africa, the Economic Community of West African States (ECOWAS), the French-speaking West African Economic Community (CEAO), which became the West African Monetary and Economic Union (UEMOA) in 1994, and the Southern African Development Community (SADC). Its successor, the African Union, has attempted to "continentalize" conflict management rather than leaving it to the subregional bodies. Most of these subregional organizations were not created for conflict reduction at all, but rather to provide a ready forum where heads of state could meet primarily for economic reasons and work out differences in the corridors; conflict reduction became a necessary precondition for carrying out their other, primary business. Indeed, this successive relationship between economic cooperation and security preconditions is the story of the founding of the continental AU as well, as discussed below. Two different types of multilateral negotiation need to be distinguished: one is the activity of ad hoc multilateral committees established to deal with specific conflicts, while the other is the business of the plenary of summit meetings of the multilateral organizations themselves.

There is no need to spend time on the major African committee envisaged in the 1960s to reduce conflict among African states: the Commission for Mediation, Arbitration and Conciliation. Indicated by the OAU Charter, it never came into existence, since it conflicted with the rapidly established characteristics of inter-African relations as being the domain of heads of state. Instead, the OAU appointed ad hoc committees to deal with conflicts as they arose on the summit agenda, with membership carefully allocated based on language, ideology, regional, experience, and other interest groups. Such careful balancing guaranteed stalemate, and the record was not good—success in one out of three cases in some two dozen instances in the first two decades of the organization.[27]

In addition, many of the successes were only temporary, with the conflict breaking out in another form later on (and requiring a new committee). On the other hand, batting .333 may not be a bad average under the circumstances. Very often conditions were not propitious, and more frequently still, the purposes of the mother organization were other than conflict resolution—as is discussed below—and these purposes therefore overrode the efforts of the committees. In addition, in a few more cases, conflict management—the reduction of the means (ostensibly leading to a reduction of the ends) of conflict—was the outcome of committee efforts rather than the settlement of basic issues. Unfortunately, it is impossible to calculate a similar batting average for the incalculable private efforts at mediation, to see whether OAU committees did better than individual heads of state.

Committee mediation was a more important function of the OAU than its record might indicate, however, and there are lessons to be learned. It overcame one major defect of private mediation, in that it provided coordination, whereas private mediators often competed among themselves. This competition then allowed the parties to the conflict to sit by and wait—or even actively campaign—for better terms to come along in the hands of other private mediators. In OAU committees, many of the members were passive, overlooking and legitimizing the activities of a few members who did the active mediation. Furthermore, OAU committees were constrained by the guidelines of the organization and its summits; they could not seek just any terms for agreement, since they were at the same time the standard-bearers of OAU principles. That dual role sometimes made it impossible to find terms of agreement to which both sides could subscribe. It is difficult to fault either the OAU committees or the private mediators in such conflicts as the Somali-Ethiopian dispute or the Western Sahara; the two contestants' positions were simply irreconcilable, the parties were alternately, not mutually, stalemated, and resolution had to await a change in the cost of holding out for one or both that would bring them to soften their positions.

Thus, an OAU committee was named to mediate the Somali-Ethiopian border problem at the 1973 summit, and when it failed, another was named at the 1976 summit. As they operated under the 1964 OAU resolution affirming the sanctity of colonial boundaries, they had little leeway to meet Somalia's grievances; instead they reaffirmed the principle. But another OAU committee extracted a promise (false, as it turned out) from Ghana not to practice subversion against Ivory Coast, Upper Volta, and Niger in 1965, in accordance with OAU charter principles, and another intervened to free Guineans held in Ghana on the way to the OAU summit the following year. In such cases, OAU committees, acting within charter principles, made it possible for transgressing states to return to behavioral norms without loss of face, a task for which multimembered OAU committees were even better suited than private mediators. After the establishment of the Mechanism for the Prevention, Management and Resolution of Conflicts within the OAU in 1993, the Special Representative of the Secretary-General (SRSG) came into use, replacing the committees and their drawbacks, without their meager advantages.

In these situations, risk, trust, persuasion, and stalemate are the same ingredients in success. The actual negotiations are accomplished by skillfully luring the erring party back from the limb on which he has crawled, while the mediator gives assurances on risk and trust and provides an atmosphere of unity and fraternity that prevents the other party from crowing. Since the conflicting parties usually have no dispute with the mediator, it becomes difficult for them to refuse his assurances and reject his atmospherics.

The OAU itself, in its biennial ministerial and annual presidential meetings, was not a conflict resolution mechanism. It provided corridors and committees, which operated as described, and principles, which provided the guidelines for solutions. The AU does much the same, despite heightened ambitions. But a body of more than fifty members is not a mechanism for resolving disputes. If it does come to the point of decreeing a solution, either the conflict on the ground has finally become stalemated or a lot of negotiation has taken place beforehand to make that solution acceptable. Otherwise, the conflict goes on. This was the fate of the major conflicts that tore the OAU apart—second (1964) Congo crisis, Biafra (1966–1970), dialogue with South Africa, Sahara (1975 to 1988, when it turned the dispute over to the UN), Chad (1980–1984), Angola (1974–2005), Rwanda (1993–1996), Burundi, the fourth (1998–1999) Congo crisis, and Ivory Coast (after 1999).

Yet in the OAU's handling of each of these conflicts, there has been some important and even skillful negotiation. A prime example which shows the possibilities of negotiation within the organization vs. the political stance of its summits is the Western Sahara conflict. The OAU revived the 1964–1967 committee to investigate the causes of the Saharan war as a committee of Wisemen to resolve the Western Saharan issue in 1978. The committee was diligent and creative in trying to bridge the positions of Algeria and Morocco. Then, at the 1981 summit, under pressure from an impending recognition of the Sahrawi Arab Democratic Republic (SADR), Morocco agreed to a referendum and the Wisemen were transformed into an Implementation Committee of the OAU. It met three times, and through painstaking negotiation with the parties, essentially established the guidelines for a referendum. The guidelines were still in place as the parties moved toward a vote under UN auspices a decade later, while at the same time holding back the efforts of various parties at various times to undo previous aspects of the evolving agreement. However, at the close of the third meeting ("Nairobi III") in February 1982, the OAU Council of Ministers disavowed its committee's work by admitting the SADR to membership. Curiously, the heads of state on the committee did not have the political commitment to put their decisions into effect.

Other cases of OAU negotiations show similar characteristics. The work of the non-OAU committee of Chad meeting in Kano and Lagos in 1979, which set up the GUNT, was followed by an OAU committee on Chad and then the 1981 summit in Nairobi. Intense negotiations produced a plan for a multinational peacekeeping force and a timetable for negotiations between the Chadian factions, elections, and the withdrawal of the African troops. Yet for all its coherence, the plan was unrealistic; funding, mission, sanctions, and contingency plans were not provided.[28] Some skillful negotiations bringing the conflicting parties close to agreement were undercut by the lack of political commitment within the OAU needed to carry the project to fruition.

Thus, the OAU summit—as distinguished from its committees—played a number of roles in regard to conflict negotiations. It set principles, appointed committees, provided a forum and corridors, but because of its own political divisions and the fear of offending other heads of state, it was unable to take forthright positions of reconciliation in African disputes. The 1989 summit assiduously avoided the bitter dispute between Senegal and Mauritania, and as described above, earlier summits were unable to follow through in their own conflict management and resolution mechanisms in the Saharan and Chadian conflicts.

Under the pressure of criticism for its inability to rid Africa of its recurrent and intermittent conflicts, particularly as expressed in the articulate and visionary call for a Conference on Security, Stability, Development and Cooperation in Africa (CSSDCA) launched by former Nigerian President Olusegun Obasanjo in Kampala in May 1991, the OAU voted at its 1993 summit to create a new division of the secretariat on conflict prevention, management and resolution.[29] The Kampala Document also called for the constitution of a Council of Elders, former heads of state who could serve as mediators and peacemakers. Former Presidents Léopold Senghor of Senegal, Julius Nyerere of Tanzania, Aristide Pereira of Cape Verde, and Obasanjo volunteered their services, but the OAU did not adopt the proposal, preferring its own ad hoc elders. The organization also undertook a more proactive role in preventive as well as resolving mediation, eliciting invitations to provide good-office missions in Togo, Congo (Brazzaville), Congo/Zaire, Rwanda, and Liberia to both forestall and to end violence. In so doing, the African universal organization took a major step to formalize its personal and ad hoc efforts to reduce conflict and facilitate negotiation among—and within—its members.

The major set of negotiations for reforming the political order on the continent, however, were those accompanying the replacement of the OAU by the African Union, its new creation, and by its pacing organization, the New Economic Partnership for African Development (NEPAD). While the substantive impetus for the creation of a new organization came out of the failures of the old, the occasion came from the Abuja Treaty of 1991, which laid out a number of steps to the creation of an African Economic Community in 2025. The 34th OAU summit at Ouagadougou in June 1998 called for organizational reform, at a time when a number of newly elected leaders began to emerge along with new ideas: Obasanjo and his Kampala movement, Thabo Mbeki and his African Renaissance and, with Abdulaziz Bouteflika, their Millennium African Partnership (MAP), soon to be joined by Senegal's new president, Abdoulaye Wade. An old prophet of a sovereign African federal state, Libya's Muammar Qaddafi, who had not attended a summit for twenty years, called an extraordinary summit at Sirte in July 1999, opening up a year of vigorous negotiations among the holders of the same opposing tenets as underlay the founding of the OAU in 1963—an invigorated union of states versus a single federation comprising all African states.[30]

When finally the new Union was approved, at the AU's 37th and final summit at Lusaka in July 2001, the negotiations for the new order had been marked by a number of salient and renewed characteristics. The dynamo behind the negotiations was Qaddafi, and the form of the Union with its parliament, court, and many other state-like (and European Union–like) institutions reflected his insistence and his purse in encouraging support. A group of moderate, sound-thinking leaders supplied the substance of the Union, which in working essence is much like its predecessor but animated by a new sense of purpose and order. Behind this diplomatic confrontation was the negotiatory work of technical commissions, parliamentarians, and legal experts. And, as at Addis Ababa nearly forty years earlier, the turning point was a galvanizing speech reminding the heads of state that progress and their reputations hung in the balance—this time delivered by Senegal's Wade.

However, the process was not complete with the foundation of the AU. The moderate leaders were still dubious of the soundness of the Union with its many, often hollow institutions, and so in the following year they inaugurated a similar pattern of negotiations, without Qaddafi. Again gathering together a number of plans for economic revival, devised by Mbeki, Bouteflika, Wade, and Obasanjo, joined by Egypt's president, Hosni Mubarak, they obtained authorization at the Lusaka summit to create a new organization modeled largely on the Kampala Document for Security, Stability, Development and Cooperation, but with the addition of a conflict management provision.[31] NEPAD was created at the subsequent summit, in Abuja in October 2001. Its main activity has been the negotiation of selected members' adherence to a peer review process not only over their internal economic stewardship, but also over their progress toward public participation and governmental accountability.

The consummating chapter in the work of the AU has been its handling of security issues. On one hand, it took over the Ivorian conflict, which had been tearing the country apart since the military coup of December 1999, and put Mbeki in charge of the mediation effort after ECOWAS efforts had reached an impasse. By 2007, a power-sharing agreement went into effect between the rebel New Forces and the government of Laurent Gbagbo but without, as yet, providing free and full participatory elections. On the other hand, in the Darfur genocide, the AU was able, after long negotiations with the government of Bashir in Sudan, to provide a peacekeeping force with a limited mandate in 2005 and then to work with a newly mandated UN force established in 2007, which has yet to bring the murderous conflict under control. The AU's new order works ever so slowly, aided not so much by ripeness as by fatigue among the warring parties.

NEGOTIATION FOR COOPERATION

Negotiation means overcoming conflict with agreement, but many negotiations lead to agreement on a new cooperative order rather than simply ending old conflict. All the regional and subregional organizations in African, including the OAU and AU, were established through negotiation, and a major multilateral set of cooperation agreements of the postwar world—the Yaounde, Lome, and then Cotonou series between the European Communities (EC) and the African and other states also involved repeated negotiations within the African side.[32] As in conflict negotiations, there is little that is uniquely or specifically African in these experiences, but at the same time it is clear that African statesmen are negotiating, and they are developing a broad experience that, when successful, underscores some important universal lessons and characteristics of the process. In African multilateral negotiations for cooperation, as in multilateral negotiations over conflict, the political purposes of the negotiating session override the technical commitments of the negotiated outcome. Indeed, cooperative negotiations can be divided into diplomatic and integrative cooperation; in the former, it is the declaration of the moment, attendance at the meeting, announcement of joining or not, that matters, whereas in the latter, it is the long-term engagement that is important. In the first case, the substance of the negotiations is needed as an occasion or a cover for the diplomatic event of the moment, but its coherence, feasibility, and reality are less important. In the second, the substance is the event, and parties do not leave the table before they have agreed to something that will work.

In 1968, for example, Zaire negotiated an Economic Union of Central Africa (UEAC) to win the Central African Republic (CAR) and Chad away from the Customs Union of the Central African States (UDEAC) of former French Equatorial Africa, including the rival state of Congo.[33] The goal was a diplomatic event in which the important matter was to see who would attend "Mobutu's party"; the substance of the Economic "Union" was secondary, and the negotiations did not waste time over its details. The CAR soon left UEAC to return to UDEAC, leaving the remaining members no longer even contiguous with each other. Although this is a particularly striking example, it is typical of a large number of cooperative negotiations, even in those cases where integrative cooperation is also present. The supposedly biennial summit meetings of the Maghrib Arab Union (UMA), the regional organization of North Africa, show how the procedural value of a meeting, or not, outweighs any substantive value of the organization.[34]

In the substance of cooperation, the technical expertise often comes from outside, since African states' technical resources are sometimes limited. The Mano River Union of Liberia, Sierra Leone, and Guinea (and, in 2007, Ivory Coast) was based on a 1972–1973 United Nations Development Program (UNDP) mission report, and the subregional economic organizations—ECOWAS, the Preferential Tariff Area (PTA) of East and Southern Africa (which became the Common Market for East and Southern Africa [COMESA] in 1997), the Economic Union of the States of Central Africa (CEEAC), and even NEPAD—were based on studies of the Economic Commission for Africa (ECA).[35] The fact that the Mano River Union, as well as CEAO, conflicted with provisions of ECOWAS, negotiated with the same members and others at about the same time, was an instance of political decision bypassing the technical engagements. In the case of African negotiations with the EC and EU, the external source of expertise has particularly difficult implications for Africa. European states are able to coordinate their political and technical diplomacy into an agreed proposal for aid and other aspects of their relationship with associated African states under the Yaounde conventions and with the African, Caribbean, and Pacific (ACP) states under the subsequent Lome and Cotonou conventions that can be presented as a take-it-or-leave-it offer.[36] Only in 1975, in the negotiation of the first Lome convention, did the African states develop enough solidarity among themselves (under the political clout of Nigerian leadership) and sufficiently coordinate technical and political inputs to be able to make proposals as a basis for discussion and finally for agreement.[37]

At the same time, when the two inputs operate together, they play a crucial role in African negotiations for cooperation, and the fact that some states effectively integrate political and technical components of their diplomacy while others do not gives the former a clear edge in specific negotiations. A country that provides a proposed text has a clear advantage over the others, and African cooperative negotiations frequently proceed on the basis of a single negotiating text. The case of the Lome I negotiations and the examples of the external proposals for subregional economic communities are echoed at the intra-African level by the Maghrib Arab Union (UMA) negotiated at Marrakech in 1989. Morocco and Algeria had minimalist and diplomatic notions of cooperation, and Libya and Mauritania were less precise in their expectations. But Tunisia came with a well-prepared draft that served as the basis of the agreement. At an earlier time of bilateral cooperation, it was Libya that came to Jerba with a political draft for a union in 1974, which Tunisia signed but then repudiated on closer examination.[38] And, at a later time of continental cooperation, it was Libya that came with an initial text for the creation of the AU.

The same characteristic marked the negotiation of the OAU itself in Addis Ababa in 1963, when Ethiopia proposed its own draft, elaborated by experts on the basis of the Rio Treaty of the Organization of American States in conjunction with the Monrovia-Lagos Group of African states; in this case, the similar Ethiopia and Monrovia-Lagos texts were confronted by a very different draft for a tighter union proposed by the Casablanca Group of African states, which provided an alternative that could be rejected as individual provisions were selected.[39] Once the single negotiating text is in hand, African multilateral diplomacy generally proceeds, in a classical fashion, by amendment and consolidation. Amendment involves the addition of proposals not contained in the main draft. An example is Tunisia's detailed proposal for the Commission for Mediation, Arbitration and Conciliation added to the OAU Charter at Addis Ababa. The degree to which additional proposals are integrated into the main proposal is an indicator of the primacy of integrating over simply diplomatic cooperation involved in the negotiations. Consolidation is often more characteristic of negotiations, referring to a watering down of proposals to the lowest common denominator in order to achieve the necessary consensus. Since consensus, rather than coherence, is required for diplomatic cooperation, consolidation by watering down is a frequent characteristic. It is also a common feature in the negotiation of OAU resolutions.

In multilateral cooperative negotiations, African state representatives behave as other negotiating parties do, but with some characteristics exhibited more strongly than others. The main emphasis in this analysis has been on the distinction between diplomatic and integrative cooperation, and the history of regional and subregional organizations of cooperation bear out the point. Such organizations do exist, even if inefficacy is often the price paid for their continued existence. More strikingly, when they die, they have to be reinvented, as the experiences of North, West, East, Central and Southern Africa all show. Their creation, maintenance, and reinvention all take negotiation, whether of the diplomatic or the integrative kind.

CONCLUSIONS

African states are becoming increasingly experienced in negotiation, and their negotiating often errs in overaccommodation rather than in overintransigence.

They know how to make a deal, more than how to keep or implement one. Negotiations are more successful in dampening or managing the current rounds of conflict or in providing frameworks for the current rounds of cooperation than in devising lasting resolutions or durable integration. Africa has piled up an almost sad list of high goals for big projects that fall flat into the dust, most notably in its dreams of regional and continental integration. There is the repeated feeling, and indeed engagement based on that feeling, that the sum of a lot of Littles adds up to a Lot. Other places (notably Europe) are seen as providing a model, but the prolonged political process that Europe went through to unite (to the extent that it is united today) or the special conditions, including a bloody war, that led the United States to begin a unification process are overlooked.

It is the security area, in particular, that has eluded Africa. While interstate wars have been rare, having turned from inconclusive military confrontations to bumpy negotiation processes, internal wars have been conducted with abandon under the impenetrable shield of sovereignty. But sovereignty is the creation of the so-called outsiders, without whose agreement the claims of the state concerned would never hold. African states will not interfere in another's intrastate conflict for fear that they will be weakening their own claims to protective sovereignty on the day that other states need to intervene should they experience internal conflict. This is no atmosphere for creative, constructive negotiations on internal conflict, as the events in Sudan, Zimbabwe, and Congo in the early 2000s so sadly show.

The current order, like the old one, is fluid. Even that, however, is no mean achievement, for it does provide limits to conflict and experience in cooperation and reinforces the nature and rules of the ongoing African system of international relations. Such behavior may be so pervasive because it finds its roots in cultural traditions, but such explanations are more likely to be exaggerated cultural determinism. The tradition of blood money in some areas and the absence of any negotiating tradition at all in others may be just as characteristic.

More important has been the role negotiation has played in achieving independence.[40] All formerly colonial African states (with the possible exception of Guinea-Bissau) achieved independence through some degree of negotiation, in most cases after only minimal violence, and in those cases where violent struggle was prolonged, such as Algeria, Zimbabwe, Namibia, Angola, and Mozambique, negotiation was all the more important to end it. Such experience and conditioning has been crucial to the establishment of contemporary political cultures and behaviors. In that sense, Africa can be said to have a culture of negotiation, although in the early 2000s it is being tested by civil conflict in important countries of the North (Algeria), East (Ethiopia, Somalia, Sudan, and Kenya), West (Ivory Coast, Nigeria), Center (Chad, Central Africa, Congo) and South (Zimbabwe).

There is a crying need to bring this culture of negotiation back into domestic relations. There, unlike interstate relations, force is the means of order and therefore the means of contesting it.[41] Negotiations to handle grievances are slow and unsatisfying; aggrieved segments of the population harken back to the cries of the political entrepreneur, and rebellion breaks out, bringing normal state and societal functions to a halt for long periods before the two sides settle down to serious negotiations. Because governments are unused to handling grievances through "normal politics," and their citizen groups have little experience in negotiation, the settlement of old and added grievances takes an inordinately long amount of time. While it is true that traditional measures for managing conflict, such as blood money, intermarriage, and ancestor-dominated pacts, took a long time to evolve, they are no longer effective, and yet contemporary Africa has not invented any new mechanisms to fill the gap.[42] Internal conflicts tear up Africa, and it badly needs some standards on which to negotiate stabilizing outcomes.

One reason why the changes that took place in South Africa in 1990–1994 and their subsequent durability have been described by many as a miracle, has been because both sides were authoritarian societies, untrained in negotiation, and yet they negotiated themselves into a new order with, arguably, no losers. The few other states/societies that have achieved comparable results, such as Mozambique, Burundi, and possibly Congo, did so only after considerable bloodshed and socioeconomic disruption. The terrible inadequacy of negotiations in Rwanda, Sudan, Somalia, Congo (Brazzaville), Chad, Ethiopia, Eritrea, Angola, and above all, Ivory Coast, leaves much to be learned and practiced before Africa can point to conflict management as a new domestic order of governance.

Because the challenge is ongoing, it is more important than ever to end with the traditional call for more research. So little work has been done on the actual practice of negotiation in Africa, as has been noted at several points above, and yet the field is rich with examples. The challenge of finding out "who said what to whom with what effect," so necessary to a deep understanding of negotiating behavior, is probably no greater in Africa than elsewhere and may actually be lessened by the importance accorded to the practice. The few studies that exist have shown that the challenge can be overcome. A better understanding of the process as it is conducted in Africa can serve to expand an understanding of the methods and potentialities of the process itself globally while also reinforcing the culture of negotiation in Africa.

NOTES

1. See I. William Zartman, "The Quest for Order in World Politics," in I. William Zartman, ed., *Imbalance of Power* (pending) (Boulder: Lynne Rienner, 2008).

2. On state-society relations, see Jean-François Bayard, *L'État en Afrique* (Paris: Fayard, 1989); Donald Rothchild and Naomi Chazan, eds., *The Precarious Balance* (Boulder: Westview, 1989); Jean-François Bayard, Stephen Ellis, and Beatrice Hibou, *Criminalization of the State* (Bloomington: Indiana University Press, 1997); Steve Kayizzi-Mugerwa, ed., *Reforming Africa's Institutions* (New York: United Nations University Press, 2003); and Mark Beissinger and Crawford Young, eds., *Beyond the State Crisis?* (Baltimore: Johns Hopkins University Press, 2002).

3. See I. William Zartman, "Conflict Prevention, Management, and Resolution," in Francis Deng and I. William Zartman, eds., *Conflict Resolution in Africa* (Washington, D.C.: Brookings Institution, 1991).

4. On Cold War efforts to limit African conflicts, see chapters by I. William Zartman, Crawford Young, and Daniel Kempton on the Horn and North, Central, and Southern African, respectively, in Roger Kanet and Edward Kolodziej, eds., *The Cold War as Cooperation* (New York: Macmillan, 1991).

5. For a discussion on the causes of African conflict, see I. William Zartman, *Ripe for Resolution: Conflict and Intervention in Africa,* 2nd ed. (New York: Oxford University Press, 1989), chap. 1. On the Somali and Moroccan irredenta, see chaps. 2 and 3; on Libya, see René Lemarchand, ed., *The Green and the Black* (Bloomington: Indiana University Press, 1988). On the stability of the status quo over settlement outcomes in the Western Saharan conflict, see Khadija Mohsen-Finan, *Le Sahara occidental: Les enjeux d'un conflit régional* (Paris: CNRS, 1997).

6. On the Moroccan-Algerian case, see Zartman, *Ripe for Resolution,* chap. 2; Nicole Grimaud, *La politique extérieure de l'Algérie* (Paris: Karthala, 1984); John Damis, *Conflict in Northwest Africa* (Stanford: Hoover, 1983); Mohsen-Finan, *Le Sahara occidental.*

7. See Robert G. Armstrong et al., *Socio-Political Aspects of the Palaver in Some African Countries* (Paris: UNESCO, 1979); Sally Engle Merry, "Mediation in Non-Industrial Societies," in Kenneth Kressel and Dean G. Pruitt, eds., *Mediation Research* (San Francisco: Jossey Bass, 1989), but cf. Laura Nader and Harry Todd, eds., *The Disputing Process: Law in Ten Societies* (New York: Columbia University Press, 1978), where mediation appears only in non-African cases; I. William Zartman, ed., *Traditional Cures for Modern Conflicts: African Conflict "Medicine"* (Boulder: Lynne Rienner, 1999). For divergent African attitudes toward negotiation and conflict management, see the "conflict resolution" sections in Zartman, *Ripe for Resolution,* chaps. 2–5.

8. For some recent studies of mediation, including African applications, see Kressel and Pruitt, eds., *Mediation Research;* Saadia Touval and I. William Zartman, eds., *International Mediation in Theory and Practice* (Boulder: Westview, 1985); Christopher Mitchell and Keith Webb, eds., *New Approaches to International Mediation* (Westport, Conn.: Greenwood, 1988); Jacob Bercovitch and Jeffrey Rubin, eds., *Mediation in*

International Relations (New York: St. Martin's, 1992); Jacob Bercovitch, ed., *Resolving International Conflicts* (Boulder: Lynne Rienner, 1996); Stephen John Stedman, "Negotiation and Mediation in Internal Conflict," in Michael Brown, ed., *The International Dimensions of Internal Conflict* (Cambridge: MIT Press, 1996); I. William Zartman, ed., *Elusive Peace: Negotiating to End Civil War* (Washington, D.C.: Brookings Institution, 1995); Jacob Bercovitch, "Mediation in International Conflict," in I. William Zartman, ed., *Peacemaking in International Conflict* (Washington, D.C.: U.S. Institute of Peace, 2007); I. William Zartman and Saadia Touval, "International Mediation," in Chester Crocker, Fen Hampson, and Pamela Aall, eds., *Leashing the Dogs of War* (Washington, D.C.: U.S. Institute of Peace, 2007); Jacob Bercovitch, "Mediation," in Jacob Bercovitch, Victor Kremenyuk, and I. William Zartman, eds., *Handbook of Conflict Resolution* (Thousand Oaks, Calif.: Sage, 2008).

9. See I. William Zartman, "Africa as a Subordinate State System," *International Organization* 21, no. 3 (1967): 545–564; Yassin el-Ayouty and I. William Zartman, eds., *The OAU after Twenty Years* (New York: Praeger, 1984), esp. chaps. 2 and 7.

10. I. William Zartman, "Internationalization of Communal Strife: Temptations and Opportunities of Triangulation," in Manus Midlarsky, ed., *Internationalization of Communal Strife* (New York: Routledge, 1993).

11. C. O. C. Amate, *Inside the OAU* (New York: St. Martin's, 1986), chap. 5.

12. I. William Zartman, "Prevention Gained, Prevention Lost: Collapse, Competition, and Coup in Congo," in Bruce Jentleson, ed., *Opportunities Missed, Opportunities Taken* (New York: Rowman and Littlefield, 1999).

13. On the three roles, see Zartman and Touval, "International Mediation."

14. Mohammed Maundi et al., *Getting In: Mediators Entry into the Settlement of African Conflicts* (Washington, D.C.: United States Peace Institute, 2005).

15. As shown by Marina Ottaway, "Eritrean and Ethiopia: A Transitional Conflict," in Zartman, ed., *Elusive Peace*, pp. 112–118.

16. Jean-Emmanuel Pondi, "The Burkinabe-Malian Border War," in I. William Zartman and Jeffrey Z. Rubin, eds., *Power and International Negotiation* (Ann Arbor: University of Michigan Press, 2000).

17. Zartman, *Ripe for Resolution*, chap. 3.

18. For three exceptional accounts, see John Stremlau, *The International Politics of the Nigerian Civil War* (Princeton: Princeton University Press, 1977), chaps. 6 and 7; Saadia Touval, *The Boundary Politics of Independent Africa* (Cambridge: Harvard University Press, 1972), chap. 9; and Timothy Sisk, *Democratization in South Africa: The Elusive Social Contract* (Princeton: Princeton University Press, 1995).

19. Jeremy Armon and Andy Carl, *The Liberian Peace Process, 1990–1996* (London: Conciliation Resources, 1996).

20. Gerard Prunier, *The Rwanda Crisis* (New York: Columbia University Press, 1995); Howard Adelman and Astride Suhrke, *The Rwandan Genocide* (New Brunswick: Transaction, 1999); Joyce Leader, *Rwanda in Crisis* (World Peace Foundation, 1998).

21. Zartman, *Ripe for Resolution*, p. 68.

22. Hizkias Assefa, *Mediation of Civil Wars* (Boulder: Westview, 1987), pp. 128ff.

23. Jeffrey Davidow, *A Peace in Southern Africa* (Boulder: Westview, 1980). Stepehen Low, "The Zimbabwe Settlement," in Saadia Touval and I. William Zartman, eds., *International Mediation in Theory and Practice* (Boulder: Westview, 1985); Stephen John Stedman, *Peacemaking in Civil War* (Boulder: Lynne Rienner, 1988). I am grateful to Robert Lloyd for bringing this case to my attention.

24. Zartman, *Ripe for Resolution,* chap. 5.

25. Chris Alden, "The UN and the Resolution of Conflict in Mozambique," *Journal of Modern Africa Studies* 33, no. 1 (1995): 103–128, at 105, 114.

26. On the evolving role of the OAU in general, see Yassin El-Ayouty, ed., *The OAU after Ten Years* (New York: Praeger, 1975); Michael Wolfers, *Politics in the Organization of African Unity* (New York: Barnes and Noble, 1976); El-Ayouty and Zartman, eds., *The OAU after Twenty Years;* Yassin El-Ayouty, ed., *The OAU after Twenty-Five Years* (New York: Greenwood, 1990); R. A. Akindele, *The Organization of African Unity, 1963–1988,* special issue, *Nigerian Journal of International Affairs* 14, no. 1 (1988); Maurice Kamto, Jean-Emmanuel Pondi, and Laurent Zang, *L'OUA: Rétrospectives et perspectives africaines* (Paris: Economica, 1990); I. William Zartman, "Mediation in Africa: The OAU in Chad and Congo-B," in Jacob Bercovitch, ed., *Studies in International Mediation* (New York: St. Martin's, 1999); and Edmond Keller and Donald Rothchild, eds., *Africa in the New International Order* (Boulder: Lynne Rienner, 1996). See also Olusegun Obasanjo, ed., *The Kampala Document* (New York: African Leadership Forum, 1991).

27. Figured from Annex 6, Mediation Efforts, in El-Ayouty and Zartman, eds., *OAU after Twenty Years.*

28. On the Chadian peacekeeping operation, see chapters by Dean Pittman and Henry Wiseman in El-Ayouty and Zartman, eds., *The OAU after Twenty Years;* and Nathan Pelkovits, "Peacekeeping: The African Experience," in Henry Wiseman, ed., *Peacekeeping: Appraisals and Proposals* (New York: Pergamon, 1983). Cf the experience of ECOWAS in Liberia, in Margaret Vogt, ed., *The Liberian Crisis and ECOMOG* (Lagos: Gambumo Publishing, 1992).

29. Obasanjo, *The Kampala Document;* Francis Deng and I. William Zartman, *A Strategic Vision for Africa: The Kampala Movement* (Washington, D.C.: Brookings Institution, 2002).

30. See I. William Zartman, "The Future of Continental Regionalism: Birth of the African Union," *Africa Contemporary Record* 27 (New York: Africana Publishing, 1998–2000). There are as yet no detailed analyses of the establishment and workings of the AU.

31. See Deng and Zartman, *A Strategic Vision for Africa.*

32. See I. William Zartman, *The Politics of Trade Negotiations between Africa and the European Communities* (Princeton: Princeton University Press, 1971); John Ravenhill, *Collective Clientelism: The Lome Convention and North-South Relations* (New York: Columbia University Press, 1985); Frans Alting von Geusau, ed., *The Lome Convention and a New International Economic Order* (Leyden: Sijtof, 1977); I. William Zartman, ed., *Europe and Africa: The New Phase* (Boulder: Lynne Rienner, 1993).

33. Cf I. William Zartman, *International Relations in the New Africa* (Lanham, Md.: University Press of America, reprint, 1987), esp. pp. 147ff.

34. I. William Zartman, "The Ups and Downs of Maghrib Unity," in Michael Hudson, ed., *Middle East Dilemma: The Politics and Economic of Arab Integration* (New York: Columbia University Press, 1999).

35. Peter Robson, *Integration, Development and Equity* (London: Allen & Unwin, 1983).

36. Zartman, *The Politics of Trade Negotiations,* p. 225 et passim; I. William Zartman, "Lome III: Relic of the 1970s or Model for the 1990s?" in C. Cosgrove and J. Jamar, eds., *The European Community's Development Policy* (Bruges: Collège d'Europe, de Tempel, 1986).

37. Ravenhill, *Collective Clientelism;* Joanna Moss, *The Lome Conventions and Their Implications for the United States* (Boulder: Westview, 1982); I. William Zartman, "An American Point of View," in Frans Alting von Geusau, ed., *The Lome Convention and a New International Economic Order* (Leyden: Sijtof, 1977), pp. 141ff; John Ravenhill, "Evolving Patterns of Lome Negotiations," in I William Zartman, ed., *Europe and Africa: The New Phase* (Boulder: Lynne Rienner, 1993).

38. Nicole Grimaud, *La Tunisie à la recherche de sa sécurité* (Paris: Presses Universitaires françaises, 1995).

39. Boutros Boutros-Ghali, *The Addis Ababa Charter* (New York: Carnegie Endowment, International Conciliation Series 546, 1964); T. O. Elias, "The Charter of the OAU," *American Journal of International Law* 59, no. 2 (1965): 243–276; Lawrence Martinelli, *The New Liberia* (New York: Praeger, 1964), pp. 138–140.

40. See Gilbert Khadiagala and Donald Rothchild, eds., *The Impact of Colonial Bargaining on Intergroup Relations in Africa,* special issue of *International Negotiation* 10, no. 2 (2005); Donald Rothchild, "Racial Stratification and Bargaining: The Kenyan Experience," in I. William Zartman, ed., *The 50% Solution* (New Haven: Yale University Press, 1987); Jeffrey Davidow, *A Peace in Southern Africa: The Lancaster House Conference in Rhodesia, 1979* (Boulder: Westview, 1984); Stedman, *Peacemaking in Civil War;* Chester Crocker, *High Noon in South Africa* (New York: Norton, 1992); Sisk, *Democratization in South Africa;* Patti Waldmer, *Anatomy of a Miracle* (New Brunswick, N.J.: Rutgers University Press, 1997); Allister Sparks, *Tomorrow Is Another Country* (University of Chicago Press, 1996); I. William Zartman, "Negotiating the South African Conflict," in I William Zartman, ed., *Elusive Peace: Negotiating to End Civil War* (Washington, D.C.: Brookings Institution, 1995); I. William Zartman, "Negotiating the South African Conflict," in Louise Nieuwmeijer and Fanie Cloete, eds., *The Dynamics of Negotiation in South Africa* (Pretoria: Human Sciences Research Council, 1991). Unfortunately, similar studies—or even historical accounts—do not exist for most African countries.

41. Zartman, ed., *Elusive Peace;* I. William Zartman, ed., *Governance as Conflict Management* (Washington, D.C.: Brookings Institution, 1995); Cynthia Arnson and I. William Zartman, eds., *Rethinking the Economics of War: The Interface of Need, Creed, and Greed* (Baltimore: Johns Hopkins University Press; and Washington, D.C.: Woodrow Wilson International Center Press, 2005).

42. Zartman, ed., *Traditional Cures for Modern Conflicts.*

Part IV

Global Engagement

Commitment, Competition, and Responsibility

10

The U.S. Role in Promoting Peaceful African Relations

DONALD ROTHCHILD

> The Ethiopia-Eritrea case demonstrates that high-level, sustained, continuous U.S. engagement in peacemaking in Africa can have a major positive impact. The case also demonstrates the importance of multilateral, coordinated leverage in the form of significant carrots and stick.
>
> —JOHN PRENDERGAST,
> *U.S. LEADERSHIP IN RESOLVING AFRICAN CONFLICT*

The outcomes of Africa's intrastate wars have been most devastating, particularly for the civilians trapped between the contending forces. These armed conflicts have caused millions of deaths, large numbers of refugees and displaced persons, and grave destruction of property. In addition, these wars have undermined political stability and have gravely hindered economic development. Nineteen armed conflicts took place around the world in 2004, with the number of significant armed conflicts in Africa rising to five. All of these conflicts were intrastate in nature, pitting states (often led by ethnic or religious elites) against oppositions that combined ethnic, ideological, and personalistic support.[1] Compared to other regions of the world, Paul Collier and Anke Hoeffler find Africa's economic characteristics to be "highly unfavorable for conflict risk," reflecting the continent's lower per capita income, slower GDP growth, and more rapid population growth.[2] These intense and often brutal civil wars proved difficult to negotiate, and because of lingering distrust after their termination, agreements were difficult to implement. Frequently, the results were weak states that remained fragile, unable to deal effectively with the difficult to resolve commitment and information problems.[3] The effect in many cases was to make third-party intervention indispensable if these constraints are to be overcome.

External intervention, which can play an important role in coping with intense identity-based conflict, occurs when the internal routes to conflict management are viewed as no longer a reliable means to achieve intergroup reconciliation. As internationally accepted norms on human rights are violated, powerful states within or outside the region may decide upon some form of noncoercive or coercive intervention to raise the costs of abusive or obstructive action. These strong states may threaten to intercede forcefully, or they may adopt various strategies of soft intrusion aimed at changing the behavior of actors on the African scene. Such soft, diplomatic approaches include conciliation, mediation, and arbitration; economic and political sanctions; the conditioning of peace assistance and trade relations; monitoring and verifying peace implementation; and utilizing a variety of threats, pressures, and incentives to alter the local parties' calculations on the distribution of gains from current policies. There is no single formula that is appropriate to all situations. Hence in utilizing a soft intervention approach public officials must adapt pragmatically to the particular challenges of each local context.

Although many African and non-African countries, individually or in coalition with others, have interceded in internal conflict situations on the continent, the United States stands out as a key potential actor in such undertakings. This reflects the U.S. government's command of extensive political, financial, and material resources and its enormous military and logistical capacities. When the United States brings pressure to bear on a conflict, as in Liberia and Sudan, it is in a strong position to change the incentives of local actors on agreeing to and maintaining the peace.[4] By 2006, however, it has become apparent that American primacy is in decline. Not only are American budgets overextended and its military power stretched thin by the engagements in Iraq and Afghanistan, but new great power competitors, such as China, are increasingly vying for African allies and challenging U.S. leverage.[5] This is counterbalanced to some extent by European Union initiatives in such conflict situations as Sierra Leone, Côte d'Ivoire, and the Democratic Republic of the Congo, but there are definite limits to such supportive actions as well. To be sure, America's ability to influence local preferences in Sudan and Zimbabwe is still evident, but there is no denying that a new element of uncertainty has to be factored into any calculations regarding its capacity to influence the conflict management process.

In addition, the scope for hard-power initiatives in Africa is circumscribed by public preferences. The United States is, in the words of Richard Haass, a "reluctant sheriff," a risk-averse country that lacks overriding material or security interests to cause it to become embroiled in large-scale military interventions in Africa.[6] American leaders and the general public seem torn between their dedication to the objectives of human rights, democracy, political stability, and conflict management, on the one hand, and their reluctance to assume the role of global peace enforcer on the other. Public opinion surveys indicate that leaders and the general public are more inclined to support U.S. interventions to protect the vulnerable and to further reconciliation that are multilateral and nonmilitary in nature (such as operations other than war or diplomatic initiatives) to those that involve military action and unilateralism.[7] Keeping this extensive U.S. aversion to high-risk interventions in mind, it is important to examine the manner and extent to which the U.S. commitment to conflict management appears to have shifted in the post–Cold War period.

In an effort to assess the extent of U.S. preparedness to intervene in a noncoercive and coercive manner to further peace and to protect Africa's vulnerable states, I analyze the American foreign policy approach in the post–Cold War period. I seek to gauge the advantages and disadvantages of adopting a soft intervention strategy. This analysis begins by focusing on the classic, low-profile American approach to external intervention to facilitate peaceful change. The American foreign policy establishment has shown itself to be a hesitant proponent of selective involvement in African conflict situations while being ever intent to avoid the costs and risks of becoming deeply embroiled in Africa's intrastate conflicts.[8] On rare occasions, however, American officials and the public at large have taken a more proactive stance, intervening with significant force in order to provide relief and to promote political stability.

As relief gave way to more far-reaching measures of peace enforcement, in Somalia for example, U.S. foreign policymakers showed themselves to be increasingly fearful of "mission creep" and unwilling to accept the potential losses arising from further humanitarian engagements in Africa. Significantly, they recoiled from major diplomatic or peacekeeping initiatives following the brief but bitter firefight in Mogadishu, Somalia, in October 1993. U.S. caution became manifest in the period afterward, as the Clinton team, guided in part by cautious policy prescriptions articulated in Presidential Decision Directive 25 of 1994, avoided becoming deeply enmeshed in the brutal strife that marked the destructive intrastate confrontations in Rwanda, Burundi, Sudan, Liberia, and the DR Congo.

TABLE 10.1 Intensity of U.S. sanctions on Africa

Target Country:	Sanction Intensity:	Years:	Primary Nation/ Organization Imposing Sanctions:	Notes:
South Africa	Limited	1962–1994	UN and U.S.	Arms embargo imposed.
	Limited	1975–1994	U.S.	**Tunney Amendment.** Temporary amendment to the Department of Defense appropriations bill terminating covert assistance to anti-Communist forces in Angola.
	Limited	1976–1985	U.S.	**Clark Amendment** (replaces Tunney Amendment). Sec. 404 of the **International Security Assistance Act of 1976**. (P.L. 94-239, later Sec. 118 of P.L. 96-533), prohibited aid that would help any group in Angola conduct military or paramilitary operations.
	Moderate	1985–1991	U.S.	**International Security and Development Cooperation Act of 1985** (replaces Clark Amendment) and Executive Order 12532 prohibited trade and certain other transactions involving South Africa, Revoked by: EO 12769, July 10, 1991.
	Extensive	1986–1991	U.S.	**Comprehensive Anti-Apartheid Act** (P.L. 99-440) sets policy objectives for the United States in South Africa, imposed a number of sanctions, banning the importation of South African goods and prohibiting American business investments in South Africa.
		1991	U.S.	Sanctions repealed under **Executive Order 12769**—Implementation of section 311 (a) of the comprehensive Anti-Apartheid Act—Signed: July 10, 1991—Revokes EO 12532, September 9, 1985; EO 12535, October 1, 1985.

TABLE 10.1 *(continued)*

Target Country:	Sanction Intensity:	Years:	Primary Nation/ Organization Imposing Sanctions:	Notes:
Sudan	Limited	1989–present	U.S.	Assistance programs suspended after the NIF-led coup.
	Limited	1992–present	U.S.	Arms embargo imposed.
	Limited	1993–present	U.S.	U.S. accuses Sudan of supporting international terrorism—on list with Cuba, Iran, Iraq, Libya, North Korea, and Syria.
	Moderate	1996–present	U.S.	Economic Sanctions and sanctions on leadership. **Antiterrorism and Effective Death Penalty Act of 1996** prohibits U.S. nationals from engaging in financial transactions with governments named on the State Department's terrorism list. President Clinton also announces a ban on senior Sudanese government officials from entering the United States (as called for in Security Council Resolution 1054).
	Moderate/ Extensive	1997–present	U.S.	Clinton Administration imposes comprehensive sanctions, under the **National Emergencies Act**, on the NIF government. The sanctions restrict imports or exports from Sudan, financial transactions, and prohibit investments.
	Extensive	2002–present	U.S.	**Sudan Peace Act** (P L 107-245) allows the Bush administration to levy the sanctions if he finds Khartoum is not negotiating in good faith with southern rebels to end civil war and condemned the government of Sudan for human rights abuses. (Passed House 359-8 on October 7, 2002. Passed Senate by unanimous consent on October 9, 2002. Signed into law October 21, 2002).

TABLE 10.1 *(continued)*

Target Country:	Sanction Intensity:	Years:	Primary Nation/ Organization Imposing Sanctions:	Notes:
Liberia	Limited	1990–1998	U.S.	U.S. and other major donors end assistance programs, except emergency humanitarian aid.
	Limited	1991–2000	U.S.	Ban on US military aid from 1991 to 2000, except assistance to ECOMOG.
	Limited	1992–present	UN and U.S.	Arms Embargo imposed.
	Limited	2000–present	U.S.	President Clinton barred President Charles Taylor, senior members of the Liberian government, and their supporters and families from entering the United States. Clinton stated that the action represented an explicit sanction against the Liberian government for its failure to end its trafficking in arms and illicit diamonds with the RUF, and thus fueling the Sierra Leonean conflict.

Sources: Hulbauer, Gary Clyde and Barbara Clegg, "The Impact of Economic Sanctions on US Trade: Andrew Rose's Gravity Model," International Economic Policy Briefs PB03-4, Institute for International Economics, April 2003; Institute for International Economics, "Table 1.1: Chronological Summary of Economic Sanctions for Foreign Policy Goals. 1914–99." http://www.iie.com/research/topics/sanctions/sanctions-timeline.htm. National Association of Manufacturers (March 1997), A Catalog of New US Unilateral Economic Sanctions For Foreign Policy Purposes 1993–1996; Jentleson, Bruce (2000), *International Conflict Resolution After the Cold War,* pp. 142–144. United Nations Department of Peacekeeping Operations, at http://www.un.org/Depts/dpko/dpko/home.shtml.

After that, President Clinton's 1998 trip to Africa signaled the beginning of a highly selective and cautious U.S. re-engagement with African conflict management, and this involvement persisted during the George W. Bush administration that followed. America's sense of guilt over its lack of decisive action in the Rwanda, Burundi, Democratic Republic of the Congo, and other crises partially explains the Bush administration's rising concern over underdevelopment and political instability in such states as Sudan and Liberia and its efforts to send peacekeeping missions to these intensely conflicted countries. But despite such efforts to protect the vulnerable, I argue that U.S. policymakers seem likely to pursue risk-adverse strategies in Africa well into the future, avoiding losses rather than taking extensive risks to promote peace.[9] As Charles Kupchan warns, "U.S. willingness to shoulder the burdens of global engagement will be diminishing in the years ahead."[10] Under these circumstances, I hypothesize that U.S. support for soft-diplomatic initiatives, emphasizing diplomatic pressure and incentives (as opposed to the projection of American military power), reflects this diminishing political will and capacity. It will be the likely scenario in most conflict situations in the years immediately ahead.

SOFT INTERVENTION

It is more and more accepted as doctrine that states have a right to intervene in the domestic affairs of other states to pursue humanitarian objectives. Sovereignty must not act as a cover for political elites engaging in destructive acts of ethnic cleansing, systematic rape, and mass murder. Sovereignty must be exercised responsibly.[11] When a state launches an attack on a section of its own citizenry or formulates and carries out genocidal programs, the international community is adversely affected and cannot remain aloof, justifying inaction in terms of the domestic jurisdiction principle. This was a lesson learned during the struggle against apartheid in South Africa and a lesson that had to be re-learned during the 1994 Rwanda genocide, where the international community stood on the sidelines as some 800,000 Tutsis and moderate Hutus were slaughtered. As President Clinton, speaking before an audience of genocide survivors in Rwanda, declared: "We in the United States and the world community did not do as much as we could have and should have done to try to limit what occurred in Rwanda in 1994." He then went on to warn somberly that "we're still not organized to deal with it."[12]

U.S. involvement in Africa's intrastate conflicts has taken many forms. These range from the relatively low-cost and easy-to-operationalize noncoercive incentives to relatively high-cost rescue and peacekeeping missions and military interventions. To gauge American and UN commitment to intervene in intense intrastate conflicts, I will concentrate on such key noncoercive areas of initiative as exhortation, diplomatic pressure, political and military alignment, sanctions, and the facilitation of peace accords.

EXHORTATION AND DIPLOMATIC PRESSURE

It is not surprising that a powerful international actor such as the United States, alone or in coalition with other states or international organizations, has interceded during the cautious engagement phase to exhort cooperative behavior and to protest abusive actions. Such interventions have long been recognized as representing "a legitimate exercise of the law of humanitarian intervention."[13] For example, the U.S. Senate took a strong stand on human rights violations in the Sudan in 1993, forcefully criticizing the Sudanese government for engaging in a campaign of "ethnic cleansing" against the Nuba people in Kordofan Province; it went on from such criticism to oppose the extension of further World Bank or IMF loans while these abuses remained present,[14] and in 1997, during a visit to Uganda, U.S. Secretary of State Madeleine Albright pointedly met with Sudanese rebel leaders and blamed Sudanese government officials for the continuing civil war in that country.[15] U.S. exhortations and criticisms of human rights abuses were also commonplace in Zimbabwe, Liberia, Darfur, and South Africa, largely because such statements were relatively easy to invoke and low in cost. They raise the costs on governments that abuse the civil and political rights of their citizens at little expense to themselves.

However, the ability of such observations to alter the policies and preferences of target governments or movements should not be overestimated. Unless these exhortations are linked to other, more coercive forms of action, their ability to induce a change of outlooks or practices remains in doubt. Where the target country's political elite is firmly ensconced in power and civil society is relatively ineffective, such noncoercive influences are important as indicators of international standards but somewhat limited in their immediate impact on local behavior.

POLITICAL AND MILITARY ALIGNMENT

Great power alignments with their African allies during and after the negotiation phase have at times had a significant impact on the nature and level of intrastate conflict. This was particularly evident in the Cold War period, when the United States and the Soviet Union conditioned their economic and political support upon African state compliance. In what amounts to an asymmetrical exchange relationship, the hegemonic power influenced African country choices by providing security in exchange for resource supplements.[16] As David A. Lake describes this transactional relationship: "Dominant states provide order and, in turn, make demands on other states; subordinate states benefit from the order and regard the demands of the dominant state necessary for that order as legitimate and, therefore, authoritative."[17] Of course, when they come to view these demands as unnecessary and contrary to their interests, partially autonomous but weaker parties may resist them and refuse to engage in further transactions.

For example, in the way that the United States joined forces with Haile Selassie's Amharic-dominated state and built up and equipped his armed forces, it strengthened state power at the expense of other nationalities in the country. Bereket Habte Selassie, the former attorney general of Ethiopia and professor of law at various universities, has noted that between 1953 and 1977, the United States extended $279 million in military aid to Ethiopia and trained over 3,500 Ethiopian military personnel in the United States. The defense pact between the United States and the Haile Selassie government "bolstered" the Ethiopian army, enabling it to occupy Eritrea and other subordinate regions.[18] In exchange, the United States strengthened its position in the region, securing an important regional ally as well as access to the defense-related Kagnew Station.[19]

A similar dynamic was at work in Liberia, where U.S. foreign policymakers strengthened the political center of a longtime ally against challengers in the periphery. In the 1980s, U.S. military assistance to the government of Samuel Doe in Liberia nearly doubled, and for a time, Liberia became the largest recipient of U.S. aid per capita of all the states in sub-Saharan Africa.[20] By aligning himself with the United States and using its aid to build up his army at the political center, Doe was in a position until late 1989 (and the emergence of Charles Taylor) to resist Libyan offers of assistance and to maintain power, brutally suppressing opposition threats to his rule.

In contrast to this common pattern of support for governments, U.S. policymakers also aligned themselves at times with insurgent forces who were opposed to Soviet-backed central authorities in Angola. Most notably, by extending economic and military assistance to the Ovimbundu-based National Union for the Total Independence of Angola (UNITA) insurgency in the 1980s, the United States helped Jonas Savimbi survive military assaults from the Angolan army and also weakened the capacity of the Luanda government to penetrate and regulate its society. Such alignments were not without political cost for the United States, for it came to be perceived as inspired by its Cold War concerns and highly partisan in its orientation.

Military assistance and political alignments have remained in evidence in the post–Cold War times. The United States has reportedly supplied military

TABLE 10.2 Total U.S. military aid to sub-Saharan Africa, 2000–2006

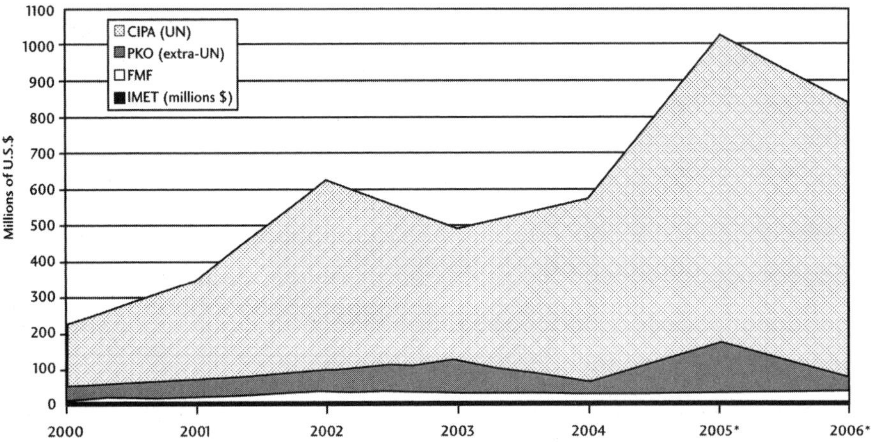

U.S. Military Aid to Africa (millions $)	2000	2001	2002	2003	2004	2005*	2006*
IMET	7.5	8.5	10.3	9.9	11.2	10.8	11
FMF	10.3	19.7	28.6	28.1	20.9	26.3	24
PKO (non-UN Peacekeeping)	36.7	46.5	54.9	78.1	30.2	133.2	41.4
CIPA (UN Peacekeeping Contributions)	170.7	264.4	526.3	372	508.8	852.2	764.9
TOTAL	225.2	339.1	620.1	488.1	571.1	1022.5	841.3

CIPA (UN Peacekeeping Contributions) (millions $)	2000	2001	2002	2003	2004	2005*	2006*
Angola	1.9						
Western Sahara		11.5	13.3	5.4	10	10	8
DR Congo	30.2	74.1	226.4	158.8	30	249	207
Rwanda	10.5	10.8	13.1	14	16	16	14
S. Leone	128.1	96.7	205.9	144.9	71	47	4
Ethiopia-Eritrea		71.3	67.6	48.9	50	50	33
Burundi					42	94	90
Liberia					290	135	159
Sudan/Darfur						250	250
TOTAL	170.7	264.4	526.3	372	508.8	852.2	764.9

Source: U.S. Department of State, "International Affairs (Function 150) Budget Request," http://www.state.gov/m/rm/rls/.

assistance, though not arms, to Uganda, Eritrea, and Ethiopia, "in an explicit effort," writes Meghan O'Sullivan, "to help them combat insurgencies fueled by the government of Sudan."[21] It has been reported that these nonlethal weapons have aided the Sudan People's Liberation Army in particular.[22]

SANCTIONS

When exhortations and moderate diplomatic pressures prove insufficient to induce a change of preferences on the part of Africa's leaders, U.S. foreign policymakers have often turned to economic, political, and military assistance sanctions. Sanctions, writes Bruce Jentleson, are the "actual or threatened denial of economic relations by one or more states (sender(s)) intended to influence the behavior of another state (target) on non-economic issues or to limit its military capabilities."[23] They seek through the use of nonmilitary punishments to raise the costs on norm-breaking regimes, thereby instilling a sense of urgency regarding a change of policies. Sanctions are less costly than direct military intervention, representing a tool of soft intervention that punishes deviant behavior and, then, rewards positive responses that reshape the priorities of targeted actors. They indicate strong disapproval with existing approaches to handling conflict issues, putting into effect either specific punitive or more comprehensive measures if the targeted actor refuses to change its practices.[24] When sanctions are backed by a wide coalition of states, inside as well as outside the region, they can raise the costs on trade and investment. In this respect, Kofi Annan notes, "the multilateral threat of economic isolation may help to encourage political dialogue, while the application of rigorous economic and political sanctions can diminish the capacity of the protagonists to sustain a prolonged fight."[25]

Certainly, the imposition of sanctions on Rhodesia, apartheid South Africa, Liberia, and Sudan did isolate the targeted regimes, increasing their costs of doing business and attracting investments. Although their effects must not be overstated, they did impose some costs, thereby contributing to a change of behavior. As U.S. Ambassador Arthur Goldberg recognized regarding the application of sanctions in the 1960s and 1970s against the continuance of Ian Smith's white minority rule in Rhodesia, sanctions would not likely have a decisive impact, but "their economy may be affected sufficiently to induce them to negotiate."[26] Clearly, the hardships of mandatory economic sanctions on Rhodesia did not prove sufficient to force policy changes on their own, but, in conjunction with the insurgent military attacks on the ground, they helped to underscore the isolation of the ruling coalition.[27] Hence their limited success often lay more in terms of local and international political symbolism and psychological relations than in the achievement of compliance with the wishes of the sending state or states.[28]

Especially in the case of relatively industrialized South Africa, sanctions created problems of acquiring the latest technology and importing petroleum products as well as complicating the ability of South Africans to compete in international sporting events, something that involved great symbolic significance for the white community. By the time the Reagan administration took office, the struggle for progressive change in South Africa had emerged as a domestic issue in American politics and the "constructive engagement" policy of working with the white-led regime, avoiding the imposition of additional sanctions, and offering to end the country's "polecat status in the world" if it cooperated on Namibian independence had failed to induce a change of priorities on the apartheid approach.[29] When a mild incentives approach did not suffice, then a more coercive incentives strategy became imperative.[30] Hence, despite the Reagan team's opposition to placing sanctions on South African trade and on its access to certain technology and services, Congress passed the 1986 Comprehensive Anti-Apartheid Act into law. The American use of the economic sanctions weapon was directed mainly at South Africa's white ruling establishment and sought to raise the costs on further governmental inaction in coming to the negotiating table and ensuring that no backsliding took place after the negotiated settlement. The 1986 law made the South African government's acceptance as a legitimate member of the world community conditional upon its reevaluation of the need for political reform. The ban on new loans and investments was damaging to the South African economy, as was the denial of access to world markets for certain goods, technology, and services. Real growth slackened, leading to a continuing rise in unemployment (some 2 million by 1991) and an estimated fall in average income of some 15 percent.[31] Only when President Nelson Mandela assumed power in South Africa and appealed to the United States to end sanctions did the Clinton team move to dismantle the existing sanctions legislation.

At different times, the United States also invoked sanctions against a number of norm-breaking states or movements in Africa, including Uganda, UNITA in Angola, Ethiopia/Eritrea, Rwanda, Nigeria/Biafra, Somalia, Libya, Sudan, and Liberia. The U.S. government publicly protested the Amin regime's harassment of its Asian citizens and subsequently went beyond this to invoke a wide range of measures, including the closure of the American embassy, the temporary cessation of bilateral aid projects, and the termination of programs by such U.S. government agencies as the Export-Import Bank and the Overseas Private Investment Corporation.[32] The effect was to further isolate a pariah regime, which was ultimately overthrown when Ugandan refugee forces linked up with Tanzanian troops to depose the dictator. The UN Security Council decision to impose an arms embargo on Ethiopia and Eritrea in May 2000 was an important step, for it sent a signal at a time of high tension "against business as usual."[33]

Sanctions of moderate intensity were also put into effect against Charles Taylor's regime in Liberia, mainly for its failure to end its illicit trafficking in military arms and conflict diamonds. U.S. sanctions followed soon after the publication of newspaper accounts in 2000–2001 of Taylor's dealings with the Sierra Leonean insurgent movement, the Revolutionary United Front. U.S. officials accused Taylor of providing the RUF with military arms in exchange for diamonds,[34] unlawfully depleting Liberian resources, and undermining "the orderly development of its political, administrative, and economic institutions and resources."[35] U.S. sanctions were put into effect on May 22, 2001 (Executive Order 13213) and then strengthened in a subsequent executive order (No. 13348 of July 27, 2004). These sanctions banned the importation of Liberian diamonds into the United States, broadened the arms embargo, and limited the ability of Taylor and his entourage to travel, move funds, or open bank accounts abroad. Although a United Nations Panel of Experts' Report on Liberia in October 2001 indicated that the Liberian government had complied with the requirement on grounding Liberian aircraft suspected of sanctions busting, it concluded that sanctions had only a limited impact. Reports provided information suggesting that the Taylor regime was still getting weapons. They also suggested that Taylor had not expelled the RUF from its territory, and that some government officials had violated the UN travel ban. Later, at the request of the newly elected government of Ellen Johnson-Sirleaf, the United States asked the UN Security Council to ease its ban on the sale of weapons to enable the Liberian security services to train their police and military services. This partial easing was agreed to in June 2006. The Security Council also lifted the embargo on Liberian timber exports but left the embargo on uncut diamonds in place for another six months, until an internationally verifiable plan was implemented.[36]

U.S. economic sanctions were also directed against the ruling National Islamic Front (NIF) government in Sudan, initially over its preparedness to provide sanctuary and support for terrorist groups and then to pressure it to negotiate in good faith with southern insurgents as well as to improve its human rights record. In an effort to demonstrate to the Sudanese government the seriousness of U.S. concerns over the Sudan government's sponsorship of state terror and its continued "prosecution of a devastating civil war," President Bill Clinton blocked Sudanese governmental assets in the United States. He also prohibited the importation of Sudanese goods into the United States and the exportation of U.S. goods to Sudan. An exception was made for the importation of gum Arabic, which was described as a product "unavailable from other sources."[37] The effect of making an exception for gum Arabic was a weakening of the force of the sanctions weapon from the very outset, however.

Then, in 2002, the U.S. Congress enacted, and President George W. Bush signed into law, the Sudan Peace Act. This Act brought the United States more directly into the ongoing peace negotiations between the Sudanese government and the Sudan People's Liberation Movement and Sudan People's Liberation Army (SPLM/SPLA). Describing the action of the Sudanese government in intensifying the prosecution of the war and in using militias to raid and enslave peoples in areas outside its control as constituting genocide, the 2002 Sudan Peace Act offered the Sudanese government incentives to move ahead with the negotiating process within a six-month period or face the consequences in terms of sanctions. Thus, if the Bush administration concluded that Sudanese authorities were not negotiating in good faith, the president was authorized to instruct U.S. spokespersons to continue to vote against international financial institution loans and credits to the government of the Sudan as well as to "take all necessary and appropriate steps, including through multilateral efforts, to deny the Government of Sudan access to oil revenues to ensure that the Government of Sudan neither directly nor indirectly utilizes any oil revenues to purchase or acquire military equipment or to finance any military activities."[38] As Meghan O'Sullivan noted, the United States had shifted from an earlier "regime change strategy" to a new emphasis on "engagement" in the negotiating process.[39] This change of emphasis made the new law part of a larger process that provided Sudanese authorities with an incentive to alter their behavior in bringing the civil war to a peaceful conclusion.

It must be recognized that sanctions are inevitably a blunt instrument. They can be difficult to apply without hurting the very people in target countries whose interests they seek to advance. Moreover, experience over the years indicates that it is not easy to organize a coalition of states prepared to bear the costs of implementing an effective sanctions policy. Sanctions involve potential economic and political costs for domestic publics in the sending countries, which governments may not be prepared to shoulder. Reportedly, the Clinton team became increasingly cautious about employing the sanctions weapon abroad as powerful American farm and business organizations expressed concerns over the potential loss of economic opportunities in the target countries. These American business interests voiced a fear that "unlimited sanctions only make foreign rivals stronger and taint us as unreliable suppliers."[40] Clearly, then, in both sender and receiver countries, sanctions cannot be used cavalierly. They may invoke fear and opposition at home and strengthen target regimes abroad, shifting blame for adverse outcomes to outsiders and causing a rally-round-the-flag effect.[41]

To act as a meaningful incentive it is important that the means of compliance, and therefore the termination of sanctions, should be specified at the outset.[42] The prospect that sanctions on oil would not be invoked under the Sudan Peace Act and, subsequently, that economic relations with the United States would be normalized if the Sudan government pursued negotiations with the South in good faith provided positive incentives for a constructive policy.[43] Clearly, unless sanctions carry with them a dynamic for change—one that enables the political elites in the initiating states to tighten or reduce their effects—they are likely to prove static and consequently ineffective.

MEDIUM-INTENSITY INTERVENTIONS

If soft, nonmilitary force interventions represent the typical U.S. response to intense intrastate conflict in Africa, occasional operations other than war (OOTW), which are somewhat harder in their approach, represent a useful contrast with this basic pattern. OOTW interventions, mainly peacekeeping and humanitarian interventions, entail military force that can involve either direct or indirect U.S. action. They can be traditional peacekeeping and provide an important incentive to maintain a cease-fire, negotiate a peace agreement, or establish a buffer between warring parties; alternatively, they can be multidimensional peacekeeping initiatives that engage not only in buffering between the adversaries but also engaging in the rebuilding of war-torn economies and overseeing demobilization, disarmament, and the reintegration of armies. "The more hostile and numerous the factions," note Michael Doyle and Nicholas Sambanis, "the more difficult is the peace process, and the more international assistance/authority is needed to establish peace."[44] When these intervening forces are sanctioned by the international community (for example, the United Nations, regional organizations, or other state groupings), they can present a trip wire that raises the costs of an attack by one of the local adversaries. Should such an attack occur, as in Charles Taylor's National Patriotic Front of Liberia 1993 offensive against the Economic Community of West African States Monitoring Group troops dug in around Monrovia, ECOMOG, with UN Security Council endorsement, launched a counteroffensive and seized some 50 percent of the country. In the current period, the United States has contributed aid to UN peacekeeping forces in Angola, Western Sahara, DR Congo, Rwanda, Sierra Leone, Ethiopia and Eritrea, Burundi, Liberia, and Sudan. U.S. peacekeeping costs have risen sharply over the years, from $171 million in 2000 to an estimated $765 million in 2006. The United

States has contributed military personnel to UN missions in four cases—Somalia, Liberia, Ethiopia-Eritrea, and Mozambique—and has pushed for a UN peacekeeping initiative to buttress the African Union Mission in the Sudan (AMIS) in Darfur.

If most of the U.S. peacekeeping efforts have been largely consistent with its low-profile approach toward Africa, the humanitarian intervention in Somalia of 1992–1994 was harder in its profile. In line with the general trajectory of cautious engagement, the Somali humanitarian intervention assumed limited objectives from the outset. Elated over its military victory in the Gulf War and prodded on by scenes of starvation and suffering in Somalia (the so-called CNN effect), the Bush I administration, with UN endorsement, dispatched a 25,000-person U.S. military force to Somalia in 1992 to ensure a stable and safe environment for the delivery of relief supplies and to begin the process of national reconciliation.[45] Overwhelming force was deemed necessary by U.S. policymakers so that there would be no doubts among factional leaders regarding the need to cooperate.[46] This force proved sufficient to enable relief agencies to distribute supplies, re-open schools, re-activate hospitals, and begin economic rehabilitation; however, the U.S. military initially resisted appeals from the UN Secretary-General to disarm the light weaponry in the hands of rival militias.[47]

The Somali intervention diverged from the normal pattern of low-profile African engagements in that U.S. policymakers were prepared to intercede in situations where the state had failed—something it had been reluctant to do in other situations. From the outset, it was unclear what would represent a successful outcome or when it would be possible to disengage. There were nagging questions early on about the mission's ability to disarm the militias and restore order in Mogadishu, to cope with the threat of national disintegration, and to undertake the diplomatic initiative necessary for political healing. The U.S. military could not be expected to impose political legitimacy on a divided society with its clan-based rivalries and ethnoregional antagonisms (i.e., the Isaak rebellion and separatism in northern Somalia).[48] All that could reasonably be expected of it was to utilize the momentary opportunity of U.S. overrule to create the conditions for internal negotiations. The military did secure the main transportation routes, pacified a sizable area of the country, and to a limited extent, began the process of putting an administrative and security system in place.

However, the peace talks that took place under the aegis of the United Nations Task Force (UNITAF) proved to be a tenuous basis for ending the conflict. Instead of encouraging the development of civil society (e.g., traditional elites and authorities, religious leaders, professionals, women's organizations, and intellectuals), American and UN diplomats promoted negotiations among the powerful warlords on the scene. The route of negotiating a pact among warlords was attractive to American authorities because it was easier to put into effect, more cost-effective, and offered incentives on inclusiveness to the major warlords. John Hirsch and Robert Oakley, describing this strategy as "pragmatic," argue that it "reduced the level of confrontation with the faction leaders and minimized the risk of casualties, it put heavy weapons out of circulation, and it quickly broke through obstacles to the delivery of food and medicine in south-central Somalia."[49] On the downside, such a pact among militia leaders meant hesitant efforts to promote disarmament and entailed dealing with the very people who had been the source of the breakdown.[50]

The diplomatic process that took place after the U.S. military intervention represented an effort to contain the most destructive elements of the conflict. Although the American team did mediate some of the local conflicts on its own, the main task of negotiating a nationwide agreement fell to Ethiopian leader Meles Zenawi and the United Nations, with the Americans playing a supporting role.[51] In March 1993, the fifteen main factional leaders met in Addis Ababa under UN sponsorship, where they agreed to establish a seventy-four-member Transitional National Council that would have included the various clan leaders plus three elected representatives (one of whom had to be a woman) selected by each of the eighteen regional councils. The Transitional National Council would have served as a legislative body, and it would have set up an independent judiciary as well as provide for the establishment of elected and regional councils.[52] All of this appeared to come apart in the ensuing months, as violence flared up anew, and the UN high command declared this provisional framework null and void.[53]

As the security environment improved and relief convoys encountered less difficulty in delivering supplies to those requiring help, the American government pressed the UN Secretary-General for a transition to United Nations authority. Not surprisingly, the UN Secretary-General resisted assuming this costly and difficult assignment, even though the United States gave assurances of continued operational support during the transition. With Somalia lacking an effective government or integrated army, and with weaponry spread widely throughout the country, the new force (the United Nations Operation in Somalia—UNOSOM II) found itself precariously placed from the beginning. In part to compensate for UNOSOM II's apparent frailty, the Security Council authorized UN commanders to use force if necessary under Chapter VII of the Charter.

By failing to disarm the militias and to set a realizable political agenda, the initial UNITAF mission left UNOSOM II in a vulnerable position when the transition came into full effect in May 1993.[54] These problems were compounded by the gap between the new, ambitious mandate the UN set for itself and its limited capabilities to achieve its objectives. Under Security Council Resolution 814, the member states emphasized "the crucial importance" of disarmament and went on to request that UNOSOM II "assume responsibility for the consolidation, expansion and maintenance of a secure environment throughout Somalia."[55] Such goals might be logical, but they were exceedingly difficult to apply in the context of a failed state. The UN, which lacked the necessary military and civilian personnel and equipment to achieve such tasks, was thinking in terms of lofty principles, not strategic realities.

This deficiency soon became apparent. In June 1993, Somali National Alliance (SNA) militiamen attacked a UNOSOM II inspection team, killing twenty-four Pakistanis and three Americans. UN Secretary-General Boutros Boutros-Ghali, pinning the responsibility for this attack on General Mohamed Farah Aidid, launched a series of raids to capture him. These forays culminated in a disastrous battle in Mogadishu on October 3 that left eighteen American soldiers and one Malaysian soldier dead, ninety U.S., Malaysian, and Pakistani soldiers wounded, and many hundreds of Somali killed or injured. The October confrontation, as Boutros-Ghali noted, was "a turning-point in the international community's involvement in Somalia."[56]

Americans generally regarded the Somali intervention as a humanitarian undertaking that did not advance U.S. national interests. Therefore, when SNA militiamen killed a number of American servicemen and dragged one of their bodies through the streets of Mogadishu, it triggered widespread public demands for withdrawal. Public opinion surveys held immediately after the October battle showed a significant segment of the American public favoring a withdrawal of American troops from Somalia in six months.[57] The American political elite was most outspoken on the need to disengage. Republican Senator Trent Lott stated unambiguously that "under no circumstances should the United States remain in Somalia."[58] On the Democratic side, Senator Sam Nunn opposed military support for an expanded UN mission. Nunn declared: "Our role is too important in areas of the world that are significant to United States military interests, security interests, and economic interests to allow our military effectiveness to be dissipated in places where we have no economic and no security interests."[59] Faced with this strong opposition, President Clinton took the pragmatic course and announced that the United States intended to withdraw its forces by March 1994. The UN soon followed in March 1995.

Clearly, American policy had shifted from a preparedness to engage in OOTW undertakings back to soft intervention. In practice, U.S. policymakers appeared most reticent to take on new, multidimensional peacekeeping operations in Africa, on their own or in support of an active UN or regional organization involvement. Thus, the U.S. government largely stood on the sidelines in the mid-1990s and beyond as intrastate conflicts and militia violence wreaked havoc not only in Somalia but also in Sudan, Burundi, Rwanda, and the DR Congo. In Somalia, a relatively hard humanitarian intervention that lacked visible objectives and substantial public support had proved brittle as it encountered growing opposition among Africans. Without local support, interveners are likely to prove ineffective and to be unable to structure the necessary incentives for political consolidation.

FACILITATION OF PEACE ACCORDS

The different strategies outlined up to this point represent approaches that third parties can use to manage the peace process. But if they are to achieve their intended purposes, noncoercive and coercive incentives must operate within a broad framework of local legitimacy and be linked to an active diplomatic effort. As Meghan O'Sullivan contends, "only when sanctions [in the Sudan] were combined with other tools of engagement did they become part of a successful equation to move Khartoum in a promising direction regarding the war."[60] An embargo on arms was also put in effect during the Ethiopian-Eritrean War along with a series of other measures, including an aid freeze, diplomatic isolation, pressure from international financial institutions that reduced lending greatly during the conflict period and provided no substantial debt relief, and heavy Congressional expressions of outrage over the extent and brutality of the fighting.[61] Because the combined thrust of diplomatic action and incentive policies can set an appropriate framework for advancing peace, it is necessary to turn at this point to one of the most prominent forms that U.S. diplomacy takes in Africa (e.g., third-party mediation) and its implications for an incentives strategy.

As indicated earlier, the United States uses a variety of soft intervention tools to bring about a cessation of civil war and to protect Africa's vulnerable peoples, but unless these tools are effectively linked to an active diplomatic process these tools by themselves may seem passive and lacking in the momentum necessary to produce a major change in policy direction. The added push for change can come from diplomatic pressure, censure, threat, coercive action, and official or nonofficial mediation. Mediation, which has an important place in a soft intervention approach, is viewed broadly here to include the extension of good offices, the provision of information, the clarification of misperceptions and misinformation, the development of a consensus on principles and objectives, the setting of an agenda, the defining of the issues in contention, the suggestion of compromises and adjustments, and the manipulation of pressures and incentives to alter payoff structures.[62] What kind of mediation—direct or indirect—is generally preferred by U.S. officials, and which type is most consistent with a soft diplomatic strategy?

It is important to note at the outset that data on civil war termination indicate that the general prospects for resolving Africa's civil wars by means of negotiation and mediation are limited. When certain circumstances have prevailed (e.g., the emergence of identifiable bargaining parties, a mutually hurting stalemate, leaders determined upon a political solution, and external pressures to reach agreement), third-party interveners have at times succeeded in bringing about an agreement in roughly one-fourth of the civil wars in the twentieth century.[63] This difficulty of mediating civil wars becomes more apparent when they involve an ethnic or religious dimension. Identity conflicts reflect the high level of emotion surrounding these encounters and the great reluctance that state authorities have for dealing with the leaders of ethnic-based guerrilla movements;[64] they fear that such diplomatic contacts may accord the insurgents a measure of international respectability, even legitimacy.[65] Moreover, the room for maneuver in a state-ethnoregional conflict is circumscribed by the nature of the "two-level" bargaining process: Not only must the negotiators deal with each other, but they must negotiate and maintain the backing of their communal members.[66] Yet despite these unpropitious bargaining conditions, third parties have sometimes managed to establish communications, set agendas for the discussion of divisive issues, and even facilitate successful negotiations.

One of the key variables that distinguish great power mediators from others is their high status and command of critical political and economic resources. Access to extensive resources enables great powers to be in a better position to influence the adversaries through offers of inducements or the threat or actual withdrawal of inducements.[67] On some occasions, various African leaders, singly or in collaboration with African or international partners, have undertaken successful mediatory initiatives in state-substate conflicts, as with Emperor Haile Selassie in the 1972 Sudanese peace negotiations; Thabo Mbeki in the 2003 Burundian political and military agreement; the Inter-Governmental Authority on Development (IGAD) in Sudan's 2005 Comprehensive Peace Agreement; the African Union in the 2006 Darfur Peace Agreement; and the Economic Community of West African States (ECOWAS) mediators' contribution to the process of returning Liberia to stable relations. Even though only a short-lived success, Foreign Minister Amara Essy of Côte d'Ivoire in 1996 mediated an agreement between the government of Sierra Leone and the insurgent opposition, the Revolutionary United Front.

Other African leaders have been less successful, however. Although Kenya's President Daniel arap Moi displayed considerable skill in hammering out an agreement on Uganda in 1985, he was constrained by the unwillingness of the negotiating parties to commit themselves credibly to what had been negotiated. President Mobutu Sese Seko's peacemaking initiative for Angola in 1989 and the various attempts by Moi, President Robert Mugabe, and President Hastings Banda to intercede in the ongoing civil war in Mozambique softened the perceptions that the adversaries held about one another, but they produced little decisive change.[68] In Burundi, the formal diplomatic track (the so-called Arusha process) organized by former Tanzanian President Julius Nyerere and backed by the countries in the Great Lakes region as well as U.S. special envoy Howard Wolpe in the 1990s failed in its efforts to bring about conclusive negotiations between the Tutsi-dominated government and the Hutu rebels.[69] And in Darfur, African Union mediators, with strong U.S. backing, succeeded in getting the Sudan government and the Minni Arkou Minnawi faction of the Sudan Liberation Movement (SLM) to sign the Darfur Peace Agreement, only to see the SLM's main military commanders and political elites officially suspend the implementation of the agreement in June 2006. African states have advantages in terms of personal rapport with political elites and knowledge of the local situation, making them particularly effective at times in facilitating agreements among disputants in neighboring countries.

By contrast, when the great powers cooperated with each other and mediated *directly* between the conflicting parties (Angola 1988), or *indirectly* backed African or other powers in their efforts to mediate intrastate disputes (Angola 1991, Mozambique 1992, Liberia 2003, Sudan 2003–2006), the prospects for successful conflict management were enhanced. Provided the great powers view their interests in terms of becoming actively involved, they can bring enormous international pressures to bear on local actors, raising the costs on intransigent resistance. According to Sudan's Foreign Minister Mustafa Ismail, "the Nuba Mountains agreement was reached because the U.S. was involved."[70] The ability of strong third-party actors to manipulate the preferences of local actors and to help alter the choices of conflicting parties on negotiating a peaceful outcome to their conflicts has not always proved sufficient (as indicated by Jonas Savimbi's renewal of the Angolan civil war in 1992), but such measures can often make a critical difference.

In line with this distinction between direct and indirect mediation, I emphasize here an American policy preference for indirect mediatory activity in dealing with African conflicts. With the end of the Cold War struggle, the international stakes at play remain relatively low, and the difficulty of coping with intrastate strife in Africa has increased noticeably. As a consequence, the tendency to become directly involved in highly consuming diplomatic initiatives that may involve a reputation cost if they fail (as in the case of Angola) has gradually given way to a preference for conflict resolution efforts under the auspices of regional and international organizations or friendly powers. The effect of this is to induce U.S. officials to favor soft diplomatic measures and indirect mediation in Africa for the most part. I explore the latter preference in the discussion that follows.

Direct Mediation

The urge to intervene directly in African disputes certainly ebbed as the Cold War passed and as the United States became aware of the moral responsibilities and costs that go with a lead role in implementing peace settlements. Even so, the temptation to play a direct role in facilitating the management of certain high-profile conflicts never disappeared entirely. As a consequence, it is important for us to note some of the forms that such direct interventions can take.

First, there is considerable scope for linkage between public and private U.S. initiatives. An example of such linkage is former President Jimmy Carter's efforts to promote an Ethiopian-Eritrean dialogue in 1989. Certainly Carter, as a past president of the United States, had exceptional entrée to people in high places as well as an aura of power associated with his former office. In addition, his attempt to bring the main protagonists together occurred with the tacit approval of the U.S. government and against a backdrop of increasing superpower cooperation on regional issues.[71] The Ethiopian government and Eritrean People's Liberation Front (EPLF) delegations, despite very different conceptions of the negotiating process, did come to the Carter Center in Atlanta prepared to talk about the issues in dispute. The results of these talks represented a hopeful beginning, for agreement was reached on ten out of thirteen points, including the agenda for the follow-up meeting, the nature of the delegations, and the official languages to be used at the meetings. Several substantive issues on the role of the chair and the nature and composition of the observers were left unsettled, however, and these contributed to the ultimate breakdown of the dialogue when the follow-up conferees reassembled in Nairobi.

Second, prominent U.S. officials, often retired from the State Department, have mediated African conflicts under United Nations auspices. In the South African case, a UN mission led by former Secretary of State Cyrus Vance in August 1992 did engage in some quiet mediatory activities between African National Congress (ANC) Secretary General Cyril Ramaphosa and Minister of Constitutional Development Roelf Meyer. Moreover, former Secretary of State James A. Baker III, acting under the auspices of the UN, mediated on the Western Sahara issue between representatives of Morocco and the *Frente Popular para la Liberacion de Saguia el-Hamra y Rio di Oro* (the Polisario Front). In meetings at Houston in September 1997, the parties reached agreement on the size of the Electoral College to be used in the upcoming referendum on the territory's self-determination.[72]

Third, officials of the U.S. government have from time to time acted as direct mediators in Africa's internal conflicts. In May 1991, as the insurgent Ethiopian People's Revolutionary Democratic Front (EPRDF) forces approached the perimeters of Addis Ababa and President Mengistu Haile Mariam fled the country, the United States interjected itself into the unfolding Ethiopian crisis. At the request of the caretaker government and the opposition movements in the field (the EPRDF, the Eritrean People's Liberation Front, and the Oromo Liberation Front), Assistant Secretary Herman Cohen convened a meeting of these parties in London on May 27 to work out a cease-fire and transition to a new regime. The situation on the ground was deteriorating rapidly. EPRDF troops remained on the outskirts of Addis Ababa, honoring a pledge to Cohen that they would not enter the city prior to the commencement of negotiations. Upon learning that the interim government was losing control of its troops and anxious to spare the city the destruction that accompanies house-to-house combat (as in Somalia), Cohen seized the initiative and publicly recommended that the EPRDF be allowed to move into the capital before the peace conference "to restore order in Addis."[73] The interim government, unable to prevent the occupation of the city by EPRDF troops, watched helplessly during the night of May 27–28 as the insurgents took charge. By sanctioning the EPRDF takeover, Cohen contended that he acted as the "conscience of the international community," sparing Addis Ababa from certain havoc.[74]

Cohen also made proposals to the Sudanese government and the SPLM/SPLA concerning a cease-fire, disengagement of forces, and the adoption of federalism in March 1990, but to no avail.[75] He did succeed in mediating an agreement in Zaire between President Mobutu Sese Seko, Archbishop Laurent Monsengwo (the president of the High Council of the Republic), and Prime Minister Etienne Tshisekedi wa Mulumba on a sharing of power during the 1992–1994 transition period, but this effort proved disappointing, for Mobutu, after accepting the compromise, refused to abide by its terms.[76]

Nevertheless, it was the complex *international* negotiations over Angola and Namibia that showed that U.S. initiatives can sometimes result in enduring settlements. From independence in November 1975 to the signing of the Angola/Namibia agreements in December 1988, the conflict among the Angolan nationalist movements (UNITA, the Popular Movement for the Liberation of Angola [MPLA], and until the early 1980s, the National Front for the Liberation of Angola [FNLA]) was a civil war exacerbated by the ties that these nationalist movements had to various external powers. Whereas the MPLA government was bolstered by Soviet military equipment and Cuban combat troops, UNITA, and for a time FNLA, received Chinese military equipment following decolonization, U.S. military assistance around independence and after 1985, and South African military assistance and combat support during all phases of the war. As the civil war continued into the 1980s, and the MPLA and UNITA forces, backed by their external allies, became locked into a costly stalemate, the various local and international actors showed themselves to be increasingly responsive to proposals for international—but not internal—negotiations. By late 1987, the time seemed ripe to make a new concerted effort to settle outstanding regional differences.[77] The opportunity for a serious peace initiative was greatly advanced by the change from adversarial to cautiously cooperative relations that took place in the mid-1980s between the United States and the Soviet Union.

With U.S. Assistant Secretary of State for African Affairs Chester A. Crocker acting as mediator, the representatives of Angola, Cuba, and South Africa met in secret in London in May 1988 to explore the Angolan proposal for a four-year withdrawal of Cuban forces. This was followed by sessions in Brazzaville, Cairo, and New York, where persistent behind-the-scenes Soviet and American communications and pressures on their allies resulted in the acceptance of general principles on Namibia's independence, a phased Cuban withdrawal, verification, and formal recognition of the U.S. role as mediator. In the Geneva talks that followed, the conferees issued a joint statement announcing a de facto cessation of hostilities and proposed dates for Namibia's independence and the exit of Cuban and South African troops from Angola. At successive meetings in the fall, the parties agreed that the Cuban troop withdrawal would take place over a 27-month period and that two-thirds of these soldiers would leave during the first year with the remainder being redeployed by stages to the north. However, this international pragmatism did not carry over to the related task of reconciling the intrastate war between the MPLA and UNITA. Only as the great powers came to recognize the urgency of reaching an internal agreement and, under the auspices of a Portuguese mediator, to exert significant influence on their respective allies did a fragile and largely ineffective peace agreement materialize.

The United States used direct mediation again in the high-stakes effort spearheaded by Senator John Danforth, President George W. Bush's special envoy in the Sudan, whose initiatives helped a U.S. State Department team to negotiate the six-month internationally monitored cease-fire in the Nuba mountains in January 2002 and then supported its implementation by setting up and funding the Joint Military Commission/Joint Monitoring Mission. Yet despite the occasional contributions of a direct mediatory approach, the United States has agreed only occasionally to assume the responsibilities of a lead mediator in Africa. This probably reflects an assessment that the risks and costs of such a mediatory role are relatively high, especially in societies that may not share Western values on bargaining and the maximization of individual interests. The result in most cases is to reinforce the strong American preference for working under the aegis of regional countries or organizations when dealing with African conflict issues. As Acting Assistant Secretary of State for African Affairs Charles R. Snyder stated, "Time and time again United States policy *is most effective* when it works to complement African efforts already underway across the continent."[79] Hence we turn now to the U.S. experience with indirect mediation.

Indirect Mediation

With U.S. political will and capacity limited in the post–Cold War period and its strategic interests in Africa constricted, it is not surprising that the Clinton and Bush administrations turned increasingly to indirect forms of mediating Africa's internal conflicts. Indirect mediatory activity, as used here, refers to U.S. backing for a formal mediatory effort mounted under the auspices of another actor. This approach can involve U.S. support for a private, informal mediator (as with former President Jimmy Carter's 1989 attempt to mediate between the Ethiopian government and the EPLF) or for a formal third-party undertaking led by another state or regional or international organization (for example, U.S. special envoy Howard Wolpe's support of the Nyerere-led mediation effort in the negotiations between the Great Lakes countries and Burundi in the late 1990s; and the backing of IGAD's mediation efforts in Sudan in the 2003–2006 period). The line between indirect mediatory activity and direct mediation can sometimes be blurred. In Somalia, following the U.S. humanitarian intervention in 1992–1993, for example, American diplomats mediated certain local conflicts on their own; however, in the critical negotiations of March 1993, where the fifteen factional leaders agreed in Addis Ababa to set up a Transitional National Council, UN and Ethiopian government leaders played a prominent third-party role, facilitated by a behind-the-scenes American diplomatic effort.

There are numerous instances of U.S. indirect mediatory action in Africa. In the case of Rhodesia (Zimbabwe), where Britain was still recognized by most countries as the colonial power, U.S. diplomats played a supporting role during the 1979 Lancaster House peace negotiations. At one critical juncture when the future constitutional arrangements were being discussed, it became necessary for the British to try to overcome the Patriotic Front's objections by offering to grant financial assistance for land resettlement and redistribution to an independent Zimbabwe. At this time, U.S. diplomats, who had been observing the procedures closely, came to the support of the British mediators, offering financial grants to an independent Zimbabwe for such broad purposes as agriculture and education. By enabling the Patriotic Front negotiators to save face, American side-payment helped to keep the conference from breaking down over the land issue.[80]

Although U.S. mediators played a central role in facilitating an international settlement in Angola in 1987–1988, it followed the lead of two middle-power mediators—Zaire and Portugal—and the United Nations when it came to negotiating an internal agreement between the MPLA government and UNITA. The first effort to mediate an internal agreement was undertaken by Zaire's President Mobutu Sese Seko, with the quiet backing of the Soviet Union and the United States, at Gbadolite, Zaire, in June 1989. After meeting separately with Angolan President José Eduardo dos Santos and UNITA leader Savimbi to work out an agreement on the summit declaration, Mobutu presented the rivals before a gathering of Africa's respected leaders, securing a handshake between the arch adversaries as well as a sketchy agreement on a cease-fire and on plans to move toward national integration. While supportive in principle of the Gbadolite peace process, U.S. policymakers did not put sufficient pressure on Savimbi to ensure that he would appear at the Kinshasa mini-summit or move toward a compromise agreement.

When it became apparent that the Gbadolite process had stalled, dos Santos called for the acceptance of a new third-party intermediary. Portugal, the former colonial power, stepped into the situation and from mid-1990 to 1991 chaired a series of talks between representatives of the Angolan government and UNITA. This time, the two great powers took a very active stance in support of the Portuguese mediators. U.S. Secretary of State James Baker met publicly in December 1990 with the Angolan foreign minister, while Soviet Foreign Minister Eduard Shevardnadze conferred with Savimbi. Then the two great powers jointly sponsored a meeting in Washington, D.C., attended by the Angolans and the Portuguese, which produced the so-called Washington Concepts Paper, a conceptual framework for the Portuguese-mediated talks. Under the terms of this paper, the coming into effect of a cease-fire would be followed by a cessation of exports of lethal materiel to the parties by the United States, the Soviet Union, and all other countries (the so-called triple-zero option); an amendment of the constitution to provide for multiparty democracy; free and fair elections; the creation of a national army; and the installation of an international monitoring force. The Washington agreement on basic negotiating principles gave a new impetus to the flagging Portuguese-led deliberations. With U.S. and Soviet observers in attendance, the negotiators at Bicesse came to an agreement on such knotty issues as the formation of a national army, the setting of dates for the cease-fire, the timing of multiparty elections, and the international monitoring process (including great power participation).

Following the first round of the presidential elections in 1992, it became apparent to Savimbi that he was unlikely to win the runoff election, and claiming fraud, he withdrew the UNITA units from the new Angolan army and renewed the civil war. At the outset, UNITA successfully occupied some 70 percent of the country; however, as the Angolan government purchased new arms from abroad and hired the services of the South African security firm Executive Outcomes, the tide of war changed, and the UNITA forces were put on the defensive.[81] Savimbi realized that it was time to return to the negotiating table.

This turn to peace was facilitated by the existence of ongoing negotiations between the Angolan government and UNITA at Lusaka, under the auspices of UN special representative Alioune Blondin Beye. In 1994, Beye, assisted by U.S. special envoy Paul Hare and other diplomats, carefully negotiated what became known as the Lusaka Protocol. The protocol reaffirmed the Bicesse accords and reestablished formal control by central authorities over the whole country, while at the same time providing UNITA with confidence-building measures. These measures included terminating Angolan army offensives, repatriating mercenaries, releasing political prisoners and captured soldiers, providing for UN monitoring of demobilization, including UNITA personnel in the police and army, and appointing UNITA party officials to high executive and administrative positions. Implementation of the protocol proved extremely difficult, mainly because Savimbi and his lieutenants appeared to engage in delaying tactics. Although the new government of national unity was installed in April 1997, Savimbi did not attend the opening ceremonies, and fighting continued in contested areas.

Indirect mediatory action was also evident on the part of U.S. officials during the critical phases of the 1992 Mozambican negotiations. In seeking to reconcile the Mozambican government and the Mozambique National Resistance (RENAMO), U.S. diplomats worked with Kenya's President Daniel arap Moi and Zimbabwe's President Robert Mugabe to mediate the conflict in August 1989. This effort soon lost its impetus, as RENAMO demanded recognition as a condition for negotiations, while the Mozambique Liberation Front (FRELIMO) government sought acceptance as the country's legitimate ruling authority.[82] In these circumstances, a new intermediary acceptable to both sides became essential. The rival parties agreed, in the summer of 1990, to begin direct talks in Rome under the joint mediation of the Italian government, the Roman Catholic lay organization Sant'Egidio, and the Roman Catholic Archbishop of Beira.

The United States, as Assistant Secretary of State for African Affairs Herman J. Cohen testified, "played a prominent facilitative role." It advanced the agenda of the talks, encouraged the parties to go to the bargaining table, and consulted with the mediators and rival interests over a two-year period.[83] In its capacity as an official observer, the United States sent legal and military experts to Rome to help iron out the details, and it consulted regularly with the contending parties over the cease-fire and military-related issues.[84] After sixteen years of war and an estimated 1 million deaths, the peace treaty signed by President Joaquim A. Chissano and RENAMO leader Afonso Dhlakama represented a major achievement. The timetables set for demobilization, disarmament, and unification of forces proved to be somewhat unrealistic and required further negotiations. Even so, a successful consolidation of the peace agreement through externally facilitated monitoring and supervision added significantly to stabilizing the peace process.

Indirect mediation efforts by the Bush administration in 2003 in Liberia and in 2003–2006 in Sudan were largely in line with this past low-profile approach. In the Liberian negotiations, prominent sources interviewed by this author emphasized that the United States was active in a supportive role, with the leadership of the peace process being an ECOWAS effort, backed by the Friends of Mediation (the United States, UN, and European Union).[85] Acting under the auspices of regional leaders, U.S. mediators facilitated the negotiation process and firmly avoided the role of primary actor.[86] In the Sudanese peace negotiations, U.S. influence came from giving advice to the parties, particularly the SPLM/SPLA, which sought its counsel, and not pressing for principles that its diplomats favored. "One of the keys to success" in Sudan, explained Acting Assistant Secretary of State Charles R. Snyder, "is actually falling in behind the work already done by the Africans, reinvigorating it, and taking it further" to include new, expanded measures.[87] This is not to say that U.S. representatives held back on all occasions from playing an assertive role in these negotiations. U.S. diplomats were forthright, for example, on the need to prevent any one of the Liberian factions from achieving a military victory; in the Sudan, they stressed the importance of preserving Sudanese unity, and they took the initiative in urging Abyei's self-administering status. In general, however, it seems reasonable to conclude that the United States sought local leadership of the negotiation process, and for the most part its diplomats shunned a prominent public role in these African interventions.

Clearly, external mediators, particularly those from great powers such as the United States, are acting prudently when they tread warily in Africa's negotiations and thereby promote a sense of African self-determination and ownership of the peace process. This often means avoiding the temptation to manipulate societal spokespersons and to act as a facilitator rather than a mediator with muscle.[88] The United States, according to public officials interviewed by this author, heeded this need for restraint in both the Liberian and Sudanese negotiations. Although an indirect mediatory strategy did not prove sufficient to bring a peaceful outcome to Darfur, the results were generally constructive in Liberia and Sudan's North-South settlement.

CONCLUSION: EVALUATING THE STRATEGIES

With the exception of such high-profile issues as South African sanctions, the mediation in Angola, the Somali humanitarian intervention, and the Sudanese diplomatic initiatives over the North-South and Darfur agreements, U.S. efforts to promote political stability and peace in Africa have been low in profile, involving limited commitments of energy and resources. The credibility of the United States was not at stake, and domestic public opinion was not mobilized to create a sense of urgent behavioral change on the part of government officials. Because of the limited American commitment, involvement in regional or global multilateral coalitions often appeared more likely to produce constructive results than higher-profile, unilateral engagements. Moreover, indirect mediation tended to be more useful in negotiating and implementing peace accords than direct mediation, an outcome that can be disappointing to well-intentioned observers determined upon creating quicker shortcuts to peaceful outcomes.

Paradoxically, in its efforts to protect Africa's vulnerable minorities, soft power has generally proved as effective, if not more effective, than hard power. In part, this is explained by the limits of American influence. In the African context, the United States does not always have the usable power attributed to it by observers at home and abroad. Its modern weaponry is not necessarily relevant, and its military forces frequently lack the support of local populations. Hence, as seen in Somalia, its army lacks the leverage necessary to influence local preferences in the desired direction. In part, this is also explained in terms of U.S. political will and preparedness to commit human lives and resources to protect vulnerable peoples and advance peace. American will and interests, then, combine to push U.S. strategists to seek to achieve their objectives in low-cost, low-risk ways. In these circumstances, human protection and peaceful relations tend to be ranked lower than the avoidance of heavy potential losses that accrue from following a principled but risky course.

But a soft intervention approach can also create problems when its tools do not prove sufficient to alter the behavior of targeted actors. U.S. denials of legitimacy or sanctions may raise costs but still prove inadequate to achieve the goals of decision makers. In Africa, indirect mediation, the preferred U.S. route, may lack enough manipulability to push the bargaining parties toward a mutually acceptable and peaceful outcome. Just as the strategies of soft intervention must be linked to active diplomacy to be effective, indirect mediation must link U.S. and European Union leadership to African determination to achieve the necessary momentum leading to peaceful outcomes. Soft intervention and indirect mediation are attractive strategies because they accommodate African sensitivities and American preferences simultaneously. They involve low risks for the sending country or countries and are respectful of local African competence and integrity. On many occasions, this is sufficient to bring about the desired change. But when it is not, a tipping point may be reached where hesitation and pragmatism must give way to stronger measures.

NOTES

I wish to express my appreciation to Nikolas Emmanuel, Timothy Sisk, John Harbeson, Matthew Hoddie, and Edith Rothchild for comments on the first draft of this chapter.

1. Lotta Harbom and Peter Wallensteen, "Appendix 3a: Patterns of Major Armed Conflicts, 1990–2004," in Renata Dwan and Caroline Holmqvist, eds., *SIPRI Yearbook, 2004* (Oxford: Oxford University Press, 2005), pp. 121–133.

2. Paul Collier and Anke Hoeffler, *On the Incidence of Civil War in Africa*, (Washington, D.C.: World Bank, 2000), p. 9.

3. David A. Lake and Donald Rothchild, *The International Spread of Ethnic Conflict: Fear, Diffusion, and Escalation* (Princeton: Princeton University Press, 1998), pp. 11–17.

4. Donald Rothchild, "U.S. Mediation of African Conflicts," 23rd Annual Conference of the SAIS African Studies Program (Washington, D.C.: SAIS–Johns Hopkins University, 2004), April 16–17.

5. Princeton N. Lyman and J. Stephen Morrison, *More Than Humanitarianism: A Strategic U.S. Approach Toward Africa*, Report No. 56 (New York: Council on Foreign Relations, 2006).

6. Richard N. Haass, *The Reluctant Sheriff: The United States After the Cold War* (New York: Council on Foreign Relations, 1997).

7. Donald Rothchild and Nikolas Emmanuel, "U.S. Intervention in Africa's Ethnic Conflicts: The Scope for Action," in Donald Rothchild and Edmond J. Keller, eds., *U.S.-Africa Relations: Strategic Encounters* (Boulder: Lynne Rienner Publishers, 2006), pp. 65–97.

8. Michael J. Smith, "Humanitarian Intervention: An Overview of the Ethical Issues," *Ethics & International Affairs* 12 (1998), p. 66.

9. Jack S, Levy, "An Introduction to Prospect Theory," in Barbara Farnham, ed., *Avoiding Losses/Taking Risks: Prospect Theory and International Conflict* (Ann Arbor: University of Michigan Press, 1994), pp. 7–22.

10. Charles A. Kupchan, *The End of the American Era* (New York: Alfred A. Knopf, 2002), p. 206.

11. Boutros Boutros-Ghali, *An Agenda for Peace* (New York: United Nations, 1992), p. 9; Olusegun Obasanjo, "A New Deal for Africa Spearheaded by Africans," in Olusegun Obasanjo and Felix G. N. Mosha, eds., *Africa: Rise to Challenge* (New York: Africa Leadership Forum, 1993), p. 338; Francis M. Deng, Sadikiel Kimaro, Terrence Lyons, Donald Rothchild, and I. William Zartman, *Sovereignty as Responsibility: Conflict Management in Africa* (Washington, D.C.: Brookings Institution, 1996), p. 172; and Solomon Gomes, "The OAU, State Sovereignty, and Regional Security," in Edmond J. Keller and Donald Rothchild, eds., *Africa in the New International Order* (Boulder: Lynne Rienner, 1996), pp. 37–51.

12. James Bennet, "Clinton Declares U.S., with World, Failed Rwandans," *New York Times*, March 26, 1998, p. A1.

13. Ernst B. Haas, "Human Rights: To Act or Not to Act?" in Kenneth Oye, Donald Rothchild, and Robert Lieber, eds., *Eagle Entangled: U.S. Foreign Policy in a Complex World* (New York: Longman, 1979), p. 181.

14. Senate Resolution 94, *Congressional Record*, 139, no. 46 (April 3, 1993), p. S4508; and House Concurrent Resolution 131, 103rd Congress, 1st Sess. (August 3, 1993), pp. 5–6.

15. Ed Warner, "Can Sudan Break Up?" *Voice of America*, no. 5–39444, April 1, 1998.

16. Donald Rothchild and Robert L. Curry Jr., *Scarcity, Choice, and Public Policy in Middle Africa* (Berkeley: University of California Press, 1978), pp. 322–327.

17. David A. Lake, "American Hegemony and the Future of East-West Relations," *International Studies Perspectives* 7, no. 1 (February 2006), p. 25.

18. Bereket Habte Selassie, *Conflict and Intervention in the Horn of Africa* (New York: Monthly Review Press, 1980), pp. 63 and 170. See also B. Selassie, "The American Dilemma on the Horn," in Gerald J. Bender, James S. Coleman, and Richard L. Sklar, eds., *African Crisis Areas and U.S. Foreign Policy* (Berkeley: University of California Press, 1985), p. 170.

19. Jeffrey A. Lefebvre, *Arms for the Horn* (Pittsburgh: University of Pittsburgh Press, 1991), pp. 139–140.

20. Yekutiel Gershoni, "War Without End and an End to a War: The Prolonged Wars in Liberia and Sierra Leone," *African Studies Review* 40, no. 3 (December 1997), p. 58.

21. Meghan L. O'Sullivan, *Shrewd Sanctions: Statecraft and State Sponsors of Terrorism* (Washington, D.C.: Brookings Institution, 2003), p. 243.

22. Ed Warner, "Can Sudan Break up?" *Voice of America*, April 1, 1998, p. 1, at Gopher.voa.gov/00/newswire/wed/CAN_SUDAN_BREAK_UP%3f.

23. Bruce W. Jentleson, "Economic Sanctions and Post–Cold War Conflict," in Paul C. Stern and Daniel Druckman, eds., *International Conflict Resolution After the Cold War* (Washington, D.C.: National Academy Press, 2000), p. 126.

24. Donald Rothchild, *Managing Ethnic Conflict in Africa: Pressures and Incentives for Cooperation* (Washington, D.C.: Brookings Institution Press, 1997), pp. 104–105.

25. Kofi Annan, "The Causes of Conflict and the Promotion of Durable Peace and Sustainable Development in Africa," Secretary General's Report to the U.N. Security Council, April 16, 1998, p. 8.

26. Bromley Smith, "Summary Notes of the 567th Meeting of the [U.S.] National Security Council," January 25, 1967, as reprinted in *Foreign Relations of the United States, 1964–1968*, "Africa," vol. 24 (Washington, D.C.: U.S. Government Printing Office, 1999), p. 941.

27. On the problems of enforcement, see David F. Gordon, "The Politics of International Sanctions: A Case Study of South Africa," in Miroslav Nincic and Peter Wallensteen, eds., *Dilemmas of Economic Coercion: Sanctions in World Politics* (New York: Praeger, 1983), pp. 195, 208.

28. James M. Lindsay, "Trade Sanctions as Policy Instruments: A Re-examination," *International Studies Quarterly* 30, no. 2 (June 1986): 155–156. See also O'Sullivan, *Shrewd Sanctions*, p. 28; and David A. Baldwin, *Economic Statecraft* (Princeton: Princeton University Press, 1985), p. 192.

29. Rothchild, *Managing Ethnic Conflict in Africa*, p. 102.

30. Pauline H. Baker, "The United States and South Africa: Persuasion and Coercion," in Richard N. Haass and Meghan L. O'Sullivan, eds., *Honey and Vinegar: Incentives, Sanctions, and Foreign Policy* (Washington, D.C.: Brookings Institution, 2000), p. 119; and Jeffrey Herbst, "Incentives and Domestic Reform in South Africa," in David Cortright, ed., *The Price of Peace: Incentives and International Conflict Prevention* (Lanham: Rowman & Littlefield, 1997), pp. 205–222.

31. Foreign Broadcast Information Service (FBIS), Sub-Saharan Africa 92, 238 (December 10, 1992), p. 20; and Donald Rothchild and John Ravenhill, "Retreat from Globalism: U.S. Policy in the 1990s," in Kenneth A. Oye, Robert J. Lieber, and Donald Rothchild, eds., *Eagle in a New World* (New York: HarperCollins, 1992), p. 399.

32. Donald Rothchild, "Africa's Ethnic Conflicts and Their Implications for United States Policy," in Robert I. Rotberg, ed., *Africa in the 1990s and Beyond: U.S. Policy Opportunities and Choices* (Algonac, Mich.: Reference Publications, 1988), pp. 277–278.

33. John Prendergast, *U.S. Leadership in Resolving African Conflict: The Case of Ethiopia-Eritrea*, U.S. Institute of Peace, Special Report (Washington, D.C.: U.S. Institute of Peace, 2001), p. 7.

34. Douglas Farah, "Liberian Pledges to Cut Sierra Leone Rebel Ties," *Washington Post*, January 20, 2001, p. A21.

35. U.S. Department of the Treasury, Office of Foreign Assets Control, *Liberia: Blocking Property of Certain Persons and Prohibiting the Importation of Certain Goods from Liberia*, July 23, 2004, pp. 1–2.

36. "UN Divided Over Sanctions," AllAfrica.com, June 13, 2006, at http://allafrica.com/stories/printable/200606130063.html.

37. President William J. Clinton, "National Emergency with Respect to Sudan," *Message to the Committee on International Relations*, House of Representatives, Document 1.1/7:105–166 (Washington, D.C.: U.S. Government Printing Office, 1997).

38. Sudan Peace Act, Public Law 107–245, 107th Congress, HR 5531 (October 21, 2002), p. 116, at http://www.state.gov/documents/organization/19897.pdf.

39. O'Sullivan, *Shrewd Sanctions*, p. 294.

40. Quoted in Eric Schmitt, "Sanctions Don't Work, U.S. Realizes," *International Herald Tribune* (Frankfurt), August 1–2, 1998, pp. 1, 8. Statement by Bill Lane, the chair of USA Engage (a coalition of 676 companies).

41. Miroslav Nincic, *Renegade Regimes: Confronting Deviant Behavior in World Politics* (New York: Columbia University Press, 2005), p. 122.

42. Carnegie Commission on Preventing Deadly Conflict, *Preventing Deadly Conflict: Final Report* (Washington, D.C.: Carnegie Commission on Preventing Deadly Conflict, 1997), p. 54.

43. For a reference to the possibility of normalization of U.S.-Sudanese relations in the future if Sudanese officials acted positively on negotiations, see "Powell Tries to Nudge Sudan Toward Peace," *New York Times*, October 22, 2003, A14.

44. Michael W. Doyle and Nicholas Sambanis, "International Peacebuilding: A Theoretical and Quantitative Analysis," *American Political Science* Review 94, no. 4 (December 2000), p. 781.

45. Raymond W. Copson and Theodros S. Dagne, *Somalia: Operation Restore Hope* (Washington D.C.: Congressional Research Service, January 19, 1993), p. 1.

46. Robert Oakley, "Remarks" to the Subcommittee on Africa of the House Committee on Foreign Affairs, Washington, D.C., March 31, 1993, p. 3 (Mimeo).

47. United Nations, *The United Nations and Somalia, 1992–1996* (New York: United Nations, 1996), p. 41. On the military's efforts to place larger weapons in quarantine, however, see United States Institute of Peace, *Restoring Hope: The Real Lessons of Somalia for the Future of Intervention* (Washington, D.C.: U.S. Institute of Peace Press, n.d.), p. 9.

48. See Hussein M. Adam, "Somalia: Militarism, Warlordism, or Democracy?" *Review of African Political Economy* 54 (1992), p. 18; and Rakiya Omaar, "Somalia: At War with Itself," *Current History* 91, no. 565 (May 1992), p. 233.

49. John L. Hirsch and Robert B. Oakley, *Somalia and Operation Restore Hope* (Washington, D.C.: U.S. Institute of Peace Press, 1995), p. 104.

50. Ken Menkhaus and Terrence Lyons, "What Are the Lessons to Be Learned from Somalia?" *CSIS Africa Notes* 144 (January 1993), p. 7.

51. Oakley, "Remarks" to the Subcommittee on Africa, p. 1.

52. *FBIS*, Sub-Saharan Africa 93, 058 (March 29, 1993): 1. On this issue, I have also benefited from discussions with Professor Abdi I. Samatar, UC–Berkeley, April 24, 1993.

53. Abdullah A. Mohamoud, "Somalia: The Futility of Peace Talks," *West Africa* (June 28–July 4, 1993), p. 1112.

54. Walter Clarke, "Failed Visions and Uncertain Mandates in Somalia," in Walter Clarke and Jeffrey Herbst, eds., *Learning from Somalia: The Lessons of Armed Humanitarian Intervention* (Boulder: Westview, 1997), p. 4.

55. United Nations, *The United Nations and Somalia*, pp. 262–263.

56. Ibid., p. 61.

57. Steven Kull and Clay Ramsay, *U.S. Public Attitudes on Involvement in Somalia* (College Park, MD: Program on International Policy Studies, Center for International and Security Studies, University of Maryland, October 26, 1993), p. 3.

58. *Congressional Record — Senate* 139, no. 133 (October 5, 1993), p. S13043.

59. *Congressional Record — Senate* 139, no. 134 (October 6, 1993), p. S13146.

60. O'Sullivan, *Shrewd Sanctions*, p. 270.

61. Prendergast, *U.S. Leadership*, p. 7.

62. Rothchild, *Managing Ethnic Conflict in Africa*, pp. 91–93.

63. Roy Licklider, "The Consequences of Negotiated Settlements in Civil Wars, 1945–1993," *American Political Science Review* 89, no. 3 (September 1995): 684; Paul R. Pillar, *Negotiating Peace: War Termination as a Bargaining Process* (Princeton: Princeton University Press, 1983); Stephen John Stedman, *Peacemaking in Civil Wars: International Mediation in Zimbabwe, 1974–1980* (Boulder: Lynne Rienner Publishers, 1987), pp. 5–9.

64. Doyle and Sambanis, "International Peacebuilding," p. 787; Caroline Hartzell, Matthew Hoddie, and Donald Rothchild, "Stabilizing the Peace After Civil War: An Investigation of Some Key Variables," *International Organization* 55, no. 1 (Winter 2001), p. 190.

65. Daniel Frei, "Conditions Affecting the Effectiveness of International Mediation," *Papers of the Peace Science Society* (International) 26 (1976): 70. Highlighting the intensity of civil wars, Paul Pillar's data indicate that nearly twice as many interstate wars ended with negotiations than did civil wars. See Pillar, *Negotiating Peace*, pp. 5–7.

66. Robert D. Putnam, "Diplomacy and Domestic Politics: The Logic of Two-Level Games," *International Organization* 42 (Summer 1988), pp. 433–435.

67. I. William Zartman, "Inter-African Negotiations and State Renewal," in John W. Harbeson and Donald Rothchild, eds., *Africa in World Politics: The African State System in Flux*, 3rd. ed. (Boulder: Westview, 2000), p. 43.

68. I am indebted to Monila Kuchena of the University of Zimbabwe for helpful comments on the impact of these mediation initiatives, Thika, Kenya, July 21, 1993. For other examples, see I. William Zartman, "Testimony to the House Foreign Affairs Africa Subcommittee," March 31, 1993, p. 8 (typescript copy).

69. "Burundi: Sanctions to Stay," *Africa Research Bulletin* (Political, Social and Cultural Series) 35, no. 2 (February 28, 1998), pp. 13012–13013.

70. John Prendergast, "Senator Danforth's Mission: The U.S. Steps In," Crimes of War, April 2002, at http://www.crimesofwar.org/print/sudan/sudan-us-print.html.

71. *Africa Confidential* 30, 17 (August 25, 1989), p. 3.

72. "Morocco/Western Sahara: Good Conduct Accord," *Africa Research Bulletin* 34, no. 9 (September 30, 1997), p. 12833.

73. Herman J. Cohen, *Intervening in Africa: Superpower Peacemaking in a Troubled Continent* (New York: St. Martin's Press, 2000), p. 49.

74. Terrence Lyons, "The Transition in Ethiopia," *CSIS Africa Notes* 127 (August 27, 1991), p. 5.

75. On the Cohen initiative, see Deng et al., *Sovereignty as Responsibility*, pp. 187–188.

76. Georges Nzongola-Ntalaja, "The Zairian Tragedy: A Challenge for the Clinton Administration," *Africa Demos* 3, no. 1 (February 1993), p. 9.

77. Donald Rothchild and Caroline Hartzell, "The Case of Angola: Four Power Intervention and Disengagement," in Ariel E. Levite, Bruce W. Jentleson, and Larry Berman, eds., *Foreign Military Intervention: The Dynamics of Protracted Conflict* (New York: Columbia University Press, 1992), p. 185; and Michael McFaul, "The Demise of the World Revolutionary Process: Soviet-Angolan Relations Under Gorbachev," *Journal of Southern African Studies* 16 (1990), pp. 182–183.

79. Bureau of International Information Programs, U.S. Department of State, "Acting Asst. Secretary Snyder Outlines U.S.-Africa Policy Priorities," *Washington File*, January 14, 2004 (italics added), at http://usinfo.state.gov.

80. Rothchild, *Managing Ethnic Conflict*, pp. 177–178.

81. Ibid., pp. 134–141.

82. Interview, Nairobi, March 1, 1991; and Witney W. Schneidman, "Conflict Resolution in Mozambique: A Status Report," *CSIS Africa Notes* 121 (February 28, 1991), p. 6.

83. Testimony by Assistant Secretary of State for African Affairs, Mr. Herman J. Cohen, Before the House Foreign Affairs Subcommittee on Africa, October 8, 1992, p. 4 (typescript copy).

84. Ibid., p. 7.

85. Confidential interview, Washington, D.C., November 14, 2003.

86. Confidential interview, Washington, D.C., November 14, 2003.

87. U.S. Department of State, "Acting Asst. Secretary Snyder Outlines U.S.-Africa Policy Priorities," *Washington File* (January 14, 2004), p. 1.

88. Kremenyuk and Zartman, "Prospect for Security," in I. William Zartman and Victor Kremenyuk, eds., *Cooperative Security: Reducing Third World Wars* (Syracuse, N.Y.: Syracuse University Press, 1995), p. 339.

11

The War on Terrorism in Africa

PRINCETON N. LYMAN

The war on terrorism in Africa did not begin on September 11, 2001. It began in Sudan in the 1990s, where Osama bin Laden operated and where an attack against Egyptian president Hosni Mubarak was organized. Three years later, in 1998, al-Qaeda cells blew up the American embassies in Nairobi and Dar es Salaam. In retaliation for these attacks, the United States, in addition to an attack in Afghanistan, bombed a chemical plant in Sudan, claiming that it was producing elements for chemical weapons for al-Qaeda. From the time of these attacks, moreover, U.S. policy in Somalia became preoccupied with searching out, capturing, and killing the perpetrators of those attacks who were believed to have taken refuge there. The seeds of later U.S. policy and all that has followed in Somalia were planted then. More recently, terrorist acts in Europe, particularly the train attack in Spain, have been linked to cells in Morocco and Algeria, which interact with North African residents in Europe, and both countries themselves have been victims of recent terrorist bombing attacks.

After 9/11, U.S. focus on terrorism in Africa became much more pronounced. For the first time since 1993, the United States deployed a sizeable contingent of American troops on the continent, with the establishment in late 2002 of the Combined Joint Task Force-Horn of Africa (CJTF-HOA) in Djibouti. In addition, President Bush announced a $100 million counterterrorism initiative for East Africa and the Horn in 2003. At the same time, the U.S. European Command (EUCOM) spearheaded a series of training and military support operations in the Sahel, aimed at the Algeria-based GLPF; the program later blossomed into the much larger Trans-Sahara Counterterrorism Initiative that now involves both North African and Sahelian states. Counterterrorism efforts became even more pronounced in U.S. Africa policy after the Islamic Courts Movement took power in Mogadishu, Somalia, in 2006, leading to the Ethiopian invasion of Somalia, with tacit U.S. support, and the current fighting that now consumes that blighted country. Most importantly, the Pentagon announced in 2007 that it would establish a new unified Africa Command (AFRICOM) to bring together its varied programs on the continent, a sign of increasing U.S. focus on security in Africa.

U.S. concern is understandable. Africa is no more immune to the threats from terrorism than any other continent. Its combination of relatively weak states, ethnic and religious diversity and sometimes discrimination, its poverty, and in many places its "ungoverned space" all lend Africa a significant susceptibility to the growth of radical and sometimes internationally connected movements that employ terrorism. Some of these are aimed specifically at African governments, for example, the radical Islamic Maitatsine and "Taliban" in Nigeria, or the pseudo-Christian Lord's Resistance Army in northern Uganda; others clearly have a more international agenda, for example, the al-Qaeda cells along the east coast of Africa and presumably the North Africans and Sudanese who have returned to their home countries from training and participating in the insurgency in Iraq.

While the "war on terrorism" usually relates to internationally linked terrorists, Africans face other security threats of equal or greater significance, posing a question of focus for American as well as African counterterrorism efforts. There are several organized rebellions or insurgencies in Africa, while not always classified as terrorists, which wreak terrible havoc on African people and threaten national stability. These include various militia in eastern Congo, who have been the target of the International Criminal Court for their crimes against humanity, the insurgents in the Niger Delta of Nigeria, and the Janjaweed militia in the Darfur region of Sudan. It is notable that the U.S. African Command lists the Lord's Resistance Army, the Army for Liberation of Rwanda, and the obscure Afrikaner Boeremag in South Africa along with a host of Islamic groups as among the "Terror Groups in Africa."[1] Clearly, noting this broad scope, Africa cannot ignore the threat of terrorism any more than can any other part of the world.

African states have responded to this threat in different ways. In West Africa, Sahelian states have welcomed American help in getting control over their ungoverned spaces but still face unrest from within those territories. Others, like Kenya and South Africa, facing the growth of Islamic terrorist groups, have struggled to balance the need for new security legislation with the preservation of newly gained civil rights and, in Kenya's case, to avoid the worst repercussions from the recent developments in Somalia through active diplomacy. Some, like Chad and the previous government of Mauritania, have used the terrorist threat to justify policies of internal suppression and anti-democratic practices, while solidifying U.S. support for their anti-terrorist policies. And at least one, Zimbabwe, has turned the issue on its head, countering U.S. and other international criticism of its anti-democratic practices by labeling its domestic opponents as "terrorists."

Two major challenges now loom in the African and American responses to terrorism. Generally, many Africans and some American critics are very concerned that the new Africa Command and other U.S. anti-terrorism programs signal an increased militarization of U.S. policy in Africa. These critics argue that only a continual intensive attack on the root causes of terrorism and violence, that is, poverty, authoritarianism, discrimination, weak states, and similar conditions, will effectively combat such threats. They contend that a focus that relies too heavily on security will encourage authoritarian practices and undermine Africa's move toward more democratic governance. The style and focus of the unified Africa Command will be a closely watched measure of whether the United States pursues its counterterrorism policies with the requisite sensitivity, breadth of programming, and balance that is required.

A second challenge relates to the continued ability of the Africa Union (AU) to provide leadership in conflict resolution and the timely provision of peacekeepers as it has done in recent years in Burundi, Darfur, and Côte d'Ivoire. The current debacle in Somalia may have dragged the AU into an untenable situation that could fundamentally undermine the promise of that organization as a force for peacemaking and improved governance. This occurs at the same time that the AU may experience diminishing support from Nigeria and perhaps South Africa, as leaders change in those countries. Should both of these factors prove to be the case, U.S. counterterrorism policies, especially in the Horn, will have had lasting negative effects on Africa's overall security.

There follows a more detailed discussion of these issues.

THE HORN OF AFRICA

The Horn of Africa is Africa's bridge to the Middle East. That fact explains much about the complex interrelationships between differing Islamic cultures within Africa, from east to west. It has a direct effect on the history of deepened terrorist activity first in Sudan and later along the east coast of the continent, the constant instability in Somalia, and the challenges facing counterterrorist efforts in the region. This complex set of relationships also poses an organizational challenge for U.S. policymakers, one that has hampered American response: The Horn of Africa comes under the policy direction of the Africa Bureau of the Department of State, the smallest and perhaps weakest of the bureaus, while key countries linked to the Horn—for example, Yemen, Egypt, and Saudi Arabia—are under the Middle East Bureau, whose focus is elsewhere.

At the same time, the Horn is the object of the most intense and the most militarized U.S. response to terrorism in Africa. Since 2002, the United States has stationed between 1,200 to 18,000 troops in Djibouti under the Combined Joint Task Force-Horn of Africa (CJTF-HOA). CJTF-HOA participates in a joint allied patrol of the Red Sea coastal area and carries out a series of civic action and military training programs throughout the Horn as well as gathering intelligence on possible terrorist infiltration. In 2003, President Bush announced a $100 million program to improve the intelligence, border control, and police capability of the states in the region, with the goal of developing a system of regional coordination that would identify and block the movement of personnel, arms, money, and other forms of support coming from the Middle East into the Horn and moving down along the coast of East Africa. In 2006, the United States gave at least tacit backing and intelligence and material support to an Ethiopian invasion of Somalia to dislodge a radical Islamic government that had taken power in the capital. As followers of that government fled south, the United States bombed what it hoped were terrorist leaders, but the results were more civilian casualties than known terrorists killed. In March 2008, the United States again bombed southern Somalia, seeking in particular to kill one of the persons suspected in the embassy bombings of 1998. Nowhere else on the African continent has the United States been so directly and heavily involved in counterterrorist activity.

The focus on the Horn is understandable. The Horn is as ripe as any region could be to the threat of terrorist infiltration. As Robert Rotberg, who believes at least Yemen should be included in any such analysis, has observed:

> The greater horn of Africa and Yemen region is bound together by recent history as a sometime target, by its geographical proximity to the homeland of Osama bin Laden and the primary object of his political anger, by long and continuing interrelationships of licit and illicit trade, by religion, by centuries of Muslim-Christian accommodation and antagonism, by renowned resistances against Western colonizers (in the Horn), and by shared poverty, poor governance, and underdevelopment. This complex web provides a tasty menu for potential terrorists.[2]

The Horn also demonstrates clearly how complex any approach to terrorism must be. Issues of terrorism, even international terrorism, which is the prime concern of the United States, are inextricably bound up with other sources of conflict, border disputes, historic grievances, and broad regional involvement. They are not amenable to simple solutions, and alliances can be as costly in the long run as they appear effective in the short term. For example, seeking to address the threat of terrorism in the Horn, the United States has been drawn, after many years of avoidance, into the byzantine world of Somali politics and has become in the process allied ever more closely with Ethiopia. The growing reliance upon Ethiopia has developed despite the fact that Ethiopia has cracked down on its political opponents and on the press, and is accused of carrying out brutal suppression of unrest in its Ogaden region.

Somalia

Somalia has become a centerpiece of counterterrorism activities in the Horn, and the policy and military actions there have largely undermined much of the hopes and plans for regional cooperation and coordination in the Horn that the United State had once envisaged. Somalia's sad state after the fall of dictator Siad Barre in 1991 is well-known. Warlords took control of the country, which led to famine, fighting, and lack of any central governmental authority. A U.S.-led humanitarian intervention in 1992–1993 ended in a disaster when eighteen U.S. servicemen were killed. U.S. and UN operations declined thereafter. For the next thirteen years, the United States basically withdrew from involvement in Somali politics, focusing solely on intelligence and activities designed to keep Somalia from becoming a training ground for international terrorists; another U.S. objective has been to find and capture those accused of participating in the bombing of American embassies in Kenya and Tanzania.

Fears that Somalia would become a terrorist training ground soon proved unfounded. As Ken Menkhaus has explained, terrorist organizations are not entirely comfortable operating in a failed state, where their own security is in jeopardy, where outside intervention (for example, by U.S. intelligence and military operations) can take place without much public attention or outcry, and where various militia can be paid to search them out, as indeed have all taken place in Somalia.[3] These factors may, however, have contributed to U.S. overconfidence about the threat from Somalia, as attention was directed to covert anti-terrorist operations, while the dynamics of Somalia's political and religious life were virtually ignored. As a result, many in the policy community were surprised when Somalia burst back onto the terrorist radar screen in mid-2006, after an Islamist movement took power in Mogadishu, defeating an alliance of U.S.-backed warlords and establishing a strict Islamist government. Radical leaders of the movement began talking about claims on Somali-inhabited regions of neighboring countries, reviving the fears that Ethiopia had had a decade earlier and exacerbating the regional crisis of war, insurgency, and instability.

The rise of a fundamentalist Islamic government had its roots in the chaos and experimentation that went on in Somalia during the previous decade. As Roland Marchal has reported, that period saw the rise of Islamic charities that fulfilled some of the social, educational, and humanitarian needs of the population. These organizations consciously competed with Western NGOs for influence. It was also a period in which the Somali business class became more religious, in part because of their reliance on business connections in the Middle East. Finally, in the confusion, chaos, and crime that dominated much of Somali daily life, the establishment of Sharia courts, backed by the militia, offered a degree of stability and predictability, which the business class, as well as some of the feuding clan leaders, welcomed. The Islamic movement provided the leadership for these courts, first in northern Somalia, then more successfully in the south.[4]

Islam in Somalia had long had cross-currents of Sufi, Wahhabi, and other influences, with Sufi "traditionalists" dominant until recent times. Fundamentalist Islamic groups began emerging during the 1990s, some more radical than others. Al-Itihaad al-Islaami (AIAI) distinguished itself by its development of an armed force and its focus on recruiting urban semi-educated youth. It also had plans to establish both a national and regional network including the Somali-inhabited areas of Ethiopia. It was responsible for several bombing attacks in Ethiopia and Somalia. The State Department labeled AIAI a terrorist organization in 1996. That same year, Ethiopian troops drove AIAI from the towns in which it had established control. For some years, AIAI seemed to be a spent force. But its leaders reemerged in the Islamic Courts Movement in the next decade.[5]

The Sharia courts, which had been established in various parts of the country, but especially in the south, began moving toward unification in 2000. Over the course of the next several years, through various alliances, clan and subclan conflicts, and shrewd political moves, as well as growing military capacity, the Islamic Courts Movement unified control of Mogadishu, and in 2006 it established a government. Warlords who had controlled much of the city were driven out or brought under its control. Although the movement had several moderate Islamic leaders and had broad business backing, the presence of former AIAI leader Hassan Dahir Aweys at its head, who was on the U.S. list of international terrorists and was resurrecting claims on neighboring Somali regions, set off alarm bells in Washington and Addis Ababa. The United States was also concerned that three prominent terrorists, suspected in involvement in the bombings of the American embassies, were being protected by the new regime. The worst fears about Somalia after 9/11 seemed about to become true. The initial U.S. response was to try to defeat the movement militarily through an ill-conceived alliance of warlords (which took the name Alliance for the Restoration of Peace and Counter-Terrorism). The Alliance was defeated in June 2006. The next step for the United States was to seek a way to strengthen a weak countergovernment in Somalia that had emerged through complex African-led negotiations described below. With support from the United States, the UN Security Council called for an Africa Union peacekeeping force to protect this government and help bring about a political settlement. The Islamic Courts Movement vowed to fight any such force.

These developments were taking place against a backdrop of longtime diplomatic efforts to find some solution to Somalia's political crisis. Various African-led attempts to put together a unified government had been launched and then floundered since the 1990s; each transitional or interim government that was established disintegrated shortly afterward in a sea of clan and subclan rivalries. In northern Somalia, a portion of the country seceded to form its own government, Somaliland, which, though it has failed to gain international recognition, exists as a relatively peaceful counterpart to the rest of the country. A somewhat autonomous region, Puntland, adjacent to Somaliland, was organized around the same time. In 2004, African-led efforts finally produced a Transitional Federal Government (TFG). However, the TFG, led largely by the Darod clan, was unable even to establish itself in the capital, Mogadishu, setting up instead in the town of Baidoa. Threatened by the Islamic Courts Movement in 2006, it turned to Ethiopia for support.

In the last half of 2006, tensions grew between the Courts Movement and Ethiopia. In December 2006, with U.S. intelligence and material support, Ethiopian troops dislodged the Courts Movement from Mogadishu in relatively short order and enabled the TFG to move there. As noted above, the United States followed up by bombing fleeing Somali elements as they approached the Kenyan border, purportedly aiming strictly at known terrorists, but, as would be expected, spawning charges of civilian casualties. Nevertheless, at first, Ethiopia's military intervention looked like a quick and successful turning back of a dangerous radical foothold on the African continent. Ethiopia promised to withdraw its troops as soon as peace was restored and when an international peacekeeping force would be in place. In an important move, with possibly far-reaching effects, the African Union not only endorsed Ethiopia's military action but pledged to replace Ethiopian troops in Somalia with an 8,000-person peacekeeping operation. The United States lobbied hard for AU support in this matter and quickly pledged $40 million for humanitarian activities within Somalia and for helping finance the AU peacekeepers. The

United States pressed other African nations to provide troops. Uganda was the first to agree, and dispatched 1,400 soldiers. But then things turned sour.

With eerie echoes of Iraq, the Ethiopians soon found themselves faced with a determined insurgency, fueled by Islamists, clan factions opposed to the leadership of the TFG, and others recruited to fight a foreign invader. In the spring of 2007, determined to root out the insurgency, the Ethiopians and its Somali allies went on an offensive in Mogadishu. At least 1,000 were killed, and subsequently hundreds of thousands of Somalis fled the capital. The fighting continues in the capital and elsewhere in the country. At least 250,000 and by some estimates as many as one million Somalis have now been displaced. In sum, the outcome has been a severe humanitarian crisis—and no real peace. In May 2008, Ugandan troops took their first casualties, with five soldiers killed and five more wounded. Although Uganda and the United States continued to urge other African countries to provide more peacekeepers, only Burundi has provided a small contingent. An American appeal to the United Nations to take over this responsibility has similarly fallen on deaf ears.

Meanwhile, the TFG has proved unable or unwilling to create the broad unity government that was needed. Initially, it reached out only reluctantly and with conditions to the moderate leadership of the Islamic movement. It was unable to make peace with the dominant Hawiye clan in Mogadishu, and its control slipped elsewhere in the country as well. In early 2008, the TFG appointed a new prime minister, Nur Hassan Hussein, who has reached out more to moderate Islamists and seems interested in a broader peace process. But he operates under the weight of TFG internal pressures and rivalries and that of Ethiopian and American policy that brooks little accommodation with former Islamist leaders. In March 2008, the United States once again bombed southern Somalia in yet another attempt to kill a person suspected in the embassy bombings of 1998. The opposition to both the TFG and the Ethiopian presence, which has grouped under an Alliance for the Re-liberation of Somalia (ARLS), is also splitting, with a more extreme group—the Shabab—carrying much of the military effort and preaching a more universal jihadist agenda than the others.[6] In March 2008 the United States designated the Shabab as a terrorist group, a designation Shabab leaders said they regarded as a badge of honor. Gradually, Somalia appears to be slipping back to the clan- and subclan-based semi-anarchy of past decades; only now there is a strong Islamic current running through the political culture and feeding the ongoing insurgency.

Like all such conflicts, Somalia's conflict involves many of its neighbors. Somalia has become part of a proxy war between Ethiopia and Eritrea, which have been feuding over a border dispute since 1998. Eritrea has been accused of providing financing and even fighters in support of the Islamic Courts Movement.

In May 2007, Eritrea hosted a group of Somali Islamic leaders pledged to fight Ethiopian occupation leading to the creation of the ARLS now based in Asmara. Included was Sheikh Ahmed, whom the United States had described as moderate but who now seemed to have joined forces with those totally opposed to the TFG. Eritrea has also been accused of providing support to at least two militant opposition groups in Ethiopia—the Ogaden National Liberation Front (ONLF) and the Oromo Liberation Movement. The ONLF has taken responsibility for an attack on Chinese and Ethiopian oil workers in April 2007, killing nine Chinese and wounding five more, as well as killing over sixty-five Ethiopians.[7] Several more Ethiopians were taken hostage. Another regional dimension was revealed when in April 2008, Ethiopia broke diplomatic relations with Qatar, charging that government with support of both rebels within Ethiopia and Somali insurgents.

One result of these developments is that Eritrean-U.S. relations have deteriorated. Accusing the United States of bias in favor of Ethiopia regarding the border dispute, and Ethiopian policy in Somalia, the Eritrean government closed down the USAID mission, refused to receive senior U.S. envoys, including the Assistant Secretary of State for African Affairs, and sharply criticized U.S. policies in the Horn. U.S. rhetoric against Eritrea has increased accordingly. The United States has hinted it might place Eritrea on the list of countries supporting terrorism. Eritrea controls much of the Red Sea coastline along which much of the infiltration of arms, people, and funding is infiltrated for support of African terrorism. With Eritrea's withdrawal from American plans and programs in the Horn, the regional counterterrorism structure has suffered a serious blow.

The United States may also have pushed the African Union beyond its limit by encouraging the organization to promise an 8,000-person African peacekeeping force to replace the Ethiopian troops in Somalia. With Ethiopia trapped in a fierce insurgency in Somalia, few African countries are willing to become engaged in its place. Following on the Africa Union's failure to establish a credible peacekeeping force in Darfur (see below), the Africa Union may be forced to pull back from its original bold promise of aggressive action on behalf of conflict resolution. Moreover, having sided so closely with the Ethiopian invasion, neither the United States nor the African Union is in a position to lead an effective peace process in Somalia. In both regards, the Africa Union's stature has suffered.

Sudan

Sudan was the first African country to become deeply enmeshed in international terrorism. Palestinian-led terrorist actions took place there in the

1980s, including an attack on the Saudi Arabian embassy and the assassination of an American ambassador. The link to a broader agenda of international terrorism began when Osama bin Laden came to Sudan in 1991, at the invitation of Hassan al-Turabi, leader of the National Islamic Front, which had just taken power in Sudan. Bin Laden lived there for five years before moving on to Afghanistan, building a network of financial and terrorist operations. Various networks of radical and terrorist groups operated in the country during that time. With radical Egyptian and al-Qaeda involvement, an attempt was launched from Sudan on the life of Egyptian president Hosni Mubarak in 1995 while Mubarak was visiting Ethiopia. The United Nations imposed sanctions on Sudan for the government's complicity in that attack. Sudan remained the home of known or suspected terrorists for some time afterward, with interplay among international movements and Sudan's own turbulent politics. Despite increased cooperation with the United States since 9/11, including intelligence sharing, Sudan remains on the U.S. list of countries supporting terrorism.[8]

The civil war in the Darfur region of Sudan, which began in 2003, has provided another opening for terrorist influence, though more rhetorical than material. In Darfur, facing a rebellion from the largely farming communities of the region, the Sudanese government has pursued a vicious policy of destroying the villages of populations suspected of supporting the rebel forces and of arming militia that have carried out murder, rape, and other crimes against humanity. These attacks have led to the displacement of more than 2.5 million people. At least 200,000 and possible as many as 400,000, have died. Facing international condemnation, the Sudanese government agreed in 2004 to a relatively weak African peacekeeping force of 7,000 provided by the AU. The force proved unable to prevent further depredations. It was in fact poorly equipped and lacked a clear mandate.

Eventually, the AU appealed for the United Nations to assist and in effect take over much of the responsibility. Only after endless negotiation, and public urging from China, one of Sudan's principal allies and protectors, and threats of further international sanctions, did the Sudanese government agree in late 2007 to a United Nations/AU peacekeeping force of 20,000 plus some 6,000 police, but the force has only begun to be deployed and faces continuous obstacles thrown up by the Sudanese government. Meanwhile, rebel forces have fractured into competing and squabbling groups, and others have entered the fray for both political and personal gain, making the peace process ever more difficult. The Sudan government has used the fluidity of the situation to continue to bomb and attack rebel positions. The crisis has spilled over into Chad and the Central African Republic, further destabilizing the region.[9]

Into this situation, al-Qaeda sought to make inroads. In April 2006, Osama bin Laden called on his followers to prepare for a jihad against Westerners who "would be occupiers" in Darfur. The Sudanese government swiftly distanced itself from the call, but it had contributed to the opening. Sudan has consistently described U.S. concern with Darfur as a cover to gain control of Sudan's oil resources, force regime change, and crush Sudan's Islamist movement.[10] Almost taking up Osama bin Laden's call, both the government and the rebels have threatened to attack the UN/AU peacekeepers once they are deployed.

In many ways, the United States has been the most active country condemning the actions of the Sudanese government in Darfur, being the only country to label these as genocide. At the same time, the United States has been accused by activists focused on Darfur of having prioritized anti-terrorist collaboration with Sudan above resolution of the humanitarian crisis there. One of the Sudanese officials indicted by the International Criminal Court for crimes in Darfur has been a close contact of the United States on terrorist matters and was flown to the United States for consultations. Although the accusations against the Bush administration in this case are somewhat exaggerated, there are disputes within the administration over whether rewarding Sudan for the cooperation the United States has received on terrorism should outweigh the repeated threats of further sanctions over Darfur. Meanwhile, Sudan feels that its cooperation on terrorism has gone unrewarded, furthering its suspicion that at heart the United States is bent on regime change.[11]

The United States walks a tightrope in Sudan: seeking full implementation of the Comprehensive Peace Agreement that ended the decades-long North-South civil war, finding a solution to the crisis in Darfur, and working with a prickly and suspicious Sudanese government on terrorism. Now on its third special envoy for Sudan in the Bush administration, the United States struggles with no clear end in sight for the crisis in Darfur, a still fragile North-South peace, and a fractious government in Khartoum.

Kenya

Although not technically part of the Horn, Kenya is deeply affected by events there. Kenya, moreover, remains a potentially prime target for terrorists in its own right. It has substantial Western tourist activity, the headquarters of the United Nations Environment Program and the United Nations Habitat Program, a large number of Western embassies, and several international businesses. Kenya sustained terrible casualties in the bombing of the U.S. embassy in 1998. That act, and the 2002 attack on Israeli facilities in Mombasa, revealed the extent of terrorist cells operating within Kenya. The cells have taken root in the Muslim community, which traces its roots to the Middle East. The community has experienced a steady decline in political and economic influence since Kenyan independence, as Kenya's African population gained power and competition for jobs increased. As conditions have declined, religious interest has risen, Muslim religious and social groups have taken on more responsibility and influence, and there has been more interchange among young people seeking opportunity in the Middle East. The radical cells that developed in this milieu represent only a small portion of the Muslim community, which itself is only about 10 percent of the Kenyan population. Nevertheless, the outsiders directly involved in the bombings of 1998 and the Mombasa attacks were clearly assisted by Kenyan citizens.[12]

Two of the foreign perpetrators of the bombing of the American embassy, Mohamed Sadek Odeh and Mohamed Rashed al-Owhali, were apprehended and turned over to American custody. Others, including some involved later in the Mombasa attacks, fled to Somalia, touching off the long U.S. intelligence and military effort to capture them there.[13] But Kenya has since been faced with the serious challenge of finding and arresting cell members, while maintaining the fragile opening to multiparty democracy and greater respect for human rights that began with the retirement of longtime ruler Daniel arap Moi in 2002. Backlash against the American pressure on terrorism among some Kenyan leaders and from leaders of the Muslim community, weakness in the police and judiciary, and bribery have impeded efforts against domestic cell members.[14] As a result, two prominent suspects escaped custody, and no Kenyan citizens, though many have been arrested and held, have yet been convicted for participation in or for support of terrorism. The proposed antiterrorism law, which the U.S. backed, has yet to pass.

Kenya also lacks basic control over parts of its own territory. Well before the most recent Somalia fighting, Kenya faced a serious problem in the border area. Ken Menkhaus described it as follows:

> Kenya has lost control over a good portion of the north-eastern hinterland; armed convoys are required for overland travel to border towns and refugee camps, and for most of the 1990s, the Kenya side of the [Somali] border was generally more lawless and dangerous than the Somali side. The lawlessness has found its way into the heart of Nairobi. The teeming Somali slum of Eastleigh has become a virtual no-go zone for the Kenyan authorities, a world unto itself where black-market activity is rife, criminals can slip away undetected and guns can be rented for the day.[15]

Not surprisingly, when supporters of the Islamic Courts Movement fled south from the Ethiopian assault in 2006–2007, Kenya closed its border, fearing the influx of new terrorist or radical personnel. Although no Kenyan

Somalis have been found to be involved in Kenya's al-Qaeda cells, the complexities of the Somali situation and the potential spillover of events in Somalia, add to the difficulty Kenya has in addressing domestic threats.

As the situation in Somalia continued to deteriorate after the Ethiopian invasion, and the implications for Kenya were becoming clearer, Kenya began in early 2008 exploring possible new diplomatic means to overcome the political impasse. However, the internal crisis in Kenya, sparked by allegations of a stolen presidential election in March 2008, followed by major riots and killings, have overtaken all such efforts. Whether Kenya will be able to resume its strong diplomatic leadership in Somalia and elsewhere in the Horn is in question. Internal political demands and restoring internal peace will surely dominate the Kenyan agenda for some time.

Overall, it is fair to say the U.S. position in the Horn remains strong. Kenya and Ethiopia are basically reliable and committed allies in the war on terrorism. The CJTF-HOA continues to reach out across the region with a mix of civic and military activities and to gather intelligence on possible terrorist activities. But the deepening crisis in Somalia, the spillover of the Ethiopia-Eritrea dispute, the complexities and cross-currents of priorities in Sudan, and the weak support from the Africa Union make the Horn a continuing source of worry. The danger of over-militarizing the U.S. response, as in support for the Ethiopian invasion of Somalia, and the difficulties of U.S. diplomatic coordination of its Africa and Middle East policies have weakened America's role in forging a broad political coalition that could address both the political and the terrorist issues in the region. The dream of a broad regional system of coordinated and cooperative counterterrorist programs seems farther than ever from achievement.

EAST AFRICA AND SOUTHERN AFRICA

The presence of al-Qaeda cells is apparent along the east coast of Africa, including Tanzania, Zambia, the Comoros, and perhaps other countries. Outside of Tanzania, the site of one of the American embassy bombings in 1998, there have been no incidents against American or other allied targets in these countries. The worry is that these cells allow international terrorists to find safety from arrest and extradition, to raise funds, and to transport people and material for terrorist purposes elsewhere. Both Zambia and South Africa have extradited known terrorists to the United Kingdom and the United States, respectively. Counterterrorism activities, as a result, focus on intelligence capacity building, sharing of information, financial controls, coastal security, and, on occasion, extradition.

In all these countries, there are reports of reinvigorated religious activity supported from abroad, particularly from Saudi Arabia and Pakistan. Much of this is in the form of building mosques, providing imams and preachers, and developing Muslim social and welfare organizations. These are normal and respectable activities. But if the experience of Kenya, Somalia, and other countries is any guide, these activities can also provide cover and openings for radical influences.

South Africa is a special case, because of its superior intelligence capabilities, its modern financial and business systems, and its strong democratic tradition since 1994. These give South Africa some advantages in combating terrorists. The Muslim population is quite small, divided between various groups that historically came from primarily South Asia and Southeast Asia. Some Muslims enjoy high status and are prominent in business, the professions, politics, and civic organizations. Three of President Mandela's original cabinet members were Muslims: Dullah Omar, Attorney General; Kader Asmal, Minister of Water and Forestry; and Mac Maharaj, Minister of Transportation. The Pahad brothers—Aziz and Essop—have played prominent roles in both the Mandela and Mbeki administrations. However, another part of the Muslim population is poor. Locked into satellite towns, they are victims of some of the same economic hardships that exist for the majority of black South Africans. It is from this latter population that a radical organization, the People Against Gangsterism and Drugs (PAGAD), organized in the 1990s purportedly to fight drugs and crimes in the townships where their constituents lived. But soon its focus shifted toward anti-Israel and anti-Western activities, and eventually to bombings of cafes and other entertainment sites. South Africa has largely quelled PAGAD through a vigorous campaign of intelligence and arrests.

Nevertheless, South Africa is attractive to terrorists because of its superior transportation links, its infrastructure, its international linkages, and its relative freedom of movement. Ronnie Kasrils, South Africa's chief of intelligence, has continuously warned of the dangers of terrorist infiltration. Another problem is the value and apparent availability of South African passports. South Africa instituted new passports after 1994, so that they are now more secure from counterfeiting, but corrupt officials within the Department of Home Affairs have been linked to the leakage of many legitimate passports. South Africa is a way station for illegal migrants, who come through South Africa to pick up false documents and then go on to the United States or Europe. Terrorists have the same desire and, apparently, the same ability to do so.

South Africa has a strong interest in containing any terrorist threats as it prepares to host the World Cup in 2010. It has thus taken the initiative to improve security throughout the Southern Africa region. The Southern African Development Community (SADC) agreed in December 2006 to establish an anti-terrorist unit in Harare, Zimbabwe, based at the Interpol Sub-Regional

Bureau. The unit aims to be the focal point for regional information-sharing on terrorist organizations and groups. Member countries will submit regular reports to the center, which will be linked with the UN Office on Drugs and Crime (UNODC). Ironically, Zimbabwe, whose autocratic government has been sharply criticized by the United States and other Western countries, has cooperated with the United States on terrorism, including intelligence-sharing and combating money laundering and other means of financing.[16]

Cooperation on counterterrorism nevertheless runs into the same problems in South Africa as in Kenya. Muslims have accused the United States of unfair harassment, and the South African government has hesitated to cooperate on some high-profile cases. South Africa, using its rights as a member of the UN Security Council in 2007, put a hold on the U.S. recommendation to place two South African nationals, Farhad Dockrat and Junaid Ismail Dockrat, on the UN terrorist list. Inclusion on the list, administered by the UN's al-Qaeda and Taliban Sanctions Committee, triggers travel bans, asset seizures, and passport revocations for the suspects. In this instance, South Africa argued that the United States must first show conclusive evidence of terrorist activities. One of the two, Farhad Dockrat, is a prominent critic of U.S. policies in Iraq and Somalia.

WEST AFRICA: THE SAHEL

Critics of U.S. counterterrorism policy complain that the frequent use of the term "ungoverned spaces"—used to describe the vast area of the Sahel, the pirate-ridden Gulf of Guinea, and some other such places in the world—exaggerate both the anarchic character and the threat that such areas present. As much as the critics may be right, the Sahel, a vast semi-desert region between North Africa and much of sub-Saharan Africa. In West Africa in particular it is an area of formidable geography, limited government presence, and a long history of smuggling, banditry, human trafficking, and violence. More recently, it has become a battleground in the war on terror, in particular to deny that space to the Algerian terrorist group al-Qaeda in the Islamic Maghreb (formerly the Salafist Group for Preaching and Combat, the GSPC) and to other terrorist groupings that might develop in the region.

The Sahel, like the Horn of Africa, presents a bureaucratic challenge to U.S. policymakers. North African Sahelian states—Morocco, Tunisia, Libya, and Algeria—come under the Department of State's Middle East Bureau, whereas Mauritania, Senegal, Niger, Mali, Chad, and Nigeria—at the southern flank of the Sahel—are under the Bureau for African Affairs. The U.S. military, under the leadership of the European Command, had no such limitations and actively promoted security cooperation among the regional states of both north and west. Here, as in the Horn, the U.S. defense establishment has gotten out ahead of the diplomatic establishment and could give the impression that U.S. counterterrorist strategy is overly militarized.

There is no question that terrorism is a serious problem in the Maghreb. Both Algeria and Morocco experienced terrorist attacks in the spring of 2007. Moroccan nationals have been implicated in several of the terrorist attacks in Europe. But the seriousness of the threat in the Sahel is questionable. It is clearly one of the poorest areas on earth. Mali and Niger are near the bottom of the countries on the United Nations Human Development Index. Chad, while having discovered oil, is still wretchedly poor, wracked by civil conflict, and suffering the spillover effects of the conflict in Darfur. Mauritania has suffered decades of declining living conditions among its nomadic population, now crowding into cities. Senegal has done better but has never reached its economic potential. Yet this region has demonstrated remarkable commitment to democracy, defying beliefs that democracy is incompatible with either Islam or poverty. Both Mali and Niger have had to address longtime unrest among northern minorities as one of the bases of their democratic frameworks. Senegal has been a consistent civilian democracy, including a transfer of leadership from one party to another. Mauritania, after a period of what one might call electoral autocracy, overthrown by a military coup, has successfully returned to civilian rule in what were reasonably well-run elections.

It is not difficult to find examples of unrest and radical thinking in the region. A study by the International Crisis Group found a significant number of Pakistani Islamic preachers in the area who were bringing radical views to their congregants. But it is necessary to distinguish the occasional signs of radicalism, for example, young people wearing Osama bin Laden T-shirts, sharp denunciations of American policy in Iraq or Somalia, growing adherence to Sharia law, and so forth, from involvement in international terrorist activities. Almost all the people in this region, whether Muslim or Christian, are primarily focused on their domestic interests and their national politics. Issues like U.S. policy in Iraq are more of an academic or rhetorical interest than active motivators of international jihad, but rather—perhaps more significant for the United States in this region—reason to become suspicious of U.S. motives closer to home. In northern Nigeria, I found interlocutors in 2005–2006 primarily concerned that what they perceived as U.S. international anti-Muslim policy was leading the United States to support a third term for Christian president Olusegun Obasanjo. A northern Mulsim elected to the presidency in 2007 should ameliorate these worries.[17]

What makes the area of concern, nevertheless, is that the mix of poverty, discrimination, and long-standing networks of criminality can produce support or openings for influence to terrorists that are present in the region. The authors of the ICG study concluded that the most serious threat of terrorism came from disaffected minority groups, for example, the Taureg in Mali, who felt discriminated against in terms of development investments in their region and who sometimes resented interference in their economic activities, which bordered on, if not crossed the line of, illegality. Herein lies a dilemma for counterterrorism programs. The steps promoted in U.S. counterterrorism programs to improve border control and intelligence about the movement of possible terrorist materials are precisely those that produce the strongest reaction from those groups who have long lived on smuggling and similar activities.

The Sahel is in fact rife with criminality. There are at least three main land routes across the Sahel into northern Africa (the gateway to Europe) and south to the ports of Nigeria, through which people and contraband flow. Drug trafficking has increased substantially in recent years, followed by an increase in illegal migration, along with more traditional smuggling of cigarettes and similar goods. Masters of this trade include the Taureg and other nomadic groups, who are the most marginalized in national politics and development. In 2002, the group then called GSPC relocated to this region from Algeria and allegedly made commercial alliances with Taureg smugglers. At least one of the GSPC attacks on a Mauritanian border garrison in 2005 is believed to be linked as much to protecting the smuggling route as to political objectives.[18]

Into this atmosphere, the United States entered in 2002 with its first counterterrorist program in the region, the Pan Sahel Initiative (PSI). The program aimed to improve the intelligence and border security capability of several of the Sahelian countries. The program scored its first big success in 2004 when, with U.S. intelligence assistance, GSPC elements were chased from Mali by that government's forces and captured and killed by Chadian forces. The United States has since moved to create a much larger program, the Trans-Saharan Counter-Terrorism Initiative (TSCTI), which involves economic, political, and public diplomacy as well as military components. Notably, EUCOM also took the lead in successfully bringing together both northern and Sahelian African states in steadily increased intelligence and other counterterrorism programs. The United States has also stepped up joint exercises in the region, for example, Operation Flintlock in 2005, which involved 1,000 U.S. Special Forces.

To the distress of Mali and Niger, these very activities have stoked a resumption of rebellion among the northern groups with whom peace accords were critical to their democratic future. In 2005, Mali and Niger, with U.S. assistance, restored a military presence in the desert regions of their countries, areas that had been demilitarized in the mid-1990s as part of the overall political settlements of the time. In response, Malian Tauregs rebelled near the Algerian border in May–June 2006. The subsequent peace accord included removing some of the army units along the main smuggling routes. But Taureg rebellion broke out once again in Mali in August 2007, demonstrating the fragility of such agreements. Niger has experienced a similar rebellion since February 2007. The Niger government accuses the rebels of involvement in drug trafficking and banditry, whereas the rebel group claims it is fighting for more profit from uranium mining in the region and more investment in health and education for their people.[19] The mix of crime, discrimination, poverty, and limited governmental capacity are apparent and no easy challenge for any security program. Whether a broader-based TSCTI will be better able to address this complex of factors remains to be seen.

Another problem in the U.S. approach has been the lack of political oversight in the counterterrorism programs. PSI involved close cooperation with an autocratic and unpopular government in Mauritania that was subsequently overthrown. U.S. forces cooperated closely with Chadian forces, as described above, in the capture of the GSPC group. Chad's president has recently enabled himself to become president for life, faces continuing rebellion from several quarters, and is not always involved constructively in the Darfur conflict. Balancing terrorism concerns with U.S. support for democracy and better governance in Africa is an important objective, especially in a region where political and economic factors are basic to the loyalty and cooperation of indigenous populations. A senior EUCOM officer told me in 2005 that he would have welcomed some overall political direction in PSI, but there was none. State Department officials assure questioners that this will be remedied in TSCTI, which is structured as a State Department program. In addition, AFRICOM will have a State Department official as one of two deputies, as well as both State and USAID personnel on its staffing. The United States also recently granted Mali over $500 million under the Millennium Challenge Account, which may assist in overcoming regional disparities. All indications are that a broader and more politically sensitive approach is being made. Yet State lacks the personnel in its embassies to closely monitor the situation in the Sahel, and the complexities of the region will remain challenging for any security program.

WEST AFRICA: NIGERIA AND THE GULF OF GUINEA

If there is a prize target for terrorism in Africa, Nigeria should be it. Nigeria, the most populous country in Africa, has the largest Muslim population on the continent, over 65 million. It is Africa's largest oil producer. Tensions between the Muslim and the equally large Christian population are persistent and often lead to violence. Evidence of successful proselytizing by either side is an explosive source of such violence, as is any sign that one side or the other is being subject to either economic or religious discrimination. Political rivalry between the largely Muslim north and largely Christian south is a constant in Nigeria, with a barely tolerated agreement on rotating national leadership between the two. Until the election of 2007, northern Nigerians smarted over a serious decline in their influence in the military and government. Politicians also often play on religious identities to provoke tension and sometimes violence, for example, in recent riots in Plateau state where the roots of the tension are more about land than religion.[20]

Add to this mix, the Muslim north is particularly poor and ranks below standards elsewhere in the country in literacy, health status, and economic activity. Of particular significance is the de-industrialization that has taken place in the north, for example, in the industrial cities of Kano and Kaduna, due to inefficient production capabilities on the part of indigenous plants and the influx of cheap consumer goods from China and other Asian countries. Many plants of long standing have closed. One major textile company that has operated in Nigeria for decades reports employment in its factories has declined from 22,000 to 7,000 with more cuts likely. All over Nigeria, not just in the north, the population has in recent decades, despite the country's oil wealth, suffered an extraordinary decline in living standards. Per capita GNP declined by two-thirds between 1980 and 1999. Nigerians are experiencing a level of poverty not seen in many years. The recent rise in oil prices has improved the macro-economy but has as yet done little to impact the grass roots.

Attitudes toward the United States in northern Nigeria traditionally tend toward sharp criticism of U.S. policies in the Middle East. The United States is considered to have a generally negative policy toward Muslim states; in the 1980s, I experienced sharp criticisms of U.S. policy toward Libya. The criticism has grown since the U.S. invasion of Iraq. The recent concern in the north that the United States was encouraging Christian president Olusegun Obasanjo to seek a third term and deny the north its "rightful" turn for leading the country has passed. Nevertheless, there are some deep-seated negative feelings about the United States, which while not general, nor is the population openly hostile, merit close monitoring.[21]

Not surprisingly, Osama bin Laden once named Nigeria as a prime target for his Islamic revolution. Yet despite some fertile ground, there is little evidence so far that al-Qaeda per se has penetrated much in Nigeria. Mainstream Islam in Nigeria has a long tradition of its own in structure, continual adjustment, and overall moderation. The main influences are through two Sufi traditions, the Tijaniyya and the Quadiriyya, which have been rivals but also sources of reform and stability. Nigeria's own Islamic beliefs and traditions have been the target of challenges from abroad. The latest come from the Wahhabis in Saudi Arabia, Iran (though Nigeria is overwhelmingly Sunni), and to a lesser extent, Pakistan. None of these have seemingly produced any strong allegiances in Nigeria to international radical movements. Twelve of

Nigeria's thirty-six states did adopt Sharia law in the early 1990s, largely in response to the election of Obasanjo but also in reaction to growing crime and seeming lawlessness that afflicted the people on the street. Contrary to the fears of some foreigners and Nigerian Christians, the adoption of Sharia has not basically changed the nature of Nigerian Islam nor resulted in any greater confrontation between Muslims and Christians than before.[22]

All that being said, there is much in Nigeria that is not well known or understood. Some al-Qaeda cells may well exist.[23] And some other radical movements have shaken the country. A long existing radical religious sect, the Maitatsine, erupts in violence every few years. This sect appears to be entirely indigenous with no known outside sponsorship. In 2006, however, a new group, calling itself the Taliban, launched an attack in the northeast city of Borno. In April 2007, the same group launched a more serious attack in Kano, killing thirteen policemen and wounding five more. In the resulting battle, the Nigerian military reported twenty-five Taliban members were killed. This group remains something of a mystery. Members were reported to be dressed in long white gowns and speaking a language not native to the region. Most appear to have escaped, traveling west rather than back to the northeast, indicting some means of organization and perhaps indigenous support.

But the biggest unrest in Nigeria is related not to Islam, nor to international terrorism, but to the militias in Nigeria's oil-producing region of the Niger Delta. This region produces at least 80 percent of Nigeria's wealth, the bulk of its foreign exchange earnings and almost all of its government revenue. Yet it has been the site of extraordinary environmental degradation and shows little if any benefits in schools or hospitals or other gains from the precious commodity it provides. A riverine area, its rivers and streams have been perhaps irreversibly damaged from oil and gas spills, its soils equally damaged, and the population left with little employment either from traditional sources such as fishing or farming nor from the oil industry, which is largely capital intensive and dependent for its personnel on highly skilled workers, not general local labor. After decades of such conditions and inadequate response from both oil companies and the Nigerian government, younger members of the region took up arms, beginning in the 1990s.

Unfortunately, what began as a demand for better conditions, reparations, and employment has morphed into something very different. The militias, in collaboration with corrupt officials—including some high-ranking officials—have become engaged in the stealing (known as bunkering) of oil. The rates of theft are contested, but the proceeds could well exceed $1 billion annually. A large part of the proceeds go into the purchase of ever more sophisticated arms. Delta militias are now capable of not only hitting local oil stations, and occasionally local oil company offices, but attacking offshore installations and taking on armed conflict with the police and the army. They regularly kidnap oil workers of every nationality, usually releasing them after a time, but some have been killed. At the same time, the militias have succeeded in shutting down a significant portion of Nigeria's legitimate production, that is, 200,000 barrels a day and sometimes more from Nigeria's more than 2 million barrels per day capacity, contributing to the sharp rise in crude oil prices on the world market.

The delta crisis does not lend itself to easy solutions. Initially, President Obasanjo tried a military approach to the problem, but the Nigerian army not only was incapable of beating the militia on their home turf of rivers and creeks but committed so many human rights violations that its presence provoked outrage from the local population. The police forces are simply too small, too ill-equipped, and, in some cases, too corrupt to help. Efforts to reduce corruption have been only partially successful. President Obasanjo cashiered four navy admirals for their involvement in bunkering, but the process continues, and other officials are surely involved.

Efforts to pump more resources into the region have foundered on corruption, ethnic rivalries, and conflicting agendas. Under the constitution, the oil producing states receive an automatic allocation of 13 percent of the country's oil and other revenue, resulting in billions of dollars flowing to regional governors and local governments each year. A Niger Delta Development Commission was established in 2000 to channel further resources to the region. But there is little to show for these efforts. Several regional governors have been impeached for corruption, but even that step has been caught up in the ethnic rivalries and complexities of the unrest. A case in point is the governor of Bayelsa, who was arrested in London carrying stacks of cash, and later arrested in Nigeria on charges of corruption. Nevertheless, his prosecution was opposed by one of the major militia, which saw the arrest as ethnic discrimination against the Ijaw people. The Yar'Adua government, elected in 2007, released him. The oil companies, ready to commit substantial resources to development in the region, find that the security problems, on the one hand, and the inefficiencies and corruption of government, on the other, make it very difficult for them to contribute substantial sums for development. As a result they have largely reverted to seeking to mollify local leaders and dissidents with small projects and minimal offers of employment, and shutting down production in the most volatile areas when that becomes necessary.

Following his election, President Yar'Adua promised to make the Niger Delta one of his main priorities. His vice president, Goodluck Johnson, is from the Niger Delta and was seen as a natural person to lead such an effort. But in fact Johnson lacks credibility beyond his own community; his house was burned right after the election as a sign of the militants' lack of confidence in him. Moreover, a rivalry exists within the Yar'Adua administration for control of Niger Delta policy, with the secretary of the presidency, Baba Gingibe, competing with Johnson for primacy. On the ground little has changed. A long promised summit has been repeatedly postponed. Promises of development projects fail to be realized, and those that are started are often attacked by militants. At bottom, there is not sufficient incentive in the system to resolve the situation. The militants and their political allies are profiting from oil sales and growing military power; high-level as well as local officials are similarly profiting; and, with oil at more than $100 a barrel, the central government can afford to have some of its production shut in and other shares stolen when nearly 2 million barrels are still being produced within the system.

The problem in the Niger Delta is but one part of a larger concern over security in the Gulf of Guinea, from which almost all of Africa's oil is shipped. It has one of the highest rates of piracy in the world. Moreover, not one of the producing states is able to provide adequate security. Concern over the safety and security of this vital oil-producing region has thus engaged the United States as much as the international terrorist threat in the region. Again, with leadership coming from EUCOM, the United States has convened oil ministers and security officials from the Gulf of Guinea region, demonstrated detection and other security techniques, and promised support to a Gulf of Guinea collaborative program for securing the area. Not all the countries have responded enthusiastically, however. In some cases, this may reflect probable official connections with illegal oil sales and other corruption; in other cases, it may be due to a lack of regional solidarity. Angola, in particular, has been hesitant to cede leadership to Nigeria, which had taken the lead in forming a Gulf of Guinea Commission. Now that the secretariat for the commission has been located in Angola, the cooperation may improve but so far the secretariat there has been inactive. Nevertheless, as is clear from the situation in the Niger Delta, a largely military solution to this problem may not be feasible and would be far from adequate. One American expert estimated that for $100 million, a nearly foolproof system of maritime coverage against bunkering out of Nigeria could be put in place. Nigerian officials, when asked if they would accept such assistance if made available, demurred. Nevertheless, AFRICOM has made the Gulf of Guinea one of its highest priorities. It continues to offer training and advice on coastal security and stands ready to provide more substantial assistance once the countries of the region request it.

THE AFRICA COMMAND (AFRICOM)

In early 2007, the United States announced that it would create a single Africa combatant command to bring together all the security programs the United

States supports on the continent. AFRICOM is expected to become fully operational in the fall of 2008. Previously, U.S. defense operations for Africa were divided among EUCOM, which covered West, Central, and Southern Africa; Central Command, which covered the Horn; and Pacific Command, which covered the island base at Diego Garcia and maritime programs related to the Middle East. The decision to create a single African command is logical and should provide a clearer focus and a more coordinated approach to security programs in Africa.

However, the announcement of the command has raised questions about the intent of U.S. security intentions in Africa. To some, the combination of stepped-up American counterterrorism efforts and growing attention to the security of oil production in the region portend a strong security-oriented emphasis in U.S. policy in Africa. In the minds of these critics, these concerns will outweigh priorities of promoting democracy, economic development, justice, and human rights.[24] In Africa, there is also concern that stepped-up U.S. security programs in the region could result in the strengthening of African militaries, which have only recently withdrawn from politics and which continue to pose a threat to fragile democracies. There is also suspicion that this portends a more security-oriented emphasis in U.S. policy in Africa.[25]

The controversy was not helped by the reluctance of U.S. planners to articulate AFRICOM's mission at the outset. Most of the early explanations focused on the processes of organization and the desirability of coordinating existing and future programs.[26] That raised some suspicion about what might be the actual purpose. But the real dilemma for AFRICOM is that it is caught between presenting itself as a largely internal bureaucratic restructuring, and trying to be more bold. AFRICOM might have continued to be described as simply a way for the United States to better organize and coordinate its security programs in Africa. That might have produced less suspicion and indeed less notice in Africa. But as plans for AFRICOM developed, and as Pentagon spokespersons traveled across the continent to explain and promote the concept, the Pentagon went out of its way to portray it as something new and different from other combatant commands. The chair of the Joint Chiefs of Staff, General Peter Pace, emphasized that the Africa Command will not be a clone of the other traditional commands. He envisages a greater emphasis on interagency cooperation in order to "build African capabilities to effectively govern." He also denied any interests in sending U.S. troops to Africa.[27]

Stressing its interagency structure and staffing—a senior State official as one of the deputies, and both State and USAID personnel in the structure—AFRICOM was put forth as being part of a broad strategy to support democracy, development, and security. Though vague, plans appeared to include

U.S. military cooperation, beyond training peacekeepers and other security-related activities, in various civilian development projects, as CJTF-HOA had been doing—wells, clinics, environmental programs, help with fisheries development, etc. Close cooperation with State and USAID programs was envisaged, though again the dimensions of this cooperation were unclear.

While this approach might well be praiseworthy, in terms of recognizing that Africa's problems were as much related to poverty as to security, it gave the appearance that AFRICOM would be playing a large role in all U.S. programs in Africa. Not just Africans but people in the State Department wonder if Africa policy might be shifting to Stuttgart, especially given the fact that AFRICOM staff would likely exceed that of the Africa Bureau of the State Department by a goodly number. USAID officials, as well as those associated with NGOs, are very concerned that their development activities will become increasingly embedded within American security and intelligence activities, as has happened in Iraq and Afghanistan. This has already occurred to some extent in the Horn of Africa. Such a shift would diminish U.S. capacity for institution building and long-term development in Africa, relegating such USAID programs to a lower priority.

The second problem for AFRICOM was projecting its eventual headquarters on the continent of Africa. This immediately fell victim to traditional African opposition to foreign military bases in Africa, and allowed African politicians the opportunity to score points against the United States by publicly opposing not only that decision but AFRICOM itself. Nigeria and South Africa in particular made strong statements to this effect.[28] South Africa said it would not cooperate with AFRICOM. A team of senior U.S. military personnel visiting South Africa in March 2008 to discuss AFRICOM was unable to meet with any senior officials.[29] Only Liberia indicated that it would welcome AFRICOM headquarters on its soil, seeing in that a way to restore its "special relationship" with the United States. But Pentagon planners did not want it located there. Fortunately, after extensive consultations in Africa, planners have agreed that for some time in the future it would be better to locate it in Stuttgart, Germany, where EUCOM is headquartered, and to contemplate small satellite presences at select sites in Africa.

CONCLUSION

Africa cannot help but be drawn into the global war on terrorism. Internationally sponsored terrorist networks have struck at American and Israeli targets on African soil, built local cells that could strike again in Africa or recruit for operations elsewhere, and found sufficiently sympathetic elements within the population to provide safe haven for terrorists fleeing from Europe or America. North Africa is far more integrated into internationally radical Islamic terrorist activity than sub-Saharan Africa. Algerians and Moroccans have figured in several terrorist acts in Europe and constitute most of the Africans who have reportedly traveled to join al-Qaeda insurgents in Iraq. But sub-Saharan Africa is not immune. It is widely recognized that terrorists seek out and have more success in developing their infrastructure in weak, rather than failed, states, utilizing the relative predictability and protection of an operating state, while exploiting its weaknesses in intelligence and other security capacity and the marginalization of disaffected elements in its population. Africa is replete with weak states.

Moreover, the Horn of Africa is intimately linked—in geographic, religious, ethnic, political, and economic terms—to the Middle East. The development of the radical Islamic Courts Movement in Somalia reflects those linkages. People, arms, money, and material flow from the Middle East along the Red Sea coast, through Somalia and south to other East African countries, while commerce and religious interaction moves in both directions. More than anywhere else on the continent, the Horn of Africa has become a front in the military battle against internationally sponsored terrorism, backed largely by the United States but involving ever more deeply the Africa Union.

Yet the vast majority of conflict and "terrorist" activity in Africa is not linked to international sponsorship or any vast conspiracy against the West. The Lords Resistance Army in Uganda, the various militia in eastern Congo, the militants in the Niger Delta, the extremist sects in Kenya, Nigeria, and elsewhere are the principal security threats to the African population. Programs that seek to bolster African capacity against internationally sponsored terrorism, the kind of most concern to the United States and Europe, must also build capacity against these threats. Yet the roots of these conflicts go much deeper and are more complex than a "global war against terrorism." They demand stronger and more just African states, significant progress on economic development, and regional peace agreements, as much as improved intelligence and military capacity. And because the conditions that breed these homegrown forms of violent activity are the same as those that open the door for internationally sponsored terrorism, any "war" on the latter must address these broader issues.

Thus, the challenge in combating terrorism in Africa is to balance a legitimate program of security improvements with a continuing and sustained attack on poor governance, poverty, and deprivation of human rights. Getting the balance right is particularly acute because the democracies in Africa are fragile, and any crackdown on terrorist activity has to be carried out with great sensitivity to the historic grievances of marginalized groups, the incipient struggle for human rights, and the relatively weak civilian oversight of the military and security institutions. This is why, despite the best efforts of the planners of AFRICOM to follow such a broad approach, the heart and center of American counterterrorism programs cannot be based within a security apparatus. U.S. support for military civic actions programs, designed to win the hearts and minds of local populations, the centerpiece of CJTF-HOA, is not the same as USAID support for the strengthening of African institutions, the building of economic infrastructure, and the support of African civil society. Nor is it a substitute for strong political leadership from the Department of State to maintain the right balance.

African institutions are at a similar crossroads. The Africa Union was met with tremendous expectations when it was created in 2000, especially in the area of conflict resolution. Departing from the more traditional and narrow defense of sovereignty of its predecessor organization, the AU has stated that conflict within any African state could affect the region. It established a Peace and Security Council and promised African leadership and responsibility in bringing such conflicts to a close. It backed this declaration by sending African peacekeepers to Burundi, Côte d'Ivoire, the Democratic Republic of the Congo, and Darfur, ahead of the United Nations. The AU and regional organizations, such as ECOWAS, IGAD, and SADC, have taken the lead in negotiating peace agreements in Burundi, Liberia, the DRC, and elsewhere.

But Somalia has brought the AU directly into the global war on terrorism. Coming on the heels of a noble but flawed AU peacekeeping operation in Darfur, the failure to mobilize a peacekeeping force in Somalia may undermine the will and capacity of the AU to play this kind of role in the future. The AU's diplomatic role may be similarly compromised in its full commitment to Ethiopia's position in Somalia. In other such situations, the AU—like the UN—has striven to be neutral, to help parties negotiate peace, and to provide peacekeepers to back up an agreed-upon settlement among the contending parties, or, as in the case of Darfur, with the agreement of the host government. If the AU's readiness and capacity to provide leadership in peacekeeping in Africa are undermined, Somalia will have cost Africa and the West a vital means to fight all the other conflict situations on the continent. It will have been a big price to pay.

A new administration in Washington will need to reexamine these issues and the totality of American counterterrorism efforts. Fortunately for the United States, most African states share the concern over terrorism and are prepared to cooperate in fighting it, for their own safety and security. They are also, however, beset with other priorities and limitations. The United States has the tools to respond broadly, with recent initiatives such as PEPFAR, the Millennium Challenge Account, and generally rising aid levels. It has skillful diplomats and the ability to call on the United Nations and others to advance complex political solutions, as will surely be needed in the Horn. Keeping these fully engaged along with direct security programs, and the benefits of a well-organized AFRICOM, the partnership with Africa in this area can be advanced and deepened.

NOTES

1. Brigadier General Jeffrey Marshall, *EUCOM Engagement in Africa,* briefing presented to the Conference on AFRICOM at Airlie House, Virginia, sponsored by the Department of Defense, September 23, 2007, p. 16.

2. Robert Rotberg, ed., *Battling Terrorism in the Horn of Africa* (Washington, D.C.: Brookings Institution, 2005), p. 2.

3. Ken Menkhaus, "Somalia and Somaliland: Terrorism, Islam, and State Collapse," in Rotberg, ed., *Battling Terrorism*, pp. 40–41.

4. Roland Marchal, "Islamic Political Dynamics in the Civil War," in Alex de Waal, ed., *Islamism and Its Enemies in the Horn of Africa* (Bloomington: Indiana University Press, 2004), pp. 115ff. The designation of the Courts movement eventually became the Council of Somali Islamic Courts (CSIC), but the courts have also been designated by the title Islamic Courts Union (ICU) as well as Supreme Council of Islamic Courts (SCIC).

5. Ibid., pp. 125–26. The Islamic Courts Movement, like most other Somali institutions, was not entirely unified nor free of clan and subclan politics. The courts were originally organized on a subclan basis and then were later brought under a central structure. The Hawiye clan, with its power base in Mogadishu, was a strong supporter. However, tensions between the Courts Movement and the Hawiye also surfaced. For more detail on these factors, see Cedric Barnes, SOAS, and Harun Hassan, SMC, *The Rise and Fall of Mogadishu's Islamic Courts* (London: Chatham House, Africa Program, AP BP 07/02, April 2007).

6. The Shabab faction has criticized the ARLS for both any broadening of the opposition movement beyond the Islamic core and the coalition's dependence on Eritrea, and preaching a more militant Islamic internationalist agenda. Daveed Gartensen-Ross, "Will Divisions Undermine Somali Rebellion?" *Middle East Times,* February 28, 2008, http://metimes.com/International/2008/02/28will_divisions_undermine_somali_rebellion?

For a full account of the Ethiopian-Eritrean conflict and its regional dimensions, see Terrence Lyons, *Avoiding Conflict in the Horn of Africa: U.S. Policy Toward Ethiopia and Eritrea,* Council on Foreign Relations, Special Report, CSR no. 21, December 2006.

7. Rob Crilly, "Chinese Oil Workers Massacred in Attack by Army of 200 Rebels Linked to Islamists," *Times* (London), April 25, 2007, at http://www.timesonline.co.uk/tol/news/world/africa/article1701450.ece.

8. For a detailed account of radical Islamist movements and terrorist activity in Sudan, see de Waal, ed., *Islamism and Its Enemies*, pp. 71–113.

9. For details of the difficulty in the negotiations and splits among the rebel groups, see Kelly Campbell, *Negotiating Peace in Darfur,* United States Peace Briefing, Washington, D.C., January 2008.

10. Cheryl O. Igiri and Princeton N. Lyman, *Giving Meaning to "Never Again": Seeking an Effective Response to the Crisis in Darfur and Beyond,* Council on Foreign Relations, Special Report, no. 5, September 2004, p. 21.

11. Andrew S. Natsios, "Beyond Darfur," *Foreign Affairs,* May/June 2008, pp. 82–83.

12. A full account of the roots of terrorism and the subsequent efforts against terrorism in Kenya can be found in Johnnie Carson, "Kenya: The Struggle Against Terrorism," in Rotberg, ed., *Battling Terrorism,* pp. 173–192. See also Gilbert Khadiagala, "Kenya: Haven or Helpless Victim of Terrorism," in *Terrorism in the Horn of Africa,* United States Institute of Peace, Special Report no. 113, January 2004.

13. The three most wanted terrorist suspects thought to have been in Somalia are Fazul Abdullah Mohammed, Saleh Ali Saleh Nabhan, and Abu Taha al-Sudani. Fazul Abdullah Mohammed twice escaped from Kenyan custody. Saleh Ali Saleh Nabhan 'was the target of the March 2008 U.S. attack on southern Somalia.

14. The lead in complaining about harassment of Muslims under the anti-terrorism program is coming from the religious community rather than the political representatives of the community, reflecting the growing role of the former. Juma Namlola, "Speak Out on Harassment, Say Muslims," *Nation* (Nairobi), May 1, 2007. Carson, "Kenya: The Struggle Against Terrorism," p. 187, makes the same point. For a summary of complaints from both religious and civil liberty groups about the implications of Kenya's anti-terrorist programs, see the report from the International Commission of Jurists, "Eminent Jurists Conclude Hearings on Terrorism and Human Rights in East Africa," March 2, 2006, at http://ejp.icj.org/hearing2.php3?id_article=4&lang+en.

15. Ken Menkhaus, *Somalia: State Collapse and the Threat of Terrorism,* Adelphi Paper 364 (Oxford: Oxford University Press, 2004), p. 52.

16. Department of State, U.S. Office for Counterterrorism, Country Reports: Africa Overview, May 2007.

17. For a number of anecdotal examples of such attitudes, see Jeffrey Tayler, *Angry Wind: Through Muslim Black Africa by Truck, Bus, Boat, and Camel* (Boston: Houghton Mifflin, 2005).

18. Oxford Analytical Daily Brief, "Africa: Trans-Saharan Criminality," May 23, 2007.

19. Claire Spiegel, "Uranium Under the Sand, Anger Above," *The Washington Post,* April 27, 2008, p. B3.

20. Muslim and Christian interlocutors both separately told me in 2005 that recent ostensibly religious riots that had taken place in Nigeria had been provoked by political leaders.

21. For further examples of such attitudes, see Princeton N. Lyman, "A Strategic Approach to Terrorism," in Donald Rothchild and Edmond J. Keller, eds., *Africa-US Relations: Strategic Encounters* (Boulder: Lynne Reinner Publishers, 2006), pp. 60–61.

22. The best recent analysis of Nigeria's Islamic traditions and their role in modern Nigerian politics can be found in John N. Paden, *Muslim Civic Cultures and Conflict*

Resolution: The Challenges of Democratic Federalism in Nigeria (Washington D.C.: Brookings Institution, 2005).

23. American officials believe there are such cells. Personal conversations with American officials in 2006–2007.

24. For a highly critical account of the rationale for the creation of AFRICOM and the motives of some of its backers, see Paul Lubeck, Michael J. Watts, and Ronnie Lipschutz, "Convergent Interests: U.S. Energy Security and the 'Securing' of Nigerian Democracy," a publication of the Center for International Policy, February 2007, http://www.ciponline.org.

25. Al Pessin, "African Officials Express Concern About U.S Africa Command Plan," at http://www.globalsecurity.org/military/library/news/2007/04/mil-0704, April 23, 2007; "The Proposed U.S. Africa Command," *This Day*, Lagos, Nigeria, May 9, 2007; and Greg Mills and Jeffrey Herbst, "Africa, Terrorism, and AFRICOM," *RUSI Journal*, April 2007, at http://www.rusi.org.

26. Council on Foreign Relations, "The Pentagon's New Africa Command," meeting with Admiral Robert Moeller and Ambassador Robert Loftus, April 11, 2007, at http://www.cfr.org/publications/13348/-25k.

27. Herman Cohen, "The U.S. Military's New Africa Command," *Peace Operations* 2, no. 5 (March–April 2007).

28. Wyndham Hartley, "More U.S. Soldiers Not Welcome in Africa, Says Lekota," *Business Day* (Johannesburg), August 30, 2007.

29. Some of this is clearly posturing. South Africa, like other African countries, continues to participate in various U.S. military training, health, and other programs that were formerly conducted out of EUCOM and that will simply shift bureaucratically to AFRICOM.

12

Euro-African Relations in the Age of Maturity

Gilbert M. Khadiagala

> If what [is] happening in Africa today . . . was happening in any other part of the world there would be such a scandal and clamor that governments would be falling over themselves to do something about it. On the edge of this new century, in an age of unprecedented wealth and economic progress by all continents, it is unacceptable that Africa drifts further from the rest of the world, unseen in its misery and ignored in its pain.
>
> —FORMER BRITISH PRIME MINISTER TONY BLAIR, JANUARY 2005

> Africans will flood the world unless more is done to develop the continent. If we do not develop Africa, if we do not make available the necessary resources to bring about this development, these people will flood the world.
>
> —FORMER FRENCH PRESIDENT JACQUES CHIRAC, JULY 2006

In March 2007, Europe celebrated fifty years since the inauguration of the Treaty of Rome that ushered in the momentous process of integration. The anniversary marked the maturation of the political integration that stemmed from the steady and incremental steps toward a common and united Europe. A confident Europe, however, has been less celebratory of its relations with Africa, relations that are still dominated by uncertainties over negotiations for new trade ties, the crisis of African migration to Europe, and Europe's diminishing role in conflict resolution in Africa. These trends symbolize a midlife crisis in Euro-African relations whereby a resurgent Europe reluctantly manages a partner that has lost its previous allure and attractiveness.

This chapter argues that the decline of the special relationship between Europe and Africa has wrought a profound sense of pessimism, putting the relationship on an uncertain path. The biggest challenge to Euro-African relations is, as Jacques Chirac notes, the growing perception of Africa as a problem to Europe as defined primarily by the issue of migration through Europe's soft belly in the Mediterranean. This dynamic of Africa-as-a-problem has increasingly whittled down the previous relationships anchored on the promise of reciprocity and partnership. For now, the dominant themes in the relationship revolve around how Europe can tame and reduce the deleterious effects of Africa's deterioration. Alongside the decline in the special relationship has been the absence of a coherent European voice to articulate African issues. Europe has ceded its Africa policy primarily to multilateral institutions, notably the Group of Eight (G8) countries. The current state of Europe's relations with Africa reflects the inevitable maturation of a relationship that has evolved in light of changing actors, times, and contexts.

NEGOTIATING ECONOMIC PARTNERSHIP AGREEMENTS (EPAS)

The Cotonou Partnership Agreement (CPA) signed in 2000 was an attempt by the European Union (EU) to manage the economic relationships with its African, Caribbean, and Pacific (ACP) associates, in light of mounting multilateral pressures for reduction of special privileges. As a reappraisal of the forty-year relationship, the Cotonou Agreement sought to take into account the expansion of the EU and the accession of countries with no historical links with Africa. Moreover, the multilateral pressures occasioned by the World Trade Organizations (WTO) forced the changes that would eliminate the generous trade regime in existence under the Lome Conventions. Cotonou envisaged the phasing out of the trade arrangements by January 2008 and their replacement by Economic Partnership Agreements (EPAs) that would fulfill the requirements of the WTO. In June 2005, the EU-ACP states signed the revised text of the Cotonou Agreement (CPA II), broadening the areas of cooperation to include security, political dialogue, transparency, and increased social responsibility.[1]

Seven years since the accession of the Cotonou Agreement, Euro-African relations have been dominated by negotiations for EPAs to meet the January 2008 deadline established by the Cotonou Agreement. In conception, EPAs had three objectives: removal of the previous nonreciprocal clause whereby African states would furnish free access to their markets to European products; the establishment of new trading blocs among African states that would negotiate free trade areas with Europe; and better coordination of EU aid programs with the EPAs.[2]

A major objective of EPAs is to rationalize African regionalism, which has been characterized by overlapping membership, incompatible goals, and unwieldy mandates. To Europe, EPAs can flourish best in subregional contexts with distinct memberships and economic interactions. This has placed countries such as Tanzania in a quandary, as it is forced to choose negotiating an EPA in the Southern African Development Community (SADC), the East African Customs Union (EACU), or the East and Southern Africa (ESA) grouping. Although in 2003 SADC proposed that Tanzania should continue negotiating EPAs under SADC, the EU demanded negotiations under the EACU. Similarly, Europe has pressured Kenya and Uganda to quit the Common Market for Eastern and Southern Africa (COMESA), despite the reluctance of these countries to negotiate under the EACU because of the infancy of the bloc and the weak economies of the member states.[3]

Sorting out the question of membership configuration has also occasioned delays in negotiations for EPAs in Southern Africa where countries are torn among three negotiating blocs-regions: the East and Southern African countries (ESA) comprising the sixteen states of COMESA and SADC (Kenya, Uganda, Burundi, Comoros, Democratic Republic of Congo, Djibouti, Eritrea, Ethiopia, Madagascar, Malawi, Mauritius, Rwanda, Seychelles, Sudan, Zambia and Zimbabwe); SADC, and the Southern African Customs Union (SACU). On one hand, South Africa, a strong member of SADC, has a bilateral free trade agreement with the EU. On the other, SACU—South Africa, Namibia, Botswana, Lesotho, and Swaziland—are SADC members negotiating EPAs in SACU. This has essentially left the remaining SADC members—Tanzania, Mozambique, and Angola—scrambling for an alternative body to join for EPA negotiations.[4]

Although EPAs are supposed to expand intraregional trade and trade links with Europe, Christopher Stevens has observed that they may erect new trade barriers among African countries, defeating the objective of integration: "By increasing the stakes, EPAs may make regional liberalization less likely. Some countries willing to remove barriers to imports from their neighbors with similar economies may be unwilling to offer the same terms to highly competitive (and possibly dumped) EU imports. Regional groups may splinter between those willing to liberalize towards the EU and the others."[5]

Apart from the regional ramifications, most of the criticisms of EPAs have focused on their potential impact on the domestic economic policies of individual African states, notably key instruments such as tariff policies, competition, and investment rules, that all developed countries have used in their stages of development. Negotiations over market access for agricultural products have, in particular, elicited considerable opposition from African states that claim European hypocrisy through subsidies to its farmers. In addition to subsidies, most critics of EPAs charge that they would present a threat to African agriculture, as they require the opening up of Africa's markets to EU goods. Furthermore, critics contend that EPAs would take away African governments' ability to use trade policy instruments to protect agriculture.[6]

Since 2004, civil society organizations have rallied under the banner of *Stop EPAs* campaigns to raise attention to the harmful facets of these agreements. In West Africa, there has been increasing opposition to EPAs because of their potential threat to regional trade and poverty reduction. In a petition to regional governments, a coalition of nongovernmental organizations (NGOs) charged that EPAs will be built on the principle of reciprocity and envisage the abolition of all tariffs for at least 90 percent of all imports in ECOWAS from the EU:

> This has de-industrialization effects and constitutes a severe threat to small, medium scale farmers, and traders in the sub-region. The immediate effect of EPAs would be the further decline in incomes of about 50–60 percent of people being employed in these sectors and will retard the poverty reduction efforts in the sub-region. We therefore call on the leaders of both countries to have the moral fortitude to call for the stoppage of the Economic Partnership Agreements in their current form.[7]

Amidst opposition from a broad spectrum of actors in Africa about agricultural provisions, the EU reversed course in late 2006, proposing the removal of all quotas and tariffs for ACP countries' access to its markets to cover products such as beef, dairy, cereals, fruits, and vegetables. These concessions would apply following the signing of EPAs, with a phase-in period for rice and sugar. Europe has made other concessions to African subregions, for instance offering 5 billion euros for infrastructure development assistance to East and Southern African states who sign EPAs. But these concessions have not mollified opponents who have maintained that Africa's farmers would continue to face enormous obstacles in accessing the EU market. In the words of one civil society actor:

> This is hardly a generous offer as the EU is offering to eliminate tariffs on the remaining 3 percent of ACP imports, and in return they demand that Africa

> eliminates 80 percent of its tariffs on EU imports. The risk and the negative impacts will be far greater for Africa. Increased competition from the EU's highly subsidized agricultural products such as maize, milk, tomatoes, and meat could mean the loss of domestic and regional markets for millions of African smallholder farmers. And the loss of markets means loss of livelihoods, which in Africa often leads to loss of life altogether.[8]

Oxfam International did a recent study that reveals that EPAs threaten to deny African countries a favorable foothold in the global economy. Specifically, the rules on liberalization of services have the potential to reduce competition, extend the monopoly power of large companies, and drive local firms out of business. The new rules in the EPA also pose a threat to poor people's access to essential services, as countries would be required to open public utilities to foreign investment. In addition, new investment rules would prevent African states from requiring foreign companies to transfer technology, train local workers, or source inputs locally. According to Oxfam, "the overall effect of these changes in the rules is to progressively undermine economic governance, transferring power from governments to largely unaccountable multinationals firms, robbing developing countries of the tools they need to develop their economies and gain a favorable foothold in global markets."[9]

To reflect on the severity of the contemplated changes, some African countries have pleaded for delays in signing EPAs, citing lack of preparedness and unfair competition. The Private Sector Foundation of Uganda (PSFU) petitioned the government in early 2007 to delay the signing of the EPA, claiming that Uganda would need a three-year extension after the expiry of the Cotonou exemptions. Wary of being flooded with European products, the PSFU further claimed that the Ugandan economy was not ready to take advantage of the reciprocity entailed in EPAs because of high production costs, a crippling power crisis, a dilapidated transport infrastructure, and costly loans and interest rates averaging a minimum of 22 percent.[10]

Uncertainties over the future of EPAs and trade relations in general underscore Europe's determination to frame the rules of partnership. Shorn of its diplomatic niceties, partnership fundamentally reflects the asymmetries in power that have long existed. But to the extent that negotiations for EPAs fragment Africa, they have deepened rather than weakened these asymmetries.

GLOBAL MULTILATERALISM AND EURO-AFRICAN RELATIONS

Negotiating a new trade regime has occurred alongside Europe's bid to cede the parameters of economic relationships with Africa to multilateral bodies, notably the annual conclave of the G8 industrialized countries. Since the mid-2000s, the G8 has assumed significance in charting the course of debates about Africa's economic future. In addition to the rotational leadership within the EU, the growing importance of the G8 forum has led to sporadic attention to African questions. Targeted invitation of African leaders to G8 gatherings has further intensified the fragmentation of African voices, while sustaining the illusion of inclusion.

Tony Blair's Commission for Africa (CfA) report exemplified Britain's leadership in finding a multilateral consensus on African development issues.[11] Coinciding with British chairmanship of the G8 and presidency of the EU in 2005, the report tried to galvanize major donors to refocus on a host of Africa's economic challenges.[12] Billed as the most serious analysis of Africa's problems for generations, the report invoked global common interests and collective responsibilities in the search for a coherent policy toward Africa. The central message of the report was the importance of shared responsibilities in a "new kind of partnership," based on "mutual respect and solidarity." On Africa's part, leadership is essential:

> Africa's development must be shaped by Africans. History has shown us that development cannot and does not work if policies are shaped and forced by outsiders. It is Africa's actions and leadership that will be the most important determinants of progress in generating resurgence in Africa, advancing living standards and taking forward the fight against poverty. The more effective the action taken by Africa itself, the stronger the case for support from outside Africa. Partnership must be constructed around Africa's leadership. This is what AU/NEPAD is all about.[13]

There is also need for wider leadership in the developed world:

> Strong and sustained action from developed countries in support of Africa's development requires action for Africa to be a domestic political issue in developed countries. That, in turn, requires both political leadership and political support. This can come from parliamentarians, the electorates, the media, the private sector and civil society as a whole. Whilst all these sources of pressure are interrelated, they all have their individual roles to play. It was political leadership prompted by civil society and development campaigners that led to the foundation of the Commission for Africa.[14]

The CfA report recommended, among other things: the tripling of aid flows to Africa to $50 billion annually by 2015, an additional $10 billion annually to fight the HIV/AIDS pandemic, complete debt forgiveness, an extra $10 billion annually for vital infrastructure, and the repatriation by banks in the developed world of money stolen by corrupt African leaders. The report also recommended a greater voice for Africa in the World Bank and the International Monetary Fund (IMF) and argued that appointments for heads of international institutions should be based on merit and not nationality. It also revisited the old issues of good governance and capacity building, reiterating the importance of the creation of socioeconomic and legal frameworks for growth and development.[15] As Zoe Ware has noted, most of these recommendations spoke to the broader objective of strengthening responsibilities and reciprocities:

> Although it has been criticized as more meaningless promises, it has signaled a reinvigorated interest in the continent. The Commission's eminent panel has given the report credence, and it has undoubtedly benefited from having Tony Blair as its "champion." The report has begun to correct the image of Africa as a hopeless beggar with an unquenchable thirst for aid by placing emphasis on a "partnership between the developed world and the continent of Africa that goes beyond the old donor/recipient relations."[16]

At the G8 summit in July 2005 in Gleneagles, Scotland, Blair attempted to convince his colleagues to embrace the recommendations and provide funding to meet the policy objectives. In the run-up to the Gleneagles summit, Britain endorsed all the recommendations of the report and mobilized considerable diplomatic efforts to obtain support from the rest of the G8 countries. But most of the G8 countries were skeptical of British African activism and agreed to increase official development assistance by $25 billion per year by 2010. The most significant concession was debt forgiveness, in the amount of $40 billion, owed by eighteen countries (most of them in Africa).[17] Blair also obtained commitment from the G8 countries to ratify the UN convention against corruption and to take action to recover and confiscate stolen assets and return them to their legitimate owners, deny entry to corrupt officials found guilty of corruption, and enforce laws against the bribery of foreign public officials.[18]

Although the report anticipated increased scaling up of resources on the HIV/AIDS epidemic, during the conference on the replenishment for the Global Fund to Fight AIDS, Tuberculosis, and Malaria in September 2005, Britain doubled its share of the fund, but other donors gave only $3.8 billion, $3.3 billion short of the target. Similarly, despite Blair's campaign for fairer trade terms for Africa, neither the G8 countries nor the WTO Doha Development Round of trade talks in December 2005 in Hong Kong made any breakthroughs on trade issues. Overall, what Blair described as the Africa 2005 agenda fell short of expectations, for reasons explained by Penny Jackson:

> Counterbalancing the Blair campaigns, however, were considerable political and economic obstacles. To begin with, it seems that some G8 members thought the diplomatic drive was an attempt by Britain to steal the high moral ground and that it gave an insufficient recognition to their own increased commitments to the continent. The Canadians and the French had already used their chairmanships to talk about African issues, and the Bush administration has taken increased interest in Africa.[19]

Not to be overshadowed by Britain, French President Chirac launched his own global initiative to address Africa's plight, proposing an international solidarity levy on air travel, which would raise $3 billion annually to finance aid commitments.

Blair's presidency of the EU produced a landmark review of Euro-African relations to coincide with the momentum unleashed by the CfA. In October 2005, the European Commission produced a report, *EU Strategy for Africa: Towards a Euro-African Pact to Accelerate African Development*, which was endorsed by the Council of Ministers in December 2005. While rehashing some of the questions raised in the revised CPA, the report brought new issues to the fore of the relationship. Among the economic components of the EU Strategy is the establishment of the European-African Business Forum (EBF), a body that would forge dialogue and closer ties between the private and public investors in Africa and Europe. As part of this initiative, the EU made a commitment to support African Chambers of Commerce in exploring business and trade opportunities in Europe. Related to the notion of EBF is the proposal of twinning partnerships in business, industries, and trade unions. Similarly, the EU Strategy gives new prominence to helping African countries to diversify products exported to Europe.[20]

The EU Strategy also laid the foundation for resolving the vexing question of migration. Promising to make migration between Africa and Europe a positive force for development, the strategy proposed finding mechanisms that would ease the sending of remittances from Europe to Africa. Additionally, it outlined ways of transforming brain drain into brain gain through innovative programs, such as "helping African countries to tap into the potential available in their diasporas in Europe and by facilitating various forms of brain circulation, including return migration and temporary or virtual return by which African migrants can make their skills available to their home countries."[21]

On political issues, the EU Strategy was less innovative, reiterating the concerns about democracy, governance, and human rights.[22] The governance initiatives, however, tried to align Europe more with the local African initiatives, notably the African Peer Review Mechanism (APRM), the flagship program of the New Partnership for African Development (NEPAD). By backing the APRM, Europe has tried to underscore the domestication of NEPAD's principles of political, economic, and corporate governance. Although domestication had met many obstacles during the 1980s, the widespread convergence around governance as a universal good and the inextricable linkages between governance and economic development have signaled the inevitability of conditionalities. The more innovative component of the strategy was the establishment of a North African Governance Facility to promote democratization in Egypt, Libya, Tunisia, and Mauritania. On human rights, the strategy went beyond the rhetorical fealty on human rights and instead proposed the establishment of an EU-Africa Human Rights Forum with the objective of encouraging the sharing of resources and expertise on human rights issues.

On African conflicts, the EU Strategy built strongly on previous documents detailing Europe's role in conflict resolution. Since the 1999 Commission's communication on EU cooperation with African countries involved in armed conflicts, Europe has emphasized the importance of conflict prevention as the key to its African policies. In April 2000, through the Cairo Declaration and Cairo Plan of Action, adopted jointly by the EU and the Organization of African Unity (OAU), the EU developed a conflict management and resolution strategy dealing with common guidelines for arms exports, post-conflict reconstruction, conflict diamonds, and small-arms proliferation. In a follow-up to the Cairo summit in November 2002, the EU and African ministers agreed to (1) exchange information on regular basis; (2) establish an inventory of institutions dealing with conflicts; (3) strengthen the institutional capacity of early warning and preventive diplomacy; and (4) foster good governance and the rule of law as essential elements in conflict prevention. Toward this end, the EU also gave 10 million euros to the African Union Peace Fund.[23]

Subsequently, as part of the EU-Africa dialogue on conflict prevention, the EU established the Peace Facility in 2004, a 250 million euro allocation hived from the European Development Fund (EDF) to foster peace, enhance early warning, and conflict prevention. The facility specifically funds peacekeeping operations in Africa that are carried out and staffed by Africans. Funds from the Peace Facility have been used in support of the African Union Mission (AMIS) in Darfur, the Central African Republic, and the European Force (EUFOR) to support the electoral process in the Democratic Republic of the Congo (DRC).[24] Building on the success of the EU-led Peace Facility, the African Union (AU) and G8 donors recently agreed to set up a fund to support peacekeeping missions in Africa to augment the AU's Complementary Peace Facility. In increasing resources available for Africa-led peace support operations, the fund will also cover budget lines that cannot be financed by the APF.[25] Under a different framework, the EU has earmarked battle-ready groups of its own soldiers for limited peace operations in Africa.[26]

In addition to being the largest donor to the AU peacekeeping missions, the EU has been engaged in the long-term capacity-building for peace through the Peace Facility. Similarly, the EU has assiduously promoted the Kimberley Process, an international mechanism forged by Western countries to restrict the sale of diamonds from conflict countries in order to undercut diamond warlords. The 2005 Strategy sought to concretize most of the policy positions on conflict prevention and peacekeeping in Africa within the framework of Europe's Common Security and Defense Identity (ESDI) and the Common Foreign and Security Policy (CFSP).

Blair's activism raised Africa's global profile, but dependence on the new multilateral institutional leadership for agenda-setting raised profound questions of continuity. Thus, in 2006, when the G8 presidency passed onto Russia, a non-EU member, the focus on Africa's problems seemed to dissipate.[27] A year after the unprecedented focus on Africa at Gleneagles, the issues barely made it on the agenda of the G8 summit at St. Petersburg.[28] It was left to the perennial African attendees at the G8 summits—South Africa's Thabo Mbeki and Olusegun Obasanjo of Nigeria—to chastise Europe and the world for "ignoring" African issues and failing to live up to the promises of Gleneagles. Typical of these condemnations was a statement by President Mbeki: "It is important that the G8 begins to understand that making commitments to Africa without implementation is not helping."[29]

Under the presidency of Germany's Angela Merkel, the G8 leaders in June 2007 reconfirmed their commitment to double Official Development Assistance (ODA) to Africa by 2010. But studies indicate that aid flows to Africa have remained static for two years and are set to drop in spite of donor promises to increase giving.[30] Germany also proposed that each G8 member sign a partnership agreement with one African country that is living up to the expectation of global governance standards, a proposal that irked many Africans who saw it as paternalistic and a departure from the policy of geographic coherence. Reflecting the general disappointment with the 2007 G8 summit, Archbishop Njongonkulu Ndungane of Cape Town criticized the failure of Western countries to keep their promise:

> Having put Africa as a key item on the agenda, the G8 has made a number of proclamations about how they would contribute to Africa's growth and development. If G8 leaders can continue to make public pronouncements committing themselves to targets that they are failing to reach, I strongly question the type of leadership that is content to make empty promises. G8 leaders need to

> start subjecting themselves to peer-review, where they account for why they are lagging behind in meeting the commitments they have made. Members of the G8 must begin to show forthright leadership by ensuring that commitments are made with a clear road map with targets and clear time frames. Just as Europe needed a strong injection of resources from the international community to recover from World War II, so does Africa now. The international community, especially the G8 have this responsibility.[31]

When Portugal assumed the EU presidency in June 2007, there were expectations that its long interaction with Africa would help reignite attention to African issues. As part of these efforts, Lisbon announced an EU-AU summit to be held in December 2007, the first Europe-Africa summit in seven years. But even before its convention, the summit was embroiled in controversy stemming from Europe's attempts to bar Zimbabwe's President Robert Mugabe from the event. To the chagrin of African states, Portugal first suggested that Mugabe would be unwelcome, but the new British prime minister, Gordon Brown, raised the ante, threatening to boycott the summit because Mugabe's presence would contravene an EU visa ban imposed on the Zimbabwean leader. Furthermore, Brown contended that while the summit would be a "serious opportunity to forge a stronger partnership between EU and Africa, in order to fight poverty, tackle climate change, and agree on new initiatives on education, health and peace-keeping . . . if he attended, President Mugabe would undermine the summit, divert attention from the important issues that need to be resolved. In those circumstances, my attendance would not be appropriate."[32]

Responding to the campaign to bar Mugabe, SADC's chair, Zambian President Levy Mwanawasa threatened to mobilize other African countries to boycott the Lisbon summit. Declaring "No Mugabe, No Summit," Mwanawasa announced, "I will not go to Portugal if Mugabe is not allowed and I don't know how many African leaders will be prepared to go to Portugal without Mugabe."[33] Similarly, Gertrude Mongella, the Tanzanian president of the Pan-African Parliament, condemned Brown's threat: "We do know there are some problems, but if somebody wants to arm-twist Zimbabwe, that's not the best way to solve the problems. I think this is again another way of manipulating Africa. Zimbabwe is an independent nation."[34]

THE DYNAMIC OF AFRICA-AS-A-PROBLEM IN EURO-AFRICAN RELATIONS

The debate on Mugabe symbolizes lingering questions about EU perceptions of the African predicament in the twenty-first century. Global multilateralism has not reversed the creeping pessimism that has dominated Euro-African relations since the late 1990s. Following decades of civil strife and economic stagnation in Africa, Afro-pessimism pervaded the development agenda, breeding aid fatigue among Western publics. Fearful of the growing domestic inertia on African issues and African marginalization, the EU has tried to redefine most of the twenty-first-century security concerns as fundamentally having African origins. At the heart of the hardheaded realism that pervades this perspective is the assumption that Africa matters because it is the source of most of the global travails—weak states, environmental degradation, the threats of terrorism, Islamic fundamentalism, the AIDS pandemic, and migration. Since these issues have the potential to create chaos with resonance in Europe, the EU has an obligation to assist Africa in dealing with these problems.

This policy perspective has found conceptual defense in the works of Patrick Chabal and Jean-Pascal Daloz that purport widespread chaos and disorder as "normal" patterns of African politics.[35] Encapsulated in the broad ideas of a Fortress Europe, this policy has fostered preventive strategies that would insulate Europe from the quandary of Africa's presence and proximity. Noting that Europe's Africa policy oscillates between tepid engagement and neglect of African concerns, one of the leading French Africanists, Jean-François Bayart, has warned of the dangers of "abandoning" Africa:

> Europe has condemned Africa to further military turmoil in the form of civil wars and interventions of a para-colonial type by some Sub-Saharan states. Europe has abandoned the field of action to religious revolutions associated with sects and charismatic movements of a frequently obscurantist nature, which are formidable vehicles of changing political values. The logical outcome, other than a frightening decline in the conditions of life and a worrying political decay, is an unstoppable wave of emigration. Fortress Europe has no response other than bureaucratic and police repression. The ravages of HIV-AIDS, tuberculosis and malaria, the incidence of crime, the destruction of the forest, and the growing brutality of wars are all indicators that should worry Europe and suggest to Europeans that their continent will not remain immune from this turbulence forever.[36]

Although interest in chaos serves to refocus public engagement with Africa, it invariably reinforces the Africa-as-a-problem dynamic that, then, precludes engagements and partnerships that go beyond these problems. A perverse form of the globalization of the "African problem" is seen in the academic and policy debates across the Pacific, appropriately labeled, the "Africanization of the South Pacific."[37]

More than any other issue, African migration underlies Europe's Africa-as-a-problem posture. Captured in President Chirac's above-quoted statement, it also finds resonance within the larger public opinion. As a European citizen wrote to the British Broadcasting Corporation, "Rather than pulling Africans to our level (in an ideal world this would be great), migration is going to sink us to their level."[38] With an estimated 40,000 people making the often perilous sea crossing from West Africa to Spain's Canary Islands in 2006 alone, stemming the illegal migration tide on the southern shores of Europe has become the dominant irritant in EU-African relations. Although the EU Strategy of 2005 covered the softer side of migration, such as remittances and the brain drain, it was silent on the more difficult questions of mass crossings in the Mediterranean.[39]

Efforts to address illegal migration occupied the attention of the EU-Africa Ministerial Conference on Migration and Development in Tripoli in November 2006. This gathering tried to find a comprehensive and balanced approach to migration, taking into account migration trends as well as links between migration and economic, social, political, and humanitarian issues.[40] In yet another critical meeting that focused attention on migration in Rabat, Morocco, in July 2006, African and European states deliberated on developing a common approach, including tougher policing action against human trafficking and measures to deal with the poverty and conflict that drive would-be migrants to seek better lives in Europe. The then French interior minister, Nicholas Sarkozy, warned that the failure to offer opportunities to African youth today would spell disaster for Europe tomorrow: "Let us offer Africa youth a future of dignity. Then it will not risk resorting to violence and extremism, or choosing, en masse, the paths of exile."[41]

Bilateral agreements, particularly between Spain and West African nations, have failed to halt the flow of African migrants to Europe. Similarly, the EU hurriedly created FRONTEX, a border patrol force to operate in the Mediterranean, but patrols and helicopter surveillance units off the coasts of Senegal, Mauritania, Cape Verde, and the Gambia have been ineffective. The influx of illegal immigrants to Europe has also occasioned clashes among EU members, as illustrated in the EU summit on migration issues in Tampere, Finland, in September 2006. At these talks, Spain pleaded for help to deal with the surge of African migrants, repeatedly stating that it was unable to cope with the influx: "These people coming from the African continent are knocking on the door of the whole of the European Union—we just happen to be the closest border country towards the African continent."[42] More poignantly, President Ricardo Melchior of the Canary Islands threatened to "send these people arriving in small ships to Madrid and Brussels so that they can understand how serious the situation is."[43] But the rest of Europe was less sympathetic to Spanish pleas. While Germany noted that Madrid should not be asking for Europe's economic support, Austria criticized Spain's decision to grant amnesty to 500,000 undocumented foreigners in 2005, a decision that had rewarded illegal immigration.[44]

CONCLUSION

The Euro-African marriage that was consummated in Rome in 1957 has reached a predictable midlife crisis. The key challenge is whether the relationship will evolve into a comfortable maturity of respect and tolerance that comes with old age, or whether it confronts perpetual crises that stem from enduring issues of incompatibility. The relationship may adapt to these realities or collapse, but the trajectories in either direction are uncertain. For now, Europe, the dominant partner, seems to be speaking to Africa with a proverbial forked tongue—selling EPAs to demonstrate the maturation of economic relationships, while perennially reneging on G8 aid promises that ultimately seek to equip African countries to absorb and deal effectively with the EPAs.[45]

Yet the negotiations for the EPAs reveal that the days of nonreciprocal trade ties are over, awaiting new arrangements that will dovetail with current imperatives. Although these negotiations are difficult, there is growing recognition that future trade relations need a more solid anchor, even though there are enormous short-term adjustment costs. Similarly, in the realm of political conditionality and conflict resolution, the acknowledgment of reciprocities and responsibilities seems to be the way out of the debilitating debates that had previously hampered discussions about these questions. As NEPAD's domestication of the donor conditionality regime reveals, policy selectivity and differentiation among African countries has gradually evolved from a broader pattern of external and internal expectations about accountability, probity, good government, and common sense. Ultimately, an exit strategy out of dependency is the cure for political conditions and external superintendence, Herculean tasks at the heart of African economic development. Initiatives such as the launch of the first Pan-African Infrastructural Development Fund being financed by Africans to focus on energy, transport, telecommunications, and water and sanitation are crucial to dependency-reduction, but they remain rare.

In the recent evolution of Europe-Africa relations, African countries have found representation at the annual summits of G8 countries. Similarly, the Davos committee has routinely invited leaders of South Africa, Nigeria, and a smattering of other African countries to the annual conclave. There was also the much-publicized presence of Tanzania's Benjamin Mkapa and Ethiopia's Meles Zenawi on the Blair Commission for Africa. These invitations connote a growing respect and recognition of African presence in shaping the global economic agenda, but they also raise deep concerns as to whether such limited and sporadic participation trivializes and, at worst, fragments African perspectives. How much of what passes for African participation at Davos and at the G8 is substantive representation, and how much of it is tokenism that sustains the illusion of movement on African questions?

NOTES

1. For recent analyses of EU-Africa relations, see Alex Nunn and Sophia Price, "Managing Development: EU and African Relations through the Evolution of the Lome and Cotonou Agreements," *Historical Materialism* 12, no. 4 (2004), pp. 203–230; and Gumisai Mutume, "Africans Fear 'Ruin' in European Trade Talks," *Africa Renewal*, July 2007, pp. 10–12.

2. Lawrence E. Hinkle and Maurice Schiff, "Economic Partnership Agreements between Sub-Saharan Africa and the EU: A Development Perspective," *World Economy* 27, no. 2 (2004); and Paul Goodison, "Six Months On: What Shift Is There in the EU Approach to EPA Negotiations?" *Review of African Political Economy* 32, no. 104 (December 2005), pp. 295–308.

3. Wilfred Edwin, "EU Wants Dar to Decide Under Which Regional Bloc It Will Negotiate EPAs," *East African* (Nairobi), April 3, 2007.

4. Ibid.

5. Christopher Stevens, "The EU, Africa, and Economic Partnership Agreements: Unintended Consequences of Policy Dialogue," *Journal of Modern African Studies* 44, no. 3 (2006), p. 447.

6. Mutume, "Africans Fear 'Ruin' in European Trade Talks," pp. 10–12.

7. Benion Herbert Oruka, "Civil Society Urges Caution on EPAs," *East African* (Nairobi), May 1, 2007, p. 13.

8. Cited in ibid.

9. Joseph Coomson, "Notes Stop the EPAs, Oxfam, Panos Tell African Leaders," *Ghanaian Chronicle* (Accra), June 28, 2007.

10. Julius Barigaba, "Uganda Could Lose Duty Free Access to EU over EPA," *East African* (Nairobi), April 22, 2007.

11. For analyses and critiques of the CfA report, see William Brown, "The Commission for Africa: Results and Prospects for the West's Africa Policy," *Journal of Modern African Studies* 44, no. 3 (2006), pp. 349–374; Cameron Duodo, "Gleneagles: What Was All the Hype About?" *New African*, August–September 2005, pp. 34–37; Martin Plaut, "Blair and Africa: The African Commission Report," *Review of African Political Economy* 31, no. 31 (2004), pp. 704–711; and Ankie Hoogvelt, "Post-Modern Intervention and Human Rights: Report of the Commission for Africa," *Review of African Political Economy* 32, no. 106 (December 2005), pp. 569–594.

12. For discussions of Blair's Africa policy, see Zoe Ware, "Reassessing Labor's Relationship with Sub-Saharan Africa," *Round Table* 95, no. 383 (January 2006), pp. 141–152; Tom Porteous, "British Government Policy in Sub-Saharan Africa Under New Labor,"

International Affairs 81, no. 2 (2005), pp. 281–297; and Ian Taylor, "'Advice Is Judged by Results, Not by Intentions': Why Gordon Brown Is Wrong about Africa," *International Affairs* 81, no. 2 (2005), pp. 311–324.

13. Commission for Africa, *Our Common Interest: Report of the Commission for Africa* (London: Commission for Africa, 2005), p. 370.

14. Ibid., p. 382.

15. Ibid.

16. Ware, "Reassessing Labor's Relationship with Sub-Saharan Africa," p. 150.

17. Nicky Oppenheimer has criticized the G8's debt relief proposals because they do not foster responsibility: "The debt cancellation plan currently proposed does not distinguish between responsible and bad governments. In so doing, it will significantly increase the difficulty for responsible African governments to develop instruments to fund their own development. Debt relief—like aid—in this way 'shorts' African economies . . . Blanket aid—such as the wholesale cancellation of debt, irrespective of the capacity of the recipient country—could have the effect of sweeping away good practices in those countries struggling to achieve it. It will also, inevitably, take responsibility for the solution to Africa's problems away from Africans themselves. There is also a tendency in all those who espouse the Big Aid concept to adopt an ever-expanding wish list of target problems, which, it is assumed, can be resolved by the ever bigger injections of aid." See Pratibha Thaker, "Africa: Hope or Hype?" *Economist,* Special Issue, *The World in 2006*, p. 57.

18. For analyses of the summit, see Penny Jackson, "Briefing: The Commission for Africa: Gleneagles, Brussels, and Beyond," *African Affairs* 104, no. 417 (2005), p. 658.

19. Penny Jackson, "Briefing: The Commission for Africa, Gleneagles, Brussels, and Beyond," p. 658. See also a *Financial Times* (London), July 14, 2005, report that noted: "Some smaller European countries have voiced frustration at G8 grandstanding. Norway, Sweden, Denmark, Luxembourg, and The Netherlands, who collectively are the world's most generous aid donors, pointed out that none of the G8 countries had yet reached the UN target of donating 0.7 per cent of their national income as aid."

20. For discussion of this strategy, see Commission of the European Communities, *Communication from the Commission to the Council, The European Parliament, and the European Social and Economic Committee: EU Strategy for Africa, Towards a Euro-African Pact to Accelerate Africa's Development* (Brussels: The European Commission, October 12, 2005). See also S. S. Kingah, "The European Union's New African Strategy: Grounds for Cautious Optimism," *European Foreign Affairs Review* 11 (2006), pp. 527–553.

21. Cited in Kingah, "The European Union's New African Strategy," p. 530.

22. For a good analysis of EU efforts at democracy promotion, see Gordon Crawford, "The European Union and Democracy Promotion in Africa: The Case of Ghana," *European Journal of Development Research* 17, no. 4 (December 2005), pp. 571–600.

23. Kingah, "The European Union's New African Strategy," pp. 535–545. Se also Charles C. Pentland, "The European Union and Civil Conflict in Africa," *International Journal* 60, no. 4 (Autumn 2005), pp. 919–936; and Alex Ramsbotham et al., "Enhanc-

ing African Peace and Security Capacity: A Useful Role for the UK and G8," *International Affairs* 81, no. 2 (March 2005), pp. 311–324.

24. Stephan Klingebiel, "Regional Security in Africa and the Role of External Support," *European Journal of Development Research* 17, no. 5 (September 2005), pp. 437–448.

25. "Fund to Support Peacekeepers," *UN Integrated Regional Information Networks,* May 16, 2007.

26. Richard Youngs, "The EU and Conflict Resolution in West Africa," *European Foreign Affairs Review* 11 (2006), pp. 333–352.

27. In an assessment of Blair's contribution to African development on the eve of his departure from office, one analyst commented, "Whether he really achieved anything of note in terms of pushing for increased aid, debt forgiveness, fairer trading relations and other issues vital to Africa is, of course, open to debate. But the important thing is that he took the initiative to put the African agenda on the global meeting place. So even if Mr. Blair leaves office with a tarnished record on many fronts, particularly his blind support for U.S. occupation of Iraq, Africa will remember him as one who genuinely cared for the continent. And Africa will be looking closely to see whether his successor, Mr. Gordon Brown, will show the same understanding and empathy for the continent." See British Broadcasting Corporation, Summary of World News, July 30, 2007.

28. Paul Redfern, "G8 Pledges for Africa No Longer Concern the West," *East African* (Nairobi), July 11, 2006.

29. "Mbeki to Talk Tough to G8 About Africa Commitments," *Business Day* (Johannesburg), July 13, 2006.

30. "Forget Foreign Aid, Rather Go for Investment," *Business Day* (Johannesburg), June 1, 2006.

31. "African Monitor's Response to the G8 Summit Declaration," *Business Day,* June 15, 2007. See also "Aid Set to Drop, Warns Monitoring Group," allAfrica.com, May 31, 2007.

32. Chuks Ohuegbe, "Gordon, British PM, Threatens to Boycott EU-Africa Summit," *Leadership* (Abuja), September 22, 2007.

33. Emmerson Muchangwe, "'Everybody's Welcome to EU-Africa Summit,'" *Times of Zambia* (Ndola), September 27, 2007.

34. "Mugabe Shrugs off Brown Boycott," British Broadcasting Corporation, September 21, 2007.

35. Patrick Chabal and Jean-Pascal Daloz, *Africa Works: Disorder as Political Instrument* (Oxford: James Currey, 1999). For a similar conceptual direction, see Taylor, "'Advice Is Judged by Results, Not by Intentions,'" pp. 299–310.

36. Jean-François Bayart, "Commentary: Towards a New Start for Africa and Europe," *African Affairs* 103, no. 412 (2004), pp. 456–457. See also Klingebiel, "Regional Security in Africa," pp. 442–444.

37. See, in particular, Ben Reilly, "The Africanization of the South Pacific," *Australian Journal of International Affairs* 54, no. 3 (2000), pp. 262–270; and David Chappell,

"'The Africanization' of the Pacific: Blaming Others for Disorder in the Periphery," *Comparative Studies in Society and History* 25, no. 2 (2005), pp. 286–317.

38. "African Immigrants Flood Europe," *British Broadcasting Corporation,* September 23, 2006. For critical analysis of this issue, see Martin-Baldwin Edwards, "'Between a Rock and Hard Place': North Africa as a Region of Emigration, Immigration, and Transit Migration," *Review of African Political Economy* 33, no. 108 (June 2006), pp. 311–324.

39. Gumisai Mutume, "African Migration: From Tensions to Solutions," *Africa Renewal* 19, no. 4 (January 2006).

40. "EU-Africa Ministerial Conference on Migration and Development Issues," African Union (Addis Ababa), November 22, 2006.

41. Michael Frendo, "Small Country, Big Problem," *International Herald Tribune,* July 16, 2006. See also Greg Noll, "The Euro-African Immigration Conference: Africa Sells Out to Europe," *International Herald Tribune,* July 14, 2006.

42. Finland's EU Presidency, *Migration Management, Extended European Solidarity in Migration, Border Control and Asylum Policies*, Tampere Ministerial Meeting, September 20–22, 2006.

43. Ibid.

44. Ibid.

45. I am indebted to John Harbeson for alerting me to this contradiction.

13

China's Engagement in Africa

*Scope, Significance, and Consequences**

DENIS M. TULL

China's vastly increased involvement in Africa over the past decade is one of the most significant recent developments in the region. It appears to contradict the idea of international marginalisation of Africa and brings significant economic and political consequences. China's Africa interest is part of a recently more active international strategy based on *multipolarity* and non-intervention. Increased aid, debt-cancellation, and a boom in Chinese-African trade, with a strategic Chinese focus on oil, have proven mutually advantageous for China and African state elites. By offering aid without preconditions, China has presented an attractive alternative to conditional Western aid and has gained valuable diplomatic support to defend its international interests. However, a generally asymmetrical relationship differing little from previous African-Western patterns, alongside support of authoritarian governments at the expense of human rights, make the economic consequences of increased Chinese involvement in Africa mixed at best, while the political consequences are bound to prove deleterious.

INTRODUCTION

The period since the end of the Cold War, when observers would invariably name the US, France and the UK as the only foreign powers to have substantial

*Reprinted with the permission of Cambridge University Press.

interests in Sub-Saharan Africa, is drawing to a close. Over the course of the past ten years or so, the People's Republic of China has established itself as an increasingly influential player across the continent. Given the impressive scale and scope of its renewed engagement, China's forays into Africa may turn out as one of the most significant developments for the region in recent years. For one thing, China's return may single-handedly invalidate the conventional wisdom on Africa's international marginalisation; even more so since other states of the global south, notably India and Brazil, are also forging closer ties with Africa. For another, China's political and economic involvement in Africa has a palpable impact on the domestic scene in many African states, which will further augment should China continue to pursue a more globally oriented foreign policy, particularly towards non-Western regions.

Taking the general transformation of Chinese foreign policy as a starting point, this article analyses China's foreign policy towards Africa since the early 1990s. The first half of the paper reviews the scale of China's political and economic involvement and examines the objectives and strategies underlying Chinese foreign policy towards Sub-Saharan Africa. Although by no means Beijing's only objective, oil interests will receive particular emphasis. The second part of the paper looks at the impact that China's renewed engagement has on the countries of the region by considering its economic and political repercussions. It is argued that China's economic impact may prove to be a mixed blessing whereas the political consequences of its return are likely to prove deleterious.

CHINA'S SHIFTING FOREIGN POLICY

China's increasing involvement on the African continent is a manifestation of the remarkable transformation of the country's foreign policy over the past 10–15 years. Although China watchers are still debating the nature and scope of that change, they mostly agree that China has been seeking a more active role in the international system in recent years. Beijing has expanded and intensified its bilateral relations throughout the world, has joined regional bodies dealing with security and economic issues and has extended its involvement in multilateral organisations. As a result, China's foreign policy as a whole is by and large considered to be more dynamic, constructive, flexible and self-confident than was the case during the preceding decades (see Medeiros & Taylor Fravel 2003; Sutter 2004). As veteran diplomat Zbigniew Brzezinski asserts: 'China is clearly assimilating into the international system.' (Brzezinski & Mearsheimer 2005:46).

Chinese efforts to conduct a more active foreign policy beyond its Asian neighbourhood set in as early as 1989.[1] The fierce reactions of Western states to the massacre in Tiananmen square (June 1989), including an arms embargo imposed by the US and the European Union (EU), and the persistent Western criticism of China's human rights record ever since induced Beijing to seek closer ties to non-Western countries. Developing countries were effectively elevated to a 'cornerstone' of Chinese foreign policy in an effort to build coalitions to shield Beijing from Western criticism. Given their numerical weight in international organisations, African states played an important role in the Chinese stratagem. Since many African leaders were themselves at the time under growing domestic and external pressure to liberalise their political systems, they were more than willing to go along with China's claims that Western demands for democracy and the respect for human rights amounted to thinly veiled imperialistic manoeuvres intent on interfering in the domestic politics of developing states and undermining their stability and progress at large. Gauging the relations between developing and developed states in terms of a North-South conflict, this discourse served as a powerful glue whereby China sought to construct a common identity with African states vis-à-vis the paternalistic West. With these considerations in mind, China moved swiftly to increase its assistance to developing countries substantially, most of which were African nations (Taylor 1998:450).

A second factor that led the Chinese leadership to steer a more active foreign policy course in the post-1989 period was the expected emergence of an uncontested international hegemony of the US which, it was feared, would hold back China's ascendancy as a global political power (Muekalia 2004:10). To address the problem, Beijing advanced the concept of *multipolarity*, defined as the construction of more or less flexible alliances to contain every form of hegemony and to build a new and just international order. Since China obviously conceived of itself as one indispensable pole in the international system, the government reached out to non-Western states to bolster its international position vis-à-vis the US, particularly its room for manoeuvre within the UN Security Council and other international bodies. The coming into office of the administration of G.W. Bush, which conceptualised China as a 'strategic competitor'—President Clinton had referred to China as a 'strategic partner'—probably reinforced Beijing's belief in the necessity of a multipolar world and the need for new allies (see Economy 2003:243–49).

At the end of the same decade a third factor corroborated Beijing's view that a global foreign policy had become a sheer necessity. While the strength of China's economy was to no small degree based on its dynamic integration into the world economy, the financial crisis in Asia in 1997 alerted the Chinese leadership to the risks of economic interdependence as it exposed the vulnerability of the country's outward-oriented economy to external shocks. By implication, regional and international stability, mainly but not exclusively in economic terms, turned into strategic objectives (Weinstein 2005). Therefore Beijing moved to modify and broaden the conceptualisation of its (inter)national interests. For if outside events could imperil the country's continued economic growth, China's precarious domestic situation, including increased social tensions, would no doubt pose a serious challenge to the political monopoly of the Communist Party. Consequently, the Chinese leadership regarded a more active foreign policy as the best strategy to defend and assert its national interests. The need to expand and strengthen China's bilateral relations, including those with the states in Africa south of the Sahara, was part of this strategy. Accordingly, China's rapidly increasing engagement in Africa is not so much reflecting a singular or specific policy towards the continent. Instead, it is part and parcel of a wider policy thrust which manifests itself equally in China's relations towards other regions of the world such as Latin America and the Middle East.[2]

TAKING STOCK OF CHINA'S INVOLVEMENT IN AFRICA

Western responses to the Tiananmen massacre in 1989 provided the initial trigger which compelled the Chinese government to seek closer ties to Africa after a lengthy period of reduced activity.[3] In the three years following the carnage, Chinese foreign minister Qian Qichan visited no less than 14 African countries and thus laid the foundation for an intense diplomacy that continues unabated until today (see Taylor 2004:87; Marchal forthcoming). During the past two years, for example, more than one hundred high-level meetings have taken place between Chinese and African diplomats and envoys (see *BBC Monitoring Newsletter* 2005). In addition, and at a time when Western states are generally inclined to roll back their diplomatic presence in Africa, China maintains embassies in every African country—except for the six states entertaining diplomatic relations with Taiwan.[4] By the same token, the number of Chinese commercial representations is growing fast.

Although an emerging economic superpower, China continues to portray itself, at least to African audiences, as a developing nation to underline the quasi-natural convergence of interests between China, 'the biggest developing country and Africa, the continent with the-largest number of developing countries' (Jiang Zemin). At the same time Beijing acknowledges its superior international standing and uses its permanent seat in the UN Security Council to position itself as a mentor of African countries. This includes China's claims to support fairer global trade and Africa's various reform-oriented institutions such as the New Partnership for Africa's Development (NEPAD) and the African Union (AU) and an enlarged UN Security Council. While most of these pledges have remained extremely vague, China's increasing involvement in UN peacekeeping missions in Africa has been substantial. In 2004, some 1,400 Chinese participated in nine UN missions on the continent. The biggest contingent (558 troops) was sent to war-torn Liberia after the incoming Liberian government (2003) ended its diplomatic relations with Taiwan.[5]

As another signal of its commitment to Africa, Beijing points to its support for debt cancellation in favour of African countries. Over the past few years, China has cancelled the bilateral debts of 31 African countries totalling some $1.27 bn (*BBC Monitoring Newsletter* 2005). Similarly, President Hu Jintao's promise to provide development assistance 'within our power' is part of Beijing's repertoire to underline its support for Africa (*The Christian Science Monitor* 6.1.2005). In 2002 some 44% of China's widely spread overall assistance to developing countries of $1.8 bn went to Africa (*The Economist* 7.2.2004; *L'Humanité* 4.2.2004). Although this represents a large amount when measured against China's GDP per capita (2002: $911), the country clearly lags behind the volumes disbursed by major Western nations.[6] As a result, it is far from clear whether China is prepared to become a dedicated donor nation, with the obligations and commitments this may entail, or whether it will continue to emphasise its own status as a developing country, defining whatever it deems to be 'within its power' and thus foregoing international agreements among donors.

However, the limited financial value of China's aid is considerably enhanced by political considerations. The Chinese government and its African counterparts frequently stress that Beijing's aid comes with little political strings attached. Contrary to Western donors, China's cooperation with or support of African governments does not hinge on conditionalities pertaining to specific political objectives or standards (i.e. human rights, democracy). Of course, the notable exception from China's purported rejection of political demands is the issue of Taiwan; that is, Beijing's insistence that it is the only legitimate representative of China. The 'One China' principle therefore remains an important objective, even though the race for recognition between both countries is no longer as important as it was in the past, partly because in recent years Beijing was considerably more successful than Taipei in its attempts to convince African countries to shift recognition away from its rival (see Taylor 2002).

Out of the wide range of Chinese activities in Africa, economic transactions provide the most powerful evidence of China's increasing interests in the continent. The skyrocketing of Chinese-African trade deserves particular emphasis. Between 1989 and 1997 the bilateral trade volume grew by 430% and since then has more than quintupled. It reached $24 bn in 2004, amounting to 6.3% of the extra-regional trade of the states south of the Sahara.[7] In the first ten months of 2005 Chinese-African trade grew by 39% to $32.17 bn (*BBC Online* 6.1.2006). As a result, China has overtaken the UK as Africa's third most important trading partner in 2005 (after the US and France). However, Africa's share of Chinese external trade is only about two per cent and the Chinese-African trade represents a mere 40% of the US-African trade volume.

Beijing's active promotion of economic interaction with Africa has significantly contributed to the impressive growth rates of bilateral trade. In institutional terms, this has been flanked by the creation of the Forum on China-Africa Cooperation in 2000 (see *IRIN News,* 17.12.2003; Muekalia 2004:8–10; Taylor 2004:89–91). Furthermore, a Chinese-African Chamber of Commerce was opened in Beijing in March 2005, which aims at promoting trade and economic relations with initially five African countries.[8] That institution is only the latest among a fast growing number of initiatives and agreements between China and Africa. As of 2005, China has bilateral trade and investment agreements with 75% of Africa's states. Of the 40 bilateral investment agreements China entered between 1995 and 2003, 18 were established with African countries (UNCTAD 2004). Enhanced Chinese economic interest in Africa is also reflected by the fact that some 700 Chinese enterprises with a total investment of about $1.5 bn are currently operating in Africa (*Beijing Time* 16.12.2003). Finally, China has signalled its willingness to negotiate the establishment of a free trade zone with southern African states (*China Daily* 26.11.2004.).

What are the factors behind the Chinese-African trade boom? The massive export of goods to Africa is part of the story. Due first to its large and cheap labour force and second to the acute poverty in vast parts of Africa, China offers low-price export goods such as textiles and clothing, electronic devices and machines, which find a huge and soaring demand. In 2003 China was the second biggest exporter of goods (11%) to the member states of the Economic Community of West African States (ECOWAS). Given its burgeoning exports to Nigeria, West Africa's largest economy, China has since then almost certainly narrowed the gap with ECOWAS' leading supplier, i.e. France. After Nigeria's imports from China had multiplied by a factor of ten in the period between 1994 and 2002, Nigerian imports from China climbed from $1.76 bn in 2003 to $2.28 bn in 2004 (*Mail & Guardian* 23.5.2005).

Chinese imports from Africa have grown even faster. In comparison to the primarily *commercial* objectives of its export trade with Africa, the *strategic* value of China's imports from the continent stands out. It is driven by Beijing's need to secure natural resources to sustain its economic boom at home (see Zweig & Janhai 2005). For instance, China's share in the increase in global demand for some mineral resources such as aluminum, nickel and copper varies between 76 and 100% (Kaplinsky 2005). Similarly, China's oil consumption will increase dramatically over the next three decades; and so will its reliance on oil imports, which accounted for 37% of its oil consumption in 2003.[9]

Africa's resource-rich countries are in a position to provide an ample percentage of China's requirements. There is little doubt that natural resources are at the core of China's economic interests in Africa—or perhaps even its overall interest in the continent. In terms of China's imports from Africa, nine out of its ten most important trading partners are resource-rich countries. Remarkably, the list even includes emerging oil-producer Chad, one of the few African countries to recognise Taiwan.

It is probably no coincidence that Beijing's rising interest in Africa comes at a time when sizeable new discoveries of oil have been made on the continent, particularly in the Gulf of Guinea. Africa's largest producers, Angola and Nigeria, are set to at least double their production within the next decade. Important oil fields have also been explored in Equatorial-Guinea, São Tomé e Principe and Chad while minor reserves are located in Mauritania and Côte d'Ivoire (Ellis 2003:135). Together with long-standing producers Congo-Brazzaville and Gabon, these new discoveries could bring Africa's oil output to seven million barrels a day within the next 10–15 years (*International Herald Tribune* 31.7.2004). Bolstered by a massive infusion of investments of $360 bn (2001–2030) that transnational companies have announced to make, production could reach 13 million barrels per day in 2020.[10]

Regardless of these projections, Africa's contribution to China's overall oil imports is already significant. In 2004 Africa's share of Chinese overall oil imports reached 28.7%, up from 25.2% in 2003.[11] Angola, Beijing's most important

TABLE 13.1 China's most important African trading partners in 2004 (imports)

	Millions of $US	%
Angola	3,422.63	27.4
South Africa	2,567.96	20.6
Sudan	1,678.60	13.4
Republic of Congo	1,224.74	9.8
Equatorial Guinea	787.96	6.3
Gabon	415.39	3.3
Nigeria	372.91	3.0
Algeria	216.11	1.7
Morocco	208.69	1.7
Chad	148.73	1.2
TOTAL	11,043.72	88.4

Source: International Monetary Fund, *Direction of Trade Statistics* (Washington, D.C.: IMF, May 2005).

African oil supplier, exported 117 million barrels to China in 2004, a 60% increase from the previous year.[12] With a share of about 13% of Chinese oil imports, Angola came close to the level provided by China's leading oil supplier, i.e. Saudi-Arabia (125 million barrels).

STRATEGIC ELEMENTS OF CHINA'S POLICY TOWARDS AFRICA

The extent to which China appears to be welcomed with open arms by many of Africa's leaders is perhaps the most striking element of recent Sino-African relations. By offering their African counterparts a mix of political and economic incentives, the Chinese government is successfully driving home the message that increased Sino-African cooperation will inevitably result in a 'win-win situation' for both sides. The power of this argument is enhanced by a subtle discourse which posits China not only as an appealing alternative partner to the West, but also as a better choice for Africa. While this is certainly debatable with respect to Africa and its ordinary citizens as a whole, there can be little doubt that sizeable benefits of China's return will accrue to state elites.

Most obviously, an important appeal stems from the fact that China stubbornly sticks to the dogma of national sovereignty. It fiercely continues to repudiate the increasingly powerful notion that outside interference into the domestic affairs of a state can be legitimate. China's donor policies reflect this state-centred orthodoxy to the degree that, the issue of Taiwan aside, no political conditions are attached to its development assistance. Western donors, in contrast, have progressively undermined the sovereignty of African states by imposing reform agendas on them: first in the guise of Structural Adjustment Programs (SAPs) in the 1980s, followed in the 1990s by demands for democratic reform. In light of the persistent stress which economic and political conditionalities have forced on African governments, it is hardly surprising that the Chinese stance on the issue of sovereignty is gratefully acknowledged by African governments. In a barely concealed complaint against the intrusive attitudes of Western donors, a spokesman of the Kenyan government no doubt echoed a widespread sentiment on the continent when he noted: 'You never hear the Chinese saying that they will not finish a project because the government has not done enough to tackle corruption. If they are going to build a road, then it will be built.'[13] Such observations underline that non-intrusive China presents an attractive partner of African governments; that is, not only for plainly authoritarian leaders, but also for the great many of African governments presiding over hybrid regimes for whom the distribution of patronage remains an exigency of political survival.[14]

That a number of African regimes have been unable to manage the political economy of reform over the past two decades, sometimes with disastrous consequences such as outbreaks of violent conflict, was not lost on the Chinese government. In conjunction with the wholesale failure of economic reforms (SAPs), these setbacks, in Beijing's view, have but confirmed its analysis that the patchy record of Western-driven reform efforts in Africa will inadvertently facilitate Chinese advances on the continent. As *Renmin Ribao*, the official newspaper of the Communist Party, noted:

> '... owing to the general failure in the West's political and economic behaviour in Africa, African nations, which were only suspicious at first, are now negating Western-style democracy and have reinitiated "Afro-Asianism" and proposed "going towards the Orient." This has opened up new opportunities for further enriching the content and elevating the quality of China-Africa cooperation' (*BBC Monitoring Newsletter* 8.1.2004).

Furthermore, Chinese aid tends to benefit the governments of receiving countries more directly than the policies of Western donors, who are preoccupied with the reduction of poverty. The Chinese, unlike Western countries, do finance grandiose and prestigious buildings (presidential palaces, football stadiums) that African leaders highly appreciate for their very own political reasons.

In return, Beijing can count on valuable diplomatic support by African governments to defend its interests on the international level, particularly in multilateral organisations with 'one country—one vote' arrangements. In the United Nations Commission on Human Rights, for instance, African countries have frequently played a prominent role in frustrating Western efforts to bring about a formal condemnation of China's human rights record.[15] More recently, intense courting led to China's recognition as a market-economy by a fair number of African states. This is a crucial status in the wake of China's WTO accession, helping to shield it from accusations of dumping.[16] Finally, diplomatic backing by African states pertains to the recognition of the principle of 'One China' and the pursuit of the concept of a multipolar world.

Although non-interference remains an article of faith for the Chinese leadership, it is but one factor explaining China's growing influence in Africa. Particularly in the economic realm, it has only limited explanatory power. What matters more are the strategies that Chinese companies pursue in their conquest of Africa's markets. Firstly, Chinese firms appear to be significantly less risk-averse than their Western counterparts, especially in war-torn states such as Angola, DR Congo and Sierra Leone, where a 'first mover advantage' plays out in favour of risk-taking entrepreneurs.[17] This is also true in a more general sense insofar as Chinese businesses seem to consider the challenging political and economic environment in many African states as an economic opportunity. Thanks to their willingness to take significant risks, Chinese firms are able derive huge profits from rates of return on Foreign Direct Investment said to be much higher in politically volatile Sub-Saharan Africa than in other parts of the developing world.[18]

Secondly, the success of Chinese businesses in Africa may also relate to their focus on specific sectors. In no small part due to the feeble presence of Western rivals, China has become a major player in the field of infrastructure (roads, railways, barrages, power plants etc.). Strictly speaking, though, many of these projects are not commercial. Some are financed through 'tied' Chinese aid. Others are not profitable because the Chinese tend to set costs below market rates. And yet, the lack of short term commercial profits does not preclude that investments will yield significant returns in the long term. Since most infrastructure projects are public sector works, China conceives its investments as goodwill projects to woo the sympathies of African state leaders. This enables China to gain political influence, which often opens the doors for commercially or strategically more attractive businesses in other sectors, e.g. to win tenders for oil and mining concessions.[19] A third advantage is noticeable in instances where China is targeting African states suffering from Western-imposed sanctions. Since Western states are still by far the most important trading partners of African states, Western sanctions de facto turn these countries into niche markets. Having no legal or political obligation to abide by Western-imposed sanctions, China can position itself as an alternative partner of 'pariah-states' (see Alden 2005b:155). China has adopted this free-riding strategy in Sudan and Zimbabwe.

CHINA'S OIL INTERESTS

Since 1998, when a White Paper of the Chinese Ministry of Defence proclaimed energy security as an integral part of China's overall security, the country's global economic, foreign and security policies have become closely intertwined.[20] In the process, Beijing stepped up its efforts both to expand its oil imports and to diversify its oil suppliers. In line with this policy, China has increased its oil imports from Africa and has augmented the number of its African suppliers. In 2004 the country was reported to have oil stakes in as many as 11 African states.[21] In January 2006, China's top offshore oil producer, CNOOC, agreed to pay \$2.3 billion for a 45% stake in a Nigerian oil and gas field, its largest-ever overseas acquisition.[22] For the time being, however, the vast bulk of Chinese oil imports from Africa is provided by two countries: Angola and Sudan. Beijing's involvement in both countries is somewhat emblematic of the approach sketched above. First, it underlines the interconnectedness of political, diplomatic and economic strategies to secure oil supplies. Second, it points to the fact that China's efforts often focus on what may be called niche markets.

From a Chinese point of view, niche countries and their oil sectors are characterised by limited competition: either because Western multinational companies have no or only limited access for political reasons such as embargoes (e.g. Sudan, Iran) and/or because the countries are relatively new or emerging oil producers offering significant opportunities. Given the inadequate financial and technological competitiveness of Chinese oil companies (*New York Times* 14.12.2004), the targeting of niche countries forms a strategic decision to secure oil stakes. China's widening demand for African oil thus corresponds to its overall energy security policy insofar as Sudan and many of West Africa's oil-producing countries in the Gulf of Guinea can be subsumed under the first and second category of niche countries respectively.

A well-considered combination of diplomacy and economic incentives forms Beijing's key instrument to lock up African oil supplies. China's major oil companies are owned by the state and act as an extended arm of the Chinese government, which supports the overseas activities of its oil companies through a variety of instruments (see Downs 2004:25, 30). As such, strategic objectives to secure oil supplies often override commercial concerns.[23] By dispensing soft loans and credit lines, development assistance, gifts and other incentives, arms deliveries and diplomatic backing, Beijing seeks to cultivate the favour of governments in oil-producing states and, by extension, obtain privileged access and opportunities for its companies.[24] Thus oil interests and bilateral relations between China and African countries go hand in hand.

Somewhat reminiscent of a mercantilist approach, this *petro-diplomacy* can be seen in Angola where Chinese imports have grown by 400% since 2001. Recently, the state-owned China Eximbank released a $2 bn loan package to Angola in exchange for 10,000 barrels a day of oil (*Africa Confidential,* 17.12.2004). The deal was of mutual benefit. While it enabled the Angolan regime to circumvent donor pressure for increased fiscal transparency, it will strengthen the Chinese foothold in the Angolan oil economy.

The strategic elements of China's energy security policy in Africa are brought into its sharpest relief in Sudan. Having acquired 40% stake in the *Greater Nile Petroleum Operating Company* (GNPOC) in 1996, American sanctions against Khartoum and the incremental withdrawal of other Western oil companies enabled China's state-owned CNPC to become the largest foreign investor in Sudan's nascent oil production.[25] When, in 2004, the full extent of

Khartoum's genocidal campaign in the Darfur provinces came to daylight, the US and other Western states sought action against Sudan in the UN Security Council. There, however, attempts to bring Khartoum to book were repeatedly frustrated by China.[26] It either abstained from casting its vote or threatened to make use of its veto right.[27]

Notwithstanding its reference to state sovereignty and the concomitant appraisal of Darfur as a 'domestic issue,' Beijing's intransigency in the Security Council was essentially linked to its oil interests. First, Sudan is a non-negligible provider of China's oil imports (6.9%). Second, the GNPOC joint venture is the largest overseas oil investment of the Chinese CNPC. Over the years an estimated $5 bn have been invested in the acquisition of exploration and drilling licenses, the construction of pipelines, refineries and other essential infrastructure. The scale of these investments highlights China's long-term strategic interests in Sudan, which is expected to increase its production of 340,000 barrels a day to 500,000 barrels a day in 2005 and 750,000 barrels a day by 2006.

It comes as no surprise therefore that Beijing opposed UN sanctions which could have jeopardised its Sudanese investments and oil supplies for many years to come.[28] In fact, Beijing perpetuated a highly advantageous status quo. Chinese companies can continue to operate without the competition of financially and technologically superior Western firms whose return to Sudan could pose a severe threat to their dominance of the Sudanese oil economy. Interestingly, the peace agreement between Khartoum and the rebels of the Sudan People's Liberation Army (SPLA) of January 2005 contains an explicit guarantee for all oil concessions, which the Sudanese government has granted during the war (Berrigan 2005). The clause undoubtedly presented a reward for China's steadfast diplomatic support for Khartoum during the diplomatic height of the Darfur crisis.

CHINA'S ECONOMIC IMPACT

China's undeniable appeal to African states, notably as a trading partner, is the flipside of their fading economic importance to the West. Partly as a result, a good number of African elites and intellectuals appear to regard China as both an appealing economic model worth emulating and a potential catalyst for socio-economic development. No less important, they conceptualise emergent South-South-relations as a historical opportunity for Africa's states to escape the neo-colonial ties to the West. And yet, it is not evident that Chinese-African trade differs significantly from Western-African trade patterns; nor is it clear that China's engagement will substantially improve Africa's prospects for development. Judging from its most important trading partners (imports), Beijing's economic interests in Africa do not vary from those of Western states.[29] This seems to suggest that rapidly growing economic exchanges between Africa and China will neither fundamentally alter Africa's asymmetrical integration into global markets, nor will they reduce Africa's dependency on a few price-volatile primary goods that account for 73% of its overall export revenues.[30] Even outside the extractive sector, there is some reason to doubt that China's economic engagement will encourage sustainable economic growth in Africa. The evidence from an examination of textile industries, one of the few African economic success stories in recent years, is ambivalent indeed.

When the US-sponsored African Growth and Opportunity Act (AGOA) came into effect in 2000, a fair number of Chinese textile companies established themselves in Africa. The move had two closely related objectives: first, to exploit the preferential access to the US market that AGOA had conceded to certain African products, including clothing and textile.[31] Second, shifting parts of the production to Africa enabled Chinese firms to circumvent the trade barriers the Agreement on Textiles and Clothing of the so-called Uruguay Round had imposed on them to protect markets in Europe and the US from cheap Asian imports. The combined effect of the AGOA agreement and the flexible strategies of Chinese companies contributed to the rise of textile industries, notably in southern and eastern Africa.

When the Agreement on Textiles and Clothing expired on 1 January 2005 and access restrictions for Asian textiles to Western markets were removed, Africa's intermittent textile boom witnessed a meltdown. American demand for African textiles plunged in favour of even cheaper garments made in China and Africa-based Chinese companies were already relocating their production back to China.[32] In the process, tens of thousands of workers have lost their jobs or risk doing so in the near future, for example in South Africa, Zimbabwe, Lesotho and Kenya.[33] Thus African textile producers will be hit by losses of global market shares whereas the efforts of African countries to diversify their economies and exports will endure a severe setback. Even South Africa, the continent's most sophisticated economy, is negatively affected. To begin with, manufactured goods as a share of exports to China fell from 50% in 1993 to eight per cent in 2003. The structure of South Africa's trade relations with China thus mirrors the wider problem of Africa's unbalanced trade relations insofar as some 90% of its exports to China consist of raw materials (e.g. ore, platinum, and diamonds). In 2004 South Africa incurred a trade deficit with China of $1.9 bn. Were it not for Beijing's imports of oil and other raw materials, the aggregated African trade with China would show a huge deficit (see Taylor 2004:98).

To make matters worse, most African producers are simply not in a position to compete with Chinese companies even in Africa's domestic markets as they are unable to undercut Chinese production costs and prices.[34] Local retailers, too, are faced with the rapidly increasing business competition from expatriate Chinese traders.[35] Although there is some evidence that the economic activities of Chinese entrepreneurs can make a positive contribution to local development (Bräutigam 2003), a cursory perusal of local press reports indicates that their remarkable presence also stirs significant local resentments (Alden 2005b:157).[36]

Although the diversification of trading partners is an encouraging sign, African countries have to recognise that China will not *per se* have a positive impact on their economies. China's foreign trade policies are not driven by altruistic motives (see Mbeki 2004). Chinese and African businesses are first and foremost economic contenders for investments and markets, in particular in the field of labour-intensive and export-oriented manufacturing like textile and clothing (see Jenkins & Edwards 2004). To date, however, nothing indicates that Africa will be able to compete successfully with China, a result of which is that its exports to China are by and large limited to capital-intensive commodities. If anything, this imbalance may have had the effect of Africa creating jobs in China while Chinese imports have undermined job markets in Africa. While this is the result of legitimate market competition, it nonetheless contravenes Chinese statements that enhanced Chinese-African interaction always results in win-win situations. The least one can say is that Beijing's high-flying rhetoric often pales in the face of stark realities. So far, for example, the relative sparseness of Chinese long-term investments in Africa outside of the extractive sector certainly belies what official Beijing likes to cast as its economic commitment to Africa. Therefore African governments would be naïve to take Beijing's rhetoric of South-South solidarity at face value. For the harsh reality is that China is no less self-serving than any other state. If any proof was needed, the recent episode in Chinese-Zimbabwean relations provided it.[37]

The Zimbabwean regime of Robert Mugabe has in recent years turned to China to soften the impact of US and EU sanctions. But when Mugabe travelled recently to China to secure a bailout from the Beijing government he returned almost empty-handed, reportedly receiving a mere $6 m for grain imports.[38] According to one report, 'the platinum concessions offered by Zimbabwe were not a sufficient incentive for China to grant funds on the scale requested by Mugabe.'[39] That China's interests supersede vague discourses on 'South-South' solidarity is also a lesson learned by South Africa. Complaining that cheap Chinese textile imports threaten to annihilate local industries, South African trade unions exhorted the Pretoria government to take recourse to the WTO to protect textile industries. Reacting to these concerns, a Chinese official dryly noted that 'any move by the South African government to restrict textile imports from China would violate the WTO free trade agreement.[40]

China's hard-nosed economic interests are also reflected in Angola where some 2,500 Chinese workers have arrived to work for Chinese companies whose work will be financed by the oil-backed loan that Beijing granted to the Angolan government. According to one source, a total of 30,000 Chinese workers are expected eventually in Angola for the same purpose (*Le Monde* 6.7.2005). The least one can say is that China's massive transfer of personnel is doubtful to have a positive impact on African job markets, the building of local capacities and the transfer of technologies (see Alden 2005a).

POLITICAL CONSEQUENCES

To assess the political impact of China's growing involvement on the continent, it may be useful to differentiate three groups of African countries. First, China's manifest return to Africa occurs at a time when many countries of the region continue to undergo difficult political transitions from authoritarian to democratic political systems (*democratising/transition countries*). The assumption that China will make a constructive contribution to support transitions to democracy in Africa's fragile states appears somewhat far-fetched. In contrast to all other major donors in the region, except Libya, the promotion of democracy is not an objective of China's foreign policy. Such a policy appears inconceivable to the extent that it does not square with Beijing's relativistic conception of individual human and political rights. In addition, the self-interest of the political elite of the one-party state does contravene the notion of democracy support abroad. Doing so would logically imply that China's Communist leaders would dent their domestic political legitimacy. This is one of the reasons why Beijing doggedly clings to the dogma of non-interference. Its defence of sovereignty, often to the benefit of unsavoury regimes, is likely to undermine existing efforts at political liberalisation at large. For revenues from trade (and taxes), development assistance and other means of support widen the margins of manoeuvre of Africa's autocrats and help them to rein in domestic demands for democracy and the respect for human rights.[41] These mutually advantageous interactions are at the core of China's attractiveness to African state leaders and they are likely to go to the detriment of ordinary Africans (see Alden 2005b:153).

Second, China's impact on *mineral-rich countries* is also a source of concern. Chinese interest in African resources comes at a time when Western non-governmental organisations, recently supported by governments, have initiated an ever more prominent debate on the relationship between mineral wealth on the one hand and its detrimental effects on developing countries on the other. It revolves around possible options and regulatory frameworks to transform mineral wealth from a 'curse' into a vector of socio-economic development. In light of its rapidly growing reliance on imports, it seems implausible that China will join these efforts, let alone subordinate its economic interests to international attempts to solve the structural problems of richly endowed countries, as these are likely to hold back its access to resources.[42]

What is more, Beijing has no economic incentive to fall in line with Western views on issues such as fiscal transparency and accountability. By rejecting regulation efforts on the grounds of non-interference, China can position itself as a free-rider and is prone to win the political favour of and, by extension, economic benefits from sovereign-conscious governments (e.g. Angola). In that regard, the case of Darfur/Sudan is illuminating in so far as it underscores the extent to which China is prepared to defend its economic interests. If Sudan provides any clue for the future, it seems inconceivable that Beijing, unencumbered by the humanitarian tragedy in Darfur, will compromise its interests for the sake of 'minor' (domestic) issues such as transparency.

A third group of countries where China's forays may be particularly perceptible are *post-conflict states.* One the one hand, China's increasing involvement in UN peacekeeping in those states is certainly a positive development, even more so since only a small minority of Western industrialised states has shown the political willingness to make troops available for peacekeeping on the continent. On the other, however, one has to question the coherence and credibility of Chinese peacekeeping efforts if the country otherwise pursues strategies which may contribute to the eruption or prolongation of violent conflicts. For example, while China is currently an important troop-contributing country to the UN Mission in Liberia, its economic interests helped President Charles Taylor to maintain himself in power. China imported almost half of Liberia's timber in 2000 and thus provided Taylor with considerable wherewithal. It was only in July 2003 that China and France, likewise an important buyer of Liberian timber, brought themselves to reluctantly nod to UN sanctions against Liberia's timber exports, which both had previously opposed on the devious grounds of 'increased unemployment' in Liberia (Johnston 2004:447). The plummeting of revenues from timber exports and rebel groups forced Taylor to leave the country in August 2003 and the peace process finally began.

CONCLUSION

Will China's powerful return to the continent and the concomitant diversification of Africa's external relations change in any meaningful way the position of African states in the international system? In political terms, this may well be the case in the future, but it appears that this question will not be decided upon in Africa, but in Beijing and Washington. Should Brzezinski's contention be correct that China is assimilating into the international system, the answer, at least in the long run, will probably be no. For if China's integration in global markets is socialising the country's foreign policy and if in turn Beijing's interests, notably energy security, will be accommodated by non-confrontational Western behaviour, China's needs for allies in Africa and other parts of the non-Western world are likely to diminish. In economic terms, China's impact on Africa's place in the global economy is equally uncertain. To begin with, the diversification of Africa's external economic ties is a potentially promising development. However, the big picture so far is one in which Chinese-African economic relations are widely unbalanced and tend to replicate Africa's asymmetrical relationships with the West—a West Beijing so vividly claims to differ from. As a result, Africa's marginal place in the global system, defined by its limited value as a provider of mineral resources, may in effect be perpetuated by the fact that China's economic interests in Africa do not differ substantially from those of Western states. As the case of textile industries demonstrates, initial economic impulses from Chinese investments may not be sustainable insofar as Chinese companies pursue cool-headed strategies in the hunt for comparative advantages in an era of economic globalisation. As for development assistance, China's aid may have a marginal socio-economic impact. Not only is much of its aid tied, it also helps to underpin the political economies of narrow state elites. Judging from its increasing influence, however, China's elite-centred modes of assistance have proven extremely effective. They help to cultivate the goodwill of African leaders who provide Beijing with diplomatic support and valuable contracts as a matter of reciprocity. In this sense, state elites are probably the economic and, by extension, the political winners of China's growing involvement in Africa.

That aspect hints at the political repercussions of China's engagement with African states. Beijing uses the pillars of its foreign policy, notably unconditional respect for state sovereignty and its corollary, non-interference, in the pursuit of its interests, be it energy security, multipolarity or the 'One China' principle. To achieve these goals, Beijing is prepared to recklessly defend autocratic regimes that commit human rights abuses and forestall democratic reforms for narrow ends of regime survival. Finally, China's increasingly prominent role as a supplier of arms to Africa is also a source of concern.

In summary, there is virtually no way around the conclusion that China's massive return to Africa presents a negative political development that 'almost certainly does not contribute to the promotion of peace, prosperity and democracy on the continent' (Taylor 2004:99). Despite this, Western decision-makers have little reason to claim the moral high-ground vis-à-vis China. A fair number of flaws and criticisms that need to be levelled against Beijing's politics in

Africa do equally apply, though to a lesser extent, to Western policies towards Africa.[43] And yet, it also needs to be borne in mind that the policies of Western governments towards Africa have come to reflect a more normative and reform-oriented edge in recent years and, despite pervasive ambiguities, have broadly sought to promote democracy, human rights and conflict prevention.

More important, however, will prove to be the nature of the relationship between Africa's international organizations (i.e. AU, NEPAD and ECOWAS) and an increasingly influential China. Beijing's support for AU and NEPAD has so far proven little more than rhetoric and is ambivalent at best. For instance, China is insisting that its support for NEPAD be channelled through the framework of the China-Africa Cooperation Forum, thereby enabling it to avoid 'the potentially awkward position of having to support the key structural elements that are ultimately necessary for NEPAD's success: transparency, democracy, free press . . . ' (Thompson 2005:2). Similar ambiguities surround China's support for the AU, which seems to be limited to warm words and smaller ad hoc payments. That the Chinese government donated $400,000 in support of the AU's mediation efforts to resolve the Darfur crisis in early 2005, a move it hailed as a contribution to peace-building in Africa, appears disconcertingly cynical.[44] This raises important questions as to the relationship between China and Africa's reform-minded bodies exactly because AU, ECOWAS and NEPAD have recently espoused procedures and principles which clearly contravene the cornerstones of Chinese statecraft (i.e. sovereignty, non-interference). The progressive pathway taken by African Union and ECOWAS in regard to the prevention and resolution of violent conflicts is particularly at odds with Beijing's political concepts, for both organisations claim far-reaching prerogatives, including military intervention, in order to prevent or terminate large-scale human rights abuses and crimes against humanity. One may also recount that NEPAD's so-called *African Peer Review Mechanism* is, at least in theory, an instrument of political interference in the domestic affairs of states, which aims at promoting development and democracy in Africa. In the final analysis, it is not obvious how these competing conceptions can be squared—provided that Africa's regional bodies are determined to put their pledges for democracy and human rights into practice.

NOTES

1. This section is based on Taylor 1998.

2. Note, however, that Beijing recently issued an official paper on its policy towards Africa. The paper (China's Africa Policy) is available on the website of the Chinese Ministry of Foreign Affairs: http://www.fmprc.gov.cn/eng/zxxx/t230615.htm.

3. For the historical background see Snow 1989.

4. These are Burkina Faso, Chad, Gambia, Malawi, São Tomé e Principe and Swaziland. In October 2005, Senegal (once more) established relations with Beijing instead of Taiwan.

5. However, China also provided 125 police officers in the UN mission in Haiti which recognises Taiwan.

6. For example, Germany's bilateral assistance to Sub-Saharan Africa was $1.34 bn in 2002.

7. Source: International Monetary Fund, *Direction of Trade Statistics.* The United Nations Development Programme (UNDP) puts the figure much higher, i.e. $29.64 bn. See http://www.undp.org.cn.

8. The creation of the institution was supported by UNDP. See UNDP Press Release, 18.3.2005.

9. See 'China struggles to fulfill spiraling energy demands'; *Jane's Intelligence Review* 2004, 16, 7:56.

10. See International Energy Agency 2003:167; *Africa Confidential* 28.5.2004.

11. For 2004, see *Dow Jones Newswire* 21.1.2005; for 2003: Institute of Energy Economics 2004.

12. See Energy Information Administration http://www.eia.doe.gov/emeu/ipsr/t11b.xls.

13. Cited in *USA Today* 21.6.2005.

14. On the political economy of reform and non-reform see van de Walle 2001.

15. See, for example, *International Herald Tribune,* 15.5.2002.

16. See *Inter Press Service* 13.6.2004; Rumbaugh & Blancher 2004:12.

17. See, for instance, *SouthScan* 30.6.2005; *Financial Times* 15.3.2005.

18. See United Nations Office on Drugs and Crime (UNODC) 2005:78.

19. For the example of Ethiopia, see *The Wall Street Journal,* 29.3.2005; on Cameroon, see *Cameroon Tribune,* 30.5.2005.

20. See 'China struggles to fulfill spiraling energy demands'; *Jane's Intelligence Review* 2004, 16, 7: 56.

21. *Africa Energy,* August 2004, 77: 12, 19; *Africa Confidential,* 28.5.2004.

22. See *The Wall Street Journal,* 9.1.2006.

23. See 'NOCs 1–IOCs 0,' *Petroleum Economist,* 2005, April issue: 4–9; see also *International Herald Tribune,* 2.3.2005.

24. According to Grimmett (2004:27), China ranked second in arms transfers agreements with African states from 2000 to 2003. See also Taylor 2004:94–97.

25. American sanctions and the pull-out of Western companies were related to Sudan's support of terrorism and human-rights violations in the oil-producing south. See Johnson 2003:162–164; Human Rights Watch 2003.

26. See *Reuters,* 15.9.2004; *The Independent,* 15.10.2004.

27. Needless to say, China does not bear the sole responsibility for the international failure in Darfur. One has also to take into account the inconsistent positions of the US government and the ambiguous role of France. See Clough 2005:24–39.

28. Oil fields in Darfur may be another reason for Beijing's position. See *New York Times,* 8.8.2004.

29. See Table 1. The pattern is also evident in regard to investments since the extractive sector attracts 50 to 80% of all foreign direct investments to Africa. See *EIU Business Africa,* 1.10.2004, 'FDI–oil be back.'

30. *EIU Business Africa,* 16.11.2004.

31. As of 2005, 37 African states are participating in AGOA.

32. International Monetary Fund (IMF) 2005:15–20.

33. *Business Report,* 20.5.2005.

34. *Independent,* 25.4.2005; *The Reporter* (Gaborone), 27.5.2005.

35. For example, some 5,000 Chinese live in Lesotho, some 3,000 in Cameroon, i.e. the country hosts by now more Chinese than French citizens. Nigeria has a population of some 50,000 Chinese. See *BBC Monitoring,* 7.8.2005; Author's interview, Yaoundé, Western diplomat, May 2005.

36. The titles of some articles are highly indicative: 'Zimbabwe's New Colonialists,' *Weekly Standard,* 25.5.2005; 'Mixed Reaction to Chinese Invasion,' *The Reporter,* 24.5.2005; 'Uganda Should Invite "Real" Chinese Investors,' *New Vision,* 10.5.2005; 'Mozambique Invaded by China, Claims Renamo,' *AIM,* 10.5.2005.

37. For an assessment of Zimbabwe's relations with China see Friedrich-Ebert-Foundation (FES) 2004.

38. *Zimbabwe Independent,* 29.7.2005. In the same week, however, China opposed discussion at the UN Security Council of a UN report into Zimbabwe's demolition campaign that left some 700,000 persons homeless.

39. *BBC Online* 1.8.2005.

40. See *IRIN News* 29.6.2005.

41. For the case of Zimbabwe, see *The Christian Science Monitor* 30.5.2005.

42. For a useful overview over the menu of options in resource-rich countries, see Bannon & Collier 2003.

43. See various contributions on Western policies towards Africa in Taylor & Williams 2004.

44. People's Republic of China, Ministry of Foreign Affairs, Press Release, 6.1.2005.

REFERENCES

Alden, C. 2005a. 'Leveraging the dragon: toward "an Africa that can say no,"' 1 March, http://yaleglobal.yale.edu/display.article?id=5336.

Alden, C. 2005b. 'China in Africa,' *Survival,* 47, 3: 147–164.

Bannon, I. & P. Collier, eds., 2003. *Natural Resources and Violent Conflict: options and actions,* Washington, D.C.: The World Bank.

BBC Online, 6.1.2006. 'China-Africa trade jumps by 39%.'

BBC Online, 1.8.2005. 'China deal 'too small' for Mugabe.'

Berrigan, F. 2005. 'Peace accord in Sudan: good news for people or oil companies?,' *Foreign Policy in Focus,* 14 January, http://www.fpif.org/fpiftxt/985.

Bräutigam, D. 2003. 'Close encounters: Chinese business networks as industrial catalysts in Sub-Sahara Africa,' *African Affairs* 102, 408: 447–467.

Brzezinski, Z. & J. Mearsheimer 2005. 'Clash of the titans,' *Foreign Policy,* 146: 46–49.

Clough, M. 2005. 'Darfur: whose responsibility to protect?,' in *World Report 2005,* Human Rights Watch: New York.

Downs, E.S. 2004. 'The Chinese energy security debate,' *The China Quarterly* 177: 21–41.

Economy, E. 2003. 'Changing course on China,' *Current History* 102, 665: 243–49.

Ellis, S. 2003. 'Briefing: West Africa and its oil,' *African Affairs* 102, 406: 135–138.

Energy Information Administration. 2005. http://www.eia.doe.gov/emeu/ipsr/t11b.xls.

Friedrich-Ebert-Foundation (FES) 2004. *The 'Look East Policy' of Zimbabwe now focuses on China,* Harare.

Grimmett, R.F. 2004. 'Conventional arms transfers to developing nations, 1996–2003,' Washington, D.C.: Congressional Research Service.

Human Rights Watch, 2003. *Sudan, Oil and Human Rights,* New York.

Institute of Energy Economics, January 2004, Japan, http://eneken.ieej.or.jp.

International Energy Agency (IEA) 2003. *World Energy Investment Outlook,* Paris.

International Monetary Fund, *Direction of Trade Statistics.* Washington, D.C.:IMF.

International Monetary Fund (IMF) 2005. *Regional Economic Outlook Sub-Saharan Africa.* Washington, D.C.:IMF.

Jane's Intelligence Review 2004. 'China struggles to fulfill spiraling energy demands,' 16, 7: 56–57.

Jenkins, R. & C. Edwards 2004. *How does China's Growth affect Poverty Reduction in Asia, Africa, and Latin America?.* Norwich: University of East Anglia.

Johnson, D.H. 2003. *The Root Causes of Sudan's Civil War,* Oxford: James Currey.

Johnston, P. 2004. 'Timber Booms, State Busts: The Political Economy of Liberian Timber,' *Review of African Political Economy* 31, 101: 441–456.

Kaplinsky, R. 2005. 'The sun rises in the East,' Commission for Africa Report Response, Institute of Development Studies, London, http://www.ids.ac.uk/ids/news/CFA%20Response/Kaplinsky Response.pdf.

Marchal, R. forthcoming. 'Comment être semblable tout en étant différent? Les relations entre la Chine et l'Afrique,' in R. Marchal, *Afrique-Asie: échanges inégaux et mondialisation subalterne.*

Mbeki, M. 2004. 'China and SA must lessen dependence on the West,' *Sunday Times,* Johannesburg, 24 October.

Medeiros, E.S. & M. Taylor Fravel 2003. 'China's new diplomacy,' *Foreign Affairs* 82, 6: 22–35.

Muekalia, D.J. 2004. 'Africa and China's strategic partnership,' *African Security Review* 13, 1: 5–11.

People's Republic of China, Ministry of Foreign Affairs, Press Release, 6.1.2005.

Rumbaugh, T & N. Blancher 2004. 'China: International Trade and WTO Accession,' IMF Working Paper (04/36), Washington, D.C.: IMF.

Snow, P. 1989. *The Star Raft: China's encounter with Africa.* Ithaca: Cornell University Press.

Sutter, R. 2004. 'Asia in the balance: America and China's 'peaceful rise',' *Current History* 103, 674: 284–289.

Taylor, I. 1998. 'China's foreign policy towards Africa in the 1990s,' *Journal of Modern African Studies* 36, 3: 443–460.

Taylor I. 2002. 'Taiwan's Foreign Policy and Africa: The Limitations of Dollar Diplomacy,' *Journal of Contemporary China* 11, 30: 125–140.

Taylor I. 2004. 'The 'all-weather friend'? Sino-African interaction in the twenty-first century,' in I. Taylor & P. Williams, eds., *Africa in International Politics: external involvement on the continent,* London: Routledge, 83–101.

Thompson D. 2005. 'China's Soft Power in Africa: From the 'Beijing Consensus' to Health Diplomacy,' *China Brief* 5, 21: 1–4.

United Nations Conference on Trade and Development (UNCTAD). 2004. *World Investment Report 2004,* Geneva.

United Nations Office on Drugs and Crime (UNODC). 2005. *Why Fighting Crime Can Assist Development in Africa.* Vienna.

UNDP Press Release, 18.3.2005, 'New public-private partnership to promote Sino-African ties.'

Van de Walle, N. 2001. *African Economies and the Politics of Permanent Crisis, 1979–1999,* Cambridge: Cambridge University Press.

Weinstein, M.A. 2005. 'China's geostrategy: playing a waiting game,' 9 January, http://www.pinr.com.

Zweig, D. & Bi Janhai 2005. 'China's Global Hunt for Energy,' *Foreign Affairs* 84, 5: 25–38.

NEWSPAPERS, NEWSLETTERS, AND MAGAZINES

Africa Confidential, London; *Africa Energy,* Hastings; *AIM,* Maputo; *BBC Monitoring Newsletter,* London; *Beijing Time,* Beijing; *Business Report,* Johannesburg; *Cameroon Tribune,* Yaoundé; *China Daily,* Beijing; *The Christian Science Monitor,* Boston, MA., *Dow Jones Newswire,* New York; *The Economist,* London; *EIU Business Africa,* London; *Financial Times,* London; *L'Humanité,* Paris; *The Independent,* London; *Inter Press Service; International Herald Tribune,* New York; IRIN News; *Mail & Guardian,* Johannesburg; *Le Monde,* Paris; *New York Times,* New York; *New Vision,* Kampala; *Petroleum Economist,* London; *Reuters,* London; *SouthScan,* London; *The Reporter,* Gaborone; *USA Today,* McLean, VA; *The Wall Street Journal,* New York; *Weekly Standard,* Harare; *Zimbabwe Independent,* Harare.

14

Reconciling Sovereignty with Responsibility

A Basis for International Humanitarian Action

FRANCIS M. DENG

INTRODUCTION

The end of the Cold War was greeted with relief throughout the world. It was assumed that the era of global tension and insecurity was over and that humanity had ushered in a new world order that would guarantee peace, security, and respect for the universal principles of human rights and democratic freedoms. The reverse has been the case. With the disappearance of the bipolar alliance system and control mechanisms of the Cold War, a process of violent disintegration became the plight of many states, especially under formerly oppressive regimes. As the situations in the former Yugoslavia, in the former Soviet Union, and on the African continent testify, since the end of the Cold War, conflicts around the world have resulted in unprecedented humanitarian tragedies and, in some cases, have led to partial and even total collapse of states. A new development that has complicated the situation further has been the emergence of international terrorism, dramatized by the horrific assault on the twin towers of the World Trade Center in New York on September 11, 2001. That event triggered a global war on terror that, while unifying the international community against terror, appears to have polarized the world in a way somewhat reminiscent of the Cold War ideological divide. As was the case in the Cold War, states are also inclined to compromise human rights protection in the name of security from a real or perceived threat of terror.

These developments combined have stimulated a multifaceted trend toward international involvement in weak, impoverished, and conflict-prone countries, both on humanitarian grounds, and to prevent them from providing a fertile ground for international terrorism. The result is a complex situation involving sometimes conflicting motivations: On the one hand, there are mounting pressures for global humanitarian action, sometimes involving forced intervention, with an urgent quest for peacemaking and peacekeeping. On the other hand, there is the ideologically driven war on terror that is polarizing the international community into those accused or suspected of supporting terror and those fighting it. The end result of both forces is the inevitable erosion of traditional concepts of sovereignty, in order to ensure international humanitarian access to protect and assist the needy population and punish actual or potential terrorists. This has in turn generated divergent reactions from the targeted states: cooperation on the part of those governments that stand to benefit from the alliance with the United States and other major allies in the war on terror, and defensive militancy on the part of those perceived as perpetrators or supporters of international terrorism. In both cases, states are becoming fearful of international intervention and are reasserting with a defensive vigor the traditional principles of sovereignty and territorial integrity. The resulting tug-of-war is acquiring a cross-cultural dimension that is confronting the international community with severe dilemmas, as both positions represent legitimate concerns.

Much has been said and written about the processes of economic, political, and cultural globalization that the post–Cold War world was supposedly undergoing. There is, however, a process of fragmentation and localization that is concurrently under way, but which has not received commensurate attention. In Africa and indeed in many parts of the world, the state is undergoing a formidable national identity crisis in which sovereignty is being contested by forces in internal confrontation and by their external supporters. This crisis is rooted primarily in the problems of racial, ethnic, cultural, and religious diversities, rendered conflictual by gross disparities in the shaping and sharing of power, national resources, and opportunities for social, cultural, and economic development.

Indeed, the fate of the state in the post–Cold War international system is essentially dualistic in nature. During the Cold War, there was a tendency to relate all the problems around the world to the ideological confrontation of the superpowers. But in the post–Cold War era, problems are now being better understood in their proper national and regional context, where internal conflicts, violations of human rights, denial of democracy, and mismanagement of the economy are the pressing problem areas. In confronting these problems, the state is being pulled in opposite directions by the demands of various local groups and by the pressures of globalization of the market economy and universalizing political and cultural trends. The assignment of responsibility for addressing these challenges must also recognize the fundamental shift that has taken place in the post–Cold War era. Dependency is being replaced by national responsibility and accountability. This new scenario implies recasting sovereignty as a concept of responsibility for the security and general welfare of the citizens, with accountability at the regional and international levels.

The guiding principle for reconciling these positions is to assume that under normal circumstances, governments that enjoy internal legitimacy are concerned about the welfare of their people, will provide them with adequate protection and assistance, and, if unable to do so, will invite or welcome foreign assistance and international cooperation to supplement their own efforts. The conflict arises only in those exceptional instances when the state has collapsed or the government lacks the requisite capacity and is unwilling to invite or permit international involvement, while the level of human suffering dictates otherwise. This is often the case in civil conflicts characterized by racial, ethnic, cultural, or religious crises of national identity in which the conflicting parties perceive the affected population as part of "the enemy." It is essentially the need to fill the vacuum of moral responsibility created by such cleavages that makes international intervention such a moral imperative.

The paradox of the compelling circumstances that necessitate such intervention is that the crisis has gone beyond prevention and has become an emergency situation in which masses of people have fallen victim to the humanitarian tragedy. Since it is more costly now to provide the needed humanitarian relief than it would have been at an earlier stage, the obvious policy implication is that the international community must develop normative and operational principles for a doctrine of preventive intervention. Such an approach would require addressing the root causes of conflict, formulating normative guidelines, establishing the mechanisms for an appropriate institutional response, and developing strategies for timely intervention.

This is indeed a tall order. The humanitarian crisis resulting from the genocidal war in the western Sudanese region of Darfur, the inability or unwillingness of the Sudanese government to stop the carnage, and the impotence of the international community to intervene effectively to protect the civilian population indicate that, often, the stakes are too high for potential international interveners. There are, however, no easy alternatives but to reaffirm the primary responsibility of the state to protect and assist its citizens and, if it lacks the capacity, to call on the international community to assist in a positive spirit of cooperation. Should it lack the capacity and/or the will to do so, the responsibility to protect must inevitably fall on the international community in its multilevel structures: subregional, regional, global, and alliances of willing and capable states preferably acting collectively, but if need be, acting unilaterally, to stop genocide, mass atrocities, or crimes against humanity. The question is how to make this phased sharing of responsibility effective.

THE MAGNITUDE OF THE CRISIS

The events in the former Yugoslavia, the latest dramatization of which was the horrific situation in Kosovo, and in several hot spots in the former Soviet Union demonstrate that the crisis is truly global. As former UN Secretary-General Boutros Boutros-Ghali observed in his *Agenda for Peace*: "Poverty, disease, famine, oppression and despair abound, joining to produce 17 million refugees, 20 million displaced persons and massive migrations of peoples within and beyond national borders. These are both sources and consequences of conflict that require the ceaseless attention and the highest priority in the efforts of the United Nations."[1] Although the global dimension of the crisis needs to be stressed, it is fair to say that some regions are more affected than others. Africa is perhaps the most devastated by internal conflicts and their catastrophic consequences. Of an estimated 20 to 25 million internally displaced persons worldwide, over 10 million are African, as are the refugees throughout the world. It was in Africa—specifically, Rwanda—that the world witnessed genocide comparable to the horrors of Nazi Germany. In the conflict in the southern region of Sudan, nearly 2 million people are estimated to have died since the resumption of the civil war in 1983; about a quarter perished as a result of war-induced famine and related humanitarian tragedies. The conflict in Darfur has resulted in the death of between 200,000 to 400,000 people, according to varying estimates, displaced over 2 million people, and forced 1 million people to seek refuge in Chad. The Democratic Republic of Congo has also been a theater of massive carnage. In Liberia and Sierra Leone, untold atrocities were perpetrated by all sides to the conflicts. And, of course, the collapse of Somalia stands out as an example of the threat looming over a number of fragile and vulnerable states on the continent. The intervention of Ethiopia, which initially promised to bring peace and stability to Somalia, has proved to be an aggravating factor.

African leaders, diplomats, scholars, and intellectuals have recognized the plight of their countries and their people and are demonstrating a responsiveness commensurate to the challenge. The OAU Mechanism for Conflict Prevention, Management and Resolution, proposed by Secretary-General Salim Ahmed Salim in the 1992 Dakar summit and adopted by the summit in Cairo in June 1993 represented the shift in attitude. In introducing his proposals to the Council of Ministers in Dakar in 1992, the secretary-general said:

> Conflicts have cast a dark shadow over the prospects for a united, secure and prosperous Africa which we seek to create. . . . Conflicts have caused immense suffering to our people and, in the worst case, death. Men, women and children have been uprooted, dispossessed, deprived of their means of livelihood and thrown into exile as refugees as a result of conflicts. This de-humanization of a large segment of our population is unacceptable and cannot be allowed to continue. Conflicts have engendered hate and division among our people and undermined the prospects of the long-term stability and unity of our countries and Africa as a whole. Since much energy, time and resources have been devoted to meeting the exigencies of conflicts, our countries have been unable to harness the energies of our people and target them to development.[2]

The change of the Organization of African Unity (OAU) to the African Union (AU) was more than a change of names. It signified a substantive and procedural shift from the old sacrosanct commitment to the narrow concept of state responsibility, and from noninterference in the internal affairs of states to a more responsible and response oversight and constructive involvement to promote peace, security, and stability within state borders. Article 4(h) of the Constitutive Act of the AU provides for "the right of the Union to intervene in a member State pursuant to a decision of the Assembly in respect of grave circumstances, namely war crimes, genocide and crimes against humanity." In promotion and protection of a democratic system of governance, sub-article (p) of Article 4 provides for the "condemnation and rejection of unconstitutional changes of government," implicitly by military coups. To meet the challenge, however, Africa must address the issue of sovereignty.

THE ISSUE OF SOVEREIGNTY

Protecting and assisting the masses of the people affected by internecine internal conflicts entail reconciling the possibility of international intervention with traditional concepts of national sovereignty. With the post–Cold War reapportionment of responsibility for addressing these problems, primary responsibility is now placed on the states concerned, with a graduated sharing of responsibility and accountability at the subregional and regional levels and, residually, throughout the international community, both multilaterally and bilaterally. In this emerging policy framework, national sovereignty, as already noted, acquires a new meaning. Instead of being perceived as a means of insulating the state against external scrutiny or involvement, it is increasingly being postulated as a normative concept of responsibility. National sovereignty requires a system of governance that is based on democratic popular citizen participation, constructive management of diversities, respect for fundamental rights, and equitable distribution of national wealth and opportunities for development. For a government or a state to claim sovereignty, it must establish legitimacy by meeting minimal standards of good governance or responsibility for the security and general welfare of its citizens and all those under its jurisdiction. Fulfillment of these standards, in turn, requires the formulation of a normative framework stipulating standards for the responsibilities of sovereignty and a system of accountability at the various interactive levels, from national to subregional and regional to international. The consensus now is that the problems are primarily internal and that, however external their sources or continued linkages, the responsibility for solutions, especially in the post–Cold War era, falls first on Africans themselves. Africans are recognizing that the time has long since come to stop blaming colonialism for Africa's persistent problems.

The irony, however, is that the principal modern agent of Africa's political and economic development and the interlocutor in the international arena is the state, itself a creature of foreign intervention. Although Africans have, for the most part, accepted the state with its colonially defined borders, African states lack the indigenous roots for internal legitimacy. And although democracy has been expanding since the end of the Cold War, it tends to be rather narrowly associated with elections that are often not entirely free and fair; indeed, the state is often not representative or responsive to the demands and expectations of its domestic constituencies. It is important in this context to distinguish between recognizing the unity and territorial integrity of the state and questioning its policy framework, which might be attributable to a regime or might be structural in nature. A structural problem would require a fundamental restructuring of the state to meet both the internal standards of good governance and the international requirements of responsible sovereignty.

Failure on the one level usually implies failure on the other. When a state fails to meet the standards prescribed for membership in the international community, thereby exposing itself to external scrutiny and possible sanctions, it is likely to assert sovereignty and cultural relativism in an attempt to barricade itself against the threat of foreign interference. Sovereignty has evolved enough not only to prescribe democratic representation but also to justify outside intervention. As one scholar of international law observed:

> In the process, the two notions have merged. Increasingly, governments recognize that their legitimacy depends on meeting a normative expectation of the community of states. This recognition has led to the emergence of a community expectation: that those who seek the validation of their empowerment patently govern with the consent of the governed. Democracy, thus, is on the way to becoming a global entitlement, one that increasingly will be promoted and protected by collective international processes.[3]

Another has argued that

> there is a clear trend away from the idea of unconditional sovereignty and toward a concept of responsible sovereignty. Governmental legitimacy that validates the exercise of sovereignty involves adherence to minimum humanitarian norms and a capacity to act effectively to protect citizens from acute threats to their security and well-being that derive from adverse conditions within a country.[4]

During the extensive consultations I conducted in connection with my UN mandate as Representative of the Secretary-General on Internally Displaced Persons, representatives of several governments commented that national sovereignty carries with it responsibilities that, if not met, put a government at risk of forfeiting its legitimacy. One spokesperson for a major power even went as far as saying, "To put it bluntly," if governments do not live up to those responsibilities (among which he specified the protection of minority rights), "the international community should intervene by force."[5] Similar views have been expressed by representatives of African countries who were voicing a global humanitarian concern.

Such pronouncements have almost become truisms that are rapidly making narrow concepts of legality obsolete. When the international community does decide to act—as it did when Iraq invaded Kuwait, when Somalia descended into chaos and starvation, and (albeit less decisively) when the former Yugoslavia disintegrated, especially in Kosovo—controversy over issues of legality become futile or of limited value as a brake to guard against precipitous change. One observer summarized the new sense of urgency regarding the need for an international response, the ambivalence of the pressures for the needed change, and the pull of traditional legal doctrines as follows:

> In the post–Cold War world . . . a new standard of intolerance for human misery and human atrocities has taken hold. Something quite significant has occurred to raise the consciousness of nations to the plight of peoples within

> sovereign borders. There is a new commitment—expressed in both moral and legal terms—to alleviate the suffering of oppressed or devastated people. To argue today that norms of sovereignty, non-use of force, and the sanctity of internal affairs are paramount to the collective human rights of people, whose lives and well-being are at risk, is to avoid the hard questions of international law and to ignore the march of history.[6]

To intervene is, however, not an easy choice. In 1991 former UN Secretary-General Javier Perez de Cuellar highlighted this dilemma when he said, "We are clearly witnessing what is probably an irresistible shift in public attitudes towards the belief that the defense of the oppressed in the name of morality should prevail over frontiers and legal documents." But he also asked, "Does [intervention] not call into question one of the cardinal principles of international law, one diametrically opposed to it, namely, the obligation of non-interference in the internal affairs of states?"[7] In his 1991 annual report, he wrote of the new balance that must be struck between sovereignty and the protection of human rights:

> It is now increasingly felt that the principle of non-interference with the essential domestic jurisdiction of States cannot be regarded as a protective barrier behind which human rights could be massively or systematically violated with impunity. . . . The case for not impinging on the sovereignty, territorial integrity and political independence of States is by itself indubitably strong. But it would only be weakened if it were to carry the implication that sovereignty, even in this day and age, includes the right of mass slaughter or of launching systematic campaigns of decimation or forced exodus of civilian populations in the name of controlling civil strife or insurrection. With the heightened international interest in universalizing a regime of human rights, there is a marked and most welcome shift in public attitudes.
>
> To try to resist it would be politically as unwise as it is morally indefensible. It should be perceived as not so much a new departure as a more focused awareness of one of the requirements of peace.[8]

Preferring to avoid confronting the issue of sovereignty, de Cuellar called for a "higher degree of cooperation and a combination of common sense and compassion," arguing that "we need not impale ourselves on the horns of a dilemma between respect for sovereignty and the protection of human rights. . . . What is involved is not the right of intervention but the collective obligation of States to bring relief and redress in human rights emergencies."[9]

In *An Agenda for Peace,* de Cuellar's successor, Boutros Boutros-Ghali, wrote that respect for sovereignty and integrity is "crucial to any common international progress"; but he went on to say that "the time of absolute and exclusive sovereignty . . . has passed," that "its theory was never matched by reality," and that it is necessary for leaders of states "to find a balance between the needs of good internal governance and the requirements of an ever more interdependent world."[10] As one commentator noted, "The clear meaning was that governments could best avoid intervention by meeting their obligations not only to other states, but also to their own citizens. If they failed, they might invite intervention."[11]

But although negative interpretations of sovereignty prevail as "a prerogative to resist claims and encroachments coming from outside national boundaries—the right to say no," the question can be, and has been, posed as to whether erasing the doctrine of sovereignty from the minds of political leaders would reduce those forms of human suffering associated with extreme governmental failure. "Would such an erasure strengthen sentiments of human solidarity on which an ethos of corrective responsibility and individual accountability depends?"[12] The withdrawal of the international community from Somalia once the humanitarian intervention proved costly in American lives, the astonishing disengagement from Rwanda in the face of genocide in 1994, and the indifference to the atrocities and gross human rights violations in Liberia, Sierra Leone, and Sudan, to mention just a few examples—as contrasted to the dramatic, high-tech intervention on behalf of the Kurds in Iraq and the Albanians in Kosovo—prompt a resounding no in answer to the question. Selectivity in the manner and scale of response is the fundamental reality.

Boutros-Ghali's successor as secretary-general was even more vocal than his predecessors on the need to curtail the constraints of sovereignty. In an address to the Commission on Human Rights on April 7, 1999, Kofi Annan said, "When civilians are attacked and massacred because of their ethnicity, as in Kosovo, the world looks to the United Nations to speak up for them. When men, women and children are assaulted and their limbs hacked off, as in Sierra Leone, here again the world looks to the United Nations. When women and girls are denied their right to equality, as in Afghanistan, the world looks to the United Nations to take a stand." Emphasizing the expectation of "our global constituency" that the UN will intervene to protect "the tortured, the oppressed, the silenced, the victims of 'ethnic cleansing' and injustice," Annan posed a rhetorical, but pertinent question: "If, in the fact of such abuses, we do not speak up and speak out, if we do not act in defense of human rights and advocate their lasting universality, how can we answer that global constituency?"[13]

Although sovereignty as such is no longer a barrier to intervention on human rights and humanitarian grounds, the determining factor is the political will of other states based on national interest, combined with a compelling level of humanitarian concern. However, assertions of sovereignty can also be invoked by powers lacking the will to become involved. Since intervention is often costly in terms of lives and material, it is convenient to avoid it unless imperative national interest dictates otherwise. Sovereignty then elicits benign conformity to the principle of noninterference or provides a convenient excuse for inaction. If the constraints of sovereignty against justifiable intervention are to be circumvented, and more importantly, if governments and other controlling authorities such as insurgent movements are to be inspired or at least motivated to discharge their obligations, it is necessary to prescribe "normative sovereignty," or "sovereignty as responsibility."[14]

The ambivalence about intervention by the international community arises not only from reluctance to become involved but also from motives for external intervention, which are by no means always altruistic. Self-interest therefore dictates an appropriate and timely action in terms of self-protection. This was the point made by the secretary-general of the Organization of African Unity, Salim Ahmed Salim, in his bold proposals for an OAU mechanism for conflict prevention and resolution. "If the OAU, first through the Secretary-General and then the Bureau of the Summit, is to play the lead role in any African conflict," he said, "it should be enabled to intervene swiftly, otherwise it cannot be ensured that whoever (apart from African regional organizations) acts will do so in accordance with African interests."[15] Criticizing the tendency to respond only to worst-case scenarios, Salim also emphasized the need for preemptive intervention: "The basis for 'intervention' may be clearer when there is a total breakdown of law and order . . . and where, with the attendant human suffering, a spill-over effect is experienced within the neighbouring countries. . . . However, pre-emptive involvement should also be permitted even in situations where tensions evolve to such a pitch that it becomes apparent that a conflict is in the making."[16]

The secretary-general went so far as to suggest that the OAU should take the lead in transcending the traditional view of sovereignty, building on the African values of kinship, solidarity, and the notion that "every African is his brother's keeper."[17] Considering that "our borders are at best artificial," Salim argued, "we in Africa need to use our own cultural and social relationships to interpret the principle of non-interference in such a way that we are enabled to apply it to our advantage in conflict prevention and resolution."[18]

In traditional Africa, third-party intervention for mediation and conciliation is always expected, regardless of the will of the parties directly involved in a conflict. Even in domestic disputes, relatives and elders intercede without being invited. Indeed, "saving face," which is critical to conflict resolution in Africa, requires that such intervention be unsolicited. But, of course, African concepts and practices under the modern conditions of the nation-state must still balance consideration for state sovereignty against the compelling humanitarian need to protect and assist the dispossessed.

Even in the modern context and sovereignty notwithstanding, as former Secretary-General Kofi Annan put it, there is a need for a third party to speak out and say, "Stop, this is enough. This cannot be allowed to happen." Elaborating on the role of a third party, Annan said, "the third party has a very important role we should never underestimate, not only in speaking out trying to get help, but it also gives inspiration and strength to those who are caught in the situation."[19] Annan was even more emphatic when he said: "Governments must not be allowed to use sovereignty as a shield to systematically deny their people of human rights and undertake gross systematic abuses of human rights. If that were to happen, shouldn't the international community have some responsibility of going to assist these people?"[20]

The normative frameworks proposed by the OAU secretary-general and the UN secretary-general's *Agenda for Peace* are predicated on respect for the sovereignty and integrity of the state as crucial to the existing international system. However, the logic of the transcendent importance of human rights as a legitimate area of concern for the international community—especially where order has broken down or where the state is incapable or unwilling to act responsibly to protect the masses of citizens—would tend to make international inaction quite indefensible. Even in less extreme cases of acute internal conflicts, the perspectives of the pivotal actors on such issues as the national or public interest are bound to be sharply divided both internally and in terms of their relationship to the outside world. After all, internal conflicts often entail a contest of the national arena of power and, hence, sovereignty. Every political intervention from outside has its internal recipients, hosts, and beneficiaries. Under those circumstances, there can hardly be said to be indivisible national sovereignty behind which the nation stands united.

Furthermore, it is not always easy to determine the degree to which a government of a country devastated by civil war is truly in control when, as often happens, sizable portions of the territory are controlled by rebel or opposing forces. Frequently, though a government may remain in effective control of the capital and the main garrisons, much of the countryside in the war zone will have practically collapsed. How would a partial but significant collapse such as this be factored into the determination of the degree to which civil order in the country has broken down? A government cannot present a clear face to the outside world when it keeps others from stepping in to offer protection and assistance in the name of sovereignty after allowing hundreds of thousands (and maybe millions) to starve to death when food can be made available to them; to be exposed to deadly elements when they could be provided with shelter; to be indiscriminately tortured, brutalized, and murdered by opposing forces, contesting the very sovereignty that is supposed to ensure their security; or to otherwise allow them to suffer in a vacuum of moral leadership and responsibility. Under such circumstances, the international community is called upon to step in and fill the vacuum created by such neglect. If the lack of protection and assistance is the result of the country's incapacity, the government would, in all likelihood, invite or welcome such international intervention. But where the neglect is a willful part of a policy emanating from internal conflict, preventive and corrective interventions become necessary.

As former secretary-general, Kofi Annan argued that the issue is more than the culpability of governments, but the limits to their capacity in the face of the globalizing challenges facing them: "I can understand a nation's right . . . to protect its sovereignty. On the other hand, . . . the traditional concept of sovereignty is being changed by the developments in the world today, from globalization—there are lots of areas governments do not control. They do not control the external factors that affect their economy. They do not control financial flows. They do not control some of the environmental issues. Why should abuse of human rights be the only area that they should insist they should be allowed to control without any interference?"[21]

It is most significant that the Security Council, in its continued examination of the secretary-general's *Agenda for Peace,* welcomed the observations contained in the report concerning the question of humanitarian assistance and its relationship to peacemaking, peacekeeping, and peacebuilding.[22] In particular, the council established that, under certain circumstances, "there may be a close relationship between acute needs for humanitarian assistance and threats to international peace and security";[23] indeed, it "[noted] with concern the incidents of humanitarian crises, including mass displacements of population becoming or aggravating threats to international peace and security."[24] The council further expressed the belief "that humanitarian assistance should help establish the basis for enhanced stability through rehabilitation and development" and "noted the importance of adequate planning in the provision of humanitarian assistance in order to improve prospects for rapid improvement of the humanitarian situation."[25]

Absolute sovereignty is clearly no longer defensible; it never was, but it has now been significantly curtailed. The critical question now is under what circumstances the international community is justified in overriding sovereignty to protect the dispossessed populations within state borders. The common assumption in international law is that such action is justified when there is a threat to international peace. The position now supported by the Security Council is that massive violations of human rights and displacement within a country's borders may constitute such a threat.[26] Others contend that a direct threat to international peace as the basis for intervention under Chapter Seven of the UN Charter has become more a legal fiction than the principle justifying international action, nearly always under conditions of extreme humanitarian tragedies.

To avoid costly emergency relief operations, the international community must develop a response to conflict situations before they deteriorate into humanitarian tragedies. Such a response calls for placing an emphasis on peacemaking through preventive diplomacy, which in turn would require an understanding of the sources of conflicts and a willingness to address them at their roots.

RECASTING SOVEREIGNTY AS RESPONSIBILITY: RECENT DEVELOPMENTS

Recasting sovereignty as responsibility is the fundamental norm that guided my work and dialogue with governments for twelve years as Representative of the U.N. Secretary-General on Internally Displaced Persons from 1992 to 2004. Two initiatives helped shape my perspective on the emerging challenge. One was the development of an African Studies Project in the Foreign Policy Studies Program at the Brookings Institution. The other was participating in the initiative of then former head of state of Nigeria and subsequently twice-elected president Olusegun Obasanjo, toward a Helsinki-like Conference on Security, Stability, Development, and Cooperation in Africa (CSSDCA).

In the Brookings Africa Project, we made an initial assessment of conflicts in Africa and the challenges they posed in the post–Cold War era.[27] Next, we undertook national and regional case studies to deepen our understanding of the issues involved.[28] A synthesis of these case studies led to the main conclusion that as conflicts were now being properly perceived as internal, they also primarily became the responsibility of governments to prevent, manage, and resolve. Governance became perceived primarily as conflict management. Within the framework of regional and international cooperation, state sovereignty was then postulated as entailing the responsibility of conflict management. The envisaged responsibility involved managing diversity, ensuring equitable distribution of wealth, services, and development opportunities, and participating effectively in regional and international arrangements for peace, security, and stability. In subsequent work, we tried to put more flesh on the skeleton of the responsibilities of sovereignty, building largely on human rights and humanitarian norms and international accountability. Since internal conflicts often spill across international borders, their consequences also spill across borders, threatening regional security and stability. In the "apportionment" of responsibilities in the post–Cold War era, regional organizations provide the second layer of the needed response. And yet, the international community remains the residual guarantor of universal human rights and humanitarian standards in the quest for global peace and security. Hence, the stipulation of sovereignty as responsibility with implicit accountability to the regional and international layers of cooperation.

The development of the Helsinki process for Africa was motivated by the concern that the post–Cold War global order was likely to result in the withdrawal of the major powers and the marginalization of Africa. It was, therefore, imperative for Africa to take charge of its destiny and observe principles that would appeal to the West and thereby provide a sound foundation for a mutually agreeable partnership. This was found in the Helsinki framework of the Economic and Security Cooperation in Europe (ESCE), which became the Organization for Security and Cooperation in Europe (OSCE). A series of meetings culminated in the 1991 conference in Kampala, Uganda, which was attended by some 500 people, including several heads of state and representatives from all walks of life. The conference produced the Kampala Document, which elaborated the four "calabashes," so termed to distinguish them from the OSCE "baskets," and give them an African orientation. The calabashes are security, stability, development, and cooperation. The adoption of the CSSDCA by the Organization of African Unity (OAU) was initially blocked by a few governments that felt threatened by its normative principles. Obasanjo's imprisonment by the Nigerian dictator Sani Abacha also removed the leverage need to exert pressure on the OAU. When Obasanjo returned to power as the elected president of Nigeria, he was able to push successfully for the incorporation of CSSDCA into the OAU mechanism for conflict prevention, management, and resolution.[29]

In connection with these initiatives, I began to focus attention on promoting the need to balance conventional notions of sovereignty with the responsibility of the state to provide protection and general welfare to citizens and all those under state jurisdiction.[30] Given the sensitivity and controversy surrounding my mandate as Representative of the U.N. Secretary-General on Internally Displaced Persons responsible for the protection and assistance of internally displaced populations worldwide, the only way to bridge the need for international protection and assistance for the internally displaced and the barricades of the negative approach to sovereignty was to build on the fundamental norm of sovereignty as a positive concept of state responsibility toward its citizens and those under its jurisdiction. Most states discharged this responsibility under normal circumstances, and if they lacked the capacity to do so, called on the international community to assist them in discharging their responsibility. But in the exceptional cases where states failed to do so, the international community needed to assume that responsibility, if necessary, by overriding state sovereignty. In making that argument in my dialogue with governments, I would end by noting that the best way for a state to protect and preserve its sovereignty is to discharge, and be seen to discharge, its responsibility to protect and assist its needy citizens, or call for international assistance to complement its efforts. Otherwise, the world will not watch innocent civilians die or suffer without intervening. As Secretary-General Kofi Annan explained: "If citizens' rights are respected, there will be no need for anyone to want to intervene either through diplomatic means or coercive means. . . . The governments should see it not as a license for people to come in and intervene. We are talking about those situations where there are serious and gross and systematic violations of human rights. I think that governments who protect their citizens and their rights and do not create that kind of situation have no reason to worry that anyone would intervene."[31] The main point however, was to persuade the governments to accept the positive recasting of sovereignty and the responsibility it entails. This approach was quite effective in the dialogue with governments.

The principle of sovereignty as responsibility has been strengthened and mainstreamed by the Canadian-sponsored Commission on Intervention and State Sovereignty and has continued to gain wide support from the international community.[32] The Secretary-General's High Panel on Threats, Challenges, and Changes also endorsed the principle. As the UN prepared for its sixtieth anniversary celebration, the secretary-general pleaded that "we must embrace the responsibility to protect."[33] The World Summit of Heads of State and Government, which convened in New York in September 2005, "stressed the need for the General Assembly to continue consideration of the responsibility to protect populations from genocide, war crimes, ethnic cleansing, and crimes against humanity."[34]

Kofi Annan, who at the beginning of his first term as secretary-general had provoked considerable controversy by calling for the right of humanitarian intervention by the international community, reflected on the progress made in stipulating the responsibility to protect:

> The Canadian Commission . . . took the concept further, and in fact gave it a better diplomatic name than I had done. I had referred to humanitarian intervention, and then took up the "responsibility to protect"—that the governments have the responsibility to protect their people, and where they fail or show unwillingness to do that or are incapable of doing it, that responsibility may fall on the international community and the membership at large, the world community, to do something about it.[35]

The challenge that postulating sovereignty as responsibility poses for the international community is that it implies accountability. Obviously, the internally displaced themselves and other victims of internal conflicts trapped within international borders, marginalized, excluded, often persecuted, have little capacity to hold their national authorities accountable. Only the international community, including subregional, regional, and international organizations, has the leverage and clout to persuade governments and other concerned actors to discharge their responsibility or otherwise fill the vacuum of irresponsible or irresponsive sovereignty. A soft, but credible threat of consequences in case of failure to discharge the responsibility of sovereignty, combined with the promise of the benefits of international legitimacy and cooperation could be an effective inducement.

However, the fact is often that governments of affected countries, even if willing to discharge the responsibility of assisting and protecting their needy populations, lack resources and the capacity to do so. Offering them support in a way that links humanitarian assistance with protection in a holistic, integrated approach to human rights should make the case more compelling and persuasive. No government deserving any legitimacy can request material assistance from the outside world and reject concern with the human rights of the people on whose behalf it requests assistance. Doing so would be like asking the international community to feed them without ensuring their safety and dignity, an implausible logic. Now that the standard of sovereignty as responsibility has been set, the focus of the international community should shift to the need for implementation and persuading the states to honor it as an essential ingredient of their legitimacy, both domestically and internationally.

ADDRESSING THE CAUSES OF CONFLICT

In most countries torn apart by war, the sources and causes of conflict are generally recognized as inherent in the traumatic experience of state-formation and nation-building, complicated by colonial intervention and repressive post-colonial policies. The starting point, as far as Africa is concerned, is the colonial nation-state, which brought together diverse groups that were paradoxically kept separate and unintegrated. Regional ethnic groups were broken up and affiliated with others within the artificial borders of the new state, and colonial masters imposed a superstructure of law and order to maintain relative peace and tranquility.

The independence movement was a collective struggle for self-determination that reinforced the notion of unity within the artificial framework of the newly established nation-state. Initially, independence came as a collective gain that did not delineate who was to get what from the legacy of the centralized power and wealth. But because colonial institutions had divested the local communities and ethnic groups of much of their indigenous autonomy and sustainable livelihood, replacing them with a degree of centralized authority and dependency on the welfare state system, the struggle for control became unavoidable once control of these institutions passed on to the nationals at independence. The outcome was often conflict—over power, wealth, and development—that led to gross violations of human rights, denial of civil liberties, disruption of economic and social life, and the consequential frustration of efforts for development.

As the Cold War raged, however, these conflicts were seen not as domestic struggles for power and resources but as extensions of the superpower ideological confrontation. Rather than help resolve them peacefully, the superpowers often worsened the conflict by providing military and economic assistance to their own allies.

Although the end of the Cold War removed this aggravating external factor, it also removed the moderating role of the superpowers, both as third parties and as mutually neutralizing allies. The results have been unmitigated brutalities and devastation from identity conflicts. It can credibly be argued that the gist of these internal conflicts is that the ethnic pieces that were put together by the colonial glue, reinforced by the old world order, are now pulling apart and that ethnic groups are reasserting their autonomy or independence. Old identities, undermined and rendered dormant by the structures and values of the nation-state system, are reemerging and demanding participation, distribution, and legitimacy. In fact, it may be even more accurate to say that the process has been going on in a variety of ways and within the context of the constraints imposed by the nation-state system.

The larger the gap in the participation and distribution patterns based on racial, ethnic, or religious identity, the more likely the breakdown of civil order and the conversion of political confrontation into violent conflict. When the conflict turns violent, the issues at stake become transformed into a fundamental contest for state power. The objectives may vary in degree from a demand for autonomy to a major restructuring of the national framework, either to be captured by the demand-making group or to be more equitably reshaped. When the conflict escalates into a contest for the "soul" of the nation, it turns into an intractable zero-sum confrontation. The critical issue then is whether the underlying sense of injustice, real or perceived, can be remedied in a timely manner, avoiding the zero-sum level of violence.

Viewing the crisis from the global perspective, it is also pertinent to recall the words of UN Secretary-General Boutros-Ghali, who observed in *An Agenda for Peace*: "One requirement for solutions to these problems lies in commitment to human rights with a special sensitivity to those of minorities, whether ethnic, religious, social or linguistic."[36] On the need to strike a balance between the unity of larger entities and respect for the sovereignty, autonomy, and diversity of various identities, the secretary-general further noted:

> The healthy globalization of contemporary life requires in the first instance solid identities and fundamental freedoms. The sovereignty, territorial integrity and independence of states within the established international system, and the principle of self-determination for peoples, both of great value and importance, must not be permitted to work against each other in the period ahead. Respect for democratic principles at all levels of social existence is crucial: in communities, within states and within the community of states. Our constant duty should be to maintain the integrity of each while finding a balanced design for all.[37]

Where discrimination or disparity is based on race, ethnicity, region, or religion, it is easy to see how it can be combated by appropriate constitutional provisions and laws protecting basic human rights and fundamental freedoms. But where discrimination or disparity arises from conflicting perspectives on national identity, especially one based on religion, the cleavages become more difficult to bridge. In some instances, religion, ethnicity, and culture become so intertwined that they are not easy to disentangle. Such is the case in the Sudan, where Islam has gained momentum and is aspiring to offer regionwide and, indeed, global ideological leadership. Islam in the Sudan has been closely associated with Arabism, which also gives the movement a composite ethnic, cultural, and religious identity, even though the Islamists themselves espouse the nonracial ideals of the faith. The composite identity of Islam and Arabism poses the threat of subordination to non-Muslims, who also perceive themselves as non-Arabs. It is consequently resisted, especially in the South.

What makes the role of religion particularly formidable is that there are legitimate arguments on both sides of the religiously based conflict. On the one hand, the Islamists, representing the Arabized Muslim majority, want to fashion the nation on the basis of their faith, which they believe does not allow the separation of religion and the state. The non-Muslims, on the other hand, reject this, seeing it as a means of inevitably relegating them to a lower status as citizens; they insist on secularism as a more mutually accommodating basis for a pluralistic process of nation-building. The dilemma is whether an Islamic framework should be used to encompass a religiously mixed society, imposing a minority status on the non-Muslims, or whether secularism should be the national framework, thereby imposing on the Muslim majority the wishes of the non-Muslim minority. The crisis in national identity that this dualism poses is that there is not yet a consensus on a framework that unquestionably establishes the unity of the country. During the colonial period, the country was governed as two separate entities in one, and since independence, it has intermittently been at war with itself over the composite factors of religion, ethnicity, race, and culture.

If responsibility for Africa's problems is now being assigned to the Africans as represented by their states, the logic should extend down to embrace citizen participation—a process that might be termed the challenge of localization. This process would broaden the basis of participation to include not only the wide array of organizations within the now popular notion of civil society but also, and primarily, Africa's indigenous, territorially defined, local communities, with their organizational structures, value systems, institutional arrangements, and ways of using their human and material resources.

Given its centrality and pervasiveness, ethnicity is a reality no country can completely afford to ignore. Thus, African governments have ambivalently tried to dismiss it, marginalize it, manipulate it, corrupt it, or combat it in a variety of ways. But no strategic formula for its constructive use has been developed[38]—this despite the fact that an overwhelming majority of Africans, however urbanized or modernized, belong to known "tribal" or ethnic origins and remain in one way or another connected to their groups. Indeed, as one African scholar noted, "urban populations straddle the two geographical spaces—urban and rural—with the result [that] the politics of one easily spills into the politics of the other."[39] The other side of this spectrum is flexibility or adaptability that allows considerable room for molding identity to suit changing conditions or serve alternating objectives, some destructive.

Ethnic identities in themselves are not conflictual, just as individuals are not inherently in conflict merely because of their different identities and characteristics. Rather, it is unmanaged or mismanaged competition for power, wealth, or status broadly defined that provides the basis for conflict. Today, virtually every African conflict has some ethno-regional dimension to it.[40] Even those conflicts that may appear to be free of ethnic concerns involve factions and alliances built around ethnic loyalties. Analysts tend to hold one of two views regarding the role of ethnicity in these conflicts. Some see ethnicity as a source of conflict; others see it as a tool used by political entrepreneurs to promote their ambitions.[41] In reality, it is both. Ethnicity, especially when combined with territorial identity, is a reality that exists independently of political maneuvers. To argue that ethnic groups are unwitting tools of political manipulation is to underestimate a fundamental social reality and to assume that members of the group lack value judgment on the issues involved. On the other hand, given the emotional fervor and the group dynamics of the identity issues it evokes, ethnicity is clearly a resource for political manipulation and entrepreneurship, which African states are loath to manage constructively.

Ethiopia, after Eritrea's breakaway, can claim credit for being the only African country that is trying to confront the problem head-on by recognizing territorially based ethnic groups, granting them not only a large measure of autonomy but also the constitutional right of self-determination, even to the extent of secession.[42] Ethiopia's leaders assert emphatically that they are committed to the right of self-determination, wherever it leads. But it can also be argued that giving the people the right to determine their destiny leads them to believe that their interests will be safeguarded, which should give them a reason to opt for unity. In fact, the Ethiopian constitution stipulates that the right to independence can only be exercised after following an elaborate process to establish the necessity and appropriateness of that ultimate step, and indeed no ethnic community has so far exercised or demanded the right to independence constitutionally. In contrast to the case of Ethiopia, the 2005 Comprehensive Peace Agreement (CPA) that ended the decades of war in Southern Sudan grants the people of the South the right of self-determination through a referendum to be held after a six-year interim period to decide whether to remain in a united Sudan under the interim arrangements of the CPA or become an independent state. The agreement, however, stipulates that during the interim period, efforts will be exerted to make unity an attractive option for the South.

As the hope for a unity vote in the stipulated referendum in the Southern Sudan indicates, self-determination does not necessarily mean secession. After all, one of the options of self-determination is to remain within the state. But perhaps even more significant is the reconceptualization of self-determination as a principle that allows people to choose their own administrative status and machinery within the country.[43] It has been noted that internal self-administration "might be more effectively used in a way that would help avoid suffering of the kind that so regrettably become commonplace when communities feel that their only option is to fight for independence."[44] In that sense, self-determination becomes closely associated with democracy and protection of minorities and not conterminous with independence. As Sir Arthur Watts, one of the principal proponents of internal self-determination, has observed, independence is a complicated process that can be traumatic. For many communities, it is not necessarily the best option. Often, no advantage is gained by insisting on independence, excluding other kinds of arrangements, especially if they would grant a community all it wants without the additional burdens of a wholly independent existence.[45]

Ultimately, the only sustainable unity is that based on mutual understanding and agreement. Unfortunately, however, the normative framework for national unity in modern Africa is not the result of consensus. Except for a very few cases, as in post-apartheid South Africa, Africans won their independence without negotiating an internal social contract that would forge and sustain national consensus. Of course, the leaders of various factions, ethnic or political, negotiated a framework that gave them the legitimacy to speak for the country in their demand for independence. Political elites certainly negotiated a common ground for independence in Zimbabwe, Namibia, and, with less satisfactory results, Angola. And independent leaders debated over federalism in Nigeria and ethnic representation in Kenya, Uganda, and the Ivory Coast (Côte d'Ivoire). Indeed, in virtually every African country, independence was preceded by intense dialogue and negotiation between various groups, parallel to negotiations with the colonial powers. But these were tactical agreements to rid the country of its colonial yoke and, in any case, were elitist negotiations that did not involve the grass roots, as the South African negotiations did through a broad-based network of political organizations and elements of civil society.

Typically, the constitutions that African countries adopted at independence were drafted for them by the colonial masters and, contrary to the authoritarian modes of government adopted by the colonial powers, were laden with idealistic principles of liberal democracy to which Africa had not previously been introduced and in which it had no experience. The regimes built on these constitutions were in essence grafted foreign conceptualizations that had no indigenous roots and therefore lacked legitimacy. In most cases, they were soon overthrown with no remorse or regrets from the public. But these upheavals involved only a rotation of like-minded elites or, worse, military dictators, intent on occupying the seat of power vacated by the colonial masters. They soon became their colonial masters' images. In the overwhelming majority of countries, the quest for unity underscored the intensity of disunity, sometimes resulting in violent conflicts, many of which have intensified in the post–Cold War era—as evidenced by Burundi, Congo, Liberia, Sierra Leone, Somalia, Rwanda, and Zaire, now the Democratic Republic of Congo. African states must respond to the demands of justice, equity, and dignity by the component elements or risk disintegration and collapse. As Michael Chege noted in a different context, "It is time to bring this highly variegated menu to African statesmen and citizens and to convince them that self-determination of groups need not always lead to the feared disintegration of the present states into a myriad of small ethnic units."[46]

There are four policy options for managing pluralistic identities. One is to create a national framework with which all can identify without any distinction based on race, ethnicity, tribe, or religion. This is clearly the most desirable option. The second option is to create a pluralistic framework to accommodate diversity in nations that are racially, ethnically, culturally, or religiously divided.

Under this option, probably a federal arrangement, groups would accommodate each other's differences with a uniting commitment to the common purpose of national identification and nondiscrimination. For more seriously divided countries, the third option may be some form of power sharing, combined with decentralization that may expand federalism into confederalism. Finally, where even this degree of accommodation is not workable, and where territorial configurations permit, partition ought to be accepted.

This is the normative framework in which the crisis in the Sudanese region of Darfur should be addressed. Although the Sudan has made appreciable progress in ending the half-century-long war in the South, including the acceptance of self-determination that includes the possibility of secession, in the hope that unity will be made attractive during the interim period, the nation is only at the beginning of its long journey toward addressing its history and reconciling the injustices of its past with the promise of a national framework that will define a country that belongs to all of its citizens. The country continues to be challenged by the tragedy in the Darfur region and the tensions that threaten eruption in the eastern Beja region and other fragile areas of the country.

In this respect, it is worth noting that the international response to Darfur tends to see the crisis in isolation rather than as an aspect of a national quest for justice and equality that began in the South in the 1950s, extended to the adjacent regions of the North in the mid-1980s, and then to the Beja region in the late 1980s, and finally to Darfur. The struggle is expected to spread to other regions, as the dominant Arab center fights ruthlessly to preserve its power against the threats posed by proliferating rebellions in the marginalized and discriminated non-Arab regions of the country.

The appropriate response from the international community should be threefold: provide humanitarian assistance to the needy, protect the civilian population, and press for a political solution to achieve peace with justice. As long as war rages on, the government will continue to use the Arab tribal militias, the infamous *Janjaweed,* as a weapon against the rebels. Whatever the government may say in response to the pressure from the international community, it will never rein in the *Janjaweed* as criminals to be punished. They are allies in the genocidal war for survival. If, on the other hand, emphasis is placed on the search for peace, there is a good chance that both parties may be induced to adopt a more positive and constructive attitude toward international support for the peace process.

THE IMPACT OF THE WAR ON TERROR

The war on terror, in the aftermath of September 11, has created a world order that, to a certain degree, calls to mind the Cold War ideological polarization into Western democratic and Eastern communist blocs, with the United States and the Soviet Union heading these blocs. The difference is that these former superpowers are no longer on opposite sides but indeed on the same side in the global war on terror. What is still in common with the Cold War ideological divide is that, from a human rights perspective, what was crucial in evaluating the performance of a given country was what bloc it fell into. The tendency was to support any government that was ideologically allied with the superpower concerned, whatever its domestic record on human rights, democracy, or good governance in general. Conversely, the evils of a government on the opposite side were considered legitimate targets for exposure and condemnation.

In a way, a similar polarization appears to have emerged with the global war on terror. This is reflected in a number of ways, including military confrontation in which many innocent civilians fall victim to the cross fire. While the obvious cases are Afghanistan and Iraq, the war against terror is also fueling the hostilities and atrocities of the chronic conflicts in the Middle East. The recent invasion of Somalia by Ethiopia, which aimed at ousting the Islamists deemed as posing a terrorist threat in the region, paradoxically aggravated a situation that seemed to have improved under the dominant Islamic courts. The war on terror is also inducing responses in the United States and other Western democracies that are restrictive of human rights and civil liberties in the name of security, as the controversy over the treatment of prisoners in Guantánamo attests. In the polarization generated by the war on terror, the tendency seems to be that as long as a government is an ally in the war, its own human rights record at home can be overlooked or criticized rhetorically without punitive action. Furthermore, governments opportunistically declare rebel movements as terrorists, however justified their struggle, and expect support, political and even military, from their allies in the war against terror.

The global war against terror has reversed the post–Cold War withdrawal of superpower strategic interests in Africa and turned the continent into a theater of confrontation with Islamic terrorists. As Lieutenant Commander Pat Paterson of the U.S. Navy Special Operations Command in Europe explained in an article titled "Into Africa: A New Frontier in the War on Terror," for the United States, in its war with a growing movement of Islamic fundamentalism, the biggest political and military concern in Africa is terrorism.[47] The dire conditions of border disputes, ethnic conflicts, corruption and mismanagement, famine, and HIV make Africa a fertile breeding ground for Muslim extremism and terrorist recruitment. "On a continent where 50% of the population is under 15 years old and where the population is expected to grow from 800 million to 2 billion by 2050, this vast pool of angry, unskilled youth is a population vulnerable to jihadist sentiment and creates a critical problem demanding immediate attention."[48] Paterson goes on to substantiate the presence and activities of Islamic terrorists on the continent: "The history of al Qaeda in Africa goes back to 1991, when Osama bin Laden used Sudan as his operating base until U.S. and international pressure forced the Sudanese government to withdraw the welcome mat for him in 1996. In August 1998 al Qaeda exploded two massive car bombs outside the U.S. embassies in Dar es Salaam, Tanzania, and Nairobi, Kenya, killing 224 people (including 12 Americans) and injuring 5,000. In response, U.S. Navy warships fired cruise missiles into suspected terror sites near Khartoum later that month during Operation Infinite Reach."[49] Evidence of terrorist activities continues in Paterson's account:

> In 2002, al Qaeda operatives killed 15 people in an Israeli-owned hotel in Mombasa, Kenya, and simultaneously fired surface-to-air missiles at an Israeli passenger jet departing Mombasa's airport. In 2003, four suicide bombers attacked Jewish, Spanish, and Belgian sites in Casablanca, Morocco, killing 33 people. The 11 March 2004 train bombings in Madrid were carried out by African jihadists and killed 191 people and wounded 1,400 others. The 7 July 2005 London bombers who killed 51 people and injured more than 700 were assisted by collaborators from Africa.
>
> In September 2005, the U.S. Department of State listed the African organization Salifist Group for Call and Combat (GSPC) as a foreign terrorist organization putting it on par with al Qaeda. The GSPC gained notoriety with its June 2003 kidnapping of 32 Western tourists in Algeria. Terrorist groups such as GSPC use the vast ungoverned expanses of the Sahara Desert to their advantage, ferrying arms, cash, and contraband along established smuggling routes.[50]

Africans are reported to be fighting the United States in Afghanistan and Iraq: "Pentagon officials estimate that 25% of the foreign fighters in Iraq—estimated to be 5,000–8,000—are Africans. The officials also indicate that a stream of veteran jihadists from the conflicts in Iraq and Afghanistan are returning to Africa to train new soldiers and use insurgent tactics against their native countries."[51]

With Africa emerging as a significant scene, if not actor, in the global war on terror, the U.S. government has quietly opened up a front in its war on terror in East Africa:

> Military spending in the four years following 9/11 has doubled the amount expended in the preceding four years. The total spent or allocated for arms, training, and regional peacekeeping operations that focus primarily on training and arming sub-Saharan militaries in the four-year period from 2002 until the end

of 2005 will amount to $597 million, whereas for 1998–2001 it was $296 million. At this rate it will take a comparatively few years to equal the $1.5 billion that some believe was spent during the three decades of the Cold War on arms for African allies.[52]

The new U.S. Africa Command, AFRICOM, which was announced in February 2007 and is expected to be operational in the fall of 2008, aims at working in concert with African partners to create a stable security environment in which political and economic growth can take place. This means combining humanitarian development assistance with helping Africans pursue the war against terrorism more effectively. As Ryan Henry, principal Defense Department Under Secretary for Policy, told reporters in June 2007, "AFRICOM will emphasize humanitarian assistance, civic action, military professionalism, border and maritime security assistance, and responses to natural disasters." He added that terrorism is a problem in Africa, and it is something African nations are very concerned about, but "it is clearly not the primary focus" of AFRICOM, which has no intention of committing troops to the continent to pursue terrorists.[53]

Generally speaking, the war on terror is posing a threat to human rights and democratic freedoms, as Jennifer Cook and Steve Morrison have pertinently cautioned:

> As Africa has become conspicuously important in the intensified global war on terror and in U.S. efforts to win support within multilateral forums for military action against Iraq, policymakers confront the risk that geopolitical goals may trump locally specific human rights, democracy, and developmental interests. If this risk is not managed effectively, the United States easily could make mistakes reminiscent of the Cold War, in which the United States based strategic partnerships overwhelmingly on African leaders' anticommunist credentials, with enduring negative consequences for African governance and U.S. credibility on the continent.[54]

Even in the Sudan, where the war on terror appeared to have produced positive results in pressuring the parties to end the war in the South, lest they be accused of terror, with severe consequences, contradictory developments have taken place. While the government in Khartoum remains on the State Department's list of states that support terrorism, and Congress continues to be vocally antagonistic to the National Islamic Front, since renamed the National Congress Party (NCP) and in control of the government in Khartoum, the Bush administration has adopted an ambivalent attitude toward Khartoum, and the NCP has shrewdly responded opportunistically to gain Washington's favor. As an observer noted, President Omar al-Bashir's regime, "having hosted Osama bin Laden in Khartoum in the 1990s, has played its hand carefully in the U.S. war on terror. Under pressure from Washington, Khartoum sent its intelligence chief, Salah Abdallah Gosh, to brief Western intelligence officials about al-Qaeda networks in Sudan and beyond."[55] As Greg Miller and Josh Meyer have reported, "Sudan has moved beyond sharing historical information on al-Qaeda into taking part in on-going counter-terrorism operations, focusing on areas where its assistance is likely to be most appreciated."[56] They go on to write:

> Sudan has secretly worked with the CIA to spy on the insurgency in Iraq, an example of how the U.S. has continued to cooperate with the Sudanese regime even while condemning its suspected role in the killing of thousands of civilians in Darfur.
>
> President Bush has denounced the killings in Sudan's western region as genocide and has imposed sanctions on the government in Khartoum. But some critics say the administration has soft-pedaled the sanctions to preserve its extensive intelligence collaboration with Sudan.
>
> The relationship underscores the complex realities of the post-Sept. 11 world, in which the United States has relied heavily on intelligence and military cooperation from countries, including Sudan and Uzbekistan, that are considered pariah states for their records on human rights.[57]

Sudan's cooperation with the United States is said to go beyond Iraq. "Sudan has helped the United States track turmoil in Somalia, working to cultivate contacts with the Islamic Courts Union and other militias in an effort to locate al-Qaeda suspects hiding there" and "has provided extensive cooperation in counter-terrorism operations, acting on U.S. requests to detain suspects as they pass through Khartoum." The paradox is that "at a time when Sudan is being condemned in the international community, its counter-terrorism work has won precious praise. The U.S. State Department recently issued a report calling Sudan a 'strong partner in the war on terror.'"[58] This ambivalent attitude toward Khartoum may be a factor in the contradictory hard-talk, soft-action attitude that the United States policy has adopted on international response to the genocidal conflict in Darfur. Indeed, the sanctions announced by the Bush administration in late May 2007 have been described as "window-dressing," designed to appear tough while putting little real pressure on the Sudan or the Arab militias, which the country is believed to be using against rebels and civilians alike in Darfur.[59]

Another paradoxical development as a result of the war on terror has been improved relations between the United States and Libya, despite Muammar Qaddafi's controversial human rights record. The United States restored full diplomatic relations with Libya in June 2006 and removed it from the State Department's list of terrorism sponsors, ending long-standing tensions in bilateral relations and U.S.-imposed sanctions. Objectively, it is noteworthy that Muammar Qaddafi has, in recent years, made significant constructive changes. He is now viewed as having played a positive role in Africa, his most striking achievement being his initiative and strong support for the African Union. He has also taken steps to align himself with the United States in an effort to gain Western trust. His government apologized for its past violence, accepted responsibility for the 1988 Lockerbie terrorist attack, dismantled its weapons of mass destruction program in 2003, and is cooperating with the United States in the war on terror. It is, however, widely contended that

> Libya's track record of human rights abuses is still among the worst in the world, calling into question whether the administration is worthy of US support. Freedom House gave Libya the lowest possible rating in all categories—political rights, civil liberties, and freedom—citing poor prison conditions, arbitrary arrest and detention, torture, domestic violence against women, the prohibition of independent human rights organizations, and the ban on independent press. Any form of political opposition is brutally and unsubtly quelled.[60]

Critics of the U.S. and European shift of policy toward Libya argue that it will entrench Libya's poor human rights record:

> The United States and the European Union face the risk that their new diplomatic partnerships with Libya will help legitimize the regime and perpetuate the country's poor conditions. Libyan dissidents claim that Qaddafi will most likely use this new relationship to consolidate his political base and continue stamping out any possibility for political reform. There are also repercussions in the international arena. The United States has portrayed the war on terror as not only a military conflict but also an ideological struggle; current nation-building processes in Iraq and Afghanistan are inextricably linked with the words and values of 'freedom,' 'liberty,' and 'democracy.' In Libya, Qaddafi's eager suppression of the opposition Libyan Islamic Fighting Group (LIFG), recognized as a terrorist organization, has only reinforced beliefs that U.S. and EU motives are not those of building democracy but of self-interested security. Critics of a Western alliance with the Qaddafi regime claim that this "Western

hypocrisy" further alienates the Muslim world and gives radical Islamists even more ammunition to attack the West.[61]

Thus, the global war on terror, while justified by the horrific events of September 11, has triggered a chain of policies and actions that threaten to reverse the progress made in the international promotion and protection of human rights. While hindsight on whether a more targeted pursuit of the individual criminals involved in that incident might have produced different results would be superfluous and futile, there is reason to think carefully about how to pursue the war on terror without compromising the human rights standards that have been painstakingly developed since the end of World War II and the creation of the United Nations. Considering that African states are already prone to the abuse of power and egregious violations of human rights, this development poses a particular danger to be guarded against in the continent.

OPERATIONAL STRATEGIES OF INTERVENTION

Although addressing the issue of sovereignty and the root causes of conflict are critical prerequisites to intervention, formulating credible operation principles is the most pivotal factor in the equation. These principles relate to institutional mechanisms and strategies for action, both preventive and corrective. Ideally, from an institutional or organizational perspective, problems should be addressed and solved within the immediate framework, with wider involvement necessitated only by the failure of the internal efforts. Hence, conflict prevention, management, or resolution progressively moves from the domestic domain to the regional and, ultimately, to the global levels of concern and action.

As already noted, those conflicts in which the state is an effective arbiter do not present particular difficulties since they are manageable within the national framework. The problem arises when the state itself is a party to the conflict. Under those conditions, external involvement becomes necessary. In the African context, it is generally agreed that the next-best level of involvement should be the AU, but there are obvious constraints on its role, as its ineffectiveness in Darfur demonstrated. One such constraint has to do with limited resources, both material and human. But perhaps even more debilitating is the question of political will, since, in the intimate context of the region, governments feel they are subject to conflicts arising from the problematic conditions of state formation and nation building and are therefore prone to resist any form of external scrutiny. And since the judge of today may well be the accused of tomorrow, there is a temptation to avoid confronting such problems. The result is evasiveness and malign neglect. Beyond the AU, the United Nations is the next logical organization, for it represents the international community in its global context. But the UN suffers from the same constraints affecting the AU, though to a lesser degree. It, too, must deal with the problem of resources and the reciprocal protectiveness of vulnerable governments.

As recent events have demonstrated, the role of the major Western powers acting unilaterally, multilaterally, or within the framework of the United Nations—though often susceptible to accusations of selectivity and self-interested strategic motivation—has become increasingly pivotal. The problem in this regard is more one of their unwillingness to become involved or their lack of adequate preparedness for such involvement. Perhaps the most important aspect of the involvement of Western industrial democracies in foreign conflicts is the fact that these nations are often moved to act by the gravity of the humanitarian tragedies involved. Thus, their involvement is both an asset in terms of arresting the tragedy and a limitation in terms of preventing the tragedy at an earlier stage. Even with respect to humanitarian intervention, lack of preparedness for an appropriate and timely response is generally acknowledged as a major limitation.[62]

Nevertheless, some argue that there is a strong presumption that the interests of these countries are powerfully engaged and that they will eventually be driven to uphold and promote such interests through humanitarian intervention in crisis situations. Industrial democracies, they further argue, cannot operate without defending standards of human rights and political procedures that are being egregiously violated. Indeed, they themselves cannot prosper in an irreversibly international economy if large, contiguous populations descend into endemic violence and economic depression. Given these compelling reasons and the lack of preparedness for any well-planned response, the United States and Western European countries are particularly prone to crisis-induced reactions that are relatively easy to execute and, indeed, more symbolic than effective in addressing the substantive issues involved.

There will always be elements in a country who welcome intervention, especially among the disadvantaged groups to whom it promises tangible benefits. But since intervention is, of course, a major intrusion from the outside, resistance on the grounds of national sovereignty or pride is also a predictable certainty. For that reason, the justification for intervention must be reliably persuasive, if not beyond reproach: "The difference between an intervention that succeeds and one that is destroyed by immune reaction would depend on the degree of spontaneous acceptance or rejection by the local population."[63]

To avoid or minimize this "immune reaction," such an intervention would have to be broadly international in character. The principles used and the objectives toward which the intervention is targeted must transcend political and cultural boundaries or traditions and concomitant nationalist sentiments. In other words, it must enjoy an effective degree of global legitimacy. "The rationale that could conceivably carry such a burden presumably involves human rights so fundamental that they are not derived from any particular political or economic ideology."[64]

The strategy for preventive or corrective involvement in conflict should constitute gathering and analyzing information and otherwise monitoring situations with a view toward establishing an early warning system through which the international community could be alerted to act. The quest for a system of response to conflict and attendant humanitarian tragedies was outlined by the then UN Secretary-General Boutros Boutros-Ghali when, referring to the surging demands on the Security Council as a central instrument for the prevention and resolution of conflicts, he wrote that the aims of the United Nations must be:

> To seek to identify at the earliest possible stage situations that could produce conflict, and to try through diplomacy to remove the sources of danger before violence results;
>
> Where conflict erupts, to engage in peacemaking aimed at resolving the issues that have led to conflict;
>
> Through peace-keeping, to work to preserve peace, however fragile, where fighting has been halted and to assist in implementing agreements achieved by the peacemakers;
>
> To stand ready to assist in peace-building in its differing contexts: rebuilding the institutions and infrastructures of nations torn by civil war and strife; and building bonds of peaceful mutual benefit among nations formerly at war;
>
> And in the largest sense, to address the deepest causes of conflict: economic despair, social injustice and political oppression. It is possible to discern an increasingly common moral perception that spans the world's nations and peoples, and which is finding expression in international laws, many owing their genesis to the work of this Organization.[65]

The action envisaged to address conflict situations and their humanitarian consequences is a four-phase strategy that would involve monitoring developments to draw early attention to impending crises, interceding in time to avert the crisis through diplomatic initiatives, mobilizing international action when necessary, and addressing the root causes to restore peace, security, and stability.[66] The first step would be to detect and identify the problem through various early-warning mechanisms for information collection, evaluation, and reporting. If a sufficient basis for concern were established, the appropriate mechanism would be invoked to take preventive diplomatic measures and avert the crisis. Initially, such initiatives might be taken within the framework of regional arrangements—for example, the Conference on Security and Co-operation in Europe, the Organization of American States, or the African Union. In the United Nations, such preventive initiatives would naturally fall on the secretary-general, acting personally or through special representatives, to bring the situation to the attention of the Security Council for appropriate action. If diplomatic initiatives did not succeed, and depending on the level of human suffering involved, the secretary-general and the Security Council might decide to mobilize international response, ranging from further diplomatic measures to forced humanitarian intervention not only to provide emergency relief but also to facilitate the search for an enduring solution to the causes of the conflict. A strategy aimed at this broader objective would require a close understanding of the causal link between the conditions and developments leading to the outbreak of the crisis and finding solutions that address the root causes to ensure sustainable peace and stability.

CONCLUSION

Africa's turbulent transformation, initiated by colonial scramble for the continent in the nineteenth century, contained by external domination for much of the first half of the twentieth century, reactivated by the independence movement at the second half of the century, and subdued by the Cold War bipolar control mechanism, is now engaging in a renewed quest of self-liberation from within. While this initially meant more self-reliance with minimum external interference, motivated by the strategic interests of the Cold War era, the global war against international terrorism in the early twenty-first century has reactivated international concern and propensity for varying forms of intervention. The context in which this is taking place is poised delicately between globalization and isolation, initially bordering on the marginalization of Africa, but in the context of the global war on terror, putting Africa back at the center as a potential breeding ground for international terrorism. Paradoxically, ideological withdrawal by the major powers is being counterbalanced by pressures for humanitarian intervention, while the war on terror threatens to relegate human rights to a lower level of concern. This situation calls for a more cost-effective sharing of responsibility, with the Africans assuming the primary role and their international partners lending a complementary affirmative, helping hand. Whether this equation is sustainable or the war on terror will take the upper hand and lead Africa back to intensifying dependency remains a question.

Whatever the answer to that question, the policy framework that apportions responsibilities in accordance with the emerging scale must place the first tier of responsibility on the state. At the next level up the international ladder, regional actors are increasingly being challenged and motivated by the realization that their own national security is closely connected with the security of their neighbors. This realization has propelled a range of initiatives in which neighbors offer their good offices for third-party mediation in internal conflicts but, if their counsel is not heeded, intervene unilaterally or collectively to achieve their objectives. But as the case of Darfur has shown, regional capacities may be inadequate for the task, and the supportive role of the international community will continue to be a necessity for effective action. The best remedy is internal peace, security, and stability.

A number of African leaders have embraced programs of political and economic reforms that would enhance regional security and stability. Some of their peers remain doggedly committed to authoritarian methods of governance. The international community, weary of shouldering responsibility for Africa's problems, is striving to win the leaders intent on reform, give them the support they need to carry out their programs, and thereby provide them with the incentive to do so in earnest. These measures imply the stipulation of national sovereignty as responsibility with regional and international accountability. The way to guard against unwelcome international intervention is to discharge the responsibilities of sovereignty and be seen to be doing so.

An important dimension of such accountability is therefore the reform of state structures, institutions, and processes to be more equitable in their management of diversities. This reform will require pushing the process of reversing Africa's international dependency to enhance the autonomy of internal actors, ethnic groups, and members of civil society in order to mobilize and engage them in self-reliant processes of governance and sustainable development. The state has been the intermediary and often the bottleneck in the chain of Africa's dependent relationship with the outside world. The required reform must broaden the scope of decision-making through extensive and genuine decentralization. It must make a more constructive use of indigenous structures, values, and institutions for self-governance and self-sustaining development from within. Governments genuinely committed to reform should have no difficulty in supporting this approach, whereas those that insist on centralization of authority wittingly or unwittingly expose their authoritarian disposition and risk regional and international scrutiny or admonition and, possibly, condemnation and reprisals.

The time is certainly opportune for reconciling sovereignty with the responsibilities of good governance. In balancing national sovereignty and the need for international action to provide protection and assistance to victims of internal conflicts and humanitarian tragedies, certain principles are becoming increasingly obvious as policy guidelines.

First, sovereignty carries with it responsibilities for the well-being of the population. It is from this precept that the legitimacy of a government derives, whatever the political system or prevailing ideology. The relationship between the controlling authority and the populace should ideally ensure the highest standards of human dignity, but at a minimum it should guarantee food, shelter, physical security, basic health services, and other essentials.

Second, in the many countries where armed conflicts and communal violence have caused massive internal displacement, the countries are so divided on fundamental issues that legitimacy and, indeed, sovereignty are sharply contested. This is why there is always a strong faction inviting or at least welcoming external intervention. Under those circumstances, the validity of sovereignty must be judged, using reasonable standards to assess how much of the population is represented, marginalized, or excluded.

Third, living up to the responsibilities of sovereignty implies that there is a transcendent authority capable of holding the supposed sovereign accountable. Some form of an international system has always existed to ensure that states conform to accepted norms or face the consequences, whether in the form of unilateral, multilateral, or collective action. Equality among sovereign entities has always been a convenient fiction; it has never been backed by realities because some powers have always been more dominant than others and therefore have been explicitly or implicitly charged with responsibility for enforcing the agreed-upon norms of behavior. Considering that hardly any African country has the requisite capacity, "hegemonic stability" has not been a pattern, although Nigeria and South Africa have exercised considerable influence in their subregions.

Fourth, such a role imposes on the dominant authority or power certain leadership responsibilities that transcend parochialism or exclusive national interests and serve the broader interests of the community or the human family, an area where African countries, with their politics of identity, have suffered a deficit.

When these principles are translated into practical action in countries torn apart by internal conflicts, a number of implications emerge. For example, sovereignty cannot be an amoral function of authority and control; respect for fundamental human rights and humanitarian principles must be among its most basic values. Similarly, the enjoyment of human rights must encompass equitable and effective participation in the political, economic, social, and cultural life of the country, at least as a widely accepted national aspiration. This system of sharing must guarantee that all individuals and groups belong to the nation on an equal footing with the rest of the people, however identified; they must also be sufficiently represented and not discriminated against on the basis of the prevailing views of identity.

To ensure that these normative goals are met or at least genuinely pursued, the international community as represented by the United Nations is the ideal authority. The imperatives of the existing power structures and processes may, however, require that authority be exercised by other powers capable of acting on behalf of the international community. Multilateral action may therefore be justified under certain circumstances. Any type of less collective action should be closely circumscribed to guard against selectivity and exploitation for less lofty objectives of a more exclusively national character—objectives that may erode the transcendent moral authority of global leadership for the good of all humankind.

As a polarity emerges between those African governments committed to participatory democracy, respect for human rights, and responsible international partnership and those bent on repression and resistance to reform, the international community should adopt a dual strategy that effectively supports reform with positive incentives and discourages resistance with punitive sanctions. Living up to the responsibilities of sovereignty implies a transcendent authority capable of holding the supposed sovereign accountable. Although the international community has made appreciable progress in responding to humanitarian tragedies, much more needs to be done to ensure that governments adhere to the responsibilities of sovereignty by ensuring the security, fundamental rights, civil liberties, and general welfare of their citizens and all those under their domestic jurisdiction.

Although the world is far from a universal government, the foundations, the pillars, and perhaps even the structures of global governance are taking shape with the emergence of a post–Cold War international order in which the internally dispossessed are bound to benefit. Unmasking sovereignty to reveal the gross violations of human rights is no longer an aspiration; it is a process that has already started. Governments and other human rights violators are being increasingly scrutinized for such violations. What is now required is to make them fully accountable and to provide international protection and assistance for the victims of human rights violations and unremedied humanitarian tragedies within their domestic jurisdiction. In other words, what is called for is not something entirely new but, rather, an intensification and improvement of what has already been unfolding.

The global war on terror is obviously a complication insofar as it creates a Cold War–type of polarization between allies and enemies. However, in the end, just as internal conflicts require internal solutions to ensure just peace, security, and stability, a global alliance against terrorism must also address the internal conditions on which international terrorism breeds. Addressing the symptoms without going to the root causes in the crisis of national identity—acute economic disparities, poverty, deprivation, and all forms of indignities in an otherwise flourishing world—experienced not only externally but also internally for the few, will continue to generate internal conflicts in Africa with external ramifications. True security must be comprehensive and inclusive, or those left out will remain a source of instability, internally and globally.

NOTES

1. Boutros Boutros-Ghali, *An Agenda for Peace: Preventive Diplomacy, Peacemaking and Peacekeeping* (New York: United Nations, 1992), p. 7.

2. Boutros Boutros-Ghali, in a statement of his proposals to the Council of Ministers in Dakar, Senegal, in 1992. The main documents in these three areas of African initiative are as follows: *The Kampala Document Toward a Conference on Security, Stability, Development and Cooperation in Africa* (Kampala, Uganda: Africa Leadership Forum and Secretariat of the Organization of African Unity and the United Nations Economic Commission for Africa, 1991); Dent Ocaya-Lakidi, *Africa's Internal Conflicts: The Search for a Response,* Report of an Arusha, Tanzania, High-Level Consultation, March 23–25, 1992, prepared for the International Peace Academy; OAU, Council of Ministers, Fifty-sixth Ordinary Session, *Report of the Secretary-General on Conflicts in Africa: Proposals for an OAU Mechanism for Conflict Prevention and Resolution*, CM/1710 (L.VI) (Addis Ababa: Organization of African Unity, June 22–27, 1992); OAU, Council of Ministers, Fifty-seventh Ordinary Session, *Interim Report of the Secretary-General on the Mechanism for Conflict Prevention, Management and Resolution*, CM/1747 (L.VI) (Addis Ababa: Organization of African Unity, February 15–19, 1993); and OAU, Council of Ministers, Fifty-seventh Ordinary Session, *Report of the Secretary-General*, CM/Plen/Rpt (L.VII) (Addis Ababa: Organization of African Unity, February 15–19, 1993). Also pertinent to the issues involved is UN Secretary-General Boutros Boutros-Ghali's report, *An Agenda for Peace,* originally published as document A/47/277 S/24111, June 17, 1992.

3. Thomas M. Franck, "The Emerging Right to Democratic Governance," *American Journal of International Law* 86 (January 1992), p. 46.

4. Richard Falk, "Sovereignty and Human Dignity: The Search for Reconciliation," in Francis M. Deng and Terrence Lyons, eds., *African Reckoning: A Quest for Good Governance* (Washington, D.C.: Brookings Institution, 1998), p. 13.

5. Francis M. Deng, *Protecting the Dispossessed: A Challenge for the International Community* (Washington, D.C.: Brookings Institution, 1993), p. 14.

6. David J. Scheffer, "Toward a Modern Doctrine of Humanitarian Intervention," *University of Toledo Law Review* 23 (Winter 1992), p. 2.

7. UN press release SG/SM/4560, April 24, 1991; cited in Gene M. Lyons and Michael Mastanduno, *Beyond Westphalia: International Intervention, State Sovereignty and the Future of International Society* (Hanover, N.H.: Dartmouth College, 1992), p. 2. Portions of this statement are also cited in Scheffer, "Toward a Modern Doctrine of Humanitarian Intervention," p. 262.

8. Javier Perez de Cuellar, *Report of the Secretary-General on the Work of the Organization* (New York: United Nations, 1991).

9. Ibid., p. 13.

10. Boutros-Ghali, *An Agenda for Peace,* p. 5.

11. Scheffer, "Toward a Modern Doctrine of Humanitarian Intervention," pp. 262–263.

12. Falk, "Sovereignty and Human Dignity," p. 12.

13. Global Policy Forum, Statement by Secretary-General Kofi Annan, April 7, 1999, at http://www.globalpolicy.org/nations/kofi2.htm.

14. Francis M. Deng, Sadikiel Kimaro, Terrence Lyons, Donald Rothchild, and I. William Zartman, eds., *Sovereignty as Responsibility: Conflict Management in Africa* (Washington, D.C.: Brookings Institution, 1996).

15. OAU, Council of Ministers, *Report of the Secretary-General on Conflicts in Africa.*

16. Ibid.

17. Ibid.

18. Ibid.

19. Kofi Annan, interview, *Frontline: Ghosts of Rwanda*, PBS, February 17, 2004, at http://www.pbs.org/wgbh/pages/frontline/shows/ghosts/interviews/annan.html.

20. Ibid.

21. Kofi Annan, interview, *Online News Hour*, PBS, October 18, 1999, at http://www.pbs.org/newshour/bb/international/july-dec99/annan_10–18.html.

22. Note by the president of the Security Council, S/25344, February 26, 1993.

23. Ibid., p. 1.

24. Ibid., p. 2.

25. Ibid.

26. Ibid.

27. Francis M. Deng and I. William Zartman, eds., *Conflict Resolution in Africa* (Washington, D.C.: Brookings Institution, 1991).

28. Deng et al., eds., *Sovereignty as Responsibility.*

29. Deng and Lyons, eds., *African Reckoning.*

30. Francis M. Deng, and I. William Zartman, *A Strategic Vision for Africa: The Kampala Movement* (Washington, D.C.: Brookings Institution Press, 2002).

31. Kofi Annan, interview, *Online News Hour*, PBS, October 19, 1999.

32. For my various contributions to the normative theme of the responsibility of sovereignty, see the following books, chapters, and articles: Terrence Lyons and Francis M. Deng, eds., *African Reckoning: A Quest for Good Governance* (Washington, D.C.: Brookings Institution, 1998); Francis M. Deng, "Sovereignty and Humanitarian Re-

sponsibility: A Challenge for NGOs in Africa and the Sudan," in *Vigilance and Vengeance*, ed. Robert I. Rotberg (Washington, D.C.: Brookings Institution and The World Peace Foundation, 1996); Francis M. Deng, Sadikiel Kimaro, Terrence Lyons, Donald Rothchild, and I. William Zartman, eds., *Sovereignty as Responsibility: Conflict Management in Africa* (Washington, D.C.: Brookings Institution, 1996); Francis M. Deng, "Reconciling Sovereignty with Responsibility: A Basis for International humanitarian Action," in *Africa in World Politics*, eds., John Harbeson and Donald Rothchild (Boulder: Westview Press, 1995); F. M. Deng, "Frontiers of Sovereignty: A Framework of Protection, Assistance and Development for the Internally Displaced," *Leiden Journal of International Law* 8, no. 2 (1995).

33. United Nations Report of the High Level Panel on Threats, Challenges, and Changes, *A More Secure World: Our Shared Responsibility*, New York, United Nations, 2004, paras 199–203; and Kofi Annan, *In Larger Freedoms: Toward Development, Security and Human Rights for All*, UN Doc. A/59/2005, March 21, 2005, para 135.

34. General Assembly 2005, *World Summit Outcome*, UN Doc. A/60/L1, September 15, 2005, para 139.

35. Kofi Annan, interview, *Frontline: Ghosts of Rwanda.*

36. Boutros-Ghali, *An Agenda for Peace*, p. 9.

37. Ibid., pp. 9–10.

38. Donald Rothchild, *Managing Ethnic Conflict in Africa* (Washington, D.C.: Brookings Institution, 1997), pp. 20–21.

39. Thandika Mkandawire, "Shifting Commitments and National Cohesion in African Countries," in Lennart Wohlgemuth, Samantha Gibson, Stephan Klasan, Emma Rothschild, eds., *Common Security and Civil Society in Africa* (Uppsala, Sweden: Nordiska Afrikainstitutet, 1999), p. 15.

40. Roberta Cohen and Francis Deng, eds., *The Forsaken People: Case Studies of the Internally Displaced* (Washington, D.C.: Brookings Institution, 1998).

41. According to one source, ethnicity is important in African politics because it serves as an "organizing principle of sound action," which makes it "basically a political . . . phenomenon." See Naomi Chazan et al., *Politics and Society in Contemporary Africa* (Boulder: Lynne Rienner Publishers, 1988), pp. 110, 120. And as UN Secretary-General Kofi Annan observed in a paper presented to an international conference on "The Therapeutics of Conflict," when he was still undersecretary-general for Peacekeeping Operations: "Many [of the civil wars] have also been perceived as showing strong symptoms of ethnic conflict. Ethnic conflict as a symptom is, at best, extremely difficult to assess. . . . Ethnic differences are not in and of themselves either symptoms or causes of conflict; in societies where they are accepted and respected, people of vastly different backgrounds live peacefully and productively together. Ethnic differences become charged—conflictual—when they are used for political ends, when ethnic groups are intentionally placed in opposition to each other." See Kofi Annan, "The Peacekeeping Prescription," in Kevin M. Cahill, M.D., ed., *Preventive Diplomacy* (New York: Basic Books, 1996), p. 176.

42. The Constitution of the Federal Democratic Republic of Ethiopia (Addis Ababa, December 8, 1994) provides in Article 39, Number 1, that "[e]very nation, nationality and people in Ethiopia has an unconditional right to self-determination, including the right to secession." It also states in Article 39, Number 3, that "[e]very nation, nationality and people in Ethiopia has the right to a full measure of self-government which includes the right to establish institutions of government in the territory that it inhabits and to equitable representation in regional and national governments."

43. This is the essence of the proposal that the state of Liechtenstein presented to the General Assembly of the United Nations in 1991—a proposal that aimed at establishing a new international legal framework in which self-determination, defined primarily as self-administration, might be pursued within the existing state framework. See Wolfgang Danspeckgruber and Sir Arthur Watts, eds., *Self-Determination and Self-Administration: A Sourcebook* (Boulder: Lynne Rienner Publishers, 1997).

44. Ibid., p. 1.

45. Sir Arthur Watts, "The Liechtenstein Draft Convention on Self-Determination Through Self-Administration," in Wolfgang Danspeckgruber and Sir Arthur Watts, eds., *Self-Determination and Self-Administration: A Sourcebook*, (Boulder: Lynne Rienner Publishers, 1997), p. 23.

46. Cited in a review of Francis M. Deng, "Africa and the New World Disorder," *Brookings Review* (Spring 1993), p. 3. For a more comprehensive discussion of ethnic diversity in the context of democratization, see Chege's article, "Remembering Africa," in *Foreign Affairs* 71, no. 1 (1992), pp. 146–163.

47. Pat Paterson, "Into Africa: A New Frontier in the War on Terror," *United States Naval Institute Proceedings* 132, no. 5 (May 2006), p. 32.

48. Ibid.

49. Ibid.

50. Ibid.

51. Ibid.

52. Sandra T. Barnes, "Global Flows: Terror, Oil, and Strategic Philanthropy," *Africa Studies Review* 48, no. 1 (2005), pp. 1–22; at 1, 6. See also Thomas P. M. Barnett, "The Americans Have Landed," *Esquire,* June 11, 2007.

53. Jim Fisher-Thompson, "New Africa Command to Have Unique Structure, Mission," USINFO, June 22, 2007, at http://usinfo.state.gov/utils/printpage.html. See also "U.S. Africa Command at Initial Operation Capacity," U.S. Africa Command, Stuttgart, Germany, Press Release 08–001, October 1, 2007, at http://usinfo-state.gov/utils/printpage.html.

54. Jennifer G. Cook and J. Stephen Morrison, "Building an Ethic of Public Policy Discourse: An Appeal to African Studies Community," *African Issues* 30, no. 2 (2002), p. 63.

55. "Africa's Year of Terror Tactics," *New York Beacon*, January 11–17, 2007, p. 10.

56. Greg Miller and Josh Meyer, "Sudan Aids CIA's Efforts in Iraq," *Los Angeles Times*, June 11, 2007.

57. Ibid. See also Hans Pienaar, "Spooks, Hacks, Party in Secretive Sudan," *Tribune,* June 10, 2007, p. 14.

58. Miller and Meyer, "Sudan Aids CIA's Efforts in Iraq."

59. Ibid.

60. Samantha Fang, "A Worthy Ally? Reconsidering U.S.-Libyan Relations," *Harvard International Review* 29, no. 3 (Spring 2007), p. 7.

61. Ibid.

62. John Steinbruner, "Civil Violence as an International Security Problem," memorandum, November 23, 1992, addressed to the Brookings Institution Foreign Policy Studies Program staff. See also Chester A. Crocker, "The Global Law and Order Deficit: Is the West Ready to Police the World's Bad Neighbors?" *Washington Post,* December 20, 1992, p. C1.

63. Steinbruner, "Civil Violence as an International Security Problem."

64. Ibid.

65. Boutros-Ghali, *An Agenda for Peace,* pp.7–8.

66. For a more elaborate discussion of these phases as applied to the crisis of the internally displaced, see the UN study in document E/CH.4/1993/35 and the revised version of that study in Francis M. Deng, *Protecting the Dispossessed: A Challenge for the International Community* (Washington, D.C.: Brookings Institution, 1993). This study was considered by the Commission on Human Rights at its forty-ninth session, during which its findings and recommendations were endorsed and the mandate of the special representative of the secretary-general was extended for two years to continue to work on the various aspects of the problem presented in the study.

About the Contributors

Thomas M. Callaghy

Thomas M. Callaghy is Professor of Political Science at the University of Pennsylvania. His Ph.D. is from UC, Berkeley, and he has also taught at the Penn State University and Columbia University. His most recent books are two edited volumes: *Intervention and Transnationalism in Africa: Global-Local Networks of Power* (Cambridge University Press, 2001) and *Right-sizing the State: The Politics of Moving Borders* (Oxford University Press, 2001). Most of his recent work is on the politics of debt; he is currently working on a book on the creation and evolution of the Paris Club debt relief process from 1956 to present.

Francis M. Deng

Francis M. Deng was appointed by UN Secretary-General Ban Ki-moon in May 2007 as the Special Adviser on the Prevention of Genocide. Deng served as Representative of the United Nations Secretary-General on Internally Displaced Persons from 1992 to 2004, as Human Rights Officer in the United Nations Secretariat from 1967 to 1972, and as the Ambassador of the Sudan to Canada, Denmark, Finland, Norway, Sweden, and the United States. He also served as Sudan's Minister of State for Foreign Affairs. After leaving his country's service, he joined a succession of think tanks, universities, and research institutions. Deng holds a Bachelor of Laws with honors from Khartoum University and a Master of Laws (LL.M.) and a Doctor of the Science of Law (JSD) from Yale University. He has authored and edited over 30 books in the fields of law, conflict resolution, internal displacement, human rights, anthropology, folklore, history, and politics and has also written two novels on the theme of the crisis of national identity in the Sudan. Among his numerous awards in his country and abroad, Deng is co-recipient with Roberta Cohen of the 2005 Grawemeyer Award for "Ideas Improving World Order" and the 2007 Merage Foundation American Dream Leadership Award. In 2000, Deng also received the Rome Prize for Peace and Humanitarian Action.

John W. Harbeson

John W. Harbeson is Professor of Political Science in the Graduate Center and at City College in the City University of New York. He is the author, editor, or co-editor of *Land Reform and National Building in Kenya*; *The Ethiopian Transformation; Civil Society and the State in Africa; The Military in African Politics*; four editions of *Africa in World Politics*; and more than 80 articles and book chapters. He has been a Jennings Randolph Senior Fellow at the U.S. Institute of Peace, and a Visiting Fellow at Princeton's Center of International Studies, and served as the U.S. Agency for International Development's Regional Democracy and Governance Advisor for Eastern and Southern Africa. He was elected to the American Political Science Association's governing council and has co-founded its Comparative Democratization section and its African Politics Conference Group's related group.

Gilbert M. Khadiagala

Gilbert M. Khadiagala is the Jan Smuts Professor of International Relations and Head of Department at the University of the Witwatersrand, Johannesburg, South Africa. He has taught political science and African studies at the University of Nairobi, Kent State University, and most recently the School of Advanced International Studies (SAIS), the Johns Hopkins University. Professor Khadiagala is the recent author of *Meddlers or Mediators? African Interveners in Civil Conflicts in Eastern Africa* (2007), co-author of *Sudan: The Elusive Quest for Peace* (2006), co-editor of *Conflict Management and African Politics* (2008), and editor of *Security Dynamics in Africa's Great Lakes Region* (2006). He is currently working on a manuscript on *Leaders, Leadership, and Institutions in Post-Conflict Africa.*

Princeton N. Lyman

Ambassador (rtd) Princeton N. Lyman is Adjunct Senior Fellow at the Council on Foreign Relations. From 2003 to 2006, he held the Ralph Bunche Chair for Africa Policy Studies at the Council on Foreign Relations. He is also Adjunct Professor at

Georgetown University. Ambassador Lyman's career in government included assignments as Deputy Assistant Secretary of State for Africa, Ambassador to Nigeria, Director of Refugee Programs, Ambassador to South Africa, and Assistant Secretary of State for International Organization Affairs. Earlier in the U.S. Agency for International Development he was Director of USAID in Addis Ababa, Ethiopia. He has published books and articles on foreign policy, African affairs, economic development, HIV/AIDS, UN reform, terrorism, and peacekeeping.

Ali A. Mazrui

Ali A. Mazrui was born in Mombasa, Kenya, in 1933, and educated in Kenya, Great Britain and the United States. He has a Masters degree from Columbia University, New York, and a doctorate from Oxford University in England. He has written more than twenty books and hundreds of articles. One of his latest books is *Islam between Globalization and Counterterrorism* (Oxford: James Currey Publishers and Trenton, NJ: Africa World press, 2006). He is best known for his television series *The Africans: A Triple Heritage* (BB/PBS, 1986). Dr. Mazrui is currently Director, Institute of Global Cultural Studies, State University of New York, Binghamton, NY; Senior Scholar in Africana Studies, Cornell University, Ithaca, NY; Chancellor, Jomo Kenyatta University of Agriculture and Technology, Nairobi, Kenya; and Albert Luthuli Professor at Large, University of Jos, Jos, Nigeria. Dr. Mazrui has received honorary doctorates in subjects which have ranged from Divinity to Humane letters and from African Studies to Development Studies. Professor Mazrui is married and has five sons and several grandchildren.

Anokhi Parikh

Anokhi Parikh studied biology, international affairs, and economics at University of California, Berkeley, and has an MSc in development economics from Oxford University. She worked as the Health Economics and HIV/AIDS Research Unit at the University of KwaZulu Natal as an Overseas Development Fellow from 2005–2007. During her time at HEARD she worked on a number of different issues related to HIV/AIDS—ranging from drug pricing to the impact of the epidemic on households.

William Reno

William Reno is an Associate Professor of Political Science at Northwestern University. He is the author of *Corruption and State Politics in Sierra Leone* (Cambridge) and *Warlord Politics and African States* (Lynne Rienner). He is completing the forthcoming *Evolution of Warfare in Independent Africa.* His current research focuses on explaining the causes of differences in the organization and behavior of contemporary armed groups in Africa and on the southern periphery of the former Soviet Union.

Donald Rothchild

The late Donald Rothchild was Professor of Political Science at the University of California at Davis from 1965 until his death in January 2007. His university awarded him a Distinguished Professorship in 2003. He was the author or editor of more than two dozen books and over seventy articles over a career spanning almost 50 years. He wrote extensively and authoritatively on a wide range of topics including conflict mediation, international political economy, U.S. foreign policy toward Africa, ethnic politics, international regimes, international security, and Africa's place in contemporary world politics. He also wrote important work on Ghana, civil society, Afro-Marxist regimes, and state-society relations. He was elected twice to the presidency of the International Political Science Association's Research Committee on Ethnicity and Politics.

Denis M. Tull

Denis M. Tull is a senior researcher at the German Institute for International and Security Affairs in Berlin, Germany. His main research interests are Africa's international relations as well as conflict, intervention, and state building in war-torn states, in particular in the Democratic Republic of Congo. He is the author of *The Reconfiguration of Political Order in Africa: A Case Study of North Kivu (DR Congo)*, Hamburg, 2005. He has also published in *African Affairs* and *International Security*. He is a member of the editorial board of the *Journal of Modern African Studies.*

Aili Mari Tripp

Aili Mari Tripp is Professor of Political Science and Women's Studies at the University of Wisconsin-Madison. She is author of *Women and Politics in Uganda* (2000) and *Changing the Rules: The Politics of Liberalization and the Urban Informal Economy in Tanzania* (1997). She has a forthcoming book co-authored with Isabel Casimiro, Joy Kwesiga, and Alice Mungwa entitled *Women In Movement: Transformations in African Political Landscapes.* Tripp has published several other edited volumes and numerous articles and book chapters on transnational feminism, women and politics in Africa; women's responses to economic reform; and transformations of associational life in Africa.

Alan Whiteside

Professor Alan Whiteside was born in Kenya and grew up in Swaziland where he attended Waterford Kamhlaba College. He has an MA from the University of East Anglia and a D.Econ. from the University of Natal. He was an Overseas Development Institute Fellow in Botswana from 1980–1983. In 1983 he joined the Economic Research Unit of the University of Natal. In 1998 he established the Health Economics and HIV/AIDS Research Division and is its Director. In 2003 he was appointed by Secretary General Kofi Annan as one of the Commissioners on the Commission for HIV/AIDS and Governance in Africa. He has written extensively on HIV/AIDS and health issues, most recently *HIV/AIDS: A Very Short Introduction* (Oxford University Press, 2008)

Crawford Young

Crawford Young is Rupert Emerson and H. Edwin Young Professor Emeritus of Political Science at the University of Wisconsin-Madison, where he taught from 1963 to 2001. He also served as visiting professor in Congo-Kinshasa, Uganda, and Senegal. His major works include *Politics in the Congo* (1965), *The Politics of Cultural Pluralism* (1976), *Cooperatives and Development: Agricultural Politics in Ghana and Uganda* (with Neal Sherman and Tim Rose, 1981), *Ideology and Development in Africa* (1982), *The Rise and Decline of the Zairian State* (with Thomas Turner, 1985), and *The African Colonial State in Comparative Perspective* (1994). *The Politics of Cultural Pluralism* won the Herskovits Prize of the African Studies Association and was co-winner of the Ralph Bunche Award of the American Political Science Association; *The African Colonial State in Comparative Perspective* won the Gregory Luebbert Prize of the Comparative Politics Section of the APSA. He is a fellow of the American Academy of Arts and Sciences.

I. William Zartman

I. William Zartman is the Jacob Blaustein Professor of International Organization and Director of the Conflict Management Program at the Paul Nitze School of Advanced International Studies of Johns Hopkins University (SAIS). For 20 years, he was director of the SAIS African Studies Program. Previously he taught at the University of South Carolina, American University in Cairo, and New York University.

He has been Olin Professor at the U.S. Naval Academy and Halevy Professor at the Institute of Political Studies in Paris. He is a past president of the Middle East Studies Association and of the American Institute of Maghrib Studies. He is the author or editor of more than twenty books, the most recent of which include *Getting In: Mediators' Entry Into the Settlement of African Conflicts; Peacemaking in International Conflict; Cowardly Lions: Missed Opportunities to Prevent Deadly Conflict and State Collapse; Negotiating With Terrorists;* and *Rethinking the Economics of War: The Intersection of Need, Creed and Greed.* He has a Ph.D. from Yale and an honorary doctorate from the Louvain.

Index